THE
OXFORD BOOK OF
BALLADS

CHOSEN AND EDITED BY

JAMES KINSLEY

Oxford   New York

OXFORD UNIVERSITY PRESS

1989

Oxford University Press, Walton Street, Oxford OX2 6DP

Oxford New York Toronto
Delhi Bombay Calcutta Madras Karachi
Petaling Jaya Singapore Hong Kong Tokyo
Nairobi Dar es Salaam Cape Town
Melbourne Auckland

and associated companies in
Berlin Ibadan

Oxford is a trade mark of Oxford University Press

First published 1969
First issued as an Oxford University Press paperback 1982
Reprinted 1982, 1989

British Library Cataloguing in Publication Data
The Oxford Book of Ballads.
1. Ballads in English,—Collections
I. Kinsley, James, 1922–1984
784.3'06
ISBN 0–19–281330–7

Library of Congress Cataloging in Publication Data
Data available

Printed in Great Britain by
Richard Clay Ltd.
Bungay, Suffolk

PREFACE

THIS is an anthology of the traditional ballads of
Scotland and England. It replaces the Oxford Book
made by Sir Arthur Quiller-Couch in 1910 which,
although it established itself as Everyman's ballad
book, 'bringing together the best Ballads out of the
whole of our national stock' in a simple and elegant
form, has in half a century fallen out of date. For in
that time our notions of what a ballad is, and of what
is excellence in balladry, have grown broader and
more critical; editorial principles and standards have
changed; and we have learned again what generations
of scholars had forgotten—that ballads are narrative
songs in which music and poetry are interdependent.

As in the earlier book, most of the ballads here are
in the F. J. Child canon; but I have taken more from
the street than 'Q' was disposed to do—he edited for a
more prudish age, and thought anyhow of the broadside as 'crab-apple' balladry—and I have rejected a
number of his which seemed to me lyric rather than
narrative, or less ballad than dialogue, carol, or shanty.
Some 'literary' ballads by known poets have been
included (nos. 143–50): these imitations are often of
great intrinsic merit, they are useful in comparative
criticism, and they are part of the history of the genre.
(I have passed over the familiar and easily accessible
ballads of Wordsworth, Coleridge, and Keats.) Robin
Hood has less space here than he had in 1910. This is
not mere Scottish prejudice—that 'tales of Robin Hood

are good for fools' is an English proverb; some of the greenwood ballads are of poor quality, and have made way for other things.

Many of the texts in 'Q' were composite: not only where a lacuna in the tale could be filled from some fuller but otherwise inferior version, but also where conflation would preserve the finest poetry in a ballad's tradition. 'Q' apprenticed himself to Scott, who seemed to have worked out the right technique. In the *Minstrelsy of the Scottish Border* some of the greatest ballads had been judiciously assembled from various copies by a master in the craft. But Scott came to repent of the dubious fashion he had set in 'editing'. 'I think', he told William Motherwell on 3 May 1825, in a letter which marks a turning-point in ballad scholarship, 'I did wrong myself in endeavouring to make the best possible set of an ancient ballad out of several copies obtained from different quarters, and that in many respects if I improved the poetry I spoiled the simplicity of the old song.' Yet neither poetry nor even simplicity is as important here as textual integrity. A true ballad 'text' is the recording of one auditory experience, one singer's song, and even the scrupulous translation of that on to the printed page is a kind of embalming. But if it must be done, for the ballad to keep, there is still a moral as well as a technical difference between editing and fabrication.

The texts in this book are, with few exceptions, based on single versions. Wherever I could, I have gone beyond Child to his manuscript and printed sources, and I have taken many ballads from Victorian and more recent oral tradition. In choosing from among several versions of a ballad I have used three main criteria: (i) coherent but economical narrative—not 'poetry', for it is the story that matters; (ii) closeness to oral tradition (which often means taking a 'late' version); and (iii) early date, where the other criteria have been met or there are evidences of decay in the tradition of the ballad. I have thus depended as little as I could on collectors like Bishop Percy, Sir Walter Scott, and Peter Buchan, who in different ways 'mended' or elaborated their material; and as much as possible on manuscripts made from recitation and probably not much edited. Except where emendation was inevitable and obvious, I have held to my copy-text. The result is a book often less 'poetic' than its predecessor, and sometimes rougher and more primitive; but I hope my text is closer to the true ballad event, the singer's song. The orthography of the copy-texts has generally been retained, but I have repunctuated as lightly as I could without obscuring the sense. I have followed the early practice, in ballad manuscripts and printings, of not using quotation marks: a poem made for singing should not need them. Substantive alterations or additions to the copy-text are enclosed in square brackets.

'When is a ballad not a ballad?' asks Professor Bronson; 'When it has no tune.' In gathering the extant tunes to the 'Child' ballads here and in America, Bronson has made the greatest single contribution to ballad scholarship in this century: for the interaction of words and music has been demonstrated on the grand scale, and the coherence of the ballad form restored. We are beginning to see how music controls rhetoric and phrasing, the shape of the dialogue, the measure of 'obliqueness' possible to the ballad poet. I have therefore found space for tunes—more than eighty—at some sacrifice of verse. But I have given only those airs which were collected or published with the texts I print, or were in the same singer's repertoire, or (at the worst) derive from the same ballad area at about the same time. I have made conservative transcripts. The reader is warned that the verse does not always run easily over the music, and that he should (as Burns advised) assimilate the air thoroughly before taking up the song.

I have not followed 'Q' in dividing the ballads into 'books', or in marking off the vulgar from the high: the thematic patterns are too fluid, the levels of style too shifting, for that. I have, however, grouped ballads which are related in theme *or* in mood, and I have placed others as links or as contrasts. I hope that in this arrangement there may be delight as well as instruction. The first three ballads are Biblical. Nos. 4–30 are tales of faery, shape-shifting, and other magic. The 'romances' follow, moving from popular versions of medieval themes (nos. 31–2) through a great variety of love-tales happy and tragic to seductions and abductions (nos. 65–74), deceit and outrage (nos. 75–80), jealousy and hate (nos. 84–8), and devotion (nos. 90–4). Nos. 97–102 are greenwood ballads. Nos. 103–30 are mainly historical, including the 'riding ballads' of the Scottish Border. The next section is a miscellany of 'witty Inventions' (nos. 131–42), and the book ends with a series of 'literary' ballads. The notes indicate sources for poetry and music.

I gratefully acknowledge my debts to the following: Professor Otto Andersson of Åbo, Finland, for permission to use his text and air for no. 27; Professor B. H. Bronson, for allowing me to follow his conjectural readings for the airs to nos. 42 and 57; Mr. Francis Collinson, Mr. Hamish Henderson, and the staff of the School of Scottish Studies in Edinburgh, for the text and air of no. 62 and other services; Mrs. Anne Ehrenpreis for allowing me to use her text of no. 149; Mr. David Murison, editor of the Scottish National Dictionary, for help with glosses; Mr. P. N. Shuldham-Shaw, for permission to use the tune of no. 17; Oliver and Boyd, Edinburgh, for permission to reprint no. 150; the Librarians of the National Library of Scotland, the Bodleian Library, the British Museum, Nottingham Public Library, and the University Librarians at Aberdeen, Edinburgh, Glasgow, Harvard, and Nottingham, for access to manuscripts and rare prints; and to Mr. R. Fleetwood of the University Library, Nottingham, for the diligent pursuit of collections of ballads.

There is no propriety in dedicating editions of other men's work. But if an editor may be allowed to declare a 'special intention', mine has been to make a ballad book for

LOUISE, MALCOLM, and GAVIN.

JAMES KINSLEY

The University
Nottingham

ix

CONTENTS

CONTENTS

CONTENTS

CONTENTS

CONTENTS

xv

CONTENTS

1. *The Cherry-tree Carol*

JOSEPH was an old man,
    And an old man was he,
When he wedded Mary
    In the land of Galilee.

Joseph and Mary walked
    Through an orchard good,
Where was cherries and berries
    So red as any blood.

Joseph and Mary walked
    Through an orchard green,
Where was berries and cherries
    As thick as might be seen.

O then bespoke Mary
    So meek and so mild:
Pluck me one cherry, Joseph,
    For I am with child.

O then bespoke Joseph
    With words most unkind:
Let him pluck thee a cherry
    That brought thee with child.

O then bespoke the Babe
  Within his Mother's womb:
Bow down then the tallest tree
  For my Mother to have some.

Then bowed down the highest tree
  Unto his Mother's hand;
Then she cried, See, Joseph,
  I have cherries at command.

O then bespake Joseph:
  I have done Mary wrong;
But cheer up, my dearest,
  And be not cast down.

Then Mary plucked a cherry
  As red as the blood,
Then Mary went home
  With her heavy load.

Then Mary took her Babe
  And sat him on her knee,
Saying, My dear Son, tell me
  What this world will be.

O I shall be as dead, Mother,
  As the stones in the wall;
O the stones in the streets, Mother,
  Shall mourn for me all.

Upon Easter-day, Mother,
  My uprising shall be;
O the sun and the moon, Mother,
  Shall both rise with me.

2. *Seynt Steuyn and Herowdes*

SEYNT Steuene was a clerk
  In kyng Herowdes halle,
And seruyd him of bred and cloþ
  As euery kyng befalle.

Steuyn out of kechone cam
  Wyth boris hed on honde;
He saw a sterre was fayr and bryȝt
  Ouer Bedlem stonde.

He kyst adoun þe boris hed
  And went in to þe halle:
I forsak þe, kyng Herowdes,
  And þi werkes alle.

I forsak þe, kyng Herowdes,
  And þi werkes alle;
þer is a chyld in Bedlem born,
  Is beter þan we alle.

Quat eylyt þe, Steuene?
  Quat is þe befalle?
Lakkyt þe eyþer mete or drynk
  In kyng Herowdes halle?

Lakit me neyþer mete ne drynk
  In kyng Herowdes halle;
þer is a chyld in Bedlem born,
  Is beter þan we alle.

of bred and cloþ] in return for food and clothing   befalle] befits
kechone] kitchen   Bedlem] Bethlehem   kyst] cast   eylyt]
is the matter with

3

Quat eylyt þe, Steuyn? art þu wod,
  Or þu gynnyst to brede?
Lakkyt þe eyþer gold or fe,
  Or ony ryche wede?

Lakyt me neyþer gold ne fe
  Ne non ryche wede;
þer is a chyld in Bedlem born,
  Sal helpyn vs at our nede.

þat is al so soþ, Steuyn,
  Al so soþ, iwys,
As þis capoun crowe sal
  þat lyþ here in myn dysh.

þat word was not so sone seyd,
  þat word in þat halle,
þe capoun crew *Cristus natus est*
  Among þe lordes alle.

Rysyt vp, myn turmentowres,
  Be to and al be on,
And ledyt Steuyn out of þis town
  And stonyt hym wyth ston!

Tokyn he Steuene
  And stonyd hym in the way,
And þerfore is his euyn
  On Crystes owyn day.

wod] mad   þu . . . brede] are you with child   wede] apparel
iwys] indeed   Rysyt . . . ledyt . . . stonyt] Rise . . . lead . . . stone
turmentowres] torturess   Be to . . . on] By two . . . one   euyn]
eve

3. *Dives and Lazarus*

As it fell out upon a day
  Rich Dives he made a feast,
And he invited all his friends
  And gentry of the best.

Then Lazarus laid him down and down
  And down at Dives' door:
Some meat, some drink, brother Dives,
  Bestow upon the poor.

Thou art none of my brother, Lazarus,
  That lies begging at my door;
No meat nor drink will I give thee
  Nor bestow upon the poor.

Then Lazarus laid him down and down
  And down at Dives' wall:
Some meat, some drink, brother Dives,
  Or with hunger starve I shall.

Thou art none of my brother, Lazarus,
  That lies begging at my wall;
No meat nor drink will I give thee
  But with hunger starve you shall.

Then Lazarus laid him down and down
  And down at Dives' gate:
Some meat, some drink, brother Dives,
  For Jesus Christ his sake.

Thou art none of my brother, Lazarus,
   That lies begging at my gate;
No meat nor drink will I give thee
   For Jesus Christ his sake.

Then Dives sent out his merry men
   To whip poor Lazarus away;
They had no power to strike a stroke
   But flung their whips away.

Then Dives sent out his hungry dogs
   To bite him as he lay;
They had no power to bite at all
   But licked his sores away.

As it fell out upon a day
   Poor Lazarus sickened and died;
Then came two angels out of heaven
   His soul therein to guide.

Rise up, rise up, brother Lazarus,
   And go along with me;
For you've a place prepared in heaven
   To sit on an angel's knee.

As it fell out upon a day
   Rich Dives sickened and died;
Then came two serpents out of hell
   His soul therein to guide.

Rise up, rise up, brother Dives,
   And go with us to see
A dismal place prepared in hell
   From which thou canst not flee.

Then Dives looked up with his eyes
  And saw poor Lazarus blest:
Give me one drop of water, brother Lazarus,
  To quench my flaming thirst.

Oh had I as many years to abide
  As there are blades of grass,
Then there would be an end, but now
  Hell's pains will ne'er be past.

Oh was I now but alive again
  The space of one half hour;
Oh that I had my peace secure;
  Then the devil should have no power.

4. *Thomas the Rhymer*

TRUE Thomas lay on Huntlie bank,
  A ferlie he spied wi' his e'e;
And there he saw a ladye bright
  Come riding down by the Eildon Tree.

Her shirt was o' the grass-green silk,
  Her mantle o' the velvet fyne;
At ilka tett of her horse's mane
  Hung fifty siller bells and nine.

Huntlie] tributary of the Tweed, near Melrose   ferlie] marvel
Eildon] hills in the parish of Melrose   ilka tett] each tuft

True Thomas, he pull'd aff his cap
   And louted low down to his knee:
All hail, thou mighty Queen of Heaven!
   For thy peer on earth I never did see.

O no, O no, Thomas, she said,
   That name does not belang to me;
I am but the Queen of fair Elfland
   That am hither come to visit thee.

Harp and carp, Thomas, she said,
   Harp and carp along wi' me,
And if ye dare to kiss my lips,
   Sure of your bodie I will be.

Betide me weal, betide me woe,
   That weird shall never daunton me.
Syne he has kissed her rosy lips
   All underneath the Eildon Tree.

Now ye maun go wi' me, she said,
   True Thomas, ye maun go wi' me;
And ye maun serve me seven years
   Thro' weal or woe, as may chance to be.

She mounted on her milk-white steed,
   She's ta'en True Thomas up behind;
And aye whene'er her bridle rung
   The steed flew swifter than the wind.

louted] bowed   carp] sing, recite   weird] fate   daunton]
cast down   Syne] then   maun] must

O they rade on, and farther on—
    The steed gaed swifter than the wind—
Untill they reach'd a desart wide
    And living land was left behind.

Light down, light down now, True Thomas,
    And lean your head upon my knee;
Abide and rest a little space
    And I will shew you ferlies three.

O see ye not yon narrow road
    So thick beset with thorns and briers?
That is the path of righteousness,
    Though after it but few enquires.

And see ye not that braid, braid road
    That lies across that lily leven?
That is the path of wickedness,
    Though some call it the road to heaven.

And see not ye that bonny road
    That winds about the fernie brae?
That is the road to fair Elfland,
    Where thou and I this night maun gae.

But Thomas, ye maun hold your tongue
    Whatever ye may hear or see,
For if you speak word in Elflyn land
    Ye'll ne'er get back to your ain countrie.

lily] lovely   leven] lea (*nonce variant*)

O they rade on, and farther on,
   And they waded through rivers aboon the knee,
And they saw neither sun nor moon
   But they heard the roaring of the sea.

It was mirk, mirk night and there was nae stern light
   And they waded through red blude to the knee;
For a' the blude that 's shed on earth
   Rins through the springs o' that countrie.

Syne they came on to a garden green
   And she pu'd an apple frae a tree:
Take this for thy wages, True Thomas,
   It will give thee the tongue that can never lie.

My tongue is mine ain, True Thomas said,
   A gudely gift ye wad gie to me;
I neither dought to buy nor sell
   At fair or tryst where I may be;

I dought neither speak to prince or peer
   Nor ask of grace from fair ladye.
Now hold thy peace, the lady said,
   For as I say, so must it be.

He has gotten a coat of the even cloth
   And a pair of shoes of velvet green;
And till seven years were gane and past
   True Thomas on earth was never seen.

mirk] dark   stern] star   dought] dare   tryst] market
even cloth] smooth cloth

5. *The Wee Wee Man*

As I was walking all alone
   Between a Water and a Wa'
And there I spyed a wee wee man
   And he was the least that ere I saw.

His Leggs were scarce a Shathmont's length
   And thick and thimber was his thigh,
Between his Brows there was a Span
   And between his Shoulders there was three.

He took up a meikle Stane
   And he flang 't as far as I could see;
Tho I had been a Wallace wight
   I couldna liften 't to my knee.

Wa'] wall   Shathmont] measurement, from the tip of the stretched
thumb across the palm; six inches   thimber] massive   Span]
measurement of the extended hand; nine inches   meikle] large
a Wallace wight] as strong as William Wallace himself   liften]
(have) lifted

O wee wee man but thou be strong,
  O tell me whare thy dwelling be;
My dwelling down at yon bonny Bower
  O will you go with me and see.

On we lap and awa we rade
  Till we came to yon bonny Green;
We lighted down for to bait our horse
  And out there came a Lady fine.

Four and twenty at her Back
  And they were a' clad out in Green;
Tho the king of Scotland had been there
  The warst o' them might hae been his Queen.

On we lap and awa we rade
  Till we cam to yon bonny ha'
Whare the roof was o' the beaten gould
  And the floor was o' the Cristal a'.

When we came to the Stair foot
  Ladies were dancing jimp and sma,
But in the twinkling of an Eye
  My wee wee man was clean awa.

lap] leapt   bait] rest and feed   jimp] graceful   sma] slender

6. *Tam Lin*

O I forbid you, maidens a'
    That wear gowd on your hair,
To come, or gae by Carterhaugh,
    For young Tom-lin is there.

There 's nane that gaes by Carterhaugh
    But they leave him a wad;
Either their rings, or green mantles,
    Or else their maidenhead.

Janet has kilted her green kirtle,
    A little aboon her knee;
And she has broded her yellow hair
    A little aboon her bree;
And she 's awa to Carterhaugh
    As fast as she can hie.

When she cam to Carterhaugh
    Tom-lin was at the well,
And there she fand his steed standing
    But away was himsel.

gowd] gold near Selkirk   Carterhaugh] where the Ettrick and Yarrow meet,
bree] eyebrow   wad] forfeit   kirtle] skirts   broded] braided
fand] found   at the well] i.e. identified as under enchantment

She had na pu'd a double rose,
  A rose but only tway,
Till up then started young Tom-lin,
  Says, Lady, thou 's pu' nae mae.

Why pu's thou the rose, Janet,
  And why breaks thou the wand?
Or why comes thou to Carterhaugh
  Withoutten my command?

Carterhaugh it is my ain,
  My daddie gave it me;
I'll come and gang by Carterhaugh
  And ask nae leave at thee.

Janet has kilted her green kirtle
  A little aboon her knee,
And she has snooded her yellow hair
  A little aboon her bree,
And she is to her father's ha,
  As fast as she can hie.

Four and twenty ladies fair
  Were playing at the ba',
And out then cam the fair Janet,
  Ance the flower amang them a'.

Four and twenty ladies fair
  Were playing at the chess,
And out then cam the fair Janet,
  As green as onie glass.

tway] two   mae] more   wand] branch, stem   snooded]
bound up in a band   the ba'] handball

Out then spak an auld grey knight,
　　Lay o'er the castle-wa',
And says, Alas, fair Janet for thee
　　But we'll be blamed a'.

Haud your tongue ye auld-fac'd knight,
　　Some ill death may ye die,
Father my bairn on whom I will,
　　I'll father nane on thee.

Out then spak her father dear,
　　And he spak meek and mild,
And ever alas, sweet Janet, he says,
　　I think thou gaes wi' child.

If that I gae wi' child, father,
　　Mysel maun bear the blame;
There's ne'er a laird about your ha',
　　Shall get the bairn's name.

If my Love were an earthly knight,
　　As he's an elfin grey;
I wad na gie my ain true-love
　　For nae lord that ye hae.

The steed that my true-love rides on,
　　Is lighter than the wind;
Wi' siller he is shod before,
　　Wi' burning gowd behind.

Janet has kilted her green kirtle
　　A little aboon her knee;
And she has snooded her yellow hair

Haud] hold　　gaes] go　　maun] must　　laird] squire

15

A little aboon her brie;
And she 's awa to Carterhaugh
   As fast as she can hie.

When she cam to Carterhaugh,
   Tom-lin was at the well;
And there she fand his steed standing,
   But away was himsel.

She had na pu'd a double rose,
   A rose but only tway,
Till up then started young Tom-lin,
   Says, Lady thou pu's nae mae.

Why pu's thou the rose Janet,
   Amang the groves sae green,
And a' to kill the bonie babe
   That we gat us between.

O tell me, tell me, Tom-lin she says,
   For's sake that died on tree,
If e'er ye was in holy chapel,
   Or Christendom did see.

Roxbrugh he was my grandfather,
   Took me with him to bide,
And ance it fell upon a day
   That wae did me betide.

Ance it fell upon a day,
   A cauld day and a snell,
When we were frae the hunting come
   That frae my horse I fell.

bide] stay   snell] bitter

The queen o' Fairies she caught me,
  In yon green hill to dwell,
And pleasant is the fairy-land;
  But, an eerie tale to tell!

Ay at the end of seven years
  We pay a tiend to hell;
I am sae fair and fu' o flesh
  I'm fear'd it be mysel.

But the night is Halloween, lady,
  The morn is Hallowday;
Then win me, win me, an ye will,
  For weel I wat ye may.

Just at the mirk and midnight hour
  The fairy folk will ride;
And they that wad their truelove win,
  At Milescross they maun bide.

But how shall I thee ken, Tom-lin,
  O how my truelove know,
Amang sae mony unco knights
  The like I never saw.

O first let pass the black, Lady,
  And syne let pass the brown;
But quickly run to the milk-white steed,
  Pu ye his rider down:

For I'll ride on the milk-white steed,
  And ay nearest the town;
Because I was an earthly knight
  They gie me that renown.

tiend] tithe   an] if   mirk] dark   Milescross] near Carterhaugh   unco] strange   syne] then

My right hand will be glov'd, lady,
   My left hand will be bare;
Cockt up shall my bonnet be,
   And kaim'd down shall my hair;
And thae's the tokens I gie thee,
   Nae doubt I will be there.

They'll turn me in your arms, lady,
   Into an ask and adder,
But hald me fast and fear me not,
   I am your bairn's father.

They'll turn me to a bear sae grim,
   And then a lion bold;
But hold me fast and fear me not,
   As ye shall love your child.

Again they'll turn me in your arms
   To a red het gaud of airn;
But hold me fast and fear me not,
   I'll do to you nae harm.

And last they'll turn me, in your arms,
   Into the burning lead;
Then throw me into well-water,
   O throw me in wi' speed!

And then I'll be your ain truelove,
   I'll turn a naked knight:
Then cover me wi' your green mantle,
   And cover me out o sight.

kaim'd] combed   thae's] these are   ask] eft, lizard   het
gaud of airn] hot iron bar

Gloomy, gloomy was the night,
  And eerie was the way,
As fair Jenny in her green mantle
  To Milescross she did gae.

About the middle o' the night
  She heard the bridles ring;
This lady was as glad at that
  As any earthly thing.

First she let the black pass by,
  And syne she let the brown;
But quickly she ran to the milk-white steed,
  And pu'd the rider down.

Sae weel she minded what he did say
  And young Tom-lin did win;
Syne cover'd him wi' her green mantle
  As blythe's a bird in spring.

Out then spak the queen o' Fairies,
  Out of a bush o' broom;
Them that has gotten young Tom-lin,
  Has gotten a stately groom.

Out then spak the queen o' Fairies,
  And an angry queen was she;
Shame betide her ill-far'd face,
  And an ill death may she die,
For she 's ta'en awa the boniest knight
  In a' my companie.

minded] remembered

But had I ken'd, Tom-lin, she says,
　　What now this night I see,
I wad hae ta'en out thy twa grey e'en,
　　And put in twa een o' tree.

tree] wood

7. *Sir Colin*

THE king luikit owre his castle wa'
　　To his nobles ane an' a',
Says, Whare is it him Sir Colin,
　　I dinna see him amang you a'?

Up it spak an eldern knicht,
　　Aye an' even up spak he:
Sir Colin 's sick for your dochter Janet,
　　He 's very sick an' like to dee.

Win up, win up, my dochter Janet,
　　I wat ye are a match most fine;
Tak the baken bread an' wine sae ried
　　An' to Sir Colin ye maun gieng.

dinna] don't　　eldern] old　　　even up] forthrightly　　Win]
get　　wat] know, believe　　maun gieng] must go

Up she rase, that fair Janet,
  An' I wat weel she was na sweer;
An' up they rase, her merrie maries,
  An' they said a' they wad gae wi' her.

No, no, said fair Janet,
  No, no such thing can be;
For a thrang to gae to a sick man's bour
  I think it wald be great folie.

How is my knicht, all last nicht?
  Very sick an' like to dee;
But if I had a kiss o' your sweet lips
  I wald lie nae langer here.

She leant her doon on his bed-side,
  I wat she gae him kisses three;
But wi' sighen said that fair Janet,
  As for your bride, I daurna be;

Unless you watch the Orlange hill,
  An' at that hill there grows a thorn;
There ne'er cam a liven man frae it
  Sin' the first nicht that I was born.

Oh I will watch the Orlange hill
  Though I waur thinkin to be slain;
But I will gie you some love tokens
  In case we never meet again.

He gae her rings to her fingers,
  Sae did he ribbons to her hair;
He gae her a broach to her briest-bane
  For fear that they sud ne'er meet mair.

na sweer] not reluctant   maries] maids, ladies   gae] go   thrang]
crowd   daurna] dare not   Orlange] ? *eldritch*, haunted
liven] living   waur thinkin] were expecting   broach] brooch

She put her hand in her pocket
   An' she took out a lang, lang wand:
As lang 's ony man this wand sall keep
   There sall not a drap o' his blude be drawn.

When e'en was come an' e'en-bells rung,
   An' a' man boun for bed,
There beheld him Sir Colin,
   Fast to the Orlange hill he rade.

The wind blew trees oot at the rutes,
   Sae did it auld castles doon;
'Twas eneuch to fricht ony Christian knicht
   To be sae far frae ony toon.

He rade up, sae did he doon,
   He rade even through the loan,
Till he spied a knicht wi' a ladie bricht,
   Wi' a bent bow intil his han'.

She cried afar ere she cam naur,
   I warn ye, kind sir, I rede ye flee;
That for the love you bear to me
   I warn ye, kind sir, that ye flee.

They faucht up, sae did they doon,
   They faucht even through the loan,
Till he cut aff the king's richt han',
   Was set aboot wi' chains [o'] goud.

wand] branch   boun] ready   eneuch] enough   loan]
cattle road   naur] near   rede] advise   goud] gold

Haud your hand now, Sir Colin,
   I wat you've dung my love richt sair;
Noo for the love ye bear to me
   See that ye ding my love nae mair.

He wooed, he wooed that fair Janet,
   He wooed her and he brocht her hame;
He wooed, he wooed that fair Janet
   An' ca'd her Dear-Coft till her name.

Haud] hold   dung] struck   Dear-Coft till] Dearly Bought for

8. *Sir Aldingar*

OUR king he kept a ffalse steward
   Men called him Sir Aldingar.
He wolde haue layen by our comely queene,
   Her deere worshipp to haue betraide;
Our queene shee was a good woman
   And euer more said him nay.

Aldingar was offended in his mind,
   With her hee was neuer content,
But he sought what meanes he cold find out
   In a fyer to haue her brent.

There came a lame lazer to the Kings gates,
   A lazar was [b]lind and lame;
He tooke the lazar vpon his backe
   Vpon the queenes bed he did him lay;

worshipp] honour, reputation   brent] burnt   lazer] leper

He said, Lye still, lazar, wheras thou lyest,
    Looke thou goe not away,
Ile make thee a whole man and a sound
    In two howres of a day.

And then went forth Sir Aldingar
    Our Queene for to betray,
And then he mett with our comlye King,
    Saies, God you saue and see!

If I had space as I haue grace,
    A message I wold say to thee.
Say on, say on, Sir Aldingar,
    Say thou on and vnto me.

I can let you now see one of [the] greiuos[est] sights
    That euer Christen King did see:
Our Queene hath chosen a new new loue,
    She will haue none of thee;

If shee had chosen a right good Knight
    The lesse had beene her shame,
But she hath chosen a Lazar man
    Which is both blinde and lame.

If this be true, thou Aldingar,
    That thou dost tell to me,
Then will I make thee a rich Knight
    Both of gold and fee.

But if it be false, Sir Aldingar,
    That thou doest tell to me,
Then looke for noe other death
    But to be hangd on a tree.

fee] property

Goe with me, saide our comly king,
   This Lazar for to see.

When the King he came into the queenes chamber,
   Standing her bed befor,
There is a lodly lome, says Harry King,
   For our dame Queene Elinor!

If thou were a man, as thou art none,
   Here thou sholdest be slaine;
But a paire of New gallowes shall be bult,
   Thoust hang on them soe hye;

And fayre fyer there salbe bett,
   And brent our Queene salbee.
Forth then walked our comlye King,
   And mett with our comly Queene.

Saies, God you saue, our Queene, Madam,
   And Christ you saue and see!
Heere you haue chosen a new new loue
   And you will haue none of mee.

If you had chosen a right good Knight
   The lesse had beene your shame,
But you haue chosen a lazar man
   That is both blind and lame.

Euer alacke, said our comly Queene,
   Sir Aldingar is false to mee;
But euer alacke, said our comly Queene,
   Euer alas, and woe is mee!

lodly lome] loathsome cripple   salbe bett] shall be kindled

I had thought sweuens had neuer been true,
    I haue prooued them true at the last;
I dreamed in my sweauen on thursday at eueninge
    In my bed wheras I lay,

I dreamed the grype and a grimlie beast
    Had carryed my crowne away,
My gorgett and my Kirtle of golde
    And all my faire heade geere;

How he wold haue worryed me with his tush
    And borne me into his nest:
Saving there came a litle hawk
    Flying out of the East,

Saving there came a litle Hawke
    Which men call a Merlion;
Vntill the ground he stroke him downe,
    That dead he did fall downe.

Giffe I were a man, as I am none,
    A battell I wold proue,
I wold fight with that false traitor;
    Att him I cast my gloue!

Seing I am able noe battell to make,
    You must grant me, my leege, a Knight
To fight with that traitor, Sir Aldingar,
    To maintaine me in my right.

sweuens] dreams   grype] griffin   grimlie] fierce   gorgett]
neckerchief   Kirtle] gown   geere] adornments   tush] tusk
proue] try

Ile giue thee forty dayes, said our King,
   To seeke thee a man therin;
If thou find not a man in forty dayes,
   In a hott fyer thou shall brenn.

Our Queene sent forth a Messenger,
   He rode fast into the South,
He rode the countryes through and through
   Soe ffar vnto Portsmouth;
He cold find never a man in the South country
   That wold fight with the Knight soe keene.

The Second messenger the Queen forth sent
   Rode far into the east,
But (blessed be God made sunn and moone)
   He sped then all of the best.

As he rode then by one riuer side
   There he mett with a litle Child;
He seemed noe more in a mans likenesse
   Then a child of four yeeres old.

He askt the Queenes Messenger how far he rode,
   Loth he was him to tell;
The litle one was offended att him,
   Bid him adew, farwell!

Said, Turne thou againe, thou Messenger,
   Greete our Queene well from me;
When Bale is att hyest, boote is att next,
   Helpe enough there may bee!

Bale] evil   boote] help

Bid our queene remember what she did dreame
 In her bedd wheras shee lay:
Shee dreamed the grype and the grimly beast
 Had carryed her crowne away,

Her gorgett and her Kirt[l]e of gold,
 Alsoe her faire head geere.
He wold haue werryed her with his tushe
 And borne her into his nest;

Saving there came a litle hawke,
 Men call him a merlyon,
Vntill the ground he did strike him downe
 That dead he did ffall downe.

Bidd the queene be merry att her hart,
 Euermore light and glad;
When bale is att hyest, boote is at next,
 Helpe enoughe there shalbe [had].

Then the Queenes messenger rode backe,
 A gladed man then was hee;
When he came before our Queene,
 A gladd woman then was shee.

Shee gaue the Messenger twenty pound
 O lord, in gold and ffee;
Saies, Spend and spare not while this doth last,
 Then feitch thou more of me.

Our Queene was put in a tunne to burne,
 She thought no thing but death.
They were ware of the litle one
 Came ryding forth of the East

tunne] barrel

With a Mu [   ]
   A louelie child was hee;
When he came to that fier
   He light the Queene full nigh.

Said, Draw away these brands of fire
   Lie burning before our Queene,
And feitch me hither Sir Aldingar
   That is a knight soe keene.

When Aldingar see that litle one
   Full litle of him hee thought;
If there had beene halfe a hundred such
   Of them he wold not haue wrought.

Hee sayd, Come hither Sir Aldingar,
   Thou see-must as bigge as a ffooder;
I trust to God, ere I haue done with thee,
   God will send to vs auger.

Saies, The first stroke thats giuen, Sir Aldingar,
   I will giue vnto thee,
And if the second giue thou may,
   Looke then thou spare not mee.

The litle one pulld forth a well good sword,
   I-wis itt was all of guilt;
It cast light there over that feild,
   It shone soe all of guilt.

He stroke the first stroke att Aldingar,
   He stroke away his leggs by his knee;
Sayes, Stand vp, stand vp, thou false traitor,
   And fight vpon thy feete;

see-must] seemest   ffooder] cask   of guilt] gilded

For and thou thriue as thou begins,
    Of a height wee salbe meete.

A preist, a preist, sayes Aldingar,
    Me for to houzle and shriue!
A preist, a preist, sayes Aldingar,
    While I am a man liuing a-liue!

I wold haue laine by our comlie Queene,
    To it shee wold neuer consent;
I thought to haue betrayd her to our King,
    In a fyer to haue had her brent.

There came a lame Lazar to the Kings gates,
    A lazar both blind and lame;
I tooke the lazar vpon my back,
    In the Queenes bed I did him lay.

I bad him lie still, Lazar, where he lay,
    Looke he went not away;
I wold make him a whole man and a sound
    In two houres of a day.

Euer alacke, sayes Sir Aldingar,
    Falsing neuer doth well;
Forgiue, forgiue me, Queene, Madam,
    For Christs loue forgiue me!
God forgaue his death, Aldingar,
    And freely I forgiue thee.

Now take thy wife, thou King Harry,
    And loue her as thou shold;
Thy wiffe shee is as true to thee
    As stone that lies on the castle wall.

For and] for if   meete] equal   houzle] administer Communion to   shriue] absolve

The Lazar vnder the gallow tree
  Was a pretty man and small,
The Lazar vnder the gallow tree
  Was made steward in king Henerys hall.

9. *The Boy and the Mantle*

IN the third day of May
  To Carleile did come
A kind curteous child
  That cold much of wisdome.

A kirtle and a Mantle
  This Child had vppon,
With brauches and ringes
  Full richelye bedone.

He had a sute of silke
  About his middle drawne;
Without he cold of curtesye,
  He thought itt much shame.

God speed thee, King Arthur,
  Sitting att thy meate;
And the goodlye Queene Gueneuer,
  I cannott her fforgett.

I tell you Lords in this hall,
  I hett you all hea[d]e,
Except you be the more surer
  Is you for to dread.

cold] knew   kirtle] tunic   brauches] brooches   bedone]
adorned   Without . . . curtesye] If he had not courtly manners
hett] bid

He plucked out of his potewer,
  And longer wold not dwell,
He pulled forth a pretty mantle
  Betweene two nut-shells.

Haue thou here, King Arthure,
  Haue thou heere of mee;
Giue itt to thy comely queene
  Shapen as itt is alreadye;

Itt shall neuer become that wiffe
  That hath once done amisse.
Then euery Knight in the Kings court
  Began to care for his.

Forth came dame Gueneuer,
  To the mantle shee her biled:
The Ladye shee was new fangle,
  But yett shee was affrayd.

When shee had taken the Mantle,
  Shee stoode as she had beene madd:
It was from the top to the toe
  As sheeres had itt shread.

One while was itt gaule,
  Another while was itt greene,
Another while was itt wadded,—
  Ill itt did her beseeme,—

potewer] pautener, purse   care for] be concerned about   biled]
led the way   new fangle] attracted by the novelty   gaule]
gules, red   wadded] woaded, blue

Another while was it blacke
  And bore the worst hue.
By my troth, quoth King Arthur,
  I thinke thou be not true.

She threw downe the mantle
  That bright was of blee.
Fast with a rudd redd
  To her chamber can shee flee;

Shee curst the weauer and the walker
  That clothe that had wrought,
And bade a vengeance on his crowne
  That hither hath itt brought;

I had rather be in a wood
  Vnder a greene tree,
Then in King Arthurs court
  Shamed for to bee.

Kay called forth his ladye,
  And bade her come neere;
Saies, Madam, and thou be guiltye,
  I pray thee hold thee there.

Forth came his Ladye
  Shortlye and anon;
Boldlye to the Mantle
  Then is shee gone.

When she had tane the Mantle
  And cast it her about,
Then was shee bare
  All aboue the Buttocckes.

blee] colour   rudd] complexion   can] did   walker] fuller
and thou] if thou

Then euery Knight
  That was in the Kings court
Talked, laughed, and showted,
  Full oft att that sport.

Shee threw downe the mantle
  That bright was of blee:
Fast with a red rudd
  To her chamber can shee flee.

Forth came an old Knight
  Pattering ore a creede,
And he proferred to this litle boy
  Twenty markes to his meede

And all the time of the Christmasse
  Willinglye to ffeede,
For why this Mantle might
  Doe his wiffe some need.

When shee had tane the mantle
  Of cloth that was made,
Shee had no more left on her
  But a tassell and a threed;
Then euery Knight in the Kings court
  Bade, Euill might shee speed.

Shee threw downe the Mantle
  That bright was of blee,
And fast with a redd rudd
  To her chamber can shee flee.

meede] reward   For why] because

34

Craddocke called forth his Ladye,
   And bade her come in;
Saith, Winne this mantle, Ladye,
   With a litle dinne:

Winne this mantle, Ladye,
   And it salbe thine
If thou neuer did amisse
   Since thou wast mine.

Forth came Craddockes Ladye
   Shortlye and anon,
But boldlye to the Mantle
   Then is shee gone.

When shee had tane the mantle
   And cast itt her about,
Vpp att her great toe
   Itt began to crinkle and crowt;
Shee said, Bowe downe, Mantle,
   And Shame me not for nought;

Once I did amisse,
   I tell you certainlye,
When I kist Craddockes mouth
   Vnder a greene tree,
When I kist Craddockes mouth
   Before he marryed mee.

When shee had her shreeuen,
   And her sines shee had tolde,
The mantle stoode about her
   Right as shee wold,

Craddocke] Carados Briefbras   dinne] ado   crowt] pucker
her shreeuen] confessed   wold] wished

Seemelye of coulour,
  Glittering like gold.
Then euery Knight in Arthurs court
  Did her behold.

Then spake dame Gueneuer
  To Arthur our King,
She hath tane yonder mantle,
  Not with wright but with wronge!

See you not yonder woman
  That maketh her selfe soe cleare?
I haue seene tane out of her bedd
  Of men fiueteene,

Preists, Clarkes, and wedded men
  From her by-deene:
Yett shee taketh the mantle
  And maketh her-selfe cleane!

Then spake the litle boy
  That kept the mantle in hold;
Sayes, King! Chasten thy wiffe!
  Of her words shee is to bold.

Shee is a bitch and a witch,
  And a whore bold!
King, in thine owne hall
  Thou art a Cuchold!

[The] litle boy stoode
  Looking ouer a dore;
He was ware of a wyld bore
  Wold haue werryed a man.

by-deene] one after another   werryed] savaged

36

He pulld forth a wood kniffe;
  Fast thither that he ran;
He brought in the bores head,
  And quitted him like a man.

He brought in the bores head,
  And was wonderous bold:
He said, There was neuer a Cucholds kniffe
  Carue itt that cold.

Some rubbed their kniues
  Vppon a whetstone;
Some threw them vnder the table,
  And said they had none.

King Arthus and the Child
  Stood looking them vpon;
All their kniues edges
  Turned backe againe.

Craddoccke had a litle kniue
  Of Iron and of steele;
He birtled the bores head
  Wonderous weele,
That euery Knight in the Kings court
  Had a morssell.

The litle boy had a horne
  Of red gold that ronge;
He said, There was noe Cuckolde
  Shall drinke of my horne,
But he shold itt sheede
  Either behind or beforne.

cold] could   birtled] cut up   ronge] rang   sheede] spill

Some shedd on their shoulder,
    And some on their knee;
He that cold not hitt his mouth
    Put it in his eye;
And he that was a Cuckold,
    Euery man might him see.

Craddoccke wan the horne
    And the bores head;
His ladye wan the mantle
    Vnto her meede.
Euerye such a louely Ladye,
    God send her well to speede!

meede] reward

10. *Gil Brenton*

GIL BRENTON has sent o'er the fame,
He 's woo'd a wife an' brought her hame.

Full sevenscore o' ships came her wi',
The lady by the greenwood tree.

There was twal' an' twal' wi' beer an' wine,
An' twal' an' twal' wi' muskadine;

An' twall an' twall wi' bouted flowr
An' twall an' twall wi' paramour;

An' twall an' twall wi' baken bread,
An' twall an' twall wi' the goud sae red.

fame] foam   twal'] twelve   muskadine] muscatel, wine
bouted] sifted   paramour] *not identified*   goud] gold

Sweet Willy was a widow's son,
An' at her stirrup-foot he did run.

An' she was dress'd i' the finest pa',
But ay she loot the tears down fa'.

An' she was deck'd wi' the fairest flow'rs,
But ay she loot the tears down pour.

O is there water i' your shee?
Or does the win' blaw i' your glee?

Or are you mourning i' your meed
That e'er you left your mither gueede?

Or are ye mourning i' your tide
That ever ye was Gil Brenton's bride?

The[re] is nae water i' my shee,
Nor does the win' blaw i' my glee:

Nor am I mourning i' my tide
That e'er I was Gil Brenton's bride:

But I am mourning i' my meed
That ever I left my mither gueede.

But, bonny boy, tell to me
What is the customs o' your country.

The customs o 't, my dame, he says,
Will ill a gentle lady please.

pa'] pall, rich purple cloth   loot] let   shee] shoe   glee] glove
meed] mood, heart   gueede] good   tide] time

Seven king's daughters has our king wedded,
An' seven king's daughters has our king bedded.

But he 's cutted the paps frae their breastbane
An' sent them mourning hame again.

But whan you come to the palace yate,
His mither a golden chair will set.

An' be you maid or be you nane,
O sit you there till the day be dane.

An' gin you're sure that you are a maid
Ye may gang safely to his bed.

But gin o' that you be na sure,
Then hire some woman o' youre bow'r.

O whan she came to the palace yate,
His mither a golden chair did set.

An' was she maid or was she nane,
She sat in it till the day was dane.

An' she 's call'd on her bow'r woman
That waiting was her bow'r within:

Five hundred pound, maid, I'll gi' to the[e],
An' sleep this night wi' the king for me.

Whan bells was rung an' mass was sung
An' a' man unto bed was gone,

yate] gate   gin] if   gang] go

Gil Brenton an' the bonny maid,
Intill ae chamber they were laid.

O speak to me, blankets, an' speak to me, sheets,
An' speak to me, cods, that under me sleeps:

Is this a maid that I ha' wedded?
Is this a maid that I ha' bedded?

It 's nae a maid that you ha' wedded,
But it 's a maid that you ha' bedded.

Your lady 's in her bigly bow'r,
An' for you she drees mony sharp show'r.

O he has ta'en him thro' the ha',
And on his mither he did ca'.

I am the most unhappy man
That ever was in christen'd lan'.

I woo'd a maiden meek an' mild,
An' I've married a woman great wi' child.

O stay, my son, intill this ha'
An' sport you wi' your merry men a';

An' I'll gang to yon painted bow'r
An' see how 't fares wi' yon base whore.

The auld queen she was stark an' strang,
She gar'd the door flee aff the ban';

ae] one   cods] pillows   bigly] pleasant   drees] suffers
intill] within   stark] violent   gar'd] made   ban'] part of
hinge fastened to the door

The auld queen she was stark an' steer,
She gar'd the door lye i' the fleer.

O is your bairn to laird or loon,
Or is it to your father's groom?

My bairn 's na to laird or loon,
Nor is it to my father's groom;

But hear me, mither, on my knee,
An' my hard wierd I'll tell to thee.

O we were sisters, sisters seven,
We was the fairest under heaven;

We had nae mair for our seven years wark
But to shape an' sue the king's son a sark.

O it fell on a Saturday's afternoon,
Whan a' our langsome wark was done,

We keist the cavils us amang,
To see which shou'd to the green wood gang.

Ohone, alas, for I was youngest,
An' ay my wierd it was the hardest.

The cavil it did on me fa',
Which was the cause of a' my wae.

For to the green wood I must gae
To pu' the nut but an' the slae,

steer] strong fleer] floor laird or loon] nobleman or peasant
wierd] fate sue] sew sark] shirt langsome] tedious
keist] cast cavils] lots Ohone] alas (*Gaelic*) but an'] and
also slae] sloe

42

To pu' the red rose an' the thyme
To strew my mother's bow'r and mine.

I had na pu'd a flow'r but ane
Till by there came a jelly hind graeme

Wi' high-coll'd hose and laigh-coll'd shoone,
An' he 'peard to be some kingis son.

An' be I maid or be I nane,
He kept me there till the day was dane;

An' be I maid or be I nae,
He kept me there till the close of day.

He gae me a lock of yellow hair
An' bade me keep it for ever mair.

He gae me a carket o' gude black beads
An' bade me keep them against my needs.

He gae to me a gay gold ring
An' bade me ke[e]p it aboon a' thing.

He gae to me a little penknife
An' bade me keep it as my life.

What did you wi' these tokens rare
That ye got frae that young man there?

O bring that coffer hear to me
And a' the tokens ye sal see.

jelly hind graeme] worthy young fellow   -coll'd] -cut   laigh-]
low-   carket] necklace   aboon] above

An' ay she ranked, an' ay she flang,
Till a' the tokens came till her han'.

O stay here, daughter, your bow'r within,
Till I gae parley wi' my son.

O she has ta'en her thro' the ha'
An' on her son began to ca':

What did you wi' that gay gold ring
I bade you keep aboon a' thing?

What did you wi' that little penknife
I bade you keep while you had life?

What did you wi' that yallow hair
I bade you keep for ever mair?

What did you wi' that good black beeds
I bade you keep against your needs?

I gae them to a lady gay
I met i' the green wood on a day.

An' I would gi' a' my father's lan'
I had that lady my yates within.

I would gi' a' my ha's an' tow'rs
I had that bright burd i' my bow'rs.

O son, keep still your father's lan';
You hae that lady your yates within.

An' keep you still your ha's an' tow'rs;
You hae that bright burd i' your bow'rs.

ranked] raged   flang] flounced   yates] gates   burd] lady

Now or a month was come an' gone
This lady bare a bonny young son;

An' it was well written on his breastbane,
Gil Brenton is my father's name.

11. *Sweet Willie*

SWEET Willie 's ta'en him o'er the faem,
He 's woo'd a wife and brought her hame.

He 's woo'd her for her yellow hair,
But 's mither wrought her mickle care;

And mickle dolour gart her dree,
For lighter can she never be;

But in her bower she sits wi' pain,
And Willy mourns o'er her in vain.

Now to his mither he is gane,
That vile rank witch o' vilest kin.

He says, My lady has a girdle,
It 's a' red goud unto the middle;

And ay at ilka silver hem
Hings fifty silver bells and ten;

That goodly gift shall be your ain,
And let her be lighter o' her young bairn.

mickle] great   gart her dree] made her suffer   goud] gold
ilka] each   And let] if you let

O' her young bairn she 's never be lighter,
Nor in her bower to shine the brighter;

But she shall die and turn to clay,
And you shall wed anither may.

Anither may I'll never wed,
Anither may I'll never bring hame;

But sighing, says that weary wight,
I wish my days were at an en'.

He did him till his mither again,
That vile rank witch o' vilest kin,

And said, My lady has a steed,
The like o' him 's nae i' the lands o' Leed;

For he is gouden shod before
And he is gouden shod behin';

And at ilka tate o' that horse mane
There 's a gouden chess and bell ringin':—

This goodly gift sall be your ain,
And lat her be lighter o' her young bairn.

O' her young bairn she 's never be lighter,
Nor in her bower to shine the brighter;

But she shall die and go to clay,
And you shall wed anither may.

she 's] she shall   may] maiden   till] to   Leed] *perh.* leed,
speech; 'lands of the living'   gouden] with gold   tate] tuft
chess] jess, strap

Anither may I'll never wed,
Anither may I'll never bring hame;

But sighing, says that weary wight,
I wish my life were at an en'.

Then out it spak the Billy Blin'—
He spak ay in a good time—

Ye do you to the market-place,
And there ye buy a leaf o' wax.

Ye shape it bairn and bairnly like,
And in twa glazen e'en ye pit;

And do you to your mither then,
And bid her to your boy's Christnin—

For dear 's the boy he's been to you—
Then notice well what she shall do;

And do you stand a little forbye,
And listen well what she will say.

He did him to the market-place,
And there he bought a leaf o' wax.

He shaped it bairn and bairnly like,
And in twa glazen e'en he pat;

He did him till his mither then,
And bade her to his boy's Christnin;

Billy Blin'] household Brownie   glazen e'en] glass eyes   pit]
put   forbye] aside

And he did stand a little forbye,
And noticed well what she did say.

O wha has loos'd the nine witch knots
That was amang that lady's locks?

And wha's ta'en out the kaimbs o' care
That was amang that lady's hair?

And wha has kill'd the master kid
That ran aneath that lady's bed?

And wha has loos'd her left-foot shee,
And latten that lady lighter be?

O Willy has loos'd the nine witch knots
That hang amang his lady's locks;

And Willy's ta'en out the kaimbs o' care
That hang amang his lady's hair;

And Willy's killed the master kid
That ran aneath his lady's bed;

And Willy's loos'd her left-foot shee,
And latten his lady lighter be.

witch knots] tied in her hair to prevent childbirth   kaimbs] combs
master] male   shee] shoe

12. May Colven

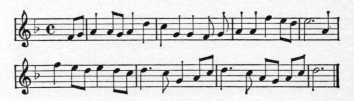

FALSE Sir John a wooing came
　　To a Maid of beauty fair,
May Colven was this Ladys name,
　　Her Fathers only Heir.

He woo'd her butt, he woo'd her ben,
　　He woo'd her in the Ha';
Until he got this Lady's consent,
　　To mount and ride awa'.

He went down to her Father's bower,
　　Where all the Steeds did stand;
And he 's taken one of the best Steeds,
　　That was in her Father's hand.

He 's got on, and she 's got on,
　　And fast as they could flee,
Untill they came to a lonesome part,
　　A Rock by the side of the Sea.

Loup off the Steed says false Sir John,
　　Your bridal bed you see;
For I have drowned Seven Young Ladies,
　　The Eight one you shall be.

butt . . . ben] in the kitchen . . . parlour　　　Loup] leap

49

Cast off, Cast off, my May Colven,
    All and your silken Gown,
For it 's o'er good, and o'er costly,
    To rot in the Salt Sea foam.

Cast off, Cast off, my May Colven,
    All and your embroider'd shoen,
For they are o'er good, and o'er costly
    To rot in the Salt Sea foam.

O turn you about O false Sir John,
    And look to the leaf of the Tree;
For it never became a Gentle Man,
    A naked Woman to see.

He turnd himself straight round about,
    To look to the leaf of the Tree;
So swift as May Colven was,
    To throw him in the Sea.

O help, O help my May Colven,
    O help, or else I'll drown;
I'll take you home to your Father's bower
    And set you down safe and sound.

No help, no help you false Sir John,
    No help nor pity thee;
Tho' Seven Kings Daughters you have drown'd
    But the Eight shall not be me.

So she went on her Fathers Steed,
    As swift as she could flee;
And she came home to her Father's bower
    Before it was break of day.

Up then spoke the pretty Parrot,
   May Colven where have you been,
What has become of false Sir John,
   That woo'd you so late the streen.

He woo'd you butt, he woo'd you ben,
   He woo'd you in the Ha',
Until he got your own consent
   For to mount and gang awa'.

O hold your tongue my pretty Parrot,
   Lay not the blame upon me,
Your Cup shall be of the flowered Gold,
   Your Cage of the Root of the Tree.

Up then spake the King himself,
   In the Bed Chamber where he lay,
What ails the Pretty Parrot,
   That prattles so long or day.

There came a Cat to my Cage Door
   It almost a worried me,
And I was calling on May Colven,
   To take the Cat from me.

the streen] yesterday evening

13. *The Twa Magicians*

THE lady stands in her bower door
   As straight as willow wand;
The blacksmith stood a little forebye
   Wi' hammer in his hand.

wand] twig   forebye] aside

Weel may ye dress ye, lady fair,
   Into your robes o' red;
Before the morn at this same time
   I'll gain your maidenhead.

Awa', awa', ye coal-black smith,
   Wou'd ye do me the wrang
To think to gain my maidenhead
   That I hae kept sae lang?

Then she has hadden up her hand
   And she sware by the mold:
I wu'dna be a blacksmith's wife
   For the full o' a chest o' gold.

I'd rather I were dead and gone
   And my body laid in grave,
Ere a rusty stock o' coal-black-smith
   My maidenhead shou'd have.

But he has hadden up his hand
   And he sware by the mass;
I'll cause ye be my light leman
   For the hauf o' that and less.

O bide, lady, bide,
   And he bade her bide:
The rusty smith your leman shall be
   For a' your muckle pride.

hadden] held   mold] earth   rusty] churlish   stock] sense-less fellow   light leman] wanton lover   hauf] half   bide] stay   muckle] great

Then she became a turtle dow
　To fly up in the air,
And he became another dow
　And they flew pair and pair.
　　O bide, lady, bide, &c.

She turn'd hersell into an eel
　To swim into yon burn,
And he became a speckled trout
　To gie the eel a turn.
　　O bide, lady, bide, &c.

Then she became a duck, a duck,
　To puddle in a peel,
And he became a rose-kaim'd drake
　To gie the duck a dreel.
　　O bide, lady, bide, &c.

She turn'd hersell into a hare
　To rin upon yon hill,
And he became a gude greyhound
　And boldly he did fill.
　　O bide, lady, bide, &c.

Then she became a gay grey mare
　And stood in yonder slack,
And he became a gilt saddle
　And sat upon her back.
　　Was she wae, he held her sae,
　　　And still he bade her bide:
　　The rusty smith her leman was
　　For a' her muckle pride.

dow] dove　　peel] pool　　rose-kaim'd] red-crested (? Muscovy)
dreel] rough handling　　fill] fulfil, perform　　slack] hollow, dip
wae] woeful

53

Then she became a het girdle
And he became a cake,
And a' the ways she turn'd hersell
The blacksmith was her make.
Was she wae, &c.

She turn'd hersell into a ship
To sail out ower the flood,
He ca'd a nail intill her tail
And syne the ship she stood.
Was she wae, &c.

Then she became a silken plaid
And stretch'd upon a bed,
And he became a green covering
And gain'd her maidenhead.
Was she wae, &c.

het girdle] hot griddle   make] match   tail] stern   syne]
then   plaid] covering

14. *Alison Gross*

O ALISON GROSS, that lives in yon tower,
The ugliest witch in the north countrie,
Has trysted me ae day up till her bower,
And mony fair speech she made to me.

She straiked my head, and she kembed my hair,
And she set me down saftly on her knee,
Says, Gin ye will be my lemman sae true,
Sae mony braw things as I would you gi'e.

trysted] enticed   ae] one   till] to   straiked] stroked
Gin] if   lemman] lover   braw] fine

She shaw'd me a mantle o' red scarlet,
　　Wi' gouden flowers and fringes fine,
Says, Gin ye will be my lemman sae true,
　　This goodly gift it sall be thine.

Awa, awa, ye ugly witch,
　　Haud far awa, and lat me be;
I never will be your lemman sae true,
　　And I wish I were out of your company.

She neist brocht a sark o' the saftest silk,
　　Weel wrought wi' pearls about the band;
Says, Gin ye will be my ain true love,
　　This goodly gift ye sall command.

She shaw'd me a cup o' the good red goud,
　　Weel set wi' jewels sae fair to see;
Says, Gin ye will be my lemman sae true,
　　This goodly gift I will you gie.

Awa, awa, ye ugly witch!
　　Haud far awa, and lat me be;
For I wadna ance kiss your ugly mouth
　　For a' the gifts that ye cou'd gie.

She 's turned her richt and round about,
　　And thrice she blew on a grass-green horn;
And she sware by the moon and the stars aboon,
　　That she'd gar me rue the day I was born.

Then out has she ta'en a silver wand,
　　And she 's turned her three times round and round;
She 's mutter'd sic words, that my strength it fail'd,
　　And I fell down senseless on the ground.

gouden] golden	Haud] keep	neist] next	sark] shirt
wadna] would not	gar] make	sic] such	

She's turn'd me into an ugly worm,
　　And gar'd me toddle about the tree;
And ay, on ilka Saturday's night,
　　My sister Maisry came to me,

Wi' silver bason, and silver kemb,
　　To kemb my headie upon her knee;
But or I had kiss'd her ugly mouth,
　　I'd rather hae toddled about the tree.

But as it fell out on last Hallowe'en,
　　When the SEELY COURT was ridin' by,
The queen lighted down on a gowan bank,
　　Nae far frae the tree whare I wont to lye.

She took me up in her milk-white hand,
　　And she straiked me three times o'er her knee;
She changed me again to my ain proper shape,
　　And I nae mair maun toddle about the tree.

worm] serpent　　ilka] every　　kemb] comb　　or] ere　　SEELY]
Fairy (happy)　　gowan] daisy　　maun] must

15. *Kempion*

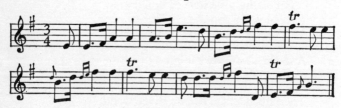

COME here, come here, you freely feed,
　　An' lay your head low on my knee;
The hardest weird I will you read
　　That e'er war read to a lady.

freely feed] beautiful child　　weird] fate　　war] was

O meikle dollour sall you dree,
   An' ay the sat seas o['e]r ye'[se] swim,
An' far mair dollour sall ye dree
   On East-muir craigs, or ye them clim.

I wot ye's be a weary wight,
   An' releived sall ye never be
Till Kempion the kingis son
   Come to the craig and thrice kiss thee.

O meickle dollour did she dree,
   An' ay the sat seas o['e]r she swam,
An' far mair dollour did she dree
   On Eastmuir craigs, or them she clim;
An ay she cried for Kempion,
   Gin he would come till her han'.

Now word has gane to Kempion
   That sich a beast was in his lan',
An' a[y] be sure she would gae mad
   Gin she gat nae help frae his han'.

Now by my sooth, says Kempion,
   This fiery beast I['ll] gang to see;
An' by my sooth, says Segramour,
   My ae brother, I'll gang you wi'.

O biggit ha' they a bonny boat
   An' they ha' set her to the sea,
An' Kempion an' Segramour
   The fiery beast ha' gane to see;
A mile afore they reach'd the shore
   I wot she gar'd the red fire flee.

meikle] great   dree] suffer   sat] salt   'se] shall   or]
ere   Kempion] Owain the champion   Gin] if   till] to
ae] only   biggit] built   gar'd . . . flee] made . . . fly

O Segramour, keep my boat afloat,
  An' lat her no the lan' so near,
For the wicked beast she'll sure gae mad
  An' set fire to the land an' mair.

O out o' my stye I winna rise—
  An' it is na for the fear o' thee—
Till Kempion the kingis son
  Come to the craig an' thrice kiss me.

He's louted him o'er the East-muir craig
  An' he has gi'en her kisses ane;
Awa' she gid an' again she came,
  The fieryest beast that ever was seen.

O out o' my stye I winna rise—
  An' it is na for fear o' thee—
Till Kempion the kingis son
  Come to the craig an' thrice kiss me.

He louted him o'er the Eastmuir craig
  An' he has gi'en her kisses twa;
Awa' she gid an' again she came,
  The fieryest beast that ever you saw.

O out o' my stye I winna rise—
  An' it is na for fear o' ye—
Till Kempion the kingis son
  Come to the craig an' thrice kiss me.

He's louted him o'er the Eastmuir craig
  An' he has gi'en her kisses three;
Awa' she gid an' again she came,
  The fairest lady that ever cou'd be.

lat] let   stye] den   louted him] stooped, leaned   gid] went

An' by my sooth, say[s] Kempion,
   My ain true love—for this is she—
O was it wolf into the wood,
   Or was it fish intill the sea,
Or was it man or wile woman,
   My true love, that mis-shapit thee?

It was na wolf into the wood
   Nor was it fish into the sea,
But it was my stepmother,
   An' wae an' weary mot she be.

O a heavier weird light her upon
   Than ever fell on wile woman;
Her hair 's grow rough an' her teeth 's grow lang,
   An' on her four feet sal she gang.

Nane sall tack pitty her upon,
   But in Wormie's Wood she sall ay won;
An' relieved sall she never be
   Till St. Mungo come o'er the sea.

mot] may   Wormie's] Dragon's   sall] shall   won] dwell

16. *The Laily Worm and the Machrel*

I WAS but seven year auld
   When my mither she did die;
My father married the ae warst woman
   The warld did ever see.

ae] one (*emphatic*)

For she has made me the laily worm
    That lies at the fit o' the tree,
An' my sister Masery she 's made
    The machrel of the sea.

An' every Saturday at noon
    The machrel comes to me,
An' she takes my laily head
    An' lays it on her knee;
She kaims it wi' a siller kaim
    An' washes 't in the sea.

Seven knights hae I slain
    Sin' I lay at the fit of the tree;
An' ye war na my ain father
    The eight ane ye should be.

Sing on your song, ye laily worm,
    That ye did sing to me.—
I never sung that song but what
    I would it sing to thee:

I was but seven year auld
    When my mither she did die;
My father married the ae warst woman
    The warld did ever see.

For she changed me to the laily worm
    That lies at the fit o' the tree,
And my sister Masery
    To the machrel of the sea.

laily worm] loathsome serpent   fit] foot   machrel] mackerel
siller kaim] silver comb   An' ye war] if ye were

And every Saturday at noon
    The machrel comes to me,
An' she takes my laily head
    An' lays it on her knee,
An' kaims it wi' a siller kame
    An' washes it i' the sea.

Seven knights hae I slain
    Sin' I lay at the fit o' the tree;
An' ye war na my ain father
    The eighth ane ye shou'd be.

He sent for his lady,
    As fast as send cou'd he:
Whar is my son that ye sent frae me,
    And my daughter, Lady Masery?

Your son is at our king's court
    Serving for meat an' fee,
An' your daughter 's at our queen's court,
    [A mary sweet an' free.]

Ye lie, ye lie, ye ill woman,
    Sae loud as I hear ye lie:
My son 's the laily worm
    That lies at the fit o' the tree,
And my daughter, Lady Masery,
    Is the machrel of the sea.

She has ta'en a siller wan'
    An' gien him strokes three,
An' he has started up the bravest knight
    That ever your eyes did see.

mary] maiden   free] gracious

She has ta'en a small horn,
    An' loud an' shrill blew she,
An' a' the fish came her untill
    But the proud machrel of the sea:
Ye shapeit me ance an unseemly shape,
    An' ye 's never mare shape me.

He has sent to the wood
    For whins and for hawthorn,
An' he has ta'en that gay lady,
    An' there he did her burn.

untill] to

17. King Orfeo

DER lived a king inta da aste,
    Scowan ürla grün;
Der lived a lady in da wast,
    Whar giorten han grün oarlac.

Dis king he has a huntin' gaen,
He 's left his Lady Isabel alane.

O I wis ye'd never gaen away,
For at your hame is döl an' wae;

Der ... da] There ... the   inta] in   aste] east   Scowan ürla
grün] The wood is early green (*Danish* Skoven årle grön)   Whar ...
oarlac] ? where the hart goes yearly (*Danish* Hvor hjorten han gồr årlig;
Child)   döl] sorrow

For da king o' Ferrie we his daert
Has pierced your lady to da hert.

 ★ ★ ★ ★ ★

And aifter dem da king has gaen,
But whan he cam it was a grey stane.

Dan he took oot his pipes ta play,
Bit sair his hert wi' döl an' wae.

And first he played da notes o' noy,
An' dan he played da notes o' joy.

An' dan he played da göd gabber reel,
Dat meicht ha' made a sick hert hale.

 ★ ★ ★ ★ ★

Noo come ye in inta wir ha',
An' come ye in among wis a'.

Now he's gaen in inta der ha',
An' he's gaen in among dem a'.

Dan he took out his pipes to play,
Bit sair his hert wi' döl an' wae.

An' first he played da notes o' noy,
An' dan he played da notes o' joy.

An' dan he played da göd gabber reel,
Dat meicht ha' made a sick hert hale.

Noo tell to us what ye will hae:
What sall we gie you for your play?

What I will hae I will you tell,
An' dat's me Lady Isabel.

Ferrie] Faery noy] grief gabber] ? merry meicht] might
wir] our wis] us

Yees tak your lady, and yees gaeng hame,
An' yees be king ower a' your ain.

He 's taen his lady, an' he 's gaen hame,
  Scowan ürla grün;
An' noo he 's king ower a' his ain,
  Whar giorten han grün oarlac.

Yees] you shall   gaeng] go   ower] over   ain] own

18. *King Henry*

LAT never a man a wooing wend
  That lacketh thingis three;
A routh o' gold, an open heart,
  Ay fu' o' Charity.

As this I speak of King Henry
  For he lay burd-alone,
An' he 's doen him to a jelly hunt's ha'
  Was seven miles frae a town.

He chas'd the deer now him before
  An' the roe down by the den,
Till the fattest buck in a' the flock
  King Henry he has slain.

routh] plenty   burd-alone] quite alone (Psalm 102: 7)   doen
him] taken himself   jelly hunt's ha'] fine hunting-lodge   den]
dean, dingle

O he has doen him to his ha'
  To make him beerly cheer,
An' in it came a griesly ghost
  Steed stappin i' the fleer.

Her head hat the reef tree o' the house,
  Her middle ye mot wel span;
He 's thrown to her his gay mantle,
  Says, Lady, hap your lingcan.

Her teeth was a' like teather stakes,
  Her nose like club or mell;
An' I ken nae thing she 'peard to be
  But the fiend that wons in hell.

Some meat, some meat, ye King Henry,
  Some meat ye gie to me!
An' what meat 's in this house, lady,
  An' what ha' I to gie?
O ye do kill your berry brown steed
  An' you bring him here to me.

O whan he slew his berry brown steed,—
  Wow but his heart was sair—
Shee eat him a' up skin an' bane,
  Left naething but hide an' hair.

Mair meat, mair meat, ye King Henry,
  Mair meat ye gi' to me!
An' what meat 's in this house, lady,
  An' what ha' I to gi'?
O ye do kill your good gray hounds
  An' ye bring them a' to me.

beerly] mighty   Steed stappin] stood stepping   fleer] floor
hat] struck   reef tree] main roof-beam   mot] might   hap]
cover   lingcan] licham, body   teather] for tethering beasts
mell] mallet   wons] dwells

O whan he slew his good gray hounds—
  Wow but his heart was sair—
She eat them a' up skin an' bane,
  Left naething but hide an' hair.

Mair meat, mair meat, ye King Henry,
  Mair meat ye gi' to me!
An' what meat 's in this house, lady,
  An' what ha' I to gi'?
O ye do kill your gay gos hawks
  An' ye bring them here to me.

O whan he slew his gay gos hawks—
  Wow but his heart was sair—
She eat them a' up skin an' bane,
  Left naething but feathers bare.

Some drink, some drink now, King Henry,
  Some drink ye bring to me!
O what drink 's i' this house, lady,
  That you're nae welcome ti?
O ye sew up your horse's hide
  An' bring in a drink to me.

[An' he 's sew'd up the bloody hide,
  A puncheon o' wine put in;
She drank it a' up at a waught,
  Left na ae drap ahin'.]

A bed, a bed now, King Henry,
  A bed you mak to me!
For ye maun pu' the heather green
  An' mak a bed to me.

puncheon] about 100 gallons   waught] draught   ae] one
ahin'] behind   maun pu'] must pull

O pu'd has he the heather green
   An' made to her a bed,
An' up has he ta'en his gay mantle
   An' o'er it has he spread.

Tak aff your claiths now, King Henry,
   An' lye down by my side!
O God forbid, says King Henry,
   That ever the like betide:
That ever the fiend that wons in hell
   Shou'd streak down by my side.

Whan night was gane and day was come,
   An' the sun shone throw the ha',
The fairest lady that ever was seen
   Lay atween him an' the wa'.

O well is me, says King Henry,
   How lang 'll this last wi' me?
Then out it spake that fair lady:
   Even till the day you dee.

For I've met wi' mony a gentle knight
   That 's gien me sic a fill,
But never before wi' a courteous knight
   That ga' me a' my will.

streak] stretch

19. *The Cruel Mother*

SHE sat down below a thorn,
  Fine flowers in the valley;
And there she has her sweet babe born,
  And the green leaves they grow rarely.

Smile na sae sweet, my bonie babe:
And ye smile sae sweet, ye'll smile me dead.

She's taen out her little penknife
And twinn'd the sweet babe o' its life.

She's howket a grave by the light o' the moon
And there she's buried her sweet babe in.

As she was going to the church
She saw a sweet babe in the porch.

O sweet babe and thou were mine
I wad cleed thee in the silk so fine.

O mother dear, when I was thine,
You didna prove to me sae kind.

And] if   penknife] sheath knife (orig. for making quill pens)
twinn'd] deprived   howket] dug   wad cleed] would clothe

68

[O cursed mother, heaven's high,
And that's where thou will neer win nigh.

O cursed mother, hell is deep,
    Fine flowers in the valley;
And there thou'll enter step by step,
    And the green leaves they grow rarely.]

win] reach, get

20. *The Cruel Sister*

THERE were two sisters sat in a bour,
    Binnorie, O Binnorie;
There came a knight to be their wooer,
    By the bonny milldams of Binnorie.

He courted the eldest with glove and ring,
But he lo'ed the youngest aboon a' thing.

He courted the eldest with broach and knife,
But he lo'ed the youngest abune his life.

The eldest she was vexed sair,
And sore envied her sister fair.

The eldest said to the youngest ane,
Will ye go and see our father's ships come in?

She 's ta'en her by the lilly hand
And led her down to the river strand.

The youngest stude upon a stane,
The eldest came and pushed her in.

She took her by the middle sma',
And dashed her bonnie back to the jaw.

O sister, sister, reach your hand,
And ye shall be heir of half my land.

O sister, I'll not reach my hand,
And I'll be heir of all your land.

Shame fa' the hand that I should take,
It 's twin'd me and my world's make.

O sister, reach me but your glove,
And sweet William shall be your love.

Sink on, nor hope for hand or glove,
And sweet William shall better be my love.

Your cherry cheeks and your yellow hair
Garr'd me gang maiden evermair.

Sometimes she sunk and sometimes she swam,
Until she came to the miller's dam.

O father, father, draw your dam,
There 's either a mermaid or a milk-white swan.

sma'] slender   jaw] wave   fa'] befal   twin'd] separated
world's make] only mate   Garr'd] made   gang] go   draw]
drain or drag

The miller hasted and drew his dam,
And there he found a drown'd woman.

You could not see her yellow hair,
For gowd and pearls that were sae rare.

You could na see her middle sma',
Her gowden girdle was sae bra'.

A famous harper passing by,
The sweet pale face he chanced to spy.

And when he looked that ladye on,
He sighed and made a heavy moan.

He made a harp of her breast-bone,
Whose sounds would melt a heart of stone.

The strings he framed of her yellow hair,
Whose notes made sad the listening ear.

He brought it to her father's hall,
And there was the court assembled all.

He laid this harp upon a stone,
And straight it began to play alone.

O yonder sits my father the king,
And yonder sits my mother the queen.

And yonder stands my brother Hugh,
And by him my William sweet and true.

gowd] gold   bra'] fine

But the last tune that the harp play'd then,
   Binnorie, O Binnorie,
Was, Woe to my sister, false Helen,
   By the bonny milldams of Binnorie.

21. *The Broomfield Hill*

THERE was a knight and a lady bright
   Had a true tryste at the broom;
The ane gaed early in the morning,
   The other in the afternoon.

And ay she sat in her mother's bower door
   And ay she made her mane:
O whether should I gang to the Broomfield Hill
   Or should I stay at hame?

For if I gang to the Broomfield Hill
   My maidenhead is gone;
And if I chance to stay at hame
   My love will ca' me mansworn.

Up then spake a witch woman,
   Ay from the room aboon:
O ye may gang to the Broomfield Hill
   And yet come maiden hame.

tryste] meeting   mane] complaint   mansworn] perjured
aboon] above

For when ye gang to the Broomfield Hill
  Ye'll find your love asleep
With a silver belt about his head
  And a broom-cow at his feet.

Take ye the blossom of the broom,
  The blossom it smells sweet,
And strew it at your true love's head
  And likewise at his feet.

Take ye the rings off your fingers,
  Put them on his right hand,
To let him know, when he doth awake,
  His love was at his command.

She pu'd the broom flower on Hive Hill
  And strew'd on 's white hals bane,
And that was to be wittering true
  That maiden she had gane.

O where were ye, my milk-white steed,
  That I hae coft sae dear,
That wadna watch and waken me
  When there was maiden here?

I stamped wi' my foot, master,
  And gar'd my bridle ring,
But na kin thing wald waken ye
  Till she was past and gane.

And wae betide ye, my gay goss hawk,
  That I did love sae dear,
That wadna watch and waken me
  When there was maiden here.

broom-cow] twig of broom   hals] neck   wittering] indication
coft] bought   gar'd] made   kin] sort of

I clapped wi' my wings, master,
    And ay my bells I rang,
And aye cry'd, Waken, waken, master,
    Before the ladye gang.

But haste and haste, my gude white steed,
    To come the maiden till,
Or a' the birds of gude green wood
    Of your flesh shall have their fill.

Ye need na burst your gude white steed
    Wi' racing o'er the howm;
Nae bird flies faster through the wood
    Than she fled through the broom.

howm] water-meadow

22. *Proud Margret*

FAIR Margret was a young ladye
    An' come of high degree;
Fair Margret was a young ladye
    An' proud as proud cou'd be.

Fair Margret was a rich ladye,
    The king's cousin was she;
Fair Margret was a rich ladye
    An' vain as vain cou'd be.

She war'd her wealth on the gay cleedin'
    That comes frae 'yont the sea;
She spent her time frae morning till night
    Adorning her fair bodye.

war'd] spent   cleedin'] clothes

Ae night she sate in her stately ha'
  Kaimin' her yellow hair,
When in there cum like a gentle knight
  An' a white scarf he did wear.

O what's your will wi' me, sir knight,
  O what's your will wi' me?
You're the likest to my ae brother
  That ever I did see.

You're the likest to my ae brother
  That ever I hae seen,
But he's buried in Dunfermline kirk
  A month an' mair bygane.

I'm the likest to your ae brother
  That ever ye did see,
But I canna get rest into my grave
  A' for the pride of thee.

Leave pride, Margret, leave pride, Margret,
  Leave pride an' vanity;
Ere ye see the sights that I hae seen
  Sair altered ye maun be.

O ye come in at the kirk-door
  Wi' the gowd plaits in your hair;
But wud ye see what I hae seen
  Ye maun them a' forbear.

O ye come in at the kirk-door
  Wi' the gowd prins i' your sleeve;
But wad ye see what I hae seen
  Ye maun gie them a' their leave.

Kaimin'] combing   ae] only   bygane] past   maun] must
gowd] gold   wud, wad] would   prins] pins

75

Leave pride, Margret, leave pride, Margret,
    Leave pride an' vanity;
Ere ye see the sights that I hae seen
    Sair altered ye maun be.

He got her in her stately ha'
    Kaimin' her yellow hair;
He left her on her sick, sick bed
    Sheding the saut, saut tear.

saut] salt

23. *Clark Sanders*

CLARKE SANDERS and may Margret
    Walkt ower yon gravel'd green,
And sad and heavy was the Love
    I wat it fell this twa between.

A bed, a bed, Clark Sanders said,
    A bed, a bed for you and I;
Fye na, fye na, the Lady said,
    Untill the day we married be.

may] maid   gravel'd green] sandy grass   wat] know

[For in] will come my seven brothers
   And a' their torches burning bright;
Thayl say, We hae but ae sister,
   And here her lying wi' a knight.

Ye'll take the sourde fray my scabbard
   An lowly lowly lift the gin,
And you may say your oth to save
   You never let Clarke Sanders in.

Yele take a napken in your hand
   And ye'l ty up baith your e'en,
An ye may say your oth to save
   That ye saw na him sen late yestreen.

Yele take me in your arms twa
   Yele carrey me ben in to your bed;
And ye may say your oth to save
   In your bower floor I never tread.

She has ta'in the sourd fray his scabbard
   And lowly lowly lifted the gin;
She was to swear her oth to save
   She never let Clark Sanders in.

She has ta'in a napken in her hand
   And she has ty'd up both her e'en;
She was to swear her oth to save
   She saw na him sine late yestreen.

She has ta'in him in her arms twa
   An carried him ben unto her bed;
She was to swear her oth to save
   He never in her bower floor tread.

ae] one   lowly] ? quietly   gin] latch   sen, sine] since
ben] through

In and came her seven brothers
　　And all their torches burning bright;
Says thay, We hae but ae sister,
　　And see there her lying wi' a knight.

Out an' speaks the first of them,
　　A wat thay hay been Lovers dear;
Out and speaks the next of them,
　　Thay hay been in Love this mony a year.

Out an' speaks the third of them,
　　It wear great sin this twa to twain;
Out an' speaks the fourth of them,
　　It wear a sin to kill a sleeping man.

Out an' speaks the fifth of them,
　　A wat thayl neer be twain'd by me;
Out an' speaks the sixt of them,
　　Wele take our leve an' gae our way.

Out and speaks the seventh of them,
　　Alltho there wear na a man but me—
[Out and speaks the seventh of them,]
　　Ise bear the brand, Ise gar him die.

And he has ta'in a bright long brand
　　And he has striped it throw the stra[e],
And throw and throw Clarke Sanders body
　　A wat he has gar'd cold iorn gae.

A wat] assuredly　　　twain] part　　　gae] go　　　Ise] I shall
brand] sword　　gar] make　　striped] drawn, whetted　　strae]
straw

CLARK SANDERS

Sanders he started an' Margret she lapt
  Intill his arms whare she lay,
An' w[i]ll and willsom was the night
  A wat it was between this twa.

And thay lay still and sleeped sound
  Untill the day begud to daw,
And kindly till him she did say
  Its time trew Love ye wear awa.

Thay lay still and sleeped sound
  Untill the sun begud to shine;
She lookt between her and [the] wa',
  And dull and heavy was his e'en.

She thought it had been a leathsome sweat
  A wat it had fallen this twa between;
But it was the blood of his fair body—
  A wat his life days wair na lang.

O Sanders Ile do for your sake
  What other Ladys wou'd na thoule;
When seven years is come an' gone
  Ther 's neer a shoe go on my sole.

O Sanders Ile do for your sake
  What other Ladys wou'd think mare;
When seven years is come an' gone
  Ther 's nere a comb go in my hair.

will and willsom] lost and desolate   begud] began   thoule]
endure

O Sanders Ile do for your sake
   What other Ladys wou'd think lack;
When seven years is come an' gone
   Ill wear nought but dowy black.

The bells gaed clinking throw the town
   To carry the dead corp to the clay,
An' sighing says her, may Margret,
   A wat I bide a doullfou' day.

       *   *   *   *   *

Hold your toung my doughter dear,
   Let all your mourning a bee;
Ile carry the dead corp to the clay
   An' I'll come back an comfort thee.

Comfort well your seven sons,
   For comforted will I never bee;
For it was neither Lord nor Loune
   That was in bower last night wi' me.

WHEN bells was rung an' mass was sung
   A wat a' men to bed were gone,
Clark Sanders came to Margrets window
   With mony a sad sigh and gro[a]n.

Are ye sleeping Margret, he says,
   Or are ye waking presentlie;
Gie me my faith an' trouth again
   A wat, trew Love, I gied to thee.

dowy] dismal   bide] await   doullfou'] doleful   Loune] peasant   trouth] troth, pledge

Your faith an' trouth yese never get
  Nor our trew Love shall never twain
Till ye come within my bower
  And kiss me both cheek and chin.

My mouth it is full cold, Margret,
  It has the smell now of the ground;
An' if I kiss thy com'ly mouth
  Thy life days will not be long.

Cocks are crowing o' merry middel [earth],
  I wat the wild fule boded day;
Gie me my faith an' trouth again
  An' let me fare me on my way.

Thy faith and trouth thou shall na' get
  Nor our trew Love shall never twin
Till ye tell me what comes of wemen
  A wat that dys in strong traveling.

Their beds are made in the heavens high
  Down at the foot of our good Lords knee,
Well set about wi' gilly flowers,
  A wat sweet company for to see.

O cocks are crowing o' merry middel [earth],
  A wat the wild foule boded day;
The salms of heaven will be sung
  And ere now Ile be miss'd away.

yese] ye shall　　　twain] break in two　　　fule] birds　　　strong
traveling] violent childbirth　　　gilly flowers] wallflowers

CLARK SANDERS

Up she has ta'in a bright long wand
   And she has straked her trouth thereon;
She has given him out at the shot window
   Wi' mony a sad sigh and heavy groan.

I thank you, Margret, I thank you, Margret,
   An' I thank you hartilie;
Gine ever the dead come for the quick
   Be sure, Margret, Ile come again for thee.

It 's hose an' shoon an' goune alane
   She clame the wall an' follow'd him,
Untill she came to a green forest,
   An' then she lost the sight of him.

Is the[re] any roome at your head, Sanders,
   Is the[re] any room at your feet,
Or any room at your twa sids
   Whare fain, fain wad I sleep?

The[re] is na room at my head, Margret,
   The[re] is na room at my feet;
There is room at my twa sids
   For Ladys for to sleep.

Cold meal is my covering owre
   But an' my winding sheet;
My bed it is full low, I say,
   Among the hungry worms I sleep.

wand] branch   straked] 'stroked', smeared (symbolic)   shot
window] hinged window, casement   quick] living   clame]
climbed   meal] mould, earth   But an'] and also

Cold meal is my covering owre
    But an' my winding sheet;
The dew it falls na sooner down
    Then ay it is full weet.

weet] wet

24. *The Carpenter's Wife*
[*The Dæmon Lover*]

O WHARE hae ye been, my dearest dear,
    These seven lang years and more?
O I am come to seek my former vows
    That ye promis'd me before.

Awa wi' your former vows, she says,
    Or else ye will breed strife;
Awa wi' your former vows, she says,
    For I'm become a wife.

I am married to a ship-carpenter,
    A ship-carpenter he 's bound;
I wadna he ken'd my mind this nicht
    For twice five hundred pound.

wadna he ken'd] would not that he knew

[I have seven ships upon the sea
　　Laden with the finest gold,
And mariners to wait us upon;
　　All these you may behold.

And I have shoes for my love's feet
　　Beaten of the purest gold,
And lined wi' the velvet soft
　　To keep my love's feet from the cold.]

She has put her foot on gude ship-board,
　　And on shipboard she's gane,
And the veil that hung oure her face
　　Was a' wi' gowd begane.

[O how do you love the ship, he said,
　　Or how do you love the sea?
And how do you love the bold mariners
　　That wait upon thee and me?

O I do love the ship, she said,
　　And I do love the sea;
But woe be to the dim mariners
　　That nowhere I can see!]

She had na sailed a league, a league,
　　A league but barely twa,
Till she did mind on the husband she left
　　And her wee young son alsua.

O haud your tongue, my dearest dear,
　　Let all your follies abee;
I'll show whare the white lillies grow
　　On the banks of Italie.

wi' gowd begane] overlaid with gold　　　　　　mind on] remember
alsua] also

She had na sailed a league, a league,
  A league but barely three,
Till grim, grim grew his countenance
  And gurly grew the sea.

O haud your tongue, my dearest dear,
  Let all your follies abee;
I'll show whare the white lillies grow
  In the bottom of the sea.

He's tane her by the milk-white hand
  And he's thrown her in the main;
And full five and twenty hundred ships
  Perish'd all on the coast of Spain.

gurly] stormy, blustery

25. *Clerk Colvill*

CLERK COLVILL and his lusty dame
  Were walking in the garden green;
The belt around her stately waist
  Cost Clerk Colvill of pounds fifteen.

O promise me now, Clerk Colvill,
  Or it will cost ye muckle strife:
Ride never by the wells of Slane
  If ye wad live and brook your life.

Now speak nae mair, my lusty dame,
  Now speak nae mair of that to me;
Did I ne'er see a fair woman
  But I wad sin with her fair body?

lusty] lively   muckle] great   brook] enjoy

He 's ta'en leave o' his gay lady
  Nought minding what his lady said,
And he 's rode by the wells of Slane
  Where washing was a bonny maid.

Wash on, wash on, my bonny maid,
  That wash sae clean your sark of silk:
And weel fa' you, fair gentleman,
  Your body 's whiter than the milk.

[He 's ta'en her by the milk-white hand
  And likewise by the grass-green sleeve;
An' laid her down upon the green,
  Nor of his lady speer'd he leave.]

Then loud, loud cry'd the Clerk Colvill,
  O my head it pains me sair;
Then take, then take, the maiden said,
  And frae my sark you'll cut a gare.

Then she 's gi'ed him a little bane-knife
  And frae h[er] sark he cut a share;
She 's ty'd it round his whey-white face,
  But ay his head it aked mair.

Then louder cry'd the Clerk Colvill,
  O sairer, sairer akes my head;
And sairer, sairer ever will,
  The maiden crys, 'till you be dead.

Out then he drew his shining blade,
  Thinking to stick her where she stood,
But she was vanish'd to a fish
  And swam far off a fair mermaid.

sark] shift   fa'] befal   speer'd] asked   gare] strip of cloth
bane-knife] knife made of bone

O mother, mother, braid my hair;
  My lusty lady, make my bed;
O brother, take my sword and spear,
  For I have seen the false mermaid.

26. *Young Hunting*

O LADY rock never your young son young
  One hour longer for me,
For I have a sweethart in Garlicks wells
  I love thrice better than thee.

The very sols of my Loves feet
  Is whiter than thy face;
But never the less na, young Hunting,
  Ye'l stay wi' me all night.

She has birl'd in him young Hunting
  The good ale and the beer
Till he was as fou drucken
  As any wild wood steer.

She has birl'd in him young Hunting
  The good ale and the wine
Till he was as fou drunken
  As any wild wood swine.

Up she has ta'in him young Hunting
  And she has had him to her bed;
And she has minded her on a little penknife

Garlicks] ? Gareloch   na] *emphatic negative*   birl'd in] poured,
plied (with)   minded her on] remembered   penknife] sheath-
knife

That hangs low down by her gore
An she has gi'n him young Hunting
  A deep wound and a sore.

Out an' spake the bonny bird
  That flew abon her head:
Lady keep well th[y] green clothing
  Fra that good Lords blood.

O better I'll keep my green clothing
  Fra that good Lords blood
Nor thou can keep thy flottering toung
  That flotters in thy head.

Light down, light down my bonny bird,
  Light down upon my hand:
O Siller, O Siller shall be thy hire
  An' goud shall be thy fee,
An' every month into the year
  Thy cage shall changed bee.

I winna light down, I shanna light down,
  I winna light on thy hand,
For soon, soon wad ye do to me
  As ye done to young Hunting.

She has booted and spir'd him, young Hunting,
  As he had been gan to ride,
A hunting horn about his neck
  An' the sharp sourd by his side;
An' she has had him to yon wan water
  For a' man calls it Clyde.

gore] skirt	flottering] waggling	Siller] silver	goud] gold
fee] reward	winna . . . shanna] won't . . . shan't		gan] going

YOUNG HUNTING

The deepest pot intill it all
　　She has puten young Hunting in,
A green truff upon his breast
　　To hold that good Lord down.

It fell ance upon a day
　　The king was going to ride,
And he sent for him young Hunting
　　To ride on his right side.

She has turn'd her right and round about,
　　She sware now by the corn:
I saw na thy son young Hunting
　　Sen yesterday at morn.

She has turn'd her right and round about,
　　She swear now by the moon:
I saw na thy son young Hunting
　　Sen yesterday at noon.

It fears me sair in Clyds water
　　That he is droun'd therein.
O thay ha' sent for the king's duckers
　　To duck for young Hunting.

Thay ducked in at the tae water bank,
　　Thay ducked out at the tither:
We'll duck no more for young Hunting
　　All tho' he wear our brother.

pot] pit, hole in the rock　　　intill] in　　　truff] turf　　　Sen]
since　　　duck(ers)] dive(rs)　　　tae ... tither] one ... other

89

Out an' speake the bonny bird
  That flew abon their heads:
O he is na drown'd in Clyds water,
  He is slain and put therein;
The Lady that lives in yon castel
  Slew him and put him in.

Leave off your ducking on the day
  And duck upon the night;
Whear ever that sakeless knight lys slain
  The candels will shine bright.

They left off their ducking on the day
  And ducked upon the night,
And whare that sackless knight lay slain
  The candels shone full bright.

The deepest pot intill it a'
  They got young Hunting in,
A green turff upon his brest
  To hold that good Lord down.

O thay ha' sent aff men to the wood
  To hew down baith thorn an' fern
That thay might get a great bonefier
  To burn that Lady in.
Put na the wyte on me, she says,
  It was her, may Catheren.

When thay had tane her may Catheren,
  In the bonefier set her in,
It wad na take upon her cheeks

sakeless] innocent   candels] corpse-lights, shining supernaturally
over a concealed body   wyte] blame   may] maid

90

Nor take upon her chin
Nor yet upon her yallow hair
To healle the deadly sin.

Out thay ha' ta'in her may Catheren
An' thay hay put that Lady in:
O it took upon her cheek, her cheek,
An' it took upon her chin
An' it took on her fair body;
She burnt like ho[ll]y gren.

holly gren] a branch of holly

27. *The Grey Selchie of Sule Skerry*

IN Norway land there lived a maid.
Hush ba loo lillie, this maid began:
I know not where my baby's father is,
Whether by land or sea does he travel in.

It happened on a certain day
When this fair lady fell fast asleep,
That in cam' a good grey selchie
And set him down at her bed feet.

Selchie] seal   Sule Skerry] sea rock 35 miles west of Orkney

Saying, Awak, awak, my pretty fair maid,
  For oh, how sound as thou dost sleep,
An' I'll tell thee where thy baby's father is:
  He's sittin close at thy bed feet.

I pray come tell to me thy name,
  Oh tell me where does thy dwelling be?
My name is good Hein Mailer,
  I earn my livin oot o' the sea.

I am a man upon the land,
  I am a selchie in the sea,
An' whin I'm far from every strand
  My dwelling is [on] Shool Skerry.

Alas, alas this woeful fate,
  This weary fate that's been laid on me,
That a man should come from the Wast o' Hoy
  To the Norway lands to have a bairn wi' me.

My dear, I'll wed thee with a ring,
  With a ring, my dear, will I wed with thee.—
Thoo may go wed thee weddens wi' whom thoo wilt,
  For I'm sure thoo'll never wed none wi' me.

Thoo will nurse my little wee son
  For seven long years upon thy knee;
An' at the end o' seven long years
  I'll come back and pay the nursing fee.

She's nursed her little wee son
  For seven long years upon her knee,
An' at the end o' seven long years
  He came back wi' gold and white monie.

Hoy] the most westerly of the Orkneys   white monie] silver

He says, My dear, I'll wed thee wi' ring,
　Wi' a ring, my dear, I'll wed wi' thee.—
Thoo mat go wed thee weddens wi' whom thoo wilt,
　For I'm sure thoo'll never wed none wi' me.

But I'll put a gold chain around his neck,
　An' a gey good gold chain it'll be,
That if ever he comes to the Norway lands
　Thoo may bae a gey good guess on he.

An thoo will get a gunner good,
　An' a gey good gunner it will be,
An' he'll gae out a May morning
　An' shoot the son an' the grey selchie.

Oh she has gotten a gunner good,
　An' a gey good gunner it was he,
An' he gaed oot on a May morning
　An' he shot the son an' the grey selchie.

[When the gunner returned and showed the Norway
woman the gold chain which he found round the neck of
the young seal she realized that her son had perished, and
gave expression to her sorrow in the last verse.]

Alas, alas this woeful fate,
　This weary fate that's been laid on me.
An' ance or twice she sobbed and sighed,
　An' her tender heart did brak in three.

mat] may　　　gey] very　　　bae . . . guess on he] get . . . inkling of
him

28. The Wife of Usher's Well

THERE lived a wife at Usher's Well
  And a wealthy wife was she;
She had three stout and stalwart sons
  And sent them o'er the sea.

They hadna been a week from her,
  A week but barely ane,
Whan word came to the carline wife
  That her three sons were gane.

They hadna been a week from her,
  A week but barely three,
Whan word came to the carline wife
  That her sons she'd never see.

I wish the wind may never cease,
  Nor fishes in the flood,
Till my three sons come hame to me
  In earthly flesh and blood.

It fell about the Martinmas
  Whan nights are lang and mirk,
The carline wife's three sons came hame
  And their hats were o' the birk.

carline] old (woman)   gane] gone, dead   fishes] *perh. corrupt.*
Scott's 'fashes, i.e. troubles' *is unconvincing*   mirk] dark   birk] birch;
a sacred plant associated with death

94

It neither grew in syke nor ditch
    Nor yet in ony sheugh,
But at the gates o' Paradise
    That birk grew fair eneugh.

Blow up the fire, my maidens,
    Bring water from the well;
For a' my house shall feast this night
    Since my three sons are well.

And she has made to them a bed,
    She's made it large and wide,
And she's ta'en her mantle her about,
    Sat down at the bed-side.

Up then crew the red, red cock
    And up and crew the gray;
The eldest to the youngest said,
    'Tis time we were away.

The cock he hadna craw'd but once
    And clapp'd his wings at a'
Whan the youngest to the eldest said,
    Brother, we must awa'.

The cock doth craw, the day doth daw,
    The channerin' worm doth chide;
Gin we be mist out o' our place
    A sair pain we maun bide.

Fare ye weel, my mother dear;
    Fareweel to barn and byre;
And fare ye weel, the bonny lass
    That kindles my mother's fire.

syke] small stream   sheugh] trench   crew] *recalling the dead*
channerin'] fretting, grumbling (in the grave)

29. *The Unquiet Grave: A Fragment*

THE wind doth blow today, my love,
 And a few small drops of rain;
I never had but one true-love,
 In cold grave she was lain.

I'll do as much for my true-love
 As any young man may:
I'll sit and mourn all at her grave
 For a twelvemonth and a day.

The twelvemonth and a day being up
 The dead began to speak:
Oh who sits weeping on my grave
 And will not let me sleep?

'Tis I, my love, sits on your grave
 And will not let you sleep;
For I crave one kiss of your clay-cold lips
 And that is all I seek.

You crave one kiss of my clay-cold lips,
 But my breath smells earthy strong;
If you have one kiss of my clay-cold lips
 Your time will not be long.

'Tis down in yon garden green,
  Love, where we used to walk,
The finest flower that ere was seen
  Is withered to a stalk.

The stalk is withered dry, my love,
  So will our hearts decay;
So make yourself content, my love,
  Till God calls you away.

30. [Hind Etin]

A. FAIR Isabel sat in her bower door
  Sewin' her silken seam,
When she heard a note in Elwin's wood
  And she wished she there had been.

She loot the seam fa' to her side,
  The needle to her tae,
And she is aff to Elwin's wood
  As fast as she can gae.

But she hadna pu'd a nut, a nut,
  Nor broken a branch but ane,
When by there cam' a young hind chiel,
  Said, Lady, lat alane.

Oh, why pu' ye the nut, the nut,
  Or why break ye the tree?
For I'm the guardian o' the wood
  And ye maun lat it be.

loot . . . fa'] let . . . fall   tae] toe   hind chiel] stripling   lat]
let (it)   maun] must

Oh, I will pu' the nut, she said,
   An' I will break the tree,
For my father 's king o' a' the realm
   An' the wood belangs to me.

But she hadna pu'd a nut, a nut,
   Nor broken a branch but three,
When by there cam' young Aiken,
   An' he gar'd her lat them be.

He 's built a bower; made it secure,
   An' plenished it weel within;
An' there she bore him seven bonnie boys
   In the depths of the forest green.

But it fell ance upon a day
   Young Aiken he thocht lang,
An' he has to the huntin' gane,
   Ta'en wi' him his eldest son.

An asking I would ask, father,
   If ye wadna angry be:
Ask on, ask on, my bonnie boy,
   You'll no be quarrelled by me.

I see my mither's cheeks aye wet,
   I seldom see them dry;
What can it be that makes my mither
   To mourn continually?

Your mother was a king's daughter
   An' far above my degree;
She might hae wed a nobleman
   Had she no been stolen by me.

gar'd] made   thocht lang] grew bored   quarrelled] found fault
with

Oh, I'll shoot the buntin on the bush,
   The linnet on the tree,
An' I'll bring them to my mither dear,
   See if she'll merrier be.

But it fell again upon a day
   Young Aiken he thocht lang,
An' he has to the huntin' gane
   But left his eldest son.

As I came thro' the wood, mither,
   I heard fine music ring;
Oh, I wish to Heaven, my son, she said,
   That I had been there alane.

Money in my pocket I hae nane,
   But royal rings I've three;
An' ye'll tak' them, my bonnie boy,
   An' ye'll gang there for me.

The first ye'll gie to the proud porter,
   He'll open an' lat ye in;
The next ye'll gie to the butler boy
   An' he will show ye ben.

An' the third ye'll gie to the minstrel
   That plays before the King;
An' he'll play success to the bonnie boy
   That cam' thro' the wood alane.

The first he gave to the proud porter,
   He opened and let him in;
The next he gave to the butler boy
   And he has shown him ben.

The third he gave to the minstrel
   That played before the King,
And he played success to the bonnie boy
   That cam' thro' the wood alane.

When he came before the King
   He fell down on his knee;
Said the King, Win up, my bonnie boy,
   What wad ye ask o' me?

Oh, tell me quickly, bonnie boy,
   What might your errand be?
For ye are sae like my daughter dear
   That my heart will break in three.

If I be like your daughter dear—
   It 's wonder it is none
If I be like your daughter dear,
   For I'm her eldest son.

Oh, tell me quickly, bonnie lad,
   Where might my daughter be?
She 's just now standing at your gates,
   An' my six brothers her wi'.

There was Charles, Vincent, Sam, and Dick,
   And likewise James and John;
And they called the eldest young Aiken,
   It was his father's name.

B. O WELL love I to ride in a mist
   And shoot in a northern wind,
And far better a lady to steal
   That 's come of a noble kind.

Win] get

Four-and-twenty ladies
  Put on that lady's sheen,
And as many young gentlemen
  Did lead her o'er the green.

Yet she preferred before them all
  Him, young Hastings the Groom;
He's coosten a mist before them all
  And away this lady has ta'en.

He's taken the lady on him behind,
  Spared neither the grass nor corn,
Till they came to the wood of Amonshaw
  Where again their loves were sworn.

And they have lived in that wood
  Full many a year and day,
And were supported from time to time
  By what he made of prey.

And seven bairns fair and fine
  There she has born to him,
And never was in good church door
  Nor never gat good kirking.

Once she took harp into her hand
  And harped them asleep;
Then she sat down at their couch side
  And bitterly did weep.

Said, Seven bairns have I born now
  To my lord in the ha';
I wish they were seven greedy rats

sheen] shoes   coosten] cast

To run upon the wa',
And I mysel' a great grey cat
To eat them ane an' a'.

For ten long years now I have lived
Within this cave of stane,
And never was at good church door
Nor got no good churching.

O then outspak her eldest child,
And a fine boy was he:
O hold your tongue, my mother dear,
I'll tell ye what to dee:

Take you the youngest in your lap,
The next youngest by the hand;
Put all the rest of us you before,
As you learnt us to gang.

And go with us into some kirk—
You say they are built of stane—
And let us all be christened,
And you get good kirking.

She took the youngest in her lap,
The next youngest by the hand—
Set all the rest of them her before,
As she learnt them to gang.

And she has left the wood with them
And to a kirk has gane,
Where the good priest them christened
And gave her good kirking.

dee] do   gang] go

31. Young Bekie

A. Young Bekie was as brave a knight
    As ever sail'd the sea,
An' he's doen him to the court of France
    To serve for meat and fee.

He had nae been i' the court of France
    A twelvemonth nor sae long,
Til he fell in love with the king's daughter
    An' was thrown in prison strong.

The king he had but ae daughter,
    Burd Isbel was her name;
An' she has to the prison-house gane
    To hear the prisoner's mane.

O gin a lady wou'd borrow me,
    At her stirrup foot I wou'd rin;
Or gin a widow wad borrow me,
    I wou'd swear to be her son.

doen him] taken himself   meat and fee] food and wages   Burd]
maid, lady   mane] complaint   gin] if   borrow] set free

Or gin a virgin wou'd borrow me,
   I wou'd wed her wi' a ring;
I'd gie her ha's, I'd gie her bowers,
   The bonny tow'rs o' Linne.

O barefoot, barefoot gaed she but
   An' barefoot came she ben;
It was no' for want o' hose an' shoone
   Nor time to put them on;

But a' for fear that her father dear
   Had heard her making din:
She 's stown the keys o' the prison house do[o]r
   An' latten the prisoner gang.

O whan she saw him, Young Bekie,
   Her heart was wondrous sair;
For the mice but an' the bold rattons
   Had eaten his yallow hair.

She 's gien him a shaver for his beard,
   A comber till his hair,
Five hunder pound in his pocket
   To spen', an' nae to spair.

She 's gien him a steed was good in need
   An' a saddle o' royal bone,
A leash o' hounds o' ae litter,
   An' Hector called one.

Linne] *a stock locality in ballads*   gaed] went   but . . . ben]
out . . . in, to . . . fro   stown] stolen   latten . . . gang] let . . .
go   but an'] and also   till] to

Atween this twa a vow was made,
  'Twas made full solemnly,
That or three years was come an' gane
  Well married they shou'd be.

He had nae been in 's ain country
  A twelvemonth till an end,
Till he 's forc'd to marry a duke's daughter
  Or than lose a' his land.

Ohon, alas, says Young Bekie,
  I know not what to dee,
For I canna win to Burd Isbel
  And she kens nae to come to me.

O it fell once upon a day
  Burd Isbel fell asleep,
An' up it starts the Belly Blin'
  An' stood at her bed feet.

O waken, waken, Burd Isbel,
  How [can] you sleep so soun',
Whan this is Bekie's wedding day
  An' the marriage gain' on?

Ye do ye to your mither's bow'r,
  Think neither sin nor shame,
An' ye tak twa o' your mither's mary's
  To keep ye frae thinking lang.

Ohon] alas (*Gaelic*)   win] reach   Belly Blin'] household
Brownie   gain'] going   Ye do ye] take yourself   mary's]
maids-of-honour   thinking lang] getting bored

Ye dress yoursel in the red scarlet
  An' your mary's in dainty green,
An' ye pit girdles about your middles
  Wou'd buy an Earldome.

O ye gang down by yon sea side
  An' down by yon sea stran';
Sae bonny will the Hollans boats
  Come rowin' till your han'.

Ye set your milk white foot abord,
  Cry, Hail ye, Domine!
An' I shal be the steerer o't
  To row you o'er the sea.

She 's tane her till her mither's bow'r,
  Thought neither sin nor shame,
An' she took twa o' her mither's marys
  To keep her frae thinking lang.

She dress'd hersel i' the red scarlet,
  Her marys i' dainty green,
And they pat girdles about their middles
  Wou'd buy an earldome.

An' they gid down by yon sea side
  An' down by yon sea stran';
Sae bonny did the Hollan boats
  Come rowin' to their han'.

She set her milk white foot on board,
  Cried, Hail ye, Domine!
An' the Belly Blin' was the steerer o 't
  To row her o'er the sea.

pit] put   Hollans boats] Dutch fishing boats   till] to

Whan she came to Young Bekie's gate
  She heard the music play;
Sae well she kent frae a' she heard
  It was his wedding day.

She 's pitten her han' in her pocket,
  Gi'n the porter guineas three:
Hae, tak ye that, ye proud porter,
  Bid the bride-groom speake to me.

O whan that he cam up the stair
  He fell low down on his knee,
He hail'd the king, an' he hail'd the queen,
  An' he hail'd him, Young Bekie.

O I've been porter at your gates
  This thirty years an' three,
But there 's three ladies at them now,
  Their like I never did see.

There 's ane o' them dress'd in red scarlet
  And twa in dainty green,
An' they hae girdles about their middles
  Wou'd buy an earldome.

Then out it spake the bierly bride,
  Was a' goud to the chin:
Gin she be braw without, she says,
  We 's be as braw within.

Then up it starts him, Young Bekie,
  An' the tears was in his e'e:
I'll lay my life it 's Burd Isbel
  Come o'er the sea to me.

bierly] stately, stalwart   goud] gold   braw] fine

107

O quickly ran he down the stair,
   An' whan he saw 't was shee,
He kindly took her in his arms
   And kiss'd her tenderly.

O hae ye forgotten, Young Bekie,
   The vow ye made to me,
Whan I took you out o' the prison strong
   Whan ye was condemn'd to die?

I gae you a steed was good in need,
   An' a saddle o' royal bone,
A leash o' hounds o' ae litter,
   An' Hector called one.

It was well kent what the lady said,
   That it was nae a lie,
For at ilka word the lady spake
   The hound fell at her knee.

Tak hame, tak hame your daughter dear,
   A blessing gae her wi',
For I maun marry my Burd Isbel
   That 's come o'er the sea to me.

Is this the custom o' your house
   Or the fashion o' your lan',
To marry a maid in a May mornin'
   An' send her back at even?

B. In London city was Bicham born,
   He long'd strange countries for to see;
But he was ta'en by a savage Moor
   Who handl'd him right cruely.

ilka] every   gae] gave   gae] go

For thro' his shoulder he put a bore,
   An' thro' the bore has pitten a tree,
An' he 's gar'd him draw the carts o' wine
   Where horse and oxen had wont to be.

He 's casten [him] in a dungeon deep
   Where he cou'd neither hear nor see;
He 's shut him up in a prison strong
   An' he 's handl'd him right cruely.

O this Moor he had but ae daughter,
   I wot her name was Shusy Pye;
She 's doen her to the prison house
   And she 's call'd Young Bicham one word by.

O hae ye ony lands or rents
   Or citys in your ain country,
Cou'd free you out of prison strong
   An' cou'd mantain a lady free?

O London city is my own,
   An' other citys twa or three,
Cou'd loose me out o' prison strong
   An' cou'd mantain a lady free.

O she has brib'd her father's men
   Wi' meikle goud and white money,
She 's gotten the key o' the prison doors
   An' she has set Young Bicham free.

bore] hole   pitten] put   tree] pole   gar'd] made
Shusy] Susie   doen her] taken herself   rents] properties
free] noble   meikle goud] much gold

She 's gi'n him a loaf o' good white bread
    But an' a flask o' Spanish wine,
An' she bad him mind on the ladie's love
    That sae kindly freed him out o' pine.

Go set your foot on good ship board
    An' haste you back to your ain country;
An' before that seven years has an end
    Come back again, love, and marry me.

It was long or seven years had an end
    She long'd fu' sair her love to see;
She 's set her foot on good ship board
    An' turn'd her back on her ain country.

She 's sail'd up, so has she doun,
    Till she came to the other side;
She 's landed at Young Bicham's yates,
    An' I hop[e] this day she sal be his bride.

Is this Young Bicham's yates? says she,
    Or is that noble prince within?
He 's up the stairs wi' his bonny bride,
    An' mony a lord and lady wi' him.

O has he ta'en a bonny bride
    An' has he clean forgotten me?
An' sighing said that gay lady,
    I wish I were i' my ain country.

But she 's pitten her han' in her pocket
    An gi'n the porter guineas three;
Says, Take ye that, ye proud porter,
    An' bid the bridegroom speak to me.

pine] suffering   yates] gates

O whan the porter came up the stair
  He 's fa'n low down upon his knee:
Won up, won up, ye proud porter,
  An' what makes a' this courtesy?

O I 've been porter at your yates
  This mair nor seven years an' three,
But there is a lady at them now
  The like of whom I never did see.

For on every finger she has a ring
  An' on the mid-finger she has three,
An' there 's as meikle goud aboon her brow
  As wou'd buy an earldome o' lan' to me.

Then up it started Young Bicham
  An' sware so loud by our Lady:
It can be nane but Shusy Pye
  That has come o'er the sea to me.

O quickly ran he down the stair,
  O' fifteen steps he has made but three;
He 's taen his bonny love in his arms
  An' a wot he kiss'd her tenderly.

O hae you tane a bonny bride?
  An' hae you quite forsaken me?
An' hae you quite forgotten her
  That ga'e you life an' liberty?

She 's lookit o'er her left shoulder
  To hide the tears stood in her e'e:
Now fare thee well, Young Bicham, she says,
  I'll strive to think nae mair on thee.

Won] get   a wot] I know, surely

Take back your daughter, Madam, he says,
　An' a double dowry I'll gi' her wi';
For I maun marry my first true love
　That's done and suffered so much for me.

He's taken his bonny love by the han'
　And led her to yon fountain stane;
He's chang'd her name frae Shusy Pye,
　An' he's cal'd her his bonny love, Lady Jane.

fountain stane] font

32. *Hynd Horn*

HYND HORN fair, and Hynd Horn free,
Where was you born and what counterie?
In good greenwood where I was born,
But my friends they hae left me a' forlorn.

I gave my love a gay gold wand,
It was to rule o'er fair Scotland;
And she gave me a gay gold ring,
To me it had virtue above all thing.

Hynd] lad　　　free] noble

As long as that ring does keep its hue,
Unto you I will prove true;
But when that ring grows pale and wan,
You'll know that I love some other man.

So he hoised his sail and away went he,
Away, away to some far counterie;
But when he looked into his ring
He knew that she loved some other man.

So he hoised his sail and home came he,
Home, home again to his ain counterie;
The first he met upon dry land
It was an auld, auld beggar man.

What news, what news, ye auld beggar man,
What news, what news hae ye to gie?
Nae news, nae news hae I to gie,
But the morn is oor queen's wedding day.

Oh you'll gie me your begging weed
And I'll gie you my riding steed.
It 's my begging weed 's nae fit for you,
And your riding steed 's too high for me.

But be it right or be it wrong,
The begging weed he has put on:
Now since I've got the begging weed,
Pray tell to me the begging lead.

Oh, you'll gang up to the heid o' yon hill,
And blaw your trumpet loud and shrill;
And you'll gang crawlin' down yon brae,
As if you could neither step nor stray.

hoised] hoisted   lead] speech, formula   gang] go   brae] hill

You'll seek frae Peter, and you'll seek frae Paul,
You'll seek frae the high to the low o' them all;
But frae nane o' them tak' ye nae thing,
Unless it comes frae the bride's ain han'.

So he socht frae Peter, and he socht frae Paul,
He socht frae the high to the low o' them all,
But frae nane o' them wad he hae nae thing
Unless it cam' frae the bride's ain han'.

So the bride came tripping down the stair
With combs of yellow gold in her hair,
With a glass o' red wine in her han'
To gie to the auld beggar man.

Out o' the glass he drank the wine,
And into it he dropped the ring:
Oh got you it by sea or got you it by lan',
Or got you it off o' a droont man's han'?

I got nae it by sea nor yet by lan',
Nor yet did I on a droont man's han';
But I got it frae you in my wooin' gay,
And I'll gie 't to you on your wedding day.

She tore the gold down frae her heid,
I'll follow you and beg my breid.
She tore the gold down frae her hair,
Says, I'll follow you for evermair.

So atween the kitchen and the ha'
And there he loot his duddy cloak fa';
He shone wi' gold aboon them a',
And the bride frae the bridegroom 's stown awa'.

ain] own   droont] drowned   loot] let   duddy] ragged
aboon] above   stown] stolen

33. *Earl Brand*

O Did you ever hear of the brave Earl Brand,
  Hey lillie, ho lillie lallie;
He's courted the King's daughter o' fair England,
  I' the brave nights so early.

She was scarcely fifteen years that tide
When sae boldly she came to his bedside:

O Earl Brand, how fain wad I see
A pack of hounds let loose on the lea.

O lady fair, I have no steed but one,
But thou shalt ride and I will run.

O Earl Brand, but my father has two,
And thou shalt have the best o' tho'.

Now they have ridden o'er moss and moor
And they have met neither rich nor poor;

Till at last they met with old Carl Hood,
He's aye for ill and never for good.

tide] time   moss] marsh   Carl Hood] Odin Síðhöttr ('Deep-
hood'), in the guise of a hooded beggar.

Now, Earl Brand, an' ye love me,
Slay this old Carl and gar him dee.

O lady fair, but that would be sair,
To slay an auld Carl that wears grey hair.

My own lady fair, I'll not do [sae],
I'll pay him his fee [and let him gae].

O where have you ridden this lee lang day,
And where have you stown this fair lady away?

I have not ridden this lee lang day,
Nor yet have I stown this fair lady away;

For she is, I trow, my sick sister,
Whom I have been bringing fra' Winchester.

If she 's been sick and nigh to dead,
What makes her wear the ribbon sae red?

If she 's been sick and like to die,
What makes her wear the gold sae high?

When came the Carl to the lady's yett,
He rudely, rudely rapped thereat:

Now where is the lady of this hall?
She 's out with her maids a-playing at the ball.

Ha, ha, ha, ye are all mista'en,
Ye may count your maidens owre again.

an'] if   Carl] man   gar him dee] make him die   sair] grievous
lee lang] livelong   stown] stolen   dead] death   yett] gate
the ball] handball

I met her far beyond the lea,
With the young Earl Brand his leman to be.

H[er] father of his best men armed fifteen,
And they're ridden after them bidene.

The lady looked owre her left shoulder, then
Says, O Earl Brand, we are both of us ta'en.

If they come on me one by one
You may stand by me till the fights be done,

But if they come on me one and all
You may stand by and see me fall.

They came upon him one by one
Till fourteen battles he has won;

And fourteen men he has them slain
Each after each upon the plain.

But the fifteenth man behind stole round
And dealt him a deep and a deadly wound.

Though he was wounded to the deid
He set his lady on her steed.

They rode till they came to the river Doune,
And there they lighted to wash his wound.

O Earl Brand, I see your heart's blood.—
It 's nothing but the glent and my scarlet hood.

leman] mistress bidene] at once deid] death Doune]
in Ayrshire glent] gleam of the river

They rode till they came to his mother's yett,
So faintly and feebly he rapped thereat.

O my son's slain, he is falling to swoon,
And it's all for the sake of an English loon.

O say not so, my dearest mother,
But marry her to my youngest brother.

To a maiden true he'll give his hand,
   Hey lillie, ho lillie lallie,
To the king's daughter o' fair England,
To a prize that was won by a slain brother's brand,
   I' the brave nights so early.

loon] whore

34. *The Douglas Tragedy*

RISE up, rise up now, Lord Douglas, she says,
   And put on your armour so bright;
Let it never be said that a daughter of thine
   Was married to a lord under night.

Rise up, rise up, my seven bold sons,
   And put on your armour so bright;
And take better care of your youngest sister
   For your eldest's awa the last night.

He 's mounted her on a milk-white steed
    And himself on a dapple grey
With a bugelet horn hung down by his side;
    And lightly they rode away.

Lord William lookit o'er his left shoulder
    To see what he could see,
And there he spy'd her seven brethren bold
    Come riding over the lee.

Light down, light down, Lady Margret, he said,
    And hold my steed in your hand,
Until that against your seven brethren bold
    And your father I mak a stand.

She held his steed in her milk-white hand
    And never shed one tear
Until that she saw her seven brethren fa',
    And her father hard fighting, who lov'd her so dear.

O hold your hand, Lord William, she said,
    For your strokes they are wondrous sair;
True lovers I can get many a ane
    But a father I can never get mair.

O she 's taen out her handkerchief,
    It was o' the holland sae fine,
And aye she dighted her father's bloody wounds
    That were redder than the wine.

O chuse, O chuse, Lady Margret, he said,
    O whether will ye gang or bide?
I'll gang, I'll gang, Lord William, she said,
    For ye have left me no other guide.

bugelet] small bugle   holland] Dutch linen   dighted] dressed

He's lifted her on a milk-white steed
   And himself on a dapple grey
With a bugelet horn hung down by his side;
   And slowly they baith rade away.

O they rade on, and on they rade,
   And a' by the light of the moon,
Until they came to yon wan water;
   And there they lighted down.

They lighted down to tak a drink
   Of the spring that ran sae clear,
And down the stream ran his gude heart's blude,
   And sair she gan to fear.

Hold up, hold up, Lord William, she says,
   For I fear that you are slain.
'Tis naething but the shadow of my scarlet cloak
   That shines in the water sae plain.

O they rade on, and on they rade,
   And a' by the light of the moon,
Until they cam to his mother's ha' door;
   And there they lighted down.

Get up, get up, lady mother, he says,
   Get up and let me in;
Get up, get up, lady mother, he says,
   For this night my fair ladye I've win.

O mak my bed, lady mother, he says,
   O mak it braid and deep;
And lay Lady Margret close at my back,
   And the sounder I will sleep.

Lord William was dead lang ere midnight,
   Lady Margret lang ere day:
And all true lovers that go thegither,
   May they have mair luck than they.

35. *Willie and Lady Margerie*

SWEET Willie was a widow's son,
   And he wore a milk-white weed O;
And weel could Willie read and write,
   Far better ride on steed O.

Lady Margerie was the first ladye
   That drank to him the wine O;
And aye as the healths gaed round and round,
   Laddy, your love is mine O.

Lady Margerie was the first ladye
   That drank to him the beer O;
And aye as the healths gaed round and round,
   Laddy, ye're welcome here O.

You must come intill my bower
   When the evening bells do ring O;
And you must come intil my bower
   When the evening mass doth sing O.

He 's ta'en four-and-twenty braid arrows
   And laced them in a whang O;
And he 's awa' to Lady Margerie's bower
   As fast as he can gang O.

weed] dress   intill] into   whang] thong   gang] go

He set his ae foot on the wa'
   And the other on a stane O;
And he 's kill'd a' the King's life guards,
   He 's kill'd them every man O.

Oh open, open, Lady Margerie,
   Open and let me in O;
The weet weets a' my yellow hair
   And the dew draps on my chin O.

With her feet as white as sleet
   She strode her bower within O;
And with her fingers lang and sma'
   She 's looten sweet Willie in O.

She 's louted down unto his foot
   To lowze sweet Willie's shoon O;
The buckles were sae stiff they wadna lowze,
   The blood had frozen in O.

O Willie, O Willie, I fear that thou
   Hast bred me dule and sorrow;
The deed that thou hast done this nicht
   Will kythe upon the morrow.

In then came her father dear
   And a braid sword by his gare O;
And he 's gi'en Willie, the widow's son,
   A deep wound and a sair O.

weet] wet, rain   sma'] slender   looten] let   louted] bent
lowze] loosen   dule] misery   kythe] be discovered   braid]
broad   gare] gown

Lye yont, lye yont, Willie, she says,
 Your sweat weets a' my side O;
Lye yont, lye yont, Willie, she says,
 For your sweat I downa bide O.

She turned her back unto the wa',
 Her face unto the room O;
And there she saw her auld father
 Fast walking up and doun O.

Woe be to you, father, she said,
 And an ill deid may you die O;
For ye've kill'd Willie, the widow's son,
 And he would have married me O.

She turned her back unto the room,
 Her face unto the wa' O;
And with a deep and heavy sich
 Her heart it brak in twa O.

yont] beyond (me)　　downa] cannot　　deid] death　　sich] sigh

36. *Glasgerion*

GLASGERION was a kings owne sonne,
 And a harper he was good,
He harped in the kings Chamber
 Where cappe and candle yoode;
And soe did hee in the Queens chamber
 Till ladies waxed wood.

cappe] wine-cup　　yoode] went, passed　　wood] wild with pleasure

And then bespake the Kings daughter,
  And these words thus sayd shee,
Saide, Strike on, strike on, Glasgerrion,
  Of thy striking doe not blinne,
Theres neuer a stroke comes ouer this harpe
  But it glads my hart within.

Faire might you fall, Lady, quoth hee;
  Who taught you now to speake?
I haue loued you, Lady, seuen yeere,
  My hart I durst neere breake.

But come to my bower, my Glasgerryon,
  When all men are att rest;
I am a ladie true of my promise,
  Thou shalt bee a welcome guest.

But home then came Glasgerryon,
  A glad man, Lord, was hee:
And come thou hither, Iacke my boy,
  Come hither vnto mee;

For the kings daughter of Normandye,
  Her loue is granted mee,
And before the cocke haue crowen
  Att her chamber must I bee.

But come you hither, Master, quoth hee,
  Lay your head downe on this stone,
For I will waken you, Master deere,
  Afore it be time to gone.

blinne] cease   Faire . . . fall] good fortune to you   durst]
dare, venture to

But vpp then rose that lither ladd
   And did on hose and shoone;
A coller he cast vpon his necke,
   Hee seemed a gentleman.

And when he came to that Ladies chamber
   He thrild vpon a pinn.
The Lady was true of her promise,
   Rose vp and lett him in.

He did not take the lady gay
   To boulster nor noe bedd,
But downe vpon her chamber flore
   Full soone he hath her layd.

He did not kisse that Lady gay
   When he came nor when he youd;
And sore mistrusted that Lady gay
   He was of some churles blood.

But home then came that lither ladd
   And did of his hose and shoone,
And cast that coller from about his necke
   (He was but a churles sonne):
Awaken, quoth hee, my Master deere,
   I hold it time to be gone.

For I haue sadled your horsse, Master,
   Well bridled I haue your steed;
Haue not I serued a good breakfast,
   When times comes I haue need.

lither] wicked   thrild] rattled   pinn] door-knocker   youd]
went

But vp then rose good Glasgerryon
   And did on both hose and shoone,
And cast a coller about his necke
   (He was a Kinges sonne).

And when he came to that Ladies chamber
   He thrild vpon a pinn;
The Lady was more then true of promise,
   Rose vp and let him in:

Saies, Whether haue you left with me
   Your braclett or your gloue,
Or are you returned backe againe
   To know more of my loue?

Glasgerryon swore a full great othe
   By oake and ashe and thorne:
Lady, I was neuer in your chamber
   Sith the time that I was borne.

O then it was your litle foote page
   Falsly hath beguiled me:
And then she pulld forth a litle pen-knife
   That hanged by her knee,
Says, There shall neuer noe churles blood
   Spring within my body.

But home then went Glasgerryon,
   A woe man, Lord, was hee,
Saies, Come hither, thou Iacke my boy,
   Come thou hither to me:

Sith] since   pen-knife] sheath-knife

For if I had killed a man to-night,
    Iacke, I wold tell it thee;
But if I haue not killed a man to-night,
    Iacke, thou hast killed three!

And he puld out his bright browne sword
    And dryed it on his sleeue,
And he smote off that lither ladds head
    And asked noe man noe leaue.

He sett the swords poynt till his brest,
    The pumill till a stone:
Thorrow that falsenese of that lither ladd
    These three liues werne all gone.

browne] burnished   till] to

37. *King Estmere*

HEARKEN to me, gentlemen,
    Come and you shall heare;
Ile tell you of two of the boldest brethren
    That ever borne y-were.

The tone of them was Adler younge,
    The tother was kyng Estmere;
The were as bolde men in their deeds,
    As any were farr and nearr.

As they were drinking ale and wine
    Within kyng Estmeres halle:
When will ye marry a wyfe, brother,
    A wyfe to glad us all?

Then bespake him kyng Estmere,
 And answered him hastilee:
I know not that ladye in any land
 That's able to marrye with mee.

Kyng Adland hath a daughter, brother,
 Men call her bright and sheene;
If I were kyng here in your stead,
 That ladye shold be my queene.

Saies, Reade me, reade me, deare brother,
 Throughout merry England,
Where we might find a messenger
 Betwixt us towe to sende.

Saies, You shal ryde yourselfe, brother,
 Ile beare you companye;
Many throughe fals messengers are deceived,
 And I feare lest soe shold wee.

Thus the [har]nisht them to ryde
 Of twoe good renisht steeds,
And when the came to king Adlands halle,
 Of redd gold shone their weeds.

And when the came to kyng Adlands hall
 Before the goodlye gate,
There they found good kyng Adland
 Rearing himselfe theratt.

sheene] shining   Reade] advise   towe] two   the harnisht
them] they accoutred themselves   renisht] fierce, wild   weeds]
garments   Rearing himselfe] leaning

Now Christ thee save, good kyng Adland;
  Now Christ you save and see.
Sayd, You be welcome, king Estmere,
  Right hartilye to mee.

You have a daughter, said Adler younge,
  Men call her bright and sheene,
My brother wold marrye her to his wiffe,
  Of Englande to be queene.

Yesterday was att my deere daughter
  Syr Bremor the kyng of Spayne;
And then she nicked him of naye,
  And I doubt sheele do you the same.

The kyng of Spayne is a foule paynim,
  And 'leeveth on Mahound;
And pitye it were that fayre ladye
  Shold marrye a heathen hound.

But grant to me, sayes kyng Estmere,
  For my love I you praye;
That I may see your daughter deere
  Before I goe hence awaye.

Although itt is seven yeers and more
  Since my daughter was in halle,
She shall come once downe for your sake
  To glad my guestes alle.

nicked ... naye] refused him with 'No'   Mahound] Mahomet

Downe then came that mayden fayre,
   With ladyes laced in pall,
And halfe a hundred of bold knightes,
   To bring her from bowre to hall;
And as many gentle squiers,
   To tend upon them all.

The talents of golde were on her head sette,
   Hanged low downe to her knee;
And everye ring on her small finger,
   Shone of the chrystall free.

Saies, God you save, my deere madam;
   Saies, God you save and see.
Said, You be welcome, kyng Estmere,
   Right welcome unto mee.

And if you love me, as you saye,
   Soe well and hartilee,
All that ever you are comen about
   Soone sped now itt shal bee.

Then bespake her father deare:
   My daughter, I saye naye;
Remember well the kyng of Spayne,
   What he sayd yesterdaye.

He wold pull downe my halles and castles,
   And reave me of my lyfe.
I cannot blame him if he doe,
   If I reave him of his wyfe.

pall] fine cloth   talents] ornaments

Your castles and your towres, father,
   Are stronglye built aboute;
And therefore of the king of Spaine
   Wee neede not stande in doubt.

Plight me your troth, nowe, kyng Estmere,
   By heaven and your righte hand,
That you will marrye me to your wyfe,
   And make me queene of your land.

Then kyng Estmere he plight his troth
   By heaven and his righte hand,
That he wolde marrye her to his wyfe,
   And make her queene of his land.

And he tooke leave of that ladye fayre,
   To goe to his owne countree,
To fetche him dukes and lordes and knightes,
   That marryed the might bee.

They had not ridden scant a myle,
   A myle forthe of the towne,
But in did come the kyng of Spayne,
   With kempes many one.

But in did come the kyng of Spayne,
   With manye a bold barone,
Tone day to marrye kyng Adlands daughter,
   Tother daye to carrye her home.

Shee sent one after kyng Estmere
   In all the spede might bee,
That he must either turne againe and fighte,
   Or goe home and loose his ladye.

kempes] fighting-men

One whyle then the page he went,
  Another while he ranne;
Till he had oretaken king Estmere,
  I wis, he never blanne.

Tydings, tydings, kyng Estmere!
  What tydinges nowe, my boye?
O tydinges I can tell to you,
  That will you sore annoye.

You had not ridden scant a mile,
  A mile out of the towne,
But in did come the kyng of Spayne
  With kempes many a one:

But in did come the kyng of Spayne
  With manye a bold barone,
Tone daye to marrye king Adlands daughter,
  Tother daye to carry her home.

My ladye fayre she greetes you well,
  And ever-more well by mee:
You must either turne againe and fighte,
  Or goe home and loose your ladye.

Saies, Reade me, reade me, deere brother,
  My reade shall ryse at thee,
Whether it is better to turne and fighte,
  Or goe home and loose my ladye.

I wis] indeed   blanne] stopped   reade shall ryse at] counsel
shall come from

Now hearken to me, sayes Adler yonge,
   And your reade must rise at me,
I quicklye will devise a waye
   To sette thy ladye free.

My mother was a westerne woman,
   And learned in gramarye,
And when I learned at the schole,
   Something shee taught itt mee.

There growes an hearbe within this field,
   And iff it were but knowne,
His color, which is whyte and redd,
   It will make blacke and browne:

His color, which is browne and blacke,
   Itt will make redd and whyte;
That sworde is not in all Englande,
   Upon his coate will byte.

And you shal be a harper, brother,
   Out of the north countrye;
And Ile be your boy, soe faine of fighte,
   And beare your harpe by your knee.

And you shal be the best harper,
   That ever tooke harpe in hand;
And I wil be the best singer,
   That ever sung in this lande.

Itt shal be written in our forheads
   All and in gramarye,
That we towe are the boldest men
   That are in all Christentye.

gramarye] (grammar), magic

133

And thus they [har]nisht them to ryde,
  On tow good renish steedes:
And when they came to king Adlands hall,
  Of redd gold shone their weedes.

And whan the came to kyng Adlands hall,
  Untill the fayre hall yate,
There they found a proud porter
  Rearing himselfe thereatt.

Sayes, Christ thee save, thou proud porter;
  Sayes, Christ thee save and see.
Nowe you be welcome, sayd the porter,
  Of what land soever ye bee.

Wee beene harpers, sayd Adler younge,
  Come out of the northe countrye;
Wee beene come hither untill this place,
  This proud weddinge for to see.

Sayd, And your color were white and redd,
  As it is blacke and browne,
I wold saye king Estmere and his brother
  Were comen untill this towne.

Then they pulled out a ryng of gold,
  Layd itt on the porters arme:
And ever we will thee, proud porter,
  Thou wilt saye us no harme.

yate] gate   Rearing himselfe] leaning   untill] to   And
your] if your

Sore he looked on kyng Estmere,
   And sore he handled the ryng,
Then opened to them the fayre hall yates,
   He lett for no kind of thyng.

Kyng Estmere he stabled his steede
   Soe fayre att the hall bord;
The froth, that came from his brydle bitte,
   Light in kyng Bremors beard.

Saies, Stable thy steed, thou proud harper,
   Saies, Stable him in the stalle;
It doth not beseeme a proud harper
   To stable him in a kyngs halle.

My ladde he is so lither, he said,
   He will doe nought that's meete;
And is there any man in this hall
   Were able him to beate?

Thou speakst proud words, sayes the king of Spaine,
   Thou harper here to mee:
There is a man within this halle,
   Will beate thy ladd and thee.

O let that man come downe, he said,
   A sight of him wold I see;
And when hee hath beaten well my ladd,
   Then he shall beate of mee.

Downe then came the kemperye man,
   And looked him in the eare;
For all the gold, that was under heaven,
   He durst not neigh him neare.

lett . . . thyng] offered no obstruction   bord] dining table   lither]
wicked   kemperye man] champion   neigh] approach

And how nowe, kempe, said the kyng of Spaine,
   And how what aileth thee?
He saies, It is writt in his forhead
   All and in gramarye,
That for all the gold that is under heaven,
   I dare not neigh him nye.

Then kyng Estmere pulld forth his harpe,
   And plaid a pretty thinge:
The ladye upstart from the borde,
   And wold have gone from the king.

Stay thy harpe, thou proud harper,
   For Gods love I pray thee
For and thou playes as thou beginns,
   Thou'lt till my bryde from mee.

He stroake upon his harpe againe,
   And playd a pretty thinge;
The ladye lough a loud laughter,
   As shee sate by the king.

Saies, sell me thy harpe, thou proud harper,
   And thy stringes all,
For as many gold nobles thou shalt have
   As heere bee ringes in the hall.

What wold ye doe with my harpe, he sayd,
   If I did sell itt yee?
To playe my wiffe and me a Fitt,
   When abed together wee bee.

till] entice   nobles] coins   Fitt] strain of music

Now 'sell me, quoth hee, thy bryde soe gay,
  As shee sitts by thy knee,
And as many gold nobles I will give,
  As leaves been on a tree.

And what wold ye doe with my bryde soe gay,
  Iff I did sell her thee?
More seemelye it is for her fayre bodye
  To lye by mee then thee.

Hee played agayne both loud and shrille,
  And Adler he did syng,
O ladye, this is thy owne true love;
  Noe harper, but a kyng.

O ladye, this is thy owne true love,
  As playnlye thou mayest see;
And Ile rid thee of that foule paynim,
  Who partes thy love and thee.

The ladye looked, the ladye blushte,
  And blushte and lookt agayne,
While Adler he hath drawn his brande,
  And hath the Sowdan slayne.

Up then rose the kemperye men,
  And loud they gan to crye:
Ah! traytors, yee have slayne our kyng,
  And therefore yee shall dye.

Kyng Estmere threwe the harpe asyde,
  And swith he drew his brand;
And Estmere he, and Adler yonge
  Right stiffe in stour can stand.

Sowdan] sultan   stiffe in stour] stalwart in battle

And aye their swordes soe sore can byte,
   Throughe help of Gramarye,
That soone they have slayne the kempery men,
   Or forst them forth to flee.

Kyng Estmere tooke that fayre ladye,
   And marryed her to his wiffe,
And brought her home to merry England
   With her to leade his life.

can] did

38. *Fair Annie*

LEARN to mak your bed, Annie,
   And learn to lie your lane,
For I maun owre the salt seas gang
   A brisk bride to bring hame.

Bind up, bind up your yellow hair,
   And tye it in your neck;
And see you look as maiden-like
   As the day that we first met.

O how can I look maiden-like
   When maiden I'll ne'er be;
When seven brave sons I've born to thee
   And the eighth is in my bodie?

The eldest of your sons, my Lord,
   Wi' red gold shines his weed;
The second of your sons, my Lord,
   Rides on a milk-white steed;

your lane] alone   maun . . . gang] must go   weed] dress

And the third of your sons, my Lord,
   He draws your beer and wine;
And the fourth of your sons, my Lord,
   Can serve you when you dine;

And the fift of your sons, my Lord,
   He can both read and write;
And the sixth of your sons, my Lord,
   Can do it most perfyte;

And the sevent of your sons, my Lord,
   Sits on the nurse's knee:
And how can I look maiden-like
   When a maid I'll never be?

But wha will bake your wedding bread
   And brew your bridal ale;
Or wha will welcome your brisk bride
   That you bring owre the dale?

I'll put cooks in my kitchen
   And stewards in my hall,
And I'll have bakers for my bread
   And brewers for my ale;
But you're to welcome my brisk bride
   That I bring owre the dale.

He set his feet into his ship
   And his cock-boat on the main;
He swore it would be year and day
   Or he returned again.

cock-boat] ship's boat

When year and day was past and gane
    Fair Annie she thocht lang,
And she is up to her bower head
    To behold both sea and land.

Come up, come up, my eldest son,
    And see now what you see;
Oh yonder comes your father dear
    And your stepmother to be.

Cast off your gown of black, mother,
    Put on your gown of brown;
And I'll put off my mourning weeds
    And we'll welcome him hame.

She 's taken wine into her hand
    And she has taken bread,
And she is down to the water side
    To welcome them indeed.

You're welcome, my lord, you're welcome, my lord,
    You're welcome home to me,
So is every lord and gentleman
    That is in your companie.

You're welcome, my lady, you're welcome, my lady,
    You're welcome home to me,
So is every lady and gentleman
    That 's in your companie.

I thank you, my girl, I thank you, my girl,
    I thank you heartily;
If I live seven years about this house
    Rewarded you shall be.

thocht lang] grew weary

She serv'd them up, she serv'd them down,
  With the wheat bread and the wine;
But aye she drank the cauld water
  To keep her colour fine.

She serv'd them up, she serv'd them down,
  With the wheat bread and the beer;
But aye she drank the cauld water
  To keep her colour clear.

When bells were rung and mass was sung
  And all were boune for rest,
Fair Annie laid her sons in bed
  And a sorrowfu' woman she was.

Will I go to the salt salt seas,
  And see the fishes swim;
Or will I go to the gay green wood
  And hear the small birds sing?

Out and spoke an aged man
  That stood behind the door:
Ye will not go to the salt salt seas
  To see the fishes swim,
Nor will ye go to the gay green wood
  To hear the small birds sing:

But ye'll take a harp into your hand,
  Go to their chamber door,
And aye ye'll harp and aye ye'll murn
  With the salt tears falling oer.

boune] ready

She's taen a harp into her hand,
　　Went to their chamber door,
And aye she harped and aye she murn'd
　　With the salt tears falling o'er.

Out and spak the brisk young bride
　　In bride bed where she lay:
I think I hear my sister Annie,
　　And I wish weel it may;
For a Scotish lord staw her awa,
　　And an ill death may he die.

Wha was your father, my girl, she says,
　　Or wha was your mother,
Or had you ever a sister dear,
　　Or had you ever a brother?

King Henry was my father dear,
　　Queen Esther was my mother,
Prince Henry was my brother dear,
　　And Fanny Flower my sister.

If King Henry was your father dear,
　　And Queen Esther was your mother,
If Prince Henry was your brother dear,
　　Then surely I'm your sister.

Come to your bed, my sister dear,
　　It ne'er was wrang'd for me,
Bot an ae kiss of his merry mouth
　　As we cam owre the sea.

staw] stole　　　Bot an ae] except for one

FAIR ANNIE

Awa, awa, ye forenoon bride,
  Awa, awa frae me;
I wudna hear my Annie greet
  For a' the gold I got wi' thee.

There were five ships of gay red gold
  Cam owre the seas with me,
It 's twa o' them will tak me hame
  And three I'll leave wi' thee.

Seven ships o' white monie
  Came owre the seas wi' me,
Five o' them I'll leave wi' thee
  And twa will take me hame;
And my mother will make my portion up
  When I return again.

forenoon] for a morning only   greet] weep

39. Fair Isabell of Rochroyall

FAIR Isabell of Rochroyall,
   She dreamed where she lay;
She dream'd a dream of her love Gregory
   A little before the day.

O huly, huly rose she up
   And huly she put on,
And huly, huly she put on
   The silks of crimsion.

Gar sadle me the black, she sayes,
   Gar sadle me the broun;
Gar sadle me the swiftest steed
   That ever rode the toun.

Rochroyall] *perh.* Rough Castle, Stirlingshire. *Other versions have*
Lochroyan (Wigtown)   huly] gently, softly   Gar sadle me]
get saddled for me

Gar shoe him with the beat silver,
   And grind him with the gold;
Gar put two bells on every side
   Till I come to some hold.

She had not rode a mile, a mile,
   A mile but barely three,
Till that she spyed a companie
   Come rakeing oe're the lee.

O whether is this the first young may
   That lighted and gaed in,
Or is this the second young may
   That ne'er the sun shined on,
Or is this Fair Isabell of Roch Royall
   Banisht from kyth and kin?

O I am not the first young may
   That lighted and gaed in,
Nor neither am I the second young may
   That ne'er the sun shone on;

But I'm Fair Isabell of Roch Royall
   Banisht from kyth and kin;
I'm seeking my true love Gregory,
   And I wou'd I had him in.

O go your way to yon castle
   And ride it round about,
And there you'll find love Gregory;
   He 's within, without any doubt.

grind] ? harness   hold] dwelling, refuge   rakeing] riding
fast   may] maid   gaed] went

O she's away to yon castle,
    She's tirled at the pin:
O open, open, love Gregory,
    And let your true love in.

His mother] If you be the lass of the Rochroyall
    As I trow not you be,
You will tell me some of our love tokens
    That was betwixt you and me.

Have you not mind, love Gregory,
    Since we sat at the wine,
When we changed the rings off our fingers
    And ay the worst fell mine?

Mine was of the massy gold
    And thine was of the tin;
Mine was true and trusty both
    And thine was false within.

If you be [the] lass of the Roch Royall
    As I trow not you be,
You will tell me some other love token
    That was betwixt you and me.

Have you not mind, love Gregory,
    Since we sat at the wine,
We changed the smocks off our two backs
    And ay the worst fell mine?

Mine was of the holland fine
    And thine was course and thin;
So many blocks have we two made
    And ay the worst was mine.

tirled] rattled   pin] door-knocker   holland] fine Dutch linen
blocks] exchanges

Love Gregory he is not at home
But he is to the sea;
If you have any word to him
I pray you leav 't with me.

———————

O who will shoe my bony foot?
Or who will glove my hand?
Or who will bind my midle jimp
With the broad lilly band?

Or who will comb my bony head
With the red river comb?
Or who will be my bairns father
Ere Gregory he come home?

Mother]   O I 's gar shoe thy bony foot
And I 's gar glove thy hand,
And I 's gar bind thy midle jimp
With the broad lilly band;

And I 's gar comb thy bony head
With the red river comb:
But there is none to be thy bairns father
Till Love Gregory he come home.

Isabell]   I'll set my foot on the shipboard,
God send me wind and more;
For there 's never a woman shall bear a son
Shall make my heart so sore.

Gregory]   I dreamed a dream now since yestreen
That I never dreamed before;
I dream'd that the lass of the Rochroyall
Was knocking at the door.

jimp] slender   bony] fair   river] *obscure*: ? ivory
gar shoe] get shod

Mother]   Ly still, ly still, my é dear son,
      Ly still and take a sleep;
  For it 's neither ane hour nor yet a half
      Since she went from the gate.

O wo be to you, ill woman,
    And ane ill death mott you die:
For you might have come to my bed side
    And then have wakened me.

Gar sadle me the black, he sayes,
    Gar sadle me the broun;
Gar sadle me the swiftest steed
    That ever rode the toun.

Gar shoe him with the beat silver,
    Gar grind him with the gold;
Cause put two bells on every side
    Till I come to some hold.

They sadled him the black, the black,
    So did they him the broun;
So did they him the swiftest steed
    That ever rode to toun.

They shoed him with the beat silver,
    They grind him with the gold;
They put two bells on every side
    Till he came to some hold.

He had not rode a mile, a mile,
    A mile but barely three,
Till that he spyed her comely corps
    Come raking oere the lee.

é] only

Set doun, set doun these comely corps,
  Let me look on the dead:
And out he 's ta'en his little pen knife
  And slitted her winding sheet.

And first he kist her cheek, her cheek,
  And then he kist her chin;
And then he kist her rosy-lips
  But there was no breath within.

Gar deall, gar deall for my love sake
  The spiced bread and the wine,
For ere the morn at this time
  So shall you deall for mine.

Gar deall, gar deall for my love sake
  The penny's that are so small,
For e're the morn at this time
  So shall you deall for all.

[And he has ta'en his little pen knife
  With a heart that was fou sair,
He has given himself a deadly wound
  And word spake never mair].

40. *Child Waters*

CHILDE WATTERS in his stable stoode
  And stroaket his milke white steede:
To him came a ffaire young Ladye
  As ere did weare womans weede.

pen knife] sheath-knife, originally for making quill pens   **Gar**
deall] have dispensed

Saies, Christ you saue, good Chyld Waters;
    Sayes, Christ you saue and see!
My girdle of gold which was too longe
    Is now to short ffor mee;

And all is with one chyld of yours
    I ffeele sturre att my side.
My gowne of greene, it is to strayght;
    Before it was to wide.

If the child be mine, faire Ellen, he sayd,
    Be mine, as you tell mee,
Take you Cheshire and Lancashire both,
    Take them your owne to bee.

If the child be mine, ffaire Ellen, he said,
    Be mine, as you doe sweare,
Take you Cheshire and Lancashire both
    And make that child your heyre.

Shee saies, I had rather haue one kisse,
    Child Waters, of thy mouth,
Then I wold haue Cheshire and Lancashire both,
    That lyes by north and south.

And I had rather haue a twinkling,
    Child Waters, of your eye,
Then I wold haue Cheshire and Lancashire both,
    To take them mine oune to bee.

Tomorrow, Ellen, I must forth ryde
    Soe ffarr into the North countrye;

gowne of greene] *a mark of defloration*   by north] to the north

The ffairest Lady that I can find,
   Ellen, must goe with mee.
And euer I pray you, Child Watters,
   Your ffootpage let me bee.

If you will my ffootpage be, Ellen,
   As you doe tell itt mee,
Then you must cutt your gownne of greene
   An inche aboue your knee;

Soe must you doe your yellow lockes
   Another inch aboue your eye;
You must tell noe man what is my name:
   My ffootpage then you shall bee.

All this long day Child Waters rode,
   Shee ran bare ffoote by his side,
Yett was he neuer soe curteous a Knight
   To say, Ellen, will you ryde?

But all this day Child Waters rode,
   Shee ran barffoote thorow the broome,
Yett he was neuer soe curteous a Knight
   As to say, Put on your shoone.

Ride softlye, shee said, Child Watters;
   Why doe you ryde soe ffast?
The child, which is no mans but yours,
   My bodye itt will burst.

He sayes, Sees thou yonder water, Ellen,
   That fflowes from banke to brim?
I trust to God, Child Waters, shee said,
   You will neuer see mee swime.

But when shee came to the waters side
    Shee sayled to the chinne:
Except the Lord of heauen be my speed
    Now must I learne to swime.

The salt waters bare vp Ellens clothes,
    Our Ladye bare vpp he[r] chinne;
And Child Waters was a woe man, good Lord,
    To see faire Ellen swime.

And when shee ouer the water was
    Shee then came to his knee;
He said, Come hither, ffaire Ellen,
    Loe yonder what I see.

Seest thou not yonder hall, Ellen?
    Of redd gold shine the yates;
Theres twentyfour ffayre ladyes,
    The ffairest is my worldlye make.

Seest thou not yonder hall, Ellen?
    Of redd gold shineth the tower;
There is twentyfour ffaire Ladyes,
    The fairest is my paramoure.

I doe see the hall now, Child Waters,
    That of redd gold shineth the yates.
God giue good then of your selfe,
    And of your worldlye make.

I doe see the hall now, Child Waters,
    That of redd gold shineth the tower.
God giue good then of your selfe
    And of your paramoure.

yates] gates   make] mate

There were twentyfour [faire] Ladyes
   Were playing at the ball;
And Ellen was the ffairest Ladye,
   Must bring his steed to the stall.

There were twentyfour faire Ladyes
   Was playing at the Chesse;
And Ellen shee was the ffairest Ladye,
   Must bring his horsse to grasse.

And then bespake Child Waters sister,
   And these were the words said shee;
You haue the prettyest ffootpage, brother,
   That euer I saw with mine eye,

But that his belly it is soe bigg,
   His girdle goes wonderous hye;
And euer I pray you, Child Waters,
   Let him goe into the Chamber with mee.

It is more meete for a litle ffootpage
   That has run through mosse and mire
To take his supper vpon his knee
   And sitt downe by the kitchin fyer,
Then goe into the chamber with any Ladye
   That weares soe [rich] attyre.

But when they had supped euery one,
   To bedd they tooke the way;
He sayd, Come hither, my litle footpage,
   Hearken what I doe say:

ball] hand-ball   mosse] bog

And goe th[ou] downe into yonder towne,
   And low into the street;
The ffa[i]rest Ladye that thou can find,
   Hyer her in mine armes to sleepe,
And take her vp in thine armes two
   For filinge of her ffeete.

Ellen is gone into the towne,
   And low into the streete;
The fairest Ladye that shee cold find,
   She hyred in his armes to sleepe,
And took her in her armes two
   For filing of her ffeete.

I pray you now, good Child Waters,
   That I may creepe in att your bedds feete,
For there is noe place about this house
   Where I may say a sleepe.

This, and itt droue now aftterward
   Till itt was neere the day:
He sayd, Rise vp, my litle ffoote page,
   And giue my steed corne and hay;
And soe doe thou the good black oates
   That he may carry me the better away.

And vp then rose ffaire Ellen
   And gaue his steed corne and hay,
And soe shee did on the good blacke oates
   That he might carry him the better away.

For filinge of] to avoid soiling   say] try   itt droue] time passed

Shee layned her backe to the Manger side
  And greiuouslye did groane;
And that beheard his mother deere
  And heard her make her moane.

Shee said, Rise vp, thou Child Waters,
  I thinke thou art a cursed man;
For yonder is a ghost in thy stable
  That grieuouslye doth groane,
Or else some woman laboures of child,
  Shee is soe woe begone.

But vp then rose Child Waters,
  And did on his shirt of silke;
Then he put on his other clothes
  On his body as white as milke.

And when he came to the stable dore
  Full still that hee did stand,
That hee might heare now faire Ellen,
  How shee made her monand.

Shee said, Lullabye, my owne deere child,
  Lullabye, deere child, deere;
I wold thy father were a king
  Thy mother layd on a beere.

Peace now, he said, good faire Ellen,
  And be of good cheere, I thee pray;
And the Bridall, and the churching both,
  They shall bee vpon one day.

monand] moaning

41. *Gil Morrice*

GIL MORRICE was an erles son,
  His name it waxed wide;
It was nae for his great riches,
  Nor yet his mickle pride;
Bot it was for a lady gay,
  That livd on Carron side.

Quhair sall I get a bonny boy,
  That will win hose and shoen;
That will gae to lord Barnards ha',
  And bid his lady cum?
And ye maun rin my errand, Willie;
  And ye maun rin wi' pride;
Quhen other boys gae on their foot,
  On horse-back ye sall ride.

O no! Oh no! my master dear!
  I dare nae for my life;
I'll no gae to the bauld baron's,
  For to triest furth his wife.

Gil] ? Julian   Carron] in Stirlingshire   gae] go   maun]
must   triest] entice

156

My bird Willie, my boy Willie;
  My dear Willie, he sayd:
How can ye strive against the stream?
  For I sall be obeyd.

Bot, O my master dear! he cryd,
  In grene wod ye're your lain;
Gi' owre sic thochts, I walde ye rede,
  For fear ye should be ta'in.
Haste, haste, I say, gae to the ha',
  Bid hir cum here wi' speid:
If ye refuse my heigh command,
  I'll gar your body bleid.

Gae bid hir take this gay mantel,
  'Tis a' gowd bot the hem;
Bid hir cum to the gude grene wode,
  And bring nane bot hir lain:
And there it is, a silken sarke,
  Her ain hand sewd the sleive;
And bid hir cum to Gill Morice,
  Speir nae bauld baron's leave.

Yes, I will gae your black errand,
  Though it be to your cost;
Sen ye by me will nae be warn'd,
  In it ye sall find frost.
The baron he is a man of might,
  He neir could bide to taunt,
As ye will see before it 's night,
  How sma' ye hae to vaunt.

your lain] alone	sic] such	walde] would	rede] counsel
gar] make	gowd] gold	hir lain] her alone	sarke] shirt
speir] ask	Sen] since	sma'] little (cause)	

And sen I maun your errand rin
   Sae sair against my will,
I'se mak a vow and keip it trow,
   It sall be done for ill.
And quhen he came to broken brigue,
   He bent his bow and swam;
And quhen he came to grass growing,
   Set down his feet and ran.

And quhen he came to Barnards ha',
   Would neither chap nor ca':
Bot set his bent bow to his breist,
   And lichtly lap the wa'.
He wauld nae tell the man his errand,
   Though he stude at the gait;
Bot straiht into the ha' he cam,
   Quhair they were set at meit.

Hail! hail! my gentle sire and dame!
   My message winna waite;
Dame, ye maun to the gude grene wod
   Before that it be late.
Ye're bidden tak this gay mantel,
   Tis a' gowd bot the hem:
You maun gae to the gude grene wode,
   Ev'n by your sel alane.

And there it is, a silken sarke,
   Your ain hand sewd the sleive;
Ye maun gae speik to Gill Morice;
   Speir nae bauld baron's leave.

I'se] I shall   brigue] bridge   chap] knock   lap] leapt
winna] won't

The lady stamped wi' hir foot,
    And winked wi' hir ee;
Bot a' that she cou'd say or do,
    Forbidden he wad nae bee.

Its surely to my bow'r-woman;
    It neir could be to me.
I brocht it to lord Barnards lady;
    I trow that ye be she.
Then up and spack the wylie nurse,
    (The bairn upon hir knee)
If it be cum frae Gill Morice,
    It 's deir welcum to mee.

Ye leid, ye leid, ye filthy nurse,
    Sae loud I heird ye lee;
I brocht it to lord Barnards lady;
    I trow ye be nae shee.
Then up and spack the bauld baron,
    An angry man was hee;
He 's ta'in the table wi' his foot,
    Sae has he wi' his knee;
Till siller cup and ezar dish
    In flinders he gar'd flee.

Gae bring a robe of your cliding,
    That hings upon the pin;
And I'll gae to the gude grene wode,
    And speik wi' your lemman.
O bide at hame, now lord Barnard,
    I warde ye bide at hame;
Neir wyte a man for violence,
    That neir wate ye wi' nane.

bow'r-woman] chambermaid   leid] lied   ezar] maplewood
flinders] smithereens   flee] fly   cliding] dresses   lemman]
lover   bide] stay   warde] advise   wyte] blame; *pa. t.* wate

Gill Morice sate in gude grene wode,
    He whistled and he sang:
O what mean a' the folk coming,
    My mother tarries lang.
The baron came to the grene wode,
    Wi' mickle dule and care,
And there he first spied Gill Morice
    Kameing his yellow hair.

Nae wonder, nae wonder, Gill Morice,
    My lady lo'ed thee weel,
The fairest part of my bodie
    Is blacker than thy heel.
Yet neir the less now, Gill Morice,
    For a' thy great beautie,
Ye 's rew the day ye eir was born;
    That head sall gae wi' me.

Now he has drawn his trusty brand,
    And slaited on the strae;
And thro' Gill Morice' fair body
    He 's gar cauld iron gae.
And he has ta'in Gill Morice' head
    And set it on a speir;
The meanest man in a' his train
    Has gotten that head to bear.

And he has ta'in Gill Morice up,
    Laid him across his steid,
And brocht him to his painted bowr
    And laid him on a bed.

mickle dule] great sorrow   Kameing] combing   's] shall
slaited] whetted   strae] straw

The lady sat on castil wa',
   Beheld baith dale and doun;
And there she saw Gill Morice' head
   Cum trailing to the toun.

Far better I loe that bluidy head,
   Both and that yellow hair,
Than lord Barnard, and a' his lands,
   As they lig here and thair.
And she has ta'in her Gill Morice,
   And kissd baith mouth and chin:
I was once as fow of Gill Morice,
   As the hip is o' the stean.

I got ye in my father's house,
   Wi' mickle sin and shame;
I brocht thee up in gude grene wode,
   Under the heavy rain.
Oft have I by thy cradle sitten,
   And fondly seen thee sleip;
But now I gae about thy grave,
   The saut tears for to weip.

And syne she kissd his bluidy cheek,
   And syne his bluidy chin:
O better I loe my Gill Morice
   Than a' my kith and kin!
Away, away, ye ill woman,
   And an il deith mait ye dee:
Gin I had kend he'd bin your son,
   He'd neir bin slain for mee.

lig] lie   fow] full   hip] rosehip   stean] stone   saut]
salt   syne] then   mait] may

42. Brown Adam

O WHA wou'd wish the win' to blaw
   Or the green leaves fa' therewith;
Or wha wad wish a leeler love
   Than Brown Adam the Smith?

His hammer's o' the beaten gold,
   His study's o' the steel,
His fingers white are my delite,
   He blows his bellows we[e]l.

But they ha' banish'd him Brown Adam
   Frae father and frae mither,
An' they ha' banish'd him Brown Adam
   Frae sister and frae brither;

And they ha' banish'd [him] Brown Adam
   Frae the flow'r o' a' his kin;
An' he's bigget a bow'r i' the good green wood
   Between his lady an' him.

O it fell once upon a day
   Brown Adam he thought lang,
An' he wou'd to the green wood gang
   To hunt some venison.

leeler] truer   study] stithy, anvil   bigget] built   thought
lang] grew bored   gang] go

He 's ta'en his bow his arm o'er,
   His bran' intill his han',
And he is to the good green wood
   As fast as he cou'd gang.

O he 's shot up an' he 's shot down
   The bird upo' the briar,
An' he 's sent it hame to his lady,
   Bade her be of good cheer.

O he 's shot up an' he 's shot down
   The bird upo' the thorn,
And sent it hame to his lady,
   And hee'd be hame the morn.

Whan he came till his lady's bow'r-door
   He stood a little foreby,
And there he heard a fu' fa'se knight
   Temptin' his gay lady.

O he 's ta'en out a gay gold ring
   Had cost him mony a poun':
O grant me love for love, lady,
   An' this sal be your own.

I loo' Brown Adam well, she says,
   I wot sae does he me,
An' I wou'd na gi' Brown Adam's love
   For nae fa'se knight I see.

Out has he ta'en a purse of gold
   Was a' fu' to the string:
Grant me but love for love, lady,
   An' a' this sal be thine.

bran' intill] sword into   the morn] on the morrow   foreby]
aside   wot] know

I loo' Brown Adam well, she says,
　　An' I ken sae does he me,
An' I wou'dna be your light leman
　　For mair nor ye cou'd gie.

Then out has he drawn his lang, lang bran'
　　And he 's flash'd it in her e'en:
Now grant me love for love, lady,
　　Or thro' you this sal gang.

O sighing said that gay lady,
　　Brown Adam tarrys lang;
Then up it starts Brown Adam,
　　Says, I'm just at your han'.

He 's gar'd him leave his bow, his bow,
　　He 's gar'd him leave his bran';
He 's gar'd him leave a better pledge,
　　Four fingers o' his right han'.

light leman] whore　　　mair nor] more than　　　gar'd] forced . . . to

43. *Jellon Grame*

O JELLON GRAME sat in Silver Wood,
　　He whistled and he sang,
And he has call'd his little foot-page
　　His errand for to gang.

Win up, my bonny boy, he says,
　　As quick as e'er you may;
For ye maun gang for Lillie Flower
　　Before the break of day.

Jellon] ? Julian　　　gang] go　　　Win] get　　　maun] must

The boy he 's buckled his belt about
    And thro' the green-wood ran,
And he came to the ladie's bower-door
    Before the day did dawn.

O sleep ye or wake ye, Lillie Flower?
    The red sun 's i' the rain:
I sleep not aft, I wake right aft;
    Wha 's that that kens my name?

Ye are bidden come to Silver Wood,
    But I fear you'll never win hame;
Ye are bidden come to Silver Wood
    And speak wi' Jellon Grame.

O I will gang to Silver Wood
    Though I shou'd never win hame;
For the thing I most desire on earth
    Is to speak wi' Jellon Grame.

She had na ridden a mile, a mile,
    A mile but barely three,
Ere she came to a new made grave
    Beneath a green oak tree.

O then up started Jellon Grame
    Out of a bush hard bye:
Light down, light down now, Lillie Flower,
    For it 's here that ye maun ly.

She lighted aff her milk-white steed
    And knelt upon her knee:
O mercy, mercy, Jellon Grame,
    For I'm nae prepar'd to die.

sun] run *MS*   aft] often   hard] close

Your bairn that stirs between my sides
   Maun shortly see the light;
But to see it weltring in my blude
   Wou'd be a piteous sight.

O shou'd I spare your life, he says,
   Until that bairn be born,
I ken fu' well your stern father
   Woud hang me on the morn.

O spare my life now, Jellon Grame,
   My father ye ne'er need dread;
I'll keep my bairn i' the good green wood
   Or wi' it I'll beg my bread.

He took nae pity on that ladie
   Tho' she for life did pray,
But pierced her thro' the fair body
   As at his feet she lay.

He felt nae pity for that ladie
   Tho' she was lying dead,
But he felt some for the bonny boy
   Lay weltring in her blude.

Up has he ta'en that bonny boy,
   Gi'en him to nurices nine,
Three to wake and three to sleep
   And three to go between.

And he 's brought up that bonny boy,
   Call'd him his sister's son;
He thought nae man would e'er find out
   The deed that he had done.

ken] know   morn] morrow

But it sae fell out upon a time,
  As a hunting they did ga[e],
That they rested them in Silver Wood
  Upon a summer-day.

Then out it spake that bonny boy
  While the tear stood in his eye:
O tell me this now, Jellon Grame,
  And I pray you dinna lie:

The reason that my mother dear
  Does never take me hame?
To keep me still in banishment
  Is baith a sin and shame.

You wonder that your mother dear
  Does never send for thee:
Lo, there's the place I slew thy mother
  Beneath that green oak tree.

Wi' that the boy has bent his bow
  (It was baith stout and lang),
And through and thro' him Jellon Grame
  He's gar'd an arrow gang.

Says, Lye you thare now, Jellon Grame,
  My mellison you wi';
The place my mother lies buried in
  Is far too good for thee.

gae] go   dinna] don't   gar'd] made   mellison] curse

44. *Little Mousgrove and the Lady Barnet*

As it fell on a light holyday,
　　As many more does in the yeere,
Little Mousgrove would to the church and pray,
　　To see the faire ladyes there.

Gallants there were of good degree,
　　For beauty exceeding faire,
Most wonderous lovely to the eie,
　　That did to that church repaire.

Some came downe in red velvet
　　And others came downe in pall;
But next came downe my Lady Barnet,
　　The fairest amongst them all.

She cast a looke upon Little Mousgrove,
　　As bright as the summer's sunne;
Full well perceived then Little Mousgrove
　　Lady Barnet 's love he had wonne.

Then Lady Barnet most meeke and mild
　　Saluted this Little Mousgrove,
Who did repay her kinde courtesie
　　With favour and gentle love.

I have a bower in merry Barnet
　　Bestrowed with cowslips sweet;
If that it please you, Little Mousgrove,
　　In love me there to meete—

pall] fine cloth

Within mine armes one night to sleepe,
   For you my heart have wonne—
You need not feare my suspicious lord
   For he from home is gone.

Betide me life, betide me death,
   This night I will sleepe with thee,
And for thy sake I'le hazzard my breath,
   So deare is thy love to me.

What shall wee doe with our little foot-page
   Our counsell for to keepe,
And watch for feare Lord Barnet comes
   Whilest wee together doe sleepe?

Red gold shall be his hier, quoth he,
   And silver shall be his fee,
If he our counsell safely doe keepe
   That I may sleepe with thee.

I will have none of your gold, said he,
   Nor none of your silver fee;
If I should keepe your counsell, sir,
   'T were great disloyaltie.

I will not be false unto my lord
   For house nor yet for land;
But if my lady doe prove untrue
   Lord Barnet shall understand.

Then swiftly runnes the little foot-page
   Unto his lord with speed,
Who then was feasting with his deare friends,
   Not dreaming of this ill deede.

fee] reward

Most speedily the page did haste,
　Most swiftly did he runne,
And when he came to the broken bridge
　He lay on his brest and swumme.

The page did make no stay at all
　But went to his lord with speed,
That he the truth might say to him
　Concerning this wicked deed.

He found his lord at supper then,
　Great merriment there they did keepe:
My lord, quoth he, this night on my word
　Mousgrove with your lady does sleepe.

If this be true, my little foot-page,
　And true as thou tellest to me,
My eldest daughter I'le give to thee
　And wedded thou shalt be.

If this be a lye, my little foot-page,
　And a lye as thou tellest to me,
A new paire of gallowes shall straight be set
　And hanged shalt thou be.

If this be a lye, my lord, said he,
　A lye that you heare from me,
Then never stay a gallowes to make
　But hang me up on the next tree.

Lord Barnet then cal'd up his merry men,
　Away with speed he would goe;
His heart was so perplext with griefe
　The truth of this he must knowe.

Saddle your horses with speed, quoth he,
   And saddle me my white steed;
If this be true as the page hath said,
   Mousgrove shall repent this deed.

He charg'd his men no noise to make
   As they rode all along on the way:
Nor winde no hornes, quoth he, on your life,
   Lest our comming it should betray.

But one of the men, that Mousgrove did love,
   And respected his friendship most deare,
To give him knowledge Lord Barnet was neere
   Did winde his bugle most cleere.

And evermore as he did blow:
   Away, Mousgrove, and away;
For if I take thee with my lady
   Then slaine thou shalt be this day.

O harke, fair lady, your lord is neere,
   I heare his little horne blow;
And if he finde me in your armes thus
   Then slaine I shall be, I know.

O lye still, lye still, Little Mousgrove,
   And keepe my backe from the cold;
I know it is my father's shepheard
   Driving sheepe to the pinfold.

Mousgrove did turne him round about,
   Sweete slumber his eyes did greet;
When he did wake he then espied
   Lord Barnet at his bed's feete.

O rise up, rise up, Little Mousgrove,
  And put thy clothes on;
It shall never be said in faire England
  I slew a naked man.

Here's two good swords, Lord Barnet said,
  Thy choice, Mousgrove, thou shalt make;
The best of them thy selfe shalt have
  And I the worst will take.

The first good blow that Mousgrove did strike
  He wounded Lord Barnet sore;
The second blow that Lord Barnet gave
  Mousgrove could strike no more.

He tooke his lady by the white hand,
  All love to rage did convert,
That with his sword in most furious sort
  He pierst her tender heart.

A grave, a grave, Lord Barnet cryde,
  Prepare to lay us in;
My lady shall lie on the upper side
  Cause she's of the better kin.

Then suddenly he slue himselfe,
  Which grieves his friends full sore;
The deaths of these thra worthy wights
  With teares they did deplore.

This sad mischance by lust was wrought:
  Then let us call for grace
That we may shun this wicked vice
  And mend our lives apace.

45. Fair Janet

Yᴇ maun gang to your father, Janet,
    Ye maun gang to him soon;
Ye maun gang to your father, Janet,
    In case that his days are dune.

Janet's awa to her father
    As fast as she could hie:
O what's your will wi' me, father?
    O what's your will wi' me?

My will wi' you, Fair Janet, he said,
    It is both bed and board;
Some say that ye lo'e Sweet Willie,
    But ye maun wed a French lord.

A French lord maun I wed, father?
    A French lord maun I wed?
Then by my sooth, quo' Fair Janet,
    He's ne'er enter my bed.

Janet's awa to her chamber
    As fast as she could go;
Wha's the first ane that tapped there
    But Sweet Willie her jo?

maun gang] must go   He's] he shall   jo] sweetheart

O we maun part this love, Willie,
  That has been lang between:
There's a French lord coming o'er the sea
  To wed me wi' a ring;
There's a French lord coming o'er the sea
  To wed and tak me hame.

If we maun part this love, Janet,
  It causeth mickle woe;
If we maun part this love, Janet,
  It makes me into mourning go.

But ye maun gang to your three sisters,
  Meg, Marion, and Jean;
Tell them to come to Fair Janet
  In case that her days are dune.

Willie's awa to his three sisters,
  Meg, Marion, and Jean:
O haste and gang to Fair Janet,
  I fear that her days are dune.

Some drew to them their silken hose,
  Some drew to them their shoon,
Some drew to them their silk manteils,
  Their coverings to put on;
And they're awa to Fair Janet
  By the hie light o' the moon.

       *   *   *   *   *

O I have born this babe, Willie,
  Wi' mickle toil and pain;
Take hame, take hame your babe, Willie,
  For nurse I dare be nane.

mickle] great   manteils] capes

FAIR JANET

He 's tane his young son in his arms
  And kisst him cheek and chin,
And he 's awa to his mother's bower
  By the hie light o' the moon.

O open, open, mother, he says,
  O open and let me in;
The rain rains on my yellow hair
  And the dew drops o'er my chin,
And I hae my young son in my arms;
  I fear that his days are dune.

With her fingers lang and sma'
  She lifted up the pin,
And with her arms lang and sma'
  Received the baby in.

Gae back, gae back now, Sweet Willie,
  And comfort your fair lady;
For where ye had but ae nourice
  Your young son shall hae three.

Willie he was scarce awa
  And the lady put to bed,
Whan in and came her father dear:
  Make haste and busk the bride.

There 's a sair pain in my head, father,
  There 's a sair pain in my side;
And ill, O ill am I, father,
  This day for to be a bride.

sma'] slender pin] latch nourice] nurse busk] dress

FAIR JANET

O ye maun busk this bonny bride
    And put a gay mantle on;
For she shall wed this auld French lord
    Gin she should die the morn.

Some put on the gay green robes
    And some put on the brown;
But Janet put on the scarlet robes
    To shine foremost throw the town.

And some they mounted the black steed,
    And some mounted the brown;
But Janet mounted the milk-white steed
    To ride foremost throw the town.

O wha will guide your horse, Janet?
    O wha will guide him best?
O wha but Willie, my true-love?
    He kens I loe him best.

And when they cam to Marie's kirk
    To tye the haly ban',
Fair Janet's cheek looked pale and wan
    And her colour gaed and cam.

When dinner it was past and done,
    And dancing to begin,
O we'll go take the bride's maidens
    And we'll go fill the ring.

O ben than cam the auld French lord
    Saying, Bride, will ye dance wi' me?
Awa, awa, ye auld French lord,
    Your face I downa see.

Gin] even if   ben] into the room   downa] cannot

O ben than cam now Sweet Willie,
   He cam wi' ane advance:
O I'll go tak the bride's maidens
   And we'll go tak a dance.

I've seen ither days wi' you, Willie,
   And so has mony mae;
Ye would hae danced wi' me mysel,
   Let a' my maidens gae.

O ben than cam now Sweet Willie,
   Saying, Bride, will ye dance wi' me?
Aye, by my sooth, and that I will,
   Gin my back should break in three.

She had nae turned her throw the dance,
   Throw the dance but thrice,
Whan she fell doun at Willie's feet
   And up did never rise.

Willie 's ta'en the key of his coffer
   And gi'en it to his man:
Gae hame and tell my mother dear
   My horse he has me slain;
Bid her be kind to my young son
   For father he has nane.

The tane was buried in Marie's kirk
   And the tither in Marie's quire;
Out of the tane there grew a birk,
   And the tither a bonny brier.

has mony mae] have many more

46. Lord Thomas and Fair Annet

LORD THOMAS and fair Annet
　　Sate a' day on a hill;
Whan night was cum, and sun was sett,
　　They had not talkt their fill.

Lord Thomas said a word in jest,
　　Fair Annet took it ill:
A'! I will nevir wed a wife
　　Against my ain friends will.

Gif ye wull nevir wed a wife,
　　A wife wull neir wed yee.
Sae he is hame to tell his mither,
　　And knelt upon his knee:

O rede, O rede, mither, he says,
　　A gude rede gie to mee:
O sall I tak the nut-browne bride,
　　And let faire Annet bee?

The nut-browne bride haes gowd and gear,
　　Fair Annet she has gat nane;
And the little beauty fair Annet has,
　　O it wull soon be gane!

rede] counsel　　　nut-browne] brown-complexioned　　　gowd and
gear] gold and livestock

And he has till his brother gane:
  Now, brother, rede ye mee;
A' sall I marrie the nut-browne bride,
  And let fair Annet bee?

The nut-browne bride has oxen, brother,
  The nut-browne bride has kye;
I wad hae ye marrie the nut-browne bride,
  And cast fair Annet bye.

Her oxen may dye i' the house, Billie,
  And her kye into the byre;
And I sall hae nothing to my sell,
  Bot a fat fadge by the fyre.

And he has till his sister gane:
  Now, sister, rede ye mee;
O sall I marrie the nut-browne bride,
  And set fair Annet free?

Ise rede ye tak fair Annet, Thomas,
  And let the browne bride alane;
Lest ye sould sigh and say, Alace!
  What is this we brought hame?

No, I will tak my mithers counsel,
  And marrie me owt o' hand;
And I will tak the nut-browne bride;
  Fair Annet may leive the land.

Up then rose fair Annets father
  Twa hours or it wer day,
And he is gane into the bower,
  Wherein fair Annet lay.

till] to   kye] cows   fadge] fat bundle   owt o' hand]
straight away   or] ere

179

Rise up, rise up, fair Annet, he says,
   Put on your silken sheene;
Let us gae to St. Maries kirke,
   And see that rich weddeen.

My maides, gae to my dressing roome,
   And dress to me my hair;
Whair-eir yee laid a plait before,
   See yee lay ten times mair.

My maids, gae to my dressing room,
   And dress to me my smock;
The one half is o' the holland fine,
   The other o' needle-work.

The horse fair Annet rade upon,
   He amblit like the wind,
Wi' siller he was shod before,
   Wi' burning gowd behind.

Four and twenty siller bells
   Wer a' tyed till his mane,
And yae tift o' the norland wind,
   They tinkled ane by ane.

Four and twenty gay gude knichts
   Rade by the fair Annets side,
And four and twenty fair ladies,
   As gin she had bin a bride.

And whan she cam to Maries kirk,
   She sat on Maries stean:
The cleading that fair Annet had on
   It skinkled in their e'en.

sheene] shoes   holland] fine Dutch linen   amblit] moved
yae] one   tift] puff   gin] if   stean] stone seat at the church
door   cleading] dress   skinkled] glittered

And whan she cam into the kirk,
　　She shimmer'd like the sun;
The belt that was about her waist,
　　Was a' wi' pearles bedone.

She sat her by the nut-browne bride,
　　And her e'en they wer sae clear,
Lord Thomas he clean forgat the bride,
　　Whan fair Annet she drew near.

He had a rose into his hand,
　　And he gave it kisses three,
And reaching by the nut-browne bride,
　　Laid it on fair Annets knee.

Up than spak the nut-browne bride,
　　She spak wi' meikle spite;
And whair gat ye that rose-water,
　　That does mak yee sae white?

O I did get the rose-water,
　　Whair ye wull neir get nane,
For I did get that very rose-water
　　Into my mithers wame.

The bride she drew a long bodkin,
　　Frae out her gay head-gear,
And strake fair Annet unto the heart,
　　That word she nevir spak mair.

Lord Thomas he saw fair Annet wex pale,
　　And marvelit what mote bee:
But whan he saw her dear hearts blude,
　　A' wood-wroth wexed hee.

　meikle] great　　　wame] womb　　　mote] might　　　wood-
wroth] mad with rage

He drew his dagger, that was sae sharp,
    That was sae sharp and meet,
And drave [it] into the nut-browne bride,
    That fell deid at his feit.

Now stay for me, dear Annet, he sed,
    Now stay, my dear, he cry'd;
Then strake the dagger untill his heart,
    And fell deid by her side.

Lord Thomas was buried without kirk-wa',
    Fair Annet within the quiere;
And o' the tane thair grew a birk,
    The other a bonny briere.

And ay they grew, and ay they threw,
    As they wad faine be neare;
And by this ye may ken right weil,
    They ware twa luvers deare.

meet] of the right size   threw] intertwined

47. *The Famous Flower of Serving-men; or, The Lady turn'd Serving-man*

Her lover being slain, her Father dead,
Her bower rob'd, her Servants fled,
She drest her self in Mans attire,
She trim'd her locks, she cut her hair,
And thereupon she chang'd her name
From Fair Elise to Sweet William.

You Beautious Ladies, great and small,
I write unto you one and all,
Whereby that you may understand
What I have suffered in this land.

I was by birth a Lady fair,
My father's chief and onely heir,
But when my good old father dy'd
Then was I made a young Knights bride.

And then my love built me a bower
Bedeckt with many a fragrant flower;
A braver bower you never did see
Then my true love did build for me.

But there came thieves late in the night,
They rob'd my bower, and slew my Knight;
And after that my Knight was slain
I could no longer there remain.

My Servants all from me did flye
In the midst of my extremity,
And left me by my self alone
With a heart more cold then any stone.

Yet though my heart was full of care
Heaven would not suffer me to despair;
Wherefore in hast I chang'd my name
From Fair Elise to Sweet William.

And therewithal I cut my hair
And drest my self in mans attire,
My Doublet, Hose, and Bever-hat,
And a golden band about my neck.

With a silver Rapier by my side
So like a gallant I did ride;
The thing that I delighted on
Was for to be a Serving-man.

braver] finer

Thus in my sumptuous mans array
I bravely rode along the way,
And at the last it chanced so
That I unto the Kings Court did go.

Then to the King I bowed full low,
My love and duty for to show,
And so much favour I did crave
That I a Serving-mans place might have.

Stand up, brave youth, the King reply'd,
Thy service shall not be deny'd;
But tell me first what thou canst do;
Thou shalt be fitted thereunto.

Wilt thou be Usher of my Hall
To wait upon my Nobles all?
Or wilt thou be taster of my Wine
To wait on me when I shall dine?

Or wilt thou be my Chamberlain
To make my bed both soft and fine?
Or wilt thou be one of my guard?
And I will give thee thy reward.

Sweet William, with a smiling face,
Said to the King, If 't please your grace
To show such favour unto me,
Your Chamberlain I fain would be.

The King then did the Nobles call
To ask the counsel of them all,
Who gave consent Sweet William he
The King's own Chamberlain should be.

Now mark what strange things came to pass:
As the King one day a hunting was
With all his Lords and noble train,
Sweet William did at home remain.

Sweet William had no company then
With him at home but an old man,
And when he saw the Coast was clear
He took a Lute which he had there.

Upon the Lute Sweet William plaid,
And to the same he sung and said
With a pleasant and most noble voice
Which made the old man to rejoyce:

My father was as brave a Lord
As ever Europe did afford;
My Mother was a Lady bright,
My Husband was a valiant Knight.

And I my self a Lady gay
Bedeckt with gorgeous rich array;
The bravest Lady in the Land
Had not more pleasures to command.

I had my musick every day,
Harmonious Lessons for to play;
I had my Virgins fair and free
Continually to wait on me.

But now, alas, my Husband 's dead
And all my friends are from me fled;
My former joys are past and gone
For now I am a Serving-man.

free] gracious

At last the King from hunting came,
And presently upon the same
He called for the good old man
And thus to speak the King began:

What news, what news, old man? quoth he,
What news hast thou to tell to me?
Brave news, the old man he did say,
Sweet William is a Lady gay.

If this be true thou tellest me
Ile make thee a Lord of high degree,
But if thy words do prove a Lye
Thou shalt be hanged up presently.

But when the King the truth had found
His joys did more and more abound;
According as the old man did say,
Sweet William was a Lady gay.

Therefore the King without delay
Put on her glorious rich array,
And upon her head a crown of gold
Which was most famous to behold.

And then, for fear of further strife,
He took Sweet William for his wife;
The like before was never seen,
A Serving-man to be a Queen.

48. *The Bents and Broom*

*   *   *   *   *

GIN I were on my milkwhite steed
  And three miles frae the toon,
I wadna fear your three bauld brithers
  Amang the bents and broom.

But he wasna weel on o' his milkwhite steed,
  Or ae mile frae the toon,
Till up it starts her three bauld brithers
  Amang the bents and broom.

I wad a wad noo, sweet Willie,
  A wad or than your life:
I hae nae wad to gie, he says,
  Unless I gie my brand.

Then he pulled out a bloody brand
  A little below his gair,
And he has killed her three bauld brithers
  And left them sprawin' there.

But when her mother heard o' that
  An angry woman was she;
And on unto the King she gaed
  As fast as gang could she;
But when her daughter heard o' that
  She was there as soon as she.

Gin] if   bents] moors covered with bent-grass   wad a wad]
lay a wager   brand] sword   gair] gown

Her mother 's in before the King,
   Bowed low down on her knee.
Win up, win up, ye gay lady,
   What is your will wi' me?
There is a knight into your court
   This day has robbed me.

Oh, has he broke your bigly bower,
   Or has he stown your fee?
Or has he stown the gay clothing
   That hangs low by your knee?

Oh, he has broke my bigly bower
   And he has stown my fee;
And he 's beguiled my ae daughter,
   And a bad woman is she.
And he has slain my three bauld sons
   Amang the bents and broom.

Ye lee, ye lee, my mother dear,
   Sae lood 's I hear ye lee;
He hasna broke your bigly bower,
   Nor has he stown your fee;
Nor has beguiled your ae daughter,
   For a good woman I'll be.

He has slain your three bauld sons
   Amang the bents and broom;
But your three sons was weel armed,
   And my love was alone.

win] get   **bigly]** fine   **stown]** stolen   **fee]** money
lee] lie

Speak on, speak on, ye gay lady,
    Your words weel pleases me;
For ae kiss o' your comely mouth
    I'll set your bonnie love free.

She 's ta'en the King in her arms
    And kissed him cheek and chin;
And he 's set her on ahin' her love
    And she 's gane singin' hame.

ae] one   ahin'] behind

49. *Rose the Red and White Lilly*

O Rose the Red and White Lilly,
    Their mother dear was dead,
And their father married an ill woman
    Wish'd them twa little guede.

Yet she had twa as fu' fair sons
    As e'er brake manis bread,
And the tane of them lo'ed her White Lilly
    An' the tither loo'd Rose the Red.

them twa] these two   guede] good   tane . . . tither] one . . .
other

O biggit ha' they a bigly bow'r
   And strawn it o'er wi' san',
And there was mair mirth i' the Ladies' bow'r
   Than in a' their father's lan'.

But out it spake their step-mother
   Wha stood a little foreby:
I hope to live and play the prank
   Sal gar your loud sang ly.

She 's call'd upon her eldest son:
   Come here, my son, to me;
It fears me sair, my eldest son,
   That ye maun sail the sea.

Gin it fear you sair, my Mither dear,
   Your bidding I maun dee,
But be never war to Rose the Red
   Than ye ha' been to me.

O had your tongue, my eldest son,
   For sma' sal be her part;
You'll nae get a kiss o' her comely mouth
   Gin your very fair heart should break.

She 's call'd upon her youngest son:
   Come here, my son, to me;
It fears me sair, my youngest son,
   That ye maun sail the sea.

biggit] built	bigly] fine, commodious	foreby] aside	Sal
gar] shall make	It fears me] I am afraid	maun] must	Gin]
if dee] do	war] worse had] hold		

Gin it fear you sair, my mither dear,
  Your bidding I maun dee,
But be never war to White Lilly
  Than ye ha' been to me.

O haud your tongue, my youngest son,
  For sma' sall be her part;
You'll ne'er get a kiss o' her comely mouth
  Tho' your very fair heart should break.

When Rose the Red and White Lilly
  Saw their twa loves were gane,
Then stopped ha' they their loud, loud sang
  And tane up the still mournin;
And their Step-mother stood listnin' by
  To hear the ladies m[ane].

Then out it spake her White Lilly:
  My sister, we'll be gane;
Why should we stay in Barnsdale
  To waste our youth in pain?

Then cutted ha' they their green cloathing
  A little below their knee,
And sae ha' they the[ir] yallow hair
  A little aboon the[ir] bree;
An' they've doen them to haely chapel
  Was christened by Our Lady.

There ha' they chang'd their ain twa names
  Sae far frae ony town,
An' the tane o' them hight Sweet Willy
  An' the tither o' them Roge the Roun'.

mane] complain		Barnsdale] *a name taken from the Robin Hood*
cycle	aboon] above	bree] brow doen them] taken them-
selves	ain] own	hight] took the name

Between this twa a vow was made,
　An' they sware it to fulfil,
That at three blasts o' bugle-horn
　She'd come her sister till.

Now Sweet Willy's gane to the kingis court
　Her true love for to see,
An' Roge the Roun' to good green wood
　Brown Robin's man to be.

As it fell out upon a day
　They a' did put the stane;
Full seven foot ayont them a'
　She gar'd the puttin-stane gang.

She lean'd her back against an oak
　And ga'e a loud Ohone,
Then out it spake him Brown Robin:
　But that 's a woman's moan!

O ken ye by my red rose lip?
　Or by my yallow hair?
Or ken ye by my milk white breast?
　For ye never saw it bare.

I ken no by your red rose lip
　Nor by your yallow hair,
Nor ken I by your milk white breast
　For I never saw it bare;
But come to your bow'r whaever sae likes
　Will find a lady there.

till] to　　　ayont] beyond　　　gar'd] made　　　gang] go
Ohone] alas (*Gaelic*)

O gin ye come to my bow'r within
  Thro' fraud, deceit, or guile,
Wi' this same bran' that 's in my han'
  I swear I will the[e] kill.

But I will come thy bow'r within
  An' spear nae leave, quoth he:
An' this same bran' that 's i' my han'
  I sall ware back on the[e].

About the tenth hour of the night
  The Ladie's bower-door was broken,
An' e'er the first hour of the day
  The bonny knave bairn was gotten.

When days were gane and months were run
  The lady took travailing,
And sair she cry'd for a bow'r woman
  For to wait her upon.

Then out it spake him Brown Robin:
  Now what needs a' this din?
For what cou'd any woman do
  But I cou'd do the same?

'T was never my mither's fashion, she says,
  Nor sall it ever be mine,
That belted knights shou'd e'er remain
  Where Ladies dree'd their pine.

But ye take up that bugle horn
  An' blaw a blast for me;
I ha' a brother i' the kingis court
  Will come me quickly ti.

bran'] sword   spear] ask   ware] bestow   knave bairn]
baby boy   travailing] labour   belted] wearing the distinctive
cincture of knighthood   dree'd their pine] suffered their pangs

193

O gin ye ha' a brither on earth
   That ye love better nor me,
'Ye blaw the horn yoursel, he says,
   For ae blast I winna gie.

She's set the horn till her mouth
   And she's blawn three blasts sae shrill;
Sweet Willy heard i' the kingis court
   And came her quickly till.

Then up it started Brown Robin,
   An' an angry man was he:
There comes nae man this bow'r within
   But first must fight wi' me.

O they hae fought that bow'r within
   Till the sun was gaing down,
Till drops o' blude frae Rose the Red
   Came hailing to the groun'.

She lean'd her back against the wa',
   Says, Robin, let a' be,
For it is a lady born and bred
   That's foughten sae well wi' thee.

O seven foot he lap a back,
   Says, Alas, and wae is me;
I never wisht in a' my life
   A woman's blude to see;
An' a' for the sake of ae fair maid
   Whose name was White Lilly.

nor] than   ae] one   winna gie] won't give   hailing]
dripping fast   's foughten] has fought

Then out it spake her White Lilly
  An' a hearty laugh leugh she:
She's lived wi' you this year an' mair
  Tho' ye kentna it was she.

Now word has gane thro' a' the lan'
  Before a month was done,
That Brown Robin's man in good green wood
  Had born a bonny young son.

The word has gane to the kingis court
  An' to the king himsel:
Now by my fay, the king could say,
  The like was never heard tell!

Then out it spake him bold Arthur
  An' a hearty laugh leugh he:
I trow some may has play'd the loon
  An' fled her ain country.

Bring me my steed, then cry'd the king,
  My bow and arrows keen;
I'l ride mysel to [the] good green wood
  An' see what's to be seen.

An't please your grace, said Bold Arthur,
  My liege, I'll gang you wi',
An' try to fin' a little foot page
  That's stray'd awa frae me.

O they've hunted i' the good green wood
  The buck but an' the rae,
An' they drew near Brown Robin's bow'r
  About the close of day.

may] maid   loon] whore   An't] if it   but an'] and also

Then out it spake the king in hast,
   Says, Arthur, look an' see
Gin that be no your little foot page
   That leans against yon tree.

Then Arthur took his bugle horn
   An' blew a blast sae shrill;
Sweet Willy started at the sound
   An' ran him quickly till.

O wanted ye your meat, Willy,
   Or wanted ye your fee?
Or gat ye ever an angry word,
   That ye ran awa frae me?

I wanted nought, my master dear,
   To me ye ay was good;
I came but to see my ae brother
   That wons in this green wood.

Then out it spake the king again,
   Says, Bonny boy, tell to me
Wha lives into yon bigly bow'r
   Stands by yon green oak tree?

O pardon me, says Sweet Willy,
   My liege, I dare no tell;
An' I pray you go no near that bow'r
   For fear they do you fell.

O haud your tongue, my bonny boy,
   For I winna be said nay;
But I will gang that bow'r within,
   Betide me weel or wae.

meat . . . fee] food . . . pay   wons] dwells   fell] kill

They've lighted off their milk white steeds
   An' saftly enter'd in,
An' there they saw her White Lilly
   Nursing her bonny yong son.

Now, by the rood, the king cou'd say,
   This is a comely sight;
I trow, instead of a forrester's man,
   This is a lady bright!

Then out it spake her Rose the Red
   An' fell low down on her knee:
O pardon us, my gracious liege,
   An' our story I'll tell thee.

Our father was a wealthy lord
   That won'd in Barnsdale,
But we had a wicked step-mother
   That wrought us meickle bale.

Yet she had twa as fu' fair sons
   As ever the sun did see,
An' the tane o' them loo'd my sister dear
   An' the tither say'd he loo'd me.

Then out it spake him Bold Arthur
   As by the king he stood:
Now, by the faith o' my body,
   This shou'd be Rose the Red!

Then in it came him Brown Robin
   Frae hunting o' the deer,
But whan he saw the king was there
   He started back for fear.

meickle bale] much harm

The king has ta'en him by the hand
  An' bade him naithing dread;
Says, Ye maun leave the good green wood,
  Come to the court wi' speed.

Then up he took White Lilly's son
  An' set him on his knee;
Says, Gin ye live to wield a bran'
  My bowman ye sall bee.

The king he sent for robes of green
  An' girdles o' shining gold;
He gart the ladies be array'd
  Most comely to behold.

They've done them unto Mary Kirk
  An' there gat fair wedding,
An' fan the news spread o'er the lan'
  For joy the bells did ring.

Then out it spake her Rose the Red,
  An' a hearty laugh leugh she:
I wonder what would our step-dame say
  Gin she this sight did see!

bran'] sword   gart] had   fan] when

50. *Babylon*

THERE were three ladies lived in a bower,
   Eh vow bonnie,
And they went out to pull a flower,
   On the bonnie banks o' Fordie.

They hadna pu'ed a flower but ane,
When up started to them a banisht man.

He's ta'en the first sister by her hand,
And he's turned her round and made her stand.

Its whether will ye be a rank robber's wife,
Or will ye die by my wee pen knife?

Its I'll not be a rank robber's wife,
But I'll rather die by your wee pen knife.

He's killed this may and he's laid her by,
For to bear the red rose company.

He's taken the second ane by the hand,
And he's turned her round and made her stand.

Fordie] near Dunkeld, Perthshire   pen knife] sheath knife (originally
for making quill pens)   may] maid

Its whether will ye be a rank robber's wife,
Or will ye die by my wee pen knife?

I'll not be a rank robber's wife,
But I'll rather die by your wee pen knife.

He 's killed this may and he 's laid her by,
For to bear the red rose company.

He 's taken the youngest ane by the hand,
And he 's turned her round and made her stand.

Says, Will ye be a rank robber's wife,
Or will ye die by my wee pen knife?

I'll not be a rank robber's wife,
Nor will I die by your wee pen knife.

For I hae a brother in this wood,
And gin ye kill me, it 's he'll kill thee.

What 's thy brother's name, come tell to me?
My brother's name is Baby Lon.

O sister, sister, what have I done,
Oh have I done this ill to thee?

O since I've done this evil deed,
Good sall never be seen o' me.

He 's taken out his wee pen knife,
    Eh vow bonnie,
And he 's twyned himsel o' his ain sweet life,
    On the bonnie banks o' Fordie.

gin] if   sall] shall   twyned] deprived

51. *The Bonny Heyn*

O MAY she comes and May she goes
  Down by yon Gardens green
And there she spied a gallant Squire
  As Squire had ever been.

And May she comes and May she goes
  Down by yon Hollen tree
And there she spied a brisk young Squire
  And a brisk young Squire was he.

Give me your green Manteel fair Maid,
  Give me your Maidenhead;
Gi[f] ye winna give me your green Manteel
  Gi' me your Maidenhead.

   *   *   *   *   *

He has ta'en her by the Milkwhite hand
  And softly laid her down,
And when he's lifted her up again
  Given her a Silver kame.

Perhaps there may be bairns kind Sir,
  Perhaps they may be Nane;
But if you be a Courtier
  You'l tell to me your Name.

I am nae Courtier fair Maid
  But new come frae the Sea;
I am nae Courtier fair Maid
  But when I courteth thee.

Hollen] holly   Gif] if   winna] won't   kame] comb

THE BONNY HEYN

They call me Jack when I'm abroad,
  Sometimes they call me John;
But when I'm in my Father's Bower
  Jock Randal is my Name.

Ye lee, Ye lee [my] bonny lad,
  Sae loud 's I hear ye lee;
For I'm Lord Randal's ae daughter,
  He has nae mair nor me.

Ye lee, Ye lee [my] bonny May,
  Sae loud 's I hear ye lee;
For I'm Lord Randal's yae yae Son
  Just now come o'er the Sea.

She 's putten her hand down by her Spare
  And out she 's ta'en a knife,
And she has put'n 't in her hearts bluid
  And ta'en away her Life.

And he has ta'en up his bonny Sister
  With the big tear in his e'en,
And he has buried his bonny Sister
  Amang the Hollins green.

And syne he 's hyed him o'er the Dale
  His Father dear to see;
Sing O, and O, for my bonny hind
  Beneath yon Hollin tree!

What needs you care for your bonny Hyn,
  For it you needna care;
There 's aught score hyns in yonder park
  And five score hyns to spare.

lee] lie   ae, yae] only   nor] than   Spare] opening in a
gown   aught] eight

202

Four score of them are siller-shod,
　　Of thae ye may get three:
But O, and O, for my bonny Hyn
　　Beneath yon Hollin Tree.

What needs you care for your bonny Hyn,
　　For it you need na care;
Take you the best, gi' me the warst
　　Since plenty is to spare.

I care no for your Hyns my Lord,
　　I care na for your Fee:
But O, and O, for my Bonny Hyn
　　Beneath the Hollin Tree.

O were ye at your Sisters Bower
　　Your Sister fair to see,
You'l think nae mair o' your bonny Hyn
　　Beneath the Hollin Tree.

★　　★　　★　　★　　★

thae] these　　　Fee] wealth

52. *Prince Robert*

PRINCE ROBERT has wedded a gay ladye,
　　He has wedded her with a ring;
Prince Robert has wedded a gay ladye
　　But he daur na bring her hame.

Your blessing, your blessing, my mother dear,
　　Your blessing now grant to me:
Instead of a blessing ye sall have my curse
　　And you'll get nae blessing frae me.

daur na] dare not

She has called upon her waiting maid
   To fill a glass of wine;
She has called upon her fause steward
   To put rank poison in.

She has put it to her roudes lip
   And to her roudes chin;
She has put it to her fause, fause mouth
   But the never a drap gaed in.

He has put it to his bonny mouth
   And to his bonny chin;
He's put it to his cherry lip
   And sae fast the rank poison ran in.

O ye hae poisoned your ae son, mother,
   Your ae son and your heir;
O ye hae poisoned your ae son, mother,
   And sons you'll never hae mair.

O where will I get a little boy
   That will win hose and shoon
To run sae fast to Darlinton
   And bid fair Eleanor come?

Then up and spake a little boy
   That wad win hose and shoon:
O I'll away to Darlinton
   And bid fair Eleanor come.

O he has run to Darlinton
   And tirled at the pin,
And wha sae ready as Eleanor's sell
   To let the bonny boy in?

roudes] hag-like, coarse   gaed] went   ae] only   tirled]
rattled   pin] door-knocker

Your gude-mother has made ye a rare dinour,
   She 's made it baith gude and fine;
Your gude-mother has made ye a gay dinour
   And ye maun cum till her and dine.

It 's twenty lang miles to Sillertoun town,
   The langest that ever were gane;
But the steed it was wight and the ladye was light
   And she cam linkin' in.

But when she cam to Sillertoun town
   And into Sillertoun ha',
The torches were burning, the ladies were mourning,
   And they were weeping a'.

O where is now my wedded lord,
   And where now can he be?
O where is now my wedded lord?
   For him I canna see.

Your wedded lord is dead, she says,
   And just gane to be laid in the clay;
Your wedded lord is dead, she says,
   And just gane to be buried the day.

Ye 'se get nane o' his gowd, ye 'se get nane o' his gear,
   Ye 'se get nae thing frae me;
Ye 'se na get an inch o' his gude broad land
   Tho' your heart suld burst in three.

I want nane o' his gowd, I want nane o' his gear,
   I want nae land frae thee;
But I'll hae the ring that 's on his finger,
   For them he did promise to me.

maun] must   till] to   linkin'] riding briskly   'se] shall
gowd] gold   gear] property

Ye 'se na get the ring that 's on his finger,
   Ye 'se na get them frae me;
Ye 'se na get the ring that 's on his finger
   An' your heart suld burst in three.

She 's turn'd her back unto the wa'
   And her face unto a rock,
And there before the mother's face
   Her very heart it broke.

The tane was buried in Marie's kirk,
   The tother in Marie's quair;
And out o' the tane there sprang a birk
   And out o' the tother a brier.

And thae twa met and thae twa plat,
   The birk but and the brier,
And by that ye may very weel ken
   They were twa lovers dear.

An'] even if   quair] choir   birk] birch   thae] these
plat] intertwined   but and] and also   ken] know

53. *Lord Livingston*

It fell about the Lammas time
   When wightsmen won their hay,
A' the squires in merry Linkum
   Went a' forth till a play.

Lammas] 1 August, harvest festival   wightsmen] husbandmen
won] took in   Linkum] a 'ballad-place'

They play'd until the evening tide,
  The sun was gaeing down;
A lady thro' plain fields was bound,
  A lily leesome thing.

Two squires that for this lady pledged
  In hopes for a renown;
The one was call'd the proud Seaton,
  The other Livingston.

When will ye, Michaell o' Livingston,
  Wad for this lady gay?
Tomorrow, tomorrow, said Livingston,
  Tomorrow, if you may.

Then they hae wadded their wagers
  And laid their pledges down;
To the high castle o' Edinbro'
  They made them ready boun.

The chamber that they did gang in,
  There it was daily dight;
The kipples were like the gude red gold
  As they stood up in hight,
And the roof-tree like the siller white,
  And shin'd like candles bright.

The lady fair into that ha'
  Was comely to be seen;
Her kirtle was made o' the pa',
  Her gowns seem'd o' the green.

plain] open   lily leesome] lovely and delightful   a renown]
prestige   wadded] waged, made   boun] *tautological*   dight]
adorned   kipples] rafters   roof-tree] main roof beam   siller]
silver   kirtle] skirt   pa'] rich cloth

Her gowns seem'd like green, like green,
    Her kirtle o' the pa';
A siller wand intill her hand
    She marshall'd ower them a'.

She ga'e every knight a lady bright,
    And every squire a may;
Her own sell chose him Livingston,
    They were a comely tway.

Then Seaton started till his foot,
    The fierce flame in his e'e:
On the next day, wi' sword in hand,
    On plain fields meet ye me.

When bells were rung and mass was sung
    And a' man bound for bed,
Lord Livingston and his fair dame
    In bed were sweetly laid.

The bed, the bed where they lay in
    Was cover'd wi' the pa';
A covering o' the gude red gowd
    Lay nightly ower the twa.

So they lay there till on the morn
    The sun shone on their feet;
Then up it raise him Livingston
    To draw to him a weed.

The firstan weed that he drew on
    Was o' the linen clear;
The nextan weed that he drew on,
    It was a weed o' weir.

may] maiden   sell] self   bound] ready   gowd] gold
weed] garment   clear] bright   weir] war

The niestan weed that he drew on
 Was gude iron and steel;
Twa gloves o' plate, a gowden helmet,
 Became that hind chiel weel.

Then out it speaks that lady gay,
 A little forbye stood she:
I'll dress mysell in men's array,
 Gae to the fields for thee.

O God forbid, said Livingston,
 That e'er I dree the shame;
My lady slain in plain fields
 And I coward knight at hame!

He scarcely travelled frae the town
 A mile but barely twa,
Till he met wi' a witch-woman;
 I pray to send her wae.

This is too gude a day, my lord,
 To gang sae far frae town;
This is too gude a day, my lord,
 On field to make you boun.

I dream'd a dream concerning thee—
 O read ill dreams to guid;
Your bower was full o' milk-white swans,
 Your bride's bed full o' bluid.

O bluid is gude, said Livingston,
 To bide it whoso may;
If I be frae yon plain fields,
 Nane knew the plight I lay.

hind chiel] young man   forbye] aside   dree] suffer   wae]
woe, ill   boun] ready   bide] endure

Then he rade on to plain fields
   As swift 's his horse cou'd hie,
And there he met the proud Seaton
   Come boldly ower the lee.

Come on to me now, Livingston,
   Or then take foot and flee;
This is the day that we must try
   Who gains the victorie.

Then they fought with sword in hand
   Till they were bluidy men;
But on the point o' Seaton's sword
   Brave Livingston was slain.

His lady lay ower castle wa'
   Beholding dale and down,
When Blenchant brave, his gallant steed,
   Came prancing to the town.

O where is now my ain gude lord?
   He stays sae far frae me:
O dinna ye see your ain gude lord
   Stand bleeding by your knee?

O live, O live, lord Livingston,
   The space o' ae half hour;
There 's nae a leech in Edinbro' town
   But I'll bring to your door.

Awa wi' your leeches, lady, he said,
   Of them I'll be the waur;
There 's nae a leech in Edinbro' town
   That can strong death debar.

lee] meadow   waur] worse

Ye'll take the lands o' Livingston
  And deal them liberallie
To the auld that may not, the young that cannot,
  And blind that does na see;
And help young maidens' marriages
  That has nae gear to gie.

My mother got it in a book
  The first night I was born,
I wou'd be wedded till a knight
  And him slain on the morn.

But I will do for my love's sake
  What ladies wou'dna thole;
Ere seven years shall hae an end
  Nae shoe 's gang on my sole.

There 's never lint gang on my head
  Nor kame gang in my hair,
Nor ever coal nor candle light
  Shine in my bower mair.

When seven years were near an end
  The lady she thought lang,
And wi' a crack her heart did brake;
  And sae this ends my sang.

gear] goods   morn] morrow   thole] endure   lint]
linen (cap)   kame] comb   thought lang] grew weary

54. Young Johnstone

YOUNG Johnstone and the young Col'nel
  Sat drinking at the wine;
O gin ye wad marry my sister
  It's I wad marry thine.

I wadna marry your sister
  For a' your houses and land,
But I'll keep her for my leman
  When I come o'er the strand.

I wadna marry your sister
  For a' your gowd so gay,
But I'll keep her for my leman
  When I come by the way.

Young Johnstone had a nut brown sword
  Hung low down by his gair,
And he ritted it through the young Col'nel,
  That word he ne'er spak mair.

gin] if   leman] mistress   gowd] gold   gair] gown
ritted] ripped, thrust

But he 's awa' to his sister's bower,
  He 's tirled at the pin;
Whare hae ye been, my dear brither,
  Sae late a coming in?
I hae been at the school, sister,
  Learning young clerks to sing.

I've dreamed a dreary dream this night,
  I wish it may be for good;
They were seeking you with hawks and hounds
  And the young Col'nel was dead.

Hawks and hounds they may seek me,
  As I trow well they be;
For I have killed the young Col'nel
  And thy own true love was he.

If ye hae killed the young Col'nel
  O dule and wae is me;
But I wish ye may be hanged on a hie gallows
  And hae nae power to flee.

And he 's awa' to his true love's bower,
  He 's tirled at the pin;
Whar hae ye been, my dear Johnstone,
  Sae late a coming in?
It 's I hae been at the school, he says,
  Learning young clerks to sing.

I have dreamed a dreary dream, she says,
  I wish it may be for good;
They were seeking you with hawks and hounds
  And the young Col'nel was dead.

tirled] rattled   pin] door-knocker   learning] teaching
clerks] scholars   dule] sorrow

213

Hawks and hounds they may seek me,
  As I trow well they be;
For I hae killed the young Col'nel
  And thy ae brother was he.

If ye hae killed the young Col'nel
  O dule and wae is me;
But I care the less for the young Col'nel
  If thy ain body be free.

Come in, come in, my dear Johnstone,
  Come in and take a sleep;
And I will go to my casement
  And carefully I will thee keep.

He had not weel been in her bower door,
  No not for half an hour,
When four and twenty belted knights
  Came riding to the bower.

Well may you sit and see, Lady,
  Well may you sit and say;
Did you not see a bloody squire
  Come riding by this way?

What colour were his hawks? she says,
  What colour were his hounds?
What colour was the gallant steed
  That bore him from the bounds?

Bloody, bloody were his hawks
  And bloody were his hounds,
But milk-white was the gallant steed
  That bore him from the bounds.

ae] only   belted] wearing the distinctive cincture of knighthood
bounds] fields

Yes, bloody, bloody were his hawks
　　And bloody were his hounds,
But milk-white was the gallant steed
　　That bore him from the bounds.

Light down, light down now, gentlemen,
　　And take some bread and wine;
And the steed be swift that he rides on,
　　He 's past the brig o' Lyne.

We thank you for your bread, fair Lady,
　　We thank you for your wine;
But I wad gie thrice three thousand pound
　　That bloody knight was ta'en.

Lie still, lie still, my dear Johnstone,
　　Lie still and take a sleep;
For thy enemies are past and gone
　　And carefully I will thee keep.

But young Johnstone had a little wee sword
　　Hung low down by his gair,
And he stabbed it in fair Annet's breast,
　　A deep wound and a sair.

What aileth thee now, dear Johnstone?
　　What aileth thee at me?
Hast thou not got my father's gold
　　Bot and my mither's fee?

And [the steed]] if　　Lyne] a water in Peeblesshire　　gie] give
gair] gown　　　Bot and] and also　　fee] property

[Ohon, alas, my lady gay,
    To come sae hastilie!
I thought it was my deadly foe
    Ye had trysted into me.]

Now live, now live, my dear Ladye,
    Now live but half an hour;
And there 's no a leech in a' Scotland
    But shall be in thy bower.

How can I live, how shall I live?
    Young Johnstone, do not you see
The red, red drops o' my bonny heart's blood
    Rin trinkling down my knee?

But take thy harp into thy hand
    And harp out owre yon plain,
And ne'er think mair on thy true love
    Than if she had never been.

He hadna weel been out o' the stable
    And on his saddle set,
Till four and twenty broad arrows
    Were thrilling in his heart.

Ohon] alas (*Gaelic*)   trysted into] enticed in to   trinkling]
trickling   owre] over   thrilling in] piercing

55. *Younge Andrew*

As I was cast in my ffirst sleepe,
    A dreadffull draught in my mind I drew;
For I was dreamed of one yong man,
    Some men called him yonge Andrew.

The moone shone bright, and itt cast a ffayre light;
    Sayes shee, Welcome, my honey, my hart, and
      my sweete!
For I haue loued thee this seuen long yeere,
    And our chance itt was wee cold neuer meete.

Then he tooke her in his armes two,
    And kissed her both cheeke and chin;
And twice or thrice he pleased this may
    Before they tow did part in twinn;

Saies, Now, good Sir, you haue had your will,
    You can demand no more of mee;
Good Sir, Remember what you said before,
    And goe to the church and marry mee.

Faire maid, I cannott doe as I wold
    [Till I am got to my own country];
Goe home and fett thy fathers redd gold,
    And Ile goe to the church and marry thee.

This Ladye is gone to her ffathers hall,
    And well she knew where his red gold lay,
And counted fforth fiue hundred pound
    Besides all other Iuells and chaines,

And brought itt all to younge Andrew;
    Itt was well counted vpon his knee.
Then he tooke her by the Lillye white hand,
    And led her vp to one hill soe hye.

Shee had vpon a gowne of blacke veluett—
    A pittyffull sight after yee shall see;
Put of thy clothes, bonny wenche, he sayes,
    For noe ffoote further thoust gang with me.

cold] could   may] maiden   twinn] twain   fett] fetch
Iuells] jewels

But then shee put of her gowne of veluett
  With many a salt teare from her eye,
And in a kirtle of ffine breaden silke
  Shee stood beffore young Andrews eye.

Sais, O put off thy kirtle of silke;
  For some and all shall goe with mee;
And to my owne Lady I must itt beare,
  Who I must needs loue better then thee.

Then shee put of her kirtle of silke
  With many a salt teare still ffrom her eye;
In a peticoate of scarlett redd
  She stood before young Andrewes eye.

Saies, O put of thy peticoate;
  For some and all of itt shall goe with mee;
And to my owne Lady I will itt beare,
  Which dwells soe ffarr in a strange countrye.

But then shee put of her peticoate
  With many a salt teare still ffrom her eye;
And in a smocke of braue white silke
  Shee stood before young Andrews eye.

Saies, O put of thy smocke of silke;
  For some and all shall goe with mee;
Vnto my owne Ladye I will it beare,
  That dwells soe ffarr in a strange countrye.

Sayes, O remember, young Andrew,
  Once of a woman you were borne;
And ffor that birth that Marye bore
  I pray you let my smocke be vpon.

kirtle] skirt   breaden] braided   braue] fine

Yes, ffayre Ladye, I know itt well,
   Once of a woman I was borne;
Yet ffor noe birth that Marye bore
   Thy smocke shall not be left here vpon.

But then shee put of her head geere ffine,
   Shee hadd billaments worth a hundred pound;
The hayre that was vpon this bony wench head
   Couered her bodye downe to the ground.

Then he pulled forth a Scottish brand
   And held itt there in his owne right hand;
Saies, Whether wilt thou dye vpon my swords point,
    Ladye,
   Or thow wilt goe naked home againe?

[O] liffe is sweet, then Sir, said shee,
   Therfore I pray you leaue mee with mine;
Before I wold dye on your swords point
   I had rather goe naked home againe.

My ffather, she sayes, is a right good Erle
   As any remaines in his countrye;
If euer he doe your body take
   Your sure to fflower a gallow tree.

And I haue seuen brethren, shee sayes,
   And they are all hardy men and bold;
Giff euer they doe your body take
   You must neuer gang quicke ouer the mold.

billaments] ornaments   brand] sword   fflower] adorn
Giff] if   mold] land

If your ffather be a right good Erle
   As any remaines in his owne countrye,
Tush! he shall neuer my body take,
   Ile gang soe ffast ouer the sea.

If you haue seuen brethren, he sayes,
   If they be neuer soe hardy or bold,
Tush! they shall neuer my body take,
   Ile gang soe ffast into the Scottish mold.

Now this Ladye is gone to her ffathers hall
   When euery body their rest did take;
But the Erle which was her ffather [deere]
   Lay waken for his deere daughters sake.

But who is that, her ffather can say,
   That soe priuilye knowes that pinn?
Its Hellen, your owne deere daughter, ffather;
   I pray you rise and lett me in.

Noe, by my hood, quoth her ffather then,
My [house] thoust neuer come within,
Without I had my red gold againe.

Nay, your gold is gone, father, said shee.
Then naked thou came into this world,
And naked thou shalt returne againe.

Nay, God fforgaue his death, father, shee sayes,
   And soe I hope you will doe mee.
Away, away, thou cursed woman;
   I pray God an ill death thou may dye!

pinn] door-knocker

220

Shee stood soe long quacking on the ground
 Till her hart itt burst in three,
And then shee ffell dead downe in a swound;
 And this was the end of this bonny Ladye.

Ithe morning when her ffather gott vp,
 A pittyffull sight there he might see;
His owne deere daughter was dead without Clothes:
 The teares they trickeled fast ffrom his eye.

Sais, Fye of gold, and ffye of fee,
For I sett soe much by my red gold
That now itt hath lost both my daughter and mee!

But after this time he neere dought good day,
But as flowers doth fade in the ffrost
Soe he did wast and weare away.

But let vs leaue talking of this Ladye,
 And talke some more of young Andrew,
For ffalse he was to this bonny Ladye;
 More pitty that itt had not beene true.

He was not gone a mile into the wild forrest
 Or halfe a mile into the hart of Wales,
But there they cought him by such a braue wyle
 That hee must come to tell noe more tales.

Full soone a wolfe did of him smell,
And shee came roaring like a beare
And gaping like a ffeend of hell.

quacking] quaking fee] wealth dought] could; had, enjoyed

Soe they ffought together like two Lyons
  And fire betweene them two glashet out;
They raught eche other such a great rappe
  That there young Andrew was slaine, well I wott.

But now young Andrew he is dead;
  But he was neuer buryed vnder mold,
For ther as the wolfe devoured him
  There lyes all this great erles gold.

glashet] flashed   raught] reached

56. *The Gay Goss Hawk*

O WELL 's me o' my gay goss hawk
  That he can speak and flee;
He'll carry a letter to my love,
  Bring back another to me.

O how can I your true love ken
  Or how can I her know,
Whan frae her mouth I never heard couth
  Nor wi' my eyes her saw?

well 's me o'] a blessing on   flee] fly   couth] ? speech

O well sal ye my true love ken
   As soon as you her see,
For of a' the flow'rs in fair Englan'
   The fairest flow'r is she.

At even at my love's bow'r door
   There grows a bowing birk,
An' sit ye down and sing thereon
   As she gangs to the Kirk.

An' four and twenty ladies fair
   Will wash and go to kirk,
But well shall ye my true love ken
   For she wears goud on her skirt.

An' four and twenty gay ladies
   Will to the mass repair,
But well sal ye my true love ken
   For she wears goud on her hair.

O even at that lady's bow'r door
   There grows a bowin' birk,
An' she set down and sang thereon
   As she ged to the kirk.

O eet and drink, my Marys a',
   The wine flows you among,
Till I gang to my shot window
   An' hear yon bonny bird's song.

Sing on, sing on, my bonny bird,
   The song ye sang the streen,
For I ken by your sweet singin'
   You're frae my true love sen'.

birk] birch   gangs] goes   goud] gold   Marys] maids
shot window] hinged window, casement   the streen] last evening

O first he sang a merry song
  An' then he sang a grave,
An' then he peck'd his feathers gray,
  To her the letter gave.

Ha', there's a letter frae your love,
  He says he sent you three;
He canna wait your love langer
  But for your sake he'll die.

He bids you write a letter to him,
  He says he's sent you five;
He canna wait your love langer,
  Tho' you're the fairest woman alive.

Ye bid him bake his bridal bread
  And brew his bridal ale,
An' I'll meet him in fair Scotlan'
  Lang, lang or it be stale.

She's doen her to her father dear,
  Fa'n low down on her knee:
A boon, a boon, my father dear,
  I pray you grant it me.

Ask on, ask on, my daughter,
  An' granted it sal be;
Except ae squire in fair Scotlan',
  An' him you sall never see.

The only boon, my father dear,
  That I do crave of the[e],
Is gin I die in southin lands
  In Scotland to bury me.

canna] cannot   doen her] taken herself   ae] one   gin] if

An' the firstin kirk that ye come till
  Ye gar the bells be rung,
An' the nextin kirk that ye come till
  Ye gar the mess be sung.

An' the thirdin kirk that ye come till
  You deal gold for my sake,
An' the fourthin kirk that ye come till
  You tarry there till night.

She 's doen her to her bigly bow'r
  As fast as she coud fare,
An' she has tane a sleepy draught
  That she had mixed wi' care.

She 's laid her down upon her bed
  An' soon she 's fa'n asleep,
And soon o'er every tender limb
  Cauld death began to creep.

Whan night was flown an' day was come
  Nae ane that did her see
But thought she was as surely dead
  As ony lady cou'd be.

Her father an' her brothers dear
  Gar'd make to her a bier;
The tae half was o' guid red gold,
  The tither o' silver clear.

Her mither an' her sisters fair
  Gar'd work for her a sark;
The tae half was o' cambrick fine,
  The tither o' needle wark.

till] to   gar] make, have   deal] distribute   tae . . . tither]
one . . . other   Gar'd work] had woven   sark] shift

The firstin kirk that they came till
   They gar'd the bells be rung,
An' the nextin kirk that they came till
   They gar'd the mess be sung.

The thirdin kirk that they came till
   They dealt gold for her sake,
An' the fourthin kirk that they came till
   Lo, there they met her make.

Lay down, lay down the bigly bier,
   Lat me the dead look on;
Wi' cherry cheeks and ruby lips
   She lay an' smil'd on him.

O ae sheave o' your bread, true-love,
   An' ae glass o' your wine,
For I hae fasted for your sake
   These fully day[is] nine.

Gang hame, gang hame, my seven bold brothers,
   Gang hame and sound your horn;
An' ye may boast in southin lan's
   Your sister 's play'd you scorn.

make] mate, lover   bigly] fine   sheave] slice

57. Brown Robin

THE king but an' his nobles a'
   Sat birling at the wine;
The king but an' his nobles a'
   Sat birling at the wine;
He would ha' nane but his ae daughter
   To wait on them at dine.

She 's serv'd them butt, she 's serv'd them ben,
   Intill a gown of green;
But her e'e was ay on Brown Robin
   That stood low under the rain.

She 's doen her to her bigly bow'r
   As fast as she cou'd gang,
An' there she 's drawn her shot window
   An' she 's harped an' she sang:

but an'] and also   birling] carousing   ae] only   butt . . .
ben] in kitchen . . . hall; to . . . fro   Intill] in   doen her] taken
herself   bigly] fine   drawn] opened   shot window] hinged
window, casement

There sits a bird i' my father's garden,
   An' O but she sings sweet;
I hope to live an' see the day
   Whan wi' my love I'll meet.

O gin that ye like me as well
   As your tongue tells to me,
What hour o' the night, my lady bright,
   At your bow'r sal I be?

Whan my father an' gay Gilbert
   Are baith set at the wine
O ready, ready I will be
   To lat my true love in.

O she has birl'd her father's porter
   Wi' strong beer an' wi' wine,
Untill he was as beastly drunk
   As ony wild wood swine;
She 's stown the keys o' her father's yates
   An' latten her true love in.

Whan night was gane an' day was come
   An' the sun shone on their feet,
Then out it spake him Brown Robin:
   I'll be discover'd yet.

Then out it spake that gay lady:
   My love, ye need na doubt;
For wi' ae wile I 've got you in,
   Wi' anither I'll bring you out.

gin] if   birl'd] plied   stown] stolen   yates] gates   doubt] fear

She 's ta'en her to her father's cellar
   As fast as she can fare,
She 's drawn a cup o' the gude red wine,
   Hung 't low down by her gare;
An' she met wi' her father dear
   Just coming down the stair.

I would na gi' that cup, daughter,
   That ye hold i' your han',
For a' the wines in my cellar,
   An' gantrees whare the[y] stan'.

O wae be to your wine, father,
   That ever 't came o'er the sea;
'T 'is pitten my head in sick a steer
   I' my bow'r I canna be.

Gang out, gang out, my daughter dear,
   Gang out an' tack the air;
Gang out an' walk i' the good green wood,
   An' a' your Marys fair.

Then out it spake the proud porter
   (Our lady wish'd him shame):
We'll send the Marys to the wood
   But we'll keep our lady at hame.

There 's thirty Marys i' my bow'r,
   There 's thirty o' them an' three;
But there 's nae ane amo' them a'
   Kens what flow'r gains for me.

gare] gown   gantrees] wooden barrel-stands   pitten] put
sick a steer] such a stir   Gang] go   Marys] maidens, ladies
Kens] knows   gains for] serves for, suits

She 's doen her to her bigly bow'r
   As fast as she could gang,
An' she has drest him Brown Robin
   Like ony bow'r woman.

The gown she pat upon her love
   Was o' the dainty green,
His hose was o' the saft, saft silk,
   His shoon o' the cordwain fine.

She 's pitten his bow in her bosom,
   His arrow in her sleeve,
His sturdy bran' her body next
   Because he was her love.

Then she is unto her bow'r door
   As fast as she cou'd gang,
But out it spake the proud porter
   (Our lady wish'd him shame):
We'll count our Marys to the wood
   An' we'll count them back again.

The firsten Mary she sent out
   Was Brown Robin by name;
Then out it spake the king himsel:
   This is a sturdy dame.

O she went out in a May morning,
   In a May morning so gay,
But she came never back again
   Her auld father to see.

cordwain] Cordovan (Spanish) leather   bran'] sword

58. Fair Margaret and Sweet William

As it fell out in a long summer's day
    Two lovers they sat on a hill;
They sat together that long summer's day,
    And could not talk their fill.

I see no harm by you, Margaret,
    And you see none by mee;
Before to-morrow at eight o' the clock
    A rich wedding you shall see.

Fair Margaret sat in her bower-window,
    Combing her yellow hair;
There she spyed sweet William and his bride,
    As they were a riding near.

Then down she layd her ivory combe,
    And braided her hair in twain:
She went alive out of her bower,
    But ne'er came alive in 't again.

When day was gone, and night was come,
   And all men fast asleep,
Then came the spirit of fair Marg'ret,
   And stood at Williams feet.

Are you awake, sweet William? shee said;
   Or, sweet William, are you asleep?
God give you joy of your gay bride-bed,
   And me of my winding-sheet.

When day was come, and night was gone,
   And all men wak'd from sleep,
Sweet William to his lady sayd,
   My dear, I have cause to weep.

I dreamt a dream, my dear ladye,
   Such dreames are never good:
I dreamt my bower was full of red swine,
   And my bride-bed full of blood.

Such dreams, such dreams, my honoured Sir,
   They never do prove good;
To dream thy bower was full of red swine,
   And thy bride-bed full of blood.

He called up his merry men all,
   By one, by two, and by three;
Saying, I'll away to fair Marg'ret's bower,
   By the leave of my ladie.

And when he came to fair Marg'ret's bower,
   He knocked at the ring;
And who so ready as her seven brethren
   To let sweet William in.

ring] door-knocker

Then he turned up the covering-sheet,
 Pray let me see the dead;
Methinks she looks all pale and wan,
 She hath lost her cherry red.

I'll do more for thee, Margaret,
 Than any of thy kin;
For I will kiss thy pale wan lips,
 Though a smile I cannot win.

With that bespake the seven brethren,
 Making most piteous mone:
You may go kiss your jolly brown bride,
 And let our sister alone.

If I do kiss my jolly brown bride,
 I do but what is right;
I neer made a vow to yonder poor corpse
 By day, nor yet by night.

Deal on, deal on, my merry men all,
 Deal on your cake and your wine:
For whatever is dealt at her funeral to-day,
 Shall be dealt to-morrow at mine.

Fair Margaret dyed to-day, to-day,
 Sweet William dyed the morrow:
Fair Margaret dyed for pure true love,
 Sweet William dyed for sorrow.

Margaret was buryed in the lower chancel,
 And William in the higher:
Out of her brest there sprang a rose,
 And out of his a briar.

deal on] share out, distribute

They grew till they grew unto the church-top,
   And then they could grow no higher;
And there they tyed in a true lovers knot,
   Which made all the people admire.

Then came the clerk of the parish,
   As you the truth shall hear,
And by misfortune cut them down,
   Or they had now been there.

59. *The Twa Brothers*

THERE were twa brethren in the north,
   They went to the school thegither;
The one unto the other said,
   Will you try a warsle, brither?

They warsled up, they warsled down,
   Till Sir John fell to the ground;
And there was a knife in Sir Willie's pouch
   Gied him a deadlie wound.

Oh brither dear, take me on your back,
   Carry me to yon burn clear;
And wash the blood from off my wound
   And it will bleed nae mair.

He took him up upon his back,
   Carried him to yon burn clear
And wash'd the blood from off his wound,
   But aye it bled the mair.

warsle] wrestle

Oh brither dear, take me on your back,
    Carry me to yon kirk-yard,
And dig a grave baith wide and deep
    And lay my body there.

He 's ta'en him up upon his back,
    Carried him to yon kirk-yard,
And dug a grave baith deep and wide
    And laid his body there.

But what will I say to my father dear,
    Gin he chance to say, Willie, whar 's John?
Oh say that he 's to England gone
    To buy him a cask of wine.

And what will I say to my mother dear,
    Gin she chance to say, Willie, whar 's John?
Oh say that he 's to England gone
    To buy her a new silk gown.

And what will I say to my sister dear,
    Gin she chance to say, Willie, whar 's John?
Oh say that he 's to England gone
    To buy her a wedding ring.

But what will I say to her you lo'e dear,
    Gin she cry, Why tarries my John?
Oh tell her I lie in Kirk-land fair,
    And home again will never come.

60. *The Cruel Brother*

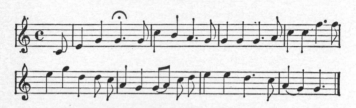

THERE was three ladies play'd at the ba',
 With a heigh-ho! and a lily gay;
There came a knight, and play'd o'er them a',
 As the primrose spreads so sweetly.

The eldest was baith tall and fair,
But the youngest was beyond compare.

The midmost had a gracefu' mien,
But the youngest look'd like Beauty's queen.

The knight bow'd low to a' the three,
But to the youngest he bent his knee.

The lady turned her head aside,
The knight he woo'd her to be his bride.

The lady blush'd a rosy red,
And said, Sir knight, I'm o'er young to wed.

O lady fair, give me your hand,
And I'll mak you ladie of a' my land.

the ba'] handball play'd o'er] surpassed

Sir knight, ere you my favour win,
Ye maun get consent frae a' my kin.

He has got consent frae her parents dear,
And likewise frae her sisters fair.

He has got consent frae her kin each one,
But forgot to speir at her brother John.

Now when the wedding day was come
The knight would take his bonny bride home.

And many a lord and many a knight
Came to behold that lady bright.

And there was nae man that did her see,
But wished himself bridegroom to be.

Her father dear led her down the stair,
And her sisters twain they kiss'd her there.

Her mother dear led her through the close,
And her brother John set her on her horse.

She lean'd her o'er the saddle-bow,
To give him a kiss ere she did go.

He has ta'en a knife baith lang and sharp
And stabb'd the bonny bride to the heart.

She hadna ridden half thro' the town
Until her heart's blood stained her gown.

maun] must   speir at] ask   close] courtyard

Ride saftly on, said the best young man,
For I think our bonny bride looks pale and wan.

O lead me gently up yon hill,
And I'll there sit down and make my will.

O what will you leave to your father dear?
The silver-shod steed that brought me here.

What will you leave to your mother dear?
My velvet pall and silken gear.

And what will ye leave to your sister Ann?
My silken scarf and my golden fan.

What will ye leave to your sister Grace?
My bloody cloaths to wash and dress.

What will ye leave to your brother John?
The gallows-tree to hang him on.

What will ye leave to your brother John's wife?
The wilderness to end her life.

This fair lady in her grave was laid,
And a mass was o'er her said.

But it would have made your heart right sair,
    With a heigh-ho! and a lily gay,
To see the bridegroom rive his hair,
    As the primrose spreads so sweetly.

pall] rich cloth   gear] apparel

238

61. Edward, Edward

QUHY dois your brand sae drop wi' bluid,
     Edward, Edward?
Quhy dois your brand sae drop wi' bluid?
  And quhy sae sad gang yee, O?
O, I hae killed my hauke sae guid,
     Mither, mither:
O, I hae killed my hauke sae guid:
  And I had nae mair bot hee, O.

Your haukis bluid was nevir sae reid,
     Edward, Edward.
Your haukis bluid was nevir sae reid,
  My deir son I tell thee, O.
O, I hae killed my reid-roan steid,
     Mither, mither:
O, I hae killed my reid-roan steid,
  That erst was sae fair and free, O.

Your steid was auld, and ye hae gat mair,
     Edward, Edward:
Your steid was auld, and ye hae gat mair,
  Sum other dule ye drie, O.
O, I hae killed my fadir deir,
     Mither, mither:
O, I hae killed my fadir deir,
  Alas! and wae is me, O!

And quhatten penance wul ye drie for that,
     Edward, Edward?
And quhatten penance will ye drie for that?
  My deir son, now tell me, O.

dule ye drie] grief you are suffering   quhatten] what

Ile set my feit in yonder boat,
      Mither, mither:
Ile set my feit in yonder boat,
  And Ile fare ovir the sea, O.

And quhat wul ye doe wi' your towirs and your ha',
      Edward, Edward?
And quhat wul ye doe wi' your towirs and your ha,'
  That were sae fair to see, O?
Ile let them stand til they doun fa',
      Mither, mither:
Ile let them stand til they doun fa',
  For here nevir mair maun I bee, O.

And quhat wul ye leive to your bairns and your wife,
      Edward, Edward?
And quhat wul ye leive to your bairns and your wife,
  Quhan ye gang ovir the sea, O?
The warldis room, let thame beg throw life,
      Mither, mither:
The warldis room, let thame beg throw life,
  For thame nevir mair wul I see, O.

And quhat wul ye leive to your ain mither deir,
      Edward, Edward?
And quhat wul ye leive to your ain mither deir?
  My deir son, now tell me, O.
The curse of hell frae me sall ye beir,
      Mither, mither:
The curse of hell frae me sall ye beir,
  Sic counseils ye gave to me, O.

maun] must   Sic] such

62. Son David

O WHAT's the blood 'at 's on your sword,
  My son David, ho son David?
What 's that blood 'at 's on your sword?
  Come promise, tell me true.

O that 's the blood of my grey meir,
  Hey lady mother, ho lady mother;
That 's the blood of my grey meir,
  Because it wadnae rule by me.

O that blood it is owre clear,
  My son David, ho son David,
That blood it is owre clear;
  Come promise, tell me true.

O that 's the blood of my grey hound,
  Hey lady mother, ho lady mother;
That 's the blood of my grey hound,
  Because it wadnae rule by me.

O that blood it is owre clear,
  My son David, ho son David,
That blood it is owre clear;
  Come promise, tell me true.

wadnae rule] would not be controlled   owre] too

SON DAVID

O that's the blood of my huntin' hawk,
  Hey lady mother, ho lady mother;
That's the blood of my huntin' hawk,
  Because it wadnae rule by me.

O that blood it is owre clear,
  My son David, ho son David;
That blood it is owre clear;
  Come promise, tell me true.

For that's the blood of my brother John,
  Hey lady mother, ho lady mother;
That's the blood of my brother John,
  Because he wadnae rule by me:

O I'm gaun awa' in a bottomless boat,
  In a bottomless boat, in a bottomless boat,
For I'm gaun awa' in a bottomless boat,
  An' I'll never return again.

O whan will you come back again,
  My son David, ho son David?
Whan will you come back again?
  Come promise, tell me true.

When the sun an' the moon meet in yon glen,
  Hey lady mother, ho lady mother;
Whan the sun an' the moon meet in yon glen,
  'Fore I'll return again.

gaun] going

63. *Lord Randal*

O WHERE ha' you been, Lord Randal my son?
And where ha' you been, my handsome young man?
I ha' been at the greenwood; mother, mak my bed soon,
For I'm wearied wi' hunting and fain wad lie down.

An' wha met ye there, Lord Randal my son?
An' wha met you there, my handsome young man?
O I met wi my true-love; mother, mak my bed soon,
For I'm wearied wi' huntin' an' fain wad lie down.

And what did she give you, Lord Randal my son?
And what did she give you, my handsome young man?
Eels fried in a pan; mother, mak my bed soon,
For I'm wearied wi' huntin' and fain wad lie down.

And wha gat your leavins, Lord Randal my son?
And wha gat your leavins, my handsom young man?
My hawks and my hounds; mother, mak my bed soon,
For I'm wearied wi' hunting and fain wad lie down.

And what becam of them, Lord Randal my son?
And what becam of them, my handsome young man?
They stretched their legs out an' died; mother, mak my
    bed soon,
For I'm wearied wi' huntin' and fain wad lie down.

O I fear you are poisoned, Lord Randal my son,
I fear you are poisoned, my handsome young man.
O yes, I am poisoned; mother, mak my bed soon,
For I'm sick at the heart and I fain wad lie down.

What d'ye leave to your mother, Lord Randal my son?
What d'ye leave to your mother, my handsome young
    man?
Four and twenty milk kye; mother, mak my bed soon,
For I'm sick at the heart and I fain wad lie down.

What d'ye leave to your sister, Lord Randal my son?
What d'ye leave to your sister, my handsome young
    man?
My gold and my silver; mother, make my bed soon,
For I'm sick at the heart an' I fain wad lie down.

What d'ye leave to your brother, Lord Randal my son?
What d'ye leave to your brother, my handsome young
    man?
My houses and my lands; mother, mak my bed soon,
For I'm sick at the heart and I fain wad lie down.

What d'ye leave to your true-love, Lord Randal my son?
What d'ye leave to your true-love, my handsome young
    man?
I leave her hell and fire; mother, mak my bed soon,
For I'm sick at the heart and I fain wad lie down.

64. The Three Rauens

THERE were three Rauens sat on a tree,
  Down a downe, hay down, hay downe,
There were three Rauens sat on a tree,
  With a downe;
There were three Rauens sat on a tree,
They were as blacke as they might be,
  With a downe derrie, derrie, derrie, downe, downe.

The one of them said to his ma[k]e,
Where shall we our breakefast take?

Downe in yonder greene field
There lies a Knight slain vnder his shield.

His hounds they lie downe at his feete,
So well they can their Master keepe.

His Haukes they flie so eagerly
There 's no fowle dare him come nie.

make] mate

Downe there comes a fallow Doe
As great with yong as she might goe.

She lift vp his bloudy hed
And kist his wounds that were so red.

She got him vp vpon her backe
And carried him to earthen lake.

She buried him before the prime,
She was dead her selfe ere euen-song time.

God send euery gentleman
Such haukes, such hounds, and such a Leman.

prime] sunrise   euen-song] vespers, sunset   Leman] lover

65. *The Courteous Knight*

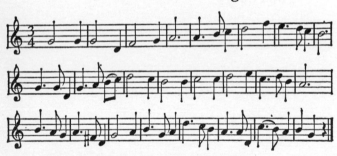

YONDER comes a courteous Knight,
    Lustily raking over the hay,
He was well ware of a bonny lass,
    As she came wandering over the way:
Then she sang down a down, Hey down derry;
Then she sang down a down, Hey down derry.

raking] riding fast

Jove you speed, fair Lady, he said,
    Amongst the leaves that be so green;
If I were a King, and wore a Crown,
    Full soon fair Lady, should thou be a Queen.
        Then she sang, *&c.*

Also *Jove* save you, fair Lady,
    Among the Roses that be so red;
If I have not my will of you,
    Full soon, fair Lady, shall I be dead.
        Then she sang, *&c.*

Then he lookt East, then he lookt West,
    He lookt North, so did he South:
He could not find a privy place,
    For all lay in the Devil's mouth.
        Then she sang, *&c.*

If you will carry me gentle Sir,
    A maid unto my father's hall;
Then you shall have your will of me
    Under purple and under Pall.
        Then she sang, *&c.*

He set her upon a steed,
    And himself upon another;
And all the day he rode her by,
    As tho' they had been sister and brother.
        Then she sang, *&c.*

all lay . . . mouth] i.e. the Devil was controlling events

When she came to her fathers hall,
   It was well walled round about;
She rode in at the wicket gate,
   And shut the four ear'd fool without.
      Then she sang, &c.

You had me (quoth she) abroad in the field,
   Among the corn, amidst the hay,
Where you might had your will of me,
   For, in good faith Sir, I ne'er said nay.
      Then she sang, &c.

You had me also amid the field,
   Among the rushes that were so brown;
Where you might had your will of me,
   But you had not the face to lay me down.
      Then she sang, &c.

He pull'd out his nut-brown sword,
   And wip'd the rust off with his sleeve:
And said: *Joves* Curse come to his heart,
   That any Woman would believe.
      Then she sang, &c.

When you have your own true love,
   A mile or twain out of the Town,
Spare not for her gay cloathing,
   But lay her body flat on the ground.
      Then she sang, &c.

four ear'd] twofold

66. Johny Faa

THE gypsies came to our Lord's yett,
  And vow but they sang sweetly;
They sang sae sweet, and sae compleat,
  That down came the fair lady.
When she came tripping down the stair,
  And a' her maids before her,
As soon as they saw her weel-far'd face
  They coost the glamer o'er her.

Gae tak frae me this gay mantile,
  And bring to me a plaidie;
For if kith and kin and a' had sworn,
  I'll follow the gypsie laddie:
Yestreen I lay in a weel-made bed,
  And my good lord beside me;

yett] gate   weel-far'd] beautiful   coost] cast   glamer]
enchantment   mantile] cape   plaidie] checkered or tartan cloth
used as a cloak   Yestreen] last night

249

This night I'll ly in a tenant's barn,
   Whatever shall betide me.

Oh! come to your bed, says Johnie Faa,
   Oh! come to your bed, my deary;
For I vow and swear by the hilt of my sword
   That your lord shall nae mair come near ye.
I'll go to bed to my Johny Faa,
   And I'll go to bed to my deary;
For I vow and swear by what past yestreen
   That my lord shall nae mair come near me.

I'll make a hap to my Johny Faa,
   And I'll make a hap to my deary;
And he 's get a' the coat gaes round,
   And my lord shall nae mair come near me.
And when our lord came hame at e'en,
   And speir'd for his fair lady,
The tane she cry'd, and the other reply'd,
   She 's awa wi' the gypsie laddie.

Gae saddle to me the black, black steed,
   Gae saddle and mak him ready;
Before that I either eat or sleep
   I'll gae seek my fair lady.—
And we were fifteen well made men,
   Altho' we were nae bonny;
And we are a' put down for ane,
   The earl of Cassilis' lady.

Johnie Faa] the gypsy chief   hap] covering   he 's] he shall
speir'd] asked   tane] one

67. *Eppie Morrie*

FOUR-AND-TWENTY Highland men
  Came a' from Carrie side,
To steal awa Eppie Morrie
  'Cause she would not be a bride.

Out it 's came her mother,
  It was a moonlight night,
She could not see her daughter,
  Their swords they shin'd so bright.

Haud far awa frae me, mother,
  Haud far awa frae me;
There 's not a man in a' Strathdon
  Shall wedded be with me.

They have taken Eppie Morrie
  And horseback bound her on,
And then awa to the minister
  As fast as horse could gang.

He 's taken out a pistol
  And set it to the minister's breast:
Marry me, marry me, minister,
  Or else I'll be your priest.

Haud far awa frae me, good sir,
  Haud far awa frae me;
For there 's not a man in all Strathdon
  That shall married be with me.

Carrie] ? Carvie Water in Strathdon, Aberdeenshire   Haud . . .
awa] keep . . . off

251

Haud far awa frae me, Willie,
  Haud far awa frae me;
For I darna vow to marry you
  Except she 's as willing as ye.

They have taken Eppie Morrie
  Since better could nae be,
And they're awa to Carrie side
  As fast as horse could flee.

When mass was sung and bells were rung,
  And all were bound for bed,
Then Willie an' Eppie Morrie
  In one bed they were laid.

Haud far awa frae me, Willie,
  Haud far awa frae me;
Before I'll lose my maidenhead
  I'll try my strength with thee.

She took the cap from off her head
  And threw it to the way,
Said, Ere I lose my maidenhead
  I'll fight with you till day.

Then early in the morning
  Before her clothes were on,
In came the maiden of Scalletter,
  Gown and shirt alone.

Get up, get up, young woman,
  And drink the wine wi' me.—
You might have called maiden,
  I'm sure as leal as thee.

bound] ready

Wally fa' you, Willie,
 That ye could nae prove a man
And ta'en the lassie's maidenhead;
 She would have hired your han'.

Haud far awa frae me, lady,
 Haud far awa frae me;
There's not a man in a' Strathdon
 The day shall wed wi' me.

Soon in there came Belbordlane
 With a pistol on every side:
Come awa hame, Eppie Morrie,
 And there you'll be my bride.

Go get to me a horse, Willie,
 And get it like a man,
And send me back to my mother
 A maiden as I cam.

The sun shines o'er the westlin hills;
 By the light lamp of the moon
Just saddle your horse, young John Forsyth,
 And whistle and I'll come soon.

Wally fa'] ill luck to   westlin] westerly

68. *Bonnie Annie Livieston*

BONNY Anny Livieston
   Went out to see the play;
By came the laird of Glenlion
   And [he 's] ta'en hir quite away.

He set hir on a milk-white steed,
   Himself upon a gray;
He 's te'en hir o'er the Highland hills
   And ta'en hir quite away.

When they came to Glenlion's gate
   The[y] lighted on the green;
There was mony a bonny lad and lass
   To wolcome the lady hame.

They led hir through high towers and bowers
   And through the buling-green,
And ay when they spake Erse to hir
   The tears blinded hir e'en.

Says, The Highlands is no for me, kind sir,
   The Highlands is no for me;
If that ye would my favour win
   Take me unto Dundee.

Glenlion] in Breadalbane, Perthshire   Erse] Gaelic

Dundee, he says, Dundee, lady—
  Dundee you shall never see;
Upon the laird of Glenlion
  Soon wadded shall ye be.

When bells were rung and mass was sung
  And all were bound for bed,
And bonny Annie Livieston
  By hir bridegroom was laid;

It 's O gin it were day, she says,
  It 's O gin it were day;
O if that it were day, she says,
  Nae langer wad I stay.

Your horse stands in a good stable
  Eating both corn and hay,
And you are in Glenlion's arms;
  Why should ye weary for day?

Glenlion's arms are good enough,
  But alais, the[y]'r no for me;
If that you would my fevour win
  Taike me unto Dundee.

Bat fetch me paper, pen and ink,
  And candle that I may see;
And I'll go write a long letter
  To Geordie in Dundee.

Where will I get a bonny boy
  That will win hose and shoon,
That will gang to my ain true-luve
  And tell him what is done?

wadded] wedded   bound] ready   gin] if   shoon] shoes

Then up then spake a bonny boy
    Near to Glenlion's kin;
Says, Many time I hae gane his erand,
    But the lady's I will rin.

O when he came to broken brigs
    He bent his bow and swame,
And when he came to grass growing
    Set down his feet and ran.

And when he came to Dundee gate
    Lap clean outo'er the wa';
Before the porter was thereat
    The boy was in the haa'.

What news, what news, bonny boy?
    What news hes thou to me?
No news, no news, said bonny boy,
    But a letter unto thee.

The first three lines he looked on,
    A loud laughter gied he;
But or he wan to the hinder en'
    The tears blinded his eie.

Gae saddle to me the black, he says,
    Gae saddle to me the broun;
Gae saddle to me the swiftest steed
    That e'er took man to towen.

Lap] leapt   or he wan to] ere he reached

He burst the black unto the slack,
　　The browen unto the brae,
But fair fa' on the siller-gray
　　That carried him ay away.

When he came to Glenlion's yett
　　He tirled at the pin,
But before that he wan up the stair
　　The lady she was gone.

O I can kiss thy cheeks, Annie,
　　O I can kiss thy chin;
O I can kiss thy clay-cold lips
　　Though there be no breath within.

Deal large at my love's buriell
　　The short bread and the wine,
And gin the morn at ten o' clock
　　Ye may deal as mukle at mine.

The taen was biried in Mary's kirk,
　　The tither in St Mary's quire,
And out of the taen there grew a birk
　　And the ither a bonny brier.

And ay they grew, and ay they threw,
　　Till they did meet aboon;
And a' that ere the same did see
　　Knew they had true lovers been.

burst] broke　　unto the slack] in the pass　　brae] hill　　fair
fa'] good fortune　　siller-] silver-　　tirled] rattled　　pin] knocker,
latch　　Deal large] distribute generously　　gin] by　　the morn]
tomorrow　　mukle] much　　taen] one　　threw] intertwined

69. *Donald of the Isles*

[*Lizie Lindsay*]

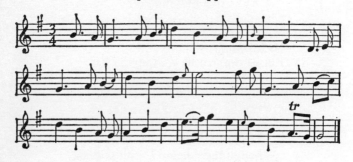

It's of a young lord o' the Hielands,
  A bonnie braw castle had he,
And he says to his lady mither:
  My boon ye will grant to me;
Sall I gae to Edinbruch city
  And fesh hame a lady wi' me?

Ye may gae to Edinbruch city
  And fesh hame a lady wi' thee,
But see that ye bring her but flattrie,
  And court her in grit povertie.

My coat, mither, sall be o' the plaiden,
  A tartan kilt oure my knee,
Wi' hosens and brogues and the bonnet;
  I'll court her wi' nae flatterie.

braw] fine   gae] go   fesh] fetch   but] without   grit]
great   plaiden] checked cloth   hosens] hose

Whan he cam to Edinbruch city
   He play'd at the ring and the ba',
And saw monie a bonnie young ladie;
   But Lizie Lindsay was first o' them a'.

Syne dress'd in his Hieland grey plaiden,
   His bonnet abune his e'e-bree,
He called on fair Lizie Lindsay;
   Says, Lizie, will ye fancy me?

And gae to the Hielands, my lassie,
   And gae, gae wi' me?
O gae to the Hielands, Lizie Lindsay,
   I'll feed ye on curds and green whey.

And ye'se get a bed o' green bracken,
   My plaidie will hap thee and me;
Ye'se lie in my arms, bonnie Lizie,
   If ye'll gae to the Hielands wi' me.

O how can I gae to the Hielands,
   Or how can I gae wi' thee,
Whan I dinna ken whare I'm gaing
   Nor wha I hae to gae wi'?

My father he is an auld shepherd,
   My mither she is an auld dey;
My name it is Donald Macdonald—
   My name I'll never deny.

O Donald, I'll gie ye five guineas
   To sit ae hour in my room,
Till I tak aff your ruddy picture;
   Whan I hae 't, I'll never think lang.

ring] riding with a lance at a ring on a stake   ba'] ? handball
abune] above   e'e-bree] eyebrow   ye'se] you shall   dinna
ken] don't know   dey] dairymaid   ae] one   tak aff] draw
ruddy] healthy, handsome   think lang] grow weary

I dinna care for your five guineas,
　　It 's ye that 's the jewel to me;
I've plenty o' kye in the Hielands
　　To feed ye wi' curds and green whey.

And ye'se get a bonnie blue plaidie
　　Wi' red and green strips thro' it a';
And I'll be the lord o' your dwalling,
　　And that 's the best picture ava.

And I am laird o' a' my possessions,
　　The king canna boast o' na mair;
And ye'se hae my true-heart in keeping,
　　There'll na ither e'en hae a share.

Sae gae to the Hielands, my lassie,
　　O gae awa' happy wi' me;
O gae to the Hielands, Lizie Lindsay,
　　And hird the wee lammies wi' me.

O how can I gae wi' a stranger
　　Oure hills and oure glens frae my hame?
I tell ye I am Donald Macdonald,
　　I'll ever be proud o' my name.

Doun cam Lizie Lindsay's ain father,
　　A knicht o' a noble degree;
Says, If ye do steal my dear daughter
　　It 's hangit ye quickly sall be.

On his heel he turn'd round wi' a bouncie,
　　And a licht lauch he did gie:
There 's nae law in Edinbruch city
　　This day that can dare to hang me.

plaidie] cloak of tartan cloth　　　e'en hae] have even　　　lammies]
lambs　　　oure] over　　　bouncie] little jump

Then up bespak Lizie's best woman,
   And a bonnie young lass was she:
Had I but a mark in my pouchie
   It 's Donald that I wad gae wi'.

O Helen, wad ye leave your coffer
   And a' your silk kirtles sae braw,
And gang wi' a bare-hough'd puir laddie
   And leave father, mither, and a'?

But I think he 's a witch or a warlock
   Or something o' that fell degree,
For I'll gae awa wi' young Donald
   Whatever my fortune may be.

Then Lizie laid doun her silk mantle
   And put on her waiting-maid's goun,
And aff and awa' to the Hielands
   She 's gane wi' this young shepherd loun.

Thro' glens and oure mountains they wander'd
   Till Lizie had scantlie a shoe;
Alas and ohone, says fair Lizie,
   Sad was the first day I saw you;
I wish I war in Edinbruch city;
   Fu' sair, sair this pastime I rue.

O haud your tongue now, bonnie Lizie,
   For yonder 's the shieling, my hame;
And there 's my guid auld honest mither
   That 's coming to meet ye her lane.

coffer] treasure (box)   kirtles] skirts, gowns   bare-hough'd]
bare-thighed   fell] evil   loun] fellow   ohone] alas (*Gaelic*)
shieling] hut, cottage   her lane] by herself

O ye're welcome, ye're welcome, Sir Donald,
  Ye're welcome hame to your ain.—
O ca' me na young Sir Donald,
  But ca' me Donald my son.—
And this they hae spoken in Erse
  That Lizie micht not understand.

The day being weetie and daggie
  The lay till 't was lang o' the day:
Win up, win up, bonnie Lizie,
  And help at the milking the kye.

O slowly raise up Lizie Lindsay,
  The saut tear blindit her e'e:
O war I in Edinbruch city
  The Hielands shou'd never see me!

He led her up to a hie mountain
  And bade her look out far and wide:
I'm Lord o' thae Isles and thae mountains,
  And ye're now my beautiful bride;

Sae rue na ye've come to the Hielands,
  Sae rue na ye've come aff wi' me;
For ye're great Macdonald's braw lady,
  And will be to the day that ye dee.

weetie] wet   daggie] misty   Win] get   thae] these

70. The Shepherd's Dochter

Chorus

THERE was a shepherd's dochter
 Kept sheep on yonder hill;
There cam a knicht o' courage bricht
 And he wad hae his will.
  Diddle, diddle, &c.

He has tane her by the milk-white hand,
 Gi'en her a gown o' green:
Take ye that, fair may, he said,
 Nae mair o' me 'll be seen.

Sin ye hae tane your wills o' me—
 Your wills o' me ye've tane—
Sin ye hae tane your wills o' me
 Pray tell to me your name.

courage bricht] lively spirit Gi'en . . . green] stained her gown on
the grass, seduced her may] maid Sin] since

O some they ca' me Jack, ladie,
  And ithers ca' me John,
But whan I am in the King's court
  Sweet William is my name.

She has kilted up her green claithing
  A little below the knee,
And she has gane to the king's court
  As fast as she could hie.

And whan she cam unto the king
  She knelt low on her knee:
There is a man into your court
  This day has robbed me.

Has he robb'd ye o' your gowd
  Or of your white money,
Or robb'd ye o' the flow'ry branch,
  The flow'r of your bodie?

He has na robb'd me of my gowd
  Nor of my white money,
But he's robb'd me o' the flow'ry branch,
  The flow'r of my bodie.

O gin he be a bondsman
  High hangit sall he be,
But gin he be a freeman
  He sall weel provide for thee.

The king has call'd on his nobles all
  By therty and by three;
Sweet William should hae been the foremost
  But the hindmost man was he.

claithing] skirts   gowd] gold   white money] silver   gin] if
By . . . three] thirty-three of them

Do ye mind yon Shepherd's dochter
  Ye met on yonder hill?
Whan a' her flocks were feeding round
  Of her ye took your will.

Then he's tane out a purse o' gowd
  Tied up intil a glove:
Sae tak ye that, fair may, he says,
  And choice for you a love.

O he's tane out three hundred pund
  Tied up intil a purse:
See, tak ye that, fair may, he says,
  And that will pay the nurse.

I'll neither have your gowd, she says,
  Nor yet your white money,
But I will hae the king's grant
  That he has granted me.

He has tane her on a milk-white steed,
  Himself upon anither,
And to his castle they hae rode
  Like sister and like brither.

O ilka nettle that they cam to:
  O weill mote you grow,
For monie a day my minnie and me
  Hae pilkit at your pow.

O ilka mill that they cam to:
  O weill mote you clap,
For monie a day my minnie and me
  Hae buckled up our lap.

mind] remember   choice] choose   ilka] each, every   mote]
may   minnie] mother   pilkit] picked   pow] head   buckled...
lap] gathered up our skirts or apron to carry away the meal

You're the king o' England's ae brither,
   I trust weill that ye be;
I'm the Earl o' Stamford's ae dochter,
   He has na mae but me.

O saw ye ere sic a near marriage
   Atween the ane and the ither;
The Earl o' Stamford's ae dochter
   And the king o' England's brither.

ae] only   sic] such   near] fit

71. *The Laird o' Ochiltree Wa's*

OH May, bonnie May is to the Yowe buchts gane
   For to milk her daddie's yowes,
And ay she sang and her voice it rang
   Out ower the tap o' the knowes, knowes, knowes,
   Out owr the tap o' the knowes.

Ther cam a troop o' gentilmen
   As they were rydand by,
And ane o' them he lichtit doun
   For to see May milkand her kye.

Yowe] ewe   buchts] folds   tap] top   knowes] knolls
lichtit doun] dismounted

Milk on, milk on, my bonnie lass,
   Milk on, milk on, said he;
For out o' the buchts I winna gang
   Till ye shaw me owr the lee.

Ryde on, ryde on, ye rank rydars,
   Your steeds are stout and strang,
For out o' the yowe buchts I winna gae
   For fear that ye do me some wrang.

He took her by the milkwhite hand
   And by the green gown sleive,
And thare he took his will o' her,
   Bot o' her he askit nae leive.

But quhan he gat his will o' her
   He loot her up again,
And a' this bonny maid said or did
   Was, Kind sir, tell me your name.

He pou't out a sillar kame,
   Sayand, Kame your yellow hair;
And gin I be na back in three quarters o' a year
   It's o' me ye'll see nae mair.

He pu't out a silken purse
   And he gied her guineas thrie,
Saying, Gin I may na be back in three quarters o' a year
   It will pay the nourice fee.

He put his fut into the stirrup
   And rade after his men;
And a' that his men said or did
   Was, Kind maister, ye've taiglit lang.

winna gang] won't go   lee] pasture   stout] sturdy   pou't]
pulled   sillar kame] silver comb   gin] if   nourice] nurse's
taiglit] loitered

I hae rade east, I hae rade wast,
   And I hae rade owr the knowes,
But the bonniest lassie that I ever saw
   Was in the yowe buchts, milkand her yowes.

She put the pail upon her heid
   And she 's gane merrilie hame;
And a' that her faither said or did
   Was, Kind dochter, ye've taiglit lang.

Oh wae be to your men, faither,
   And an ill deth may they die,
For they cawit a' the yowes out owre the knowes
   And they left naebody wi' me.

There cam a tod unto the bucht,
   The like I never saw,
An' afore that he took the ane that he took
   I wad leifar he had tane ither twa.

There cam a tod unto the bucht,
   The like I never did see,
And ay as he spak he liftit his hat,
   And he had a bonnie twinkland e'e.

It was on a day . . . a fine simmer day,
   She was cawing out her faither's kye,
Ther cam a troup o' gentilmen
   And they rade ways the lass near by.

 Quha has dune to you this ill, my dear?
   Quha has dune to you this wrang?
And she had na a word to say for hersell
   But, Kind sir, I hae a man o' my ain.

cawit] drove   tod] fox   wad leifar] would rather   cawing]
driving   kye] cows

Ye lie, ye lie, bonnie May, he says,
    Aloud I hear ye lie;
For dinna ye mind yon bonie simmer nicht
    Whan ye war in the yowe buchts wi' me?

Licht doun, licht doun, my foremaist man,
    Licht doun and let her on,
For monie a time she cawit her faither's kye
    But she'll ne'ir caw them again.

For I am the laird o' Ochiltree Wawis,
    I hae threttie pleuchs and thrie;
And I hae tane awa' the bonniest lass
    That is in a' the north countrie.

dinna ye mind] don't you remember   Wawis] Walls   threttie
pleuchs] thirty ploughs

72. *The Baron of Leys*

THE Laird of Leys is on to Edinbrugh
    To shaw a fit o' his follie;
He drest himsel in the crimson-brown
    An' he prov'd a rantin laddie.

Ben came a weel-fair'd lass,
    Says, Laddie, how do they ca' ye?
They ca' me this an' they ca' me that,
    Ye wudna ken fat they ca' me;
But whan I'm at hame on bonnie Deeside
    They ca' me The Rantin Laddie.

They sought her up, they sought her down,
    They sought her in the parlour;
She coudna be got but whar she was,
    In the bed wi' The Rantin Laddie.

Laird of Leys] one of the Burnetts of Leys, Kincardine   rantin]
riotous, merry   weel-fair'd] handsome   ca'] name   ken
fat] know what

Tell me, tell me, Baron of Leys,
   Ye tell me how they ca' ye;
Your gentle blood moves in my side
   An' I dinna ken how they ca' ye.

They ca' me this an' they ca' me that,
   Ye couldna ken how they ca' me;
But whan I'm at hame on bonnie Deeside
   They ca' me The Rantin Laddie.

Tell me, tell me, Baron of Leys,
   Ye tell me how they ca' ye;
Your gentle blood moves in my side
   An' I dinna ken how to ca' ye.

Baron of Leys it is my stile,
   Alexander Burnett they ca' me;
Whan I'm at hame on bonnie Deeside
   My name is The Rantin Laddie.

Gin your name be Alexander Burnett,
   Alas that ever I saw ye;
For ye hae a wife and bairns at hame,
   An' alas for lyin sae near ye!

But I'se gar ye be headit or hang't,
   Or marry me the morn;
Or else pay down ten thousand crowns
   For gi'ein o' me the scorn.

For my head, I canna want;
   I love my lady dearly;
But some o' my lands I maun lose in the case,
   Alas for lyin sae near ye!

I'se gar ye be headit] I'll have you beheaded   the morn] tomorrow
canna want] cannot do without (it)

Word has gane to the Lady of Leys
   That the laird he had a bairn;
The warst word she said to that was,
   I wish I had it in my arms.

For I will sell my jointure-lands—
   I am broken an' I'm sorry—
An' I'll sell a', to my silk gowns,
   An' get hame my rantin laddie.

73. [*The Fair Flower of Northumberland*]

IT was a Knight in *Scotland* borne,
   Follow my loue, leap ouer the strand:
Was taken prisoner and left forlorne
   Euen by the good Earle of *Northumberland.*

Then was he cast in prison strong,
   Follow my loue, leap ouer the strand:
Where he could not walke nor lye along,
   Euen by the good Earle of *Northumberland.*

And as in sorrow thus he lay,
   Follow my loue, come ouer the strand:
The Earles sweet Daughter walkt that way,
   And she the faire flower of *Northumberland.*

And passing by, like an Angell bright,
   Follow my loue, come ouer the strand:
This prisoner had of her a sight,
   And she the faire flower of *Northumberland.*

And lowd to her this knight did cry,
   Follow my loue, come ouer the strand:
The salt teares standing in his eie,
   And she the faire flower of *Northumberland.*

Faire Lady (he said) take pitty on me,
   Follow my loue, come ouer the strand:
And let me not in prison dye,
   And you the faire flower of *Northumberland.*

Faire Sir, how should I take pitty on thee,
   Follow my loue, come ouer the strand:
Thou being a foe to our Country,
   And I the faire flower of *Northumberland.*

Faire Lady, I am no foe (he said)
   Follow my loue, come ouer the strand:
Through thy sweete loue here was I staid,
   For thee the faire flower of *Northumberland.*

Why shouldst thou come here for loue of me,
   Follow my loue, come ouer the strand:
Hauing wife and children in thy Countrie,
   And I the faire flower of *Northumberland.*

I sweare by the blessed Trinitie,
   Follow my loue, come ouer the strand:
I haue no wife nor children I,
   Nor dwelling at home in merry *Scotland.*

If courteously you will set me free,
   Follow my loue, come ouer the strand:
I vow that I will marry thee,
   So soone as I come in merry *Scotland.*

Thou shalt be Lady of Castles and Towres,
  Follow my loue, come ouer the strand:
And sit like a Queen in princely bowers,
  When I am at home in faire *Scotland*.

Then parted hence this Lady gay,
  Follow my loue, come ouer the strand:
And got her fathers ring away,
  To help this sad knight into faire *Scotland*.

Likewise much gold she got by sleight,
  Follow my loue, come ouer the strand:
And all to help this forlorne knight
  To wend from her father to faire *Scotland*.

Two gallant steeds both good and able,
  Follow my loue, come ouer the strand:
She likewise tooke out of the stable,
  To ride with this knight into fair *Scotland*.

And to the Jaylor she sent this ring,
  Follow my loue, come ouer the strand:
The knight from prison forth to bring,
  To wend with her into faire *Scotland*.

This token set this prisoner free,
  Follow my loue, come ouer the strand:
Who straight went to this faire Lady,
  To wend with her into faire *Scotland*.

A gallant steed he did bestride,
  Follow my loue, come ouer the strand:
And with the Lady away did ride,
  And she the faire flower of *Northumberland*.

They rode till they came to a water cleere,
  Follow my loue, come ouer the strand:
Good sir how should I follow you here,
  And I the faire flower of *Northumberland*.

The water is rough and wonderfull deep,
  Follow my loue, come ouer the strand:
And on my saddle I shall not keep,
  And I the faire flower of *Northumberland*.

Feare not the foord, faire Lady (quoth he),
  Follow my loue, come ouer the strand:
For long I cannot stay for thee,
  And thou the faire flower of *Northumberland*.

The Lady prickt her wanton steed,
  Follow my loue, come ouer the strand:
And ouer the river swom with speed,
  And she the faire flower of *Northumberland*.

From top to toe all wet was she,
  Follow my loue, come ouer the strand:
This haue I done for loue of thee,
  And I the faire flower of *Northumberland*.

Thus rode she all one winters night,
  Follow my loue, come ouer the strand:
Till *Edenborow* they saw in sight,
  The chiefest towne in all *Scotland*.

Now chuse (quoth he) thou wanton flower,
  Follow my loue, come ouer the strand:
Whether thou wilt be my Paramour,
  Or get thee home to *Northumberland*.

For I haue wife and children fiue,
   Follow my loue, come ouer the strand:
In *Edenborow* they be aliue;
   Then get thee home to faire *England*.

This fauour shalt thou haue to boote,
   Follow my loue, come ouer the strand:
Ile haue thy horse, goe thou a foote,
   Goe get thee home to *Northumberland*.

O false and faithlesse knight (quoth she)
   Follow my loue, come ouer the strand:
And canst thou deale so bad with me,
   And I the faire flower of *Northumberland*?

Dishonour not a Ladies name,
   Follow my loue, come ouer the strand:
But draw thy sword, and end my shame,
   And I the faire flower of *Northumberland*.

He tooke her from her stately Steed,
   Follow my loue, come ouer the strand:
And left her there in extreme need,
   And she the faire flower of *Northumberland*.

Then sat she downe full heauily,
   Follow my loue, come ouer the strand:
At length two knights came riding by,
   Two gallant knights of faire *England*.

She fell downe humbly on her knee,
   Follow my loue, come ouer the strand:
Saying, Courteous Knights take pitty on me,
   And I the faire flower of *Northumberland*.

I haue offended my father deere,
　　Follow my loue, come ouer the strand:
And by a false knight that brought me here,
　　From the good Earle of *Northumberland.*

They tooke her up behinde [them] then,
　　Follow my loue, come ouer the strand:
And brought her to her fathers againe,
　　And he the good Earle of *Northumberland.*

All you faire maidens be warned by me,
　　Follow my loue, come ouer the strand:
Scots were neuer true, nor neuer will be,
　　To Lord, nor Lady, nor faire *England.*

74. *The False Lover*

THE sun shines high on yonder hill,
　　And low on yonder den;
And the place where my bonnie lovie does dwell,
　　The sun goes never doon, bonnie lovie,
　　The sun goes never doon.

den] dingle

277

Saddle me the black, the black,
　　And saddle me the broon,
That I may ride a' roon, bonnie lovie,
　　That I may ride a' roon.

When will ye come back, bonnie lovie,
　　And when will ye be hame?
When the heather hills are nine times brunt
　　And a' grown green again, bonnie lovie,
　　And a' grown green again.

That 's owre lang awa', bonnie lovie,
　　Oh, that 's owre lang frae hame;
Your baby that is yet unborn
　　Will be owre lang wantin' its name, bonie lovie,
　　Will be owre lang wantin' its name.

He turned his high horse head about,
　　And fast, fast on rode he;
She kilted up her gay clothing,
　　And fast, fast followed she, bonie lovie,
　　And fast, fast followed she.

At the first toon that they cam' till
　　He bought her stockings and sheen;
He bade her rue and return noo,
　　And gang nae further wi' 'im, bonnie lovie,
　　And gang nae further wi' 'im.

It 's love for love that I do want,
　　It 's love for love again;
It 's hard that I love you sae weel,
　　And you nae me again, bonnie lovie,
　　And you nae me again.

a' roon] all around　　　brunt] burnt　　　owre lang] too long
till] to　　　sheen] shoes　　gang] go

At the next toon that they cam' till
  He bought her a wedding goon;
He bade her rue and return noo,
  And gang nae further wi' im, bonnie lovie,
  And gang nae further wi' 'im.

It's love for love that I do want,
  It's love for love again;
It's hard that I love you sae weel,
  And you nae me again, bonnie lovie,
  And you nae me again.

At the next toon that they cam' till
  He bought her a brooch and a ring;
He bade her dry up her red rosy cheeks,
  And he wad tak' 'er wi' 'im, bonnie lovie,
  And he wad tak' 'er wi' 'im.

There's comfort for the comfortless,
  And honey for the bee;
There's comfort for the comfortless,
  But nane but thee for me, bonie lovie,
  But nane but thee for me.

but thee] without thee

75. Fa'se Footrage

KING EASTER has courted her for her gowd,
  King Wester for her fee,
King Honor for her lands sae braid
  And for her fair body.

gowd] gold   fee] property   braid] broad

They had not been four months married,
   As I have heard them tell,
Until the nobles of the land
   Against them did rebel.

And they cast kaivles them amang
   And kaivles them between,
And they cast kaivles them amang
   Wha shoud gae kill the king.

O some said yea and some said nay,
   Their words did not agree;
Till up it gat him Fa'se Footrage
   And sware it shoud be he.

When bells were rung and mass was sung
   And a' man boon to bed,
King Honor and his gay ladie
   In a hie chamer were laid.

Then up it raise him Fa'se Footrage
   While a' were fast asleep,
And slew the porter in his lodge
   That watch and ward did keep.

O four and twenty silver keys
   Hang hie upon a pin,
And ay as a door he did unlock
   He has fasten'd it him behind.

Then up it raise him King Honor,
   Says, What means a' this din?
Now what's the matter, Fa'se Footrage,
   O wha was 't loot you in?

kaivles] lots   gae] go and   boon to] ready for   loot] let

O ye my errand well shall learn
   Before that I depart;
Then drew a knife baith lang and sharp
   And pierced him thro' the heart.

Then up it got the Queen hersell
   And fell low down on her knee:
O spare my life now, Fa'se Footrage,
   For I never injured thee.

O spare my life now, Fa'se Footrage,
   Until I lighter be,
And see gin it be lad or lass
   King Honor has left me wi'.

O gin it be a lass, he says,
   Well nursed she shall be;
But gin it be a lad-bairn
   He shall be hanged hie.

I winna spare his tender age
   Nor yet his hie, hie kin;
But as soon as e'er he born is
   He shall mount the gallows-pin.

O four and twenty valiant knights
   Were set the Queen to guard,
And four stood ay at her bower-door
   To keep baith watch and ward.

But when the time drew till an end
   That she should lighter be,
She cast about to find a wile
   To set her body free.

lighter] i.e. of my baby   gin] if   winna] won't   gallows-pin] gibbet-beam

O she has birled these merry young men
   Wi' strong beer and wi' wine,
Until she made them a' as drunk
   As any wallwood swine.

O narrow, narrow is this window
   And big, big am I grown!
Yet thro' the might of Our Ladie
   Out at it she has won.

She wander'd up, she wander'd down,
   She wander'd out and in,
And at last into the very swines' stye
   The Queen brought forth a son.

Then they cast kaivles them amang
   Wha should gae seek the Queen,
And the kaivle fell upon Wise William
   And he 's sent his wife for him.

O when she saw Wise William's wife
   The Queen fell on her knee.
Win up, win up, madame, she says,
   What means this courtesie?

O out of this I winna rise
   Till a boon ye grant to me,
To change your lass for this lad-bairn
   King Honor left me wi'.

And ye maun learn my gay gose-hawke
   Well how to breast a steed,
And I shall learn your turtle-dow
   As well to write and read.

birled] plied   wallwood] wild-wood   won] reached, managed
Win] get   maun learn] must teach   breast] mount   -dow] -dove

And ye maun learn my gay gose-hawke
   To wield baith bow and brand,
And I shall learn your turtle-dow
   To lay gowd wi' her hand.

At kirk or market where we meet
   We dare nae mair avow
But, Dame, how does my gay gose-hawk?
   Madame, how does my dow?

When days were gane and years came on
   Wise William he thought long;
Out has he ta'en King Honor's son
   A hunting for to gang.

It sae fell out at their hunting
   Upon a summer's day,
That they cam by a fair castle,
   Stood on a sunny brae.

O dinna ye see that bonny castle
   Wi' wa's and towers sae fair?
Gin ilka man had back his ain
   Of it you shou'd be heir.

How I shou'd be heir of that castle
   In sooth I canna see,
When it belongs to Fa'se Footrage,
   And he 's nae kin to me.

brand] sword   lay gowd] embroider in gold   At . . . market]
in public   avow] declare, say   thought long] grew weary of
waiting   gang] go   brae] hill   dinna] don't   Gin
ilka] if every   ain] own

O gin ye shou'd kill him Fa'se Footrage
   You wou'd do what is right,
For I wot he kill'd your father dear
   Ere ever you saw the light.

Gin ye should kill him Fa'se Footrage
   There is nae man durst you blame,
For he keeps your mother a prisoner
   And she dares no take you hame.

The boy stared wild like a gray gose-hawke,
   Says, What may a' this mean?
My boy, you are King Honor's son
   And your mother 's our lawful queen.

O gin I be King Honor's son,
   By Our Ladie I swear
This day I will that traytour slay
   And relieve my mother dear.

He has set his bent bow till his breast
   And lap the castle-wa',
And soon he 's siesed on Fa'se Footrage
   Wha loud for help gan ca'.

O hold your tongue now, Fa'se Footrage,
   Frae me you shanna flee:
Syne pierced him through the foul fa'se heart
   And set his mother free.

And he has rewarded Wise William
   With the best half of his land,
And sae has he the turtle-dow
   Wi' the truth of his right hand.

wot] know   durst] dare   lap] jumped   shanna] shall not
Syne] then (he)   truth] pledge

76. *The Lord of Lorn and the Fals Steward*

IT was a worthy Lord of Lorn,
   He was a Lord of high degree;
He sent [his son] unto the Schoole
   To learn some civility.

He learned more learning in one day
   Then other children did in three;
And then bespake the Schoolmaster
   Unto him tenderly.

In faith thou art the honestest Boy
   That ere I blinkt on with mine eye;
I hope thou art some Easterling born,
   The Holy Ghost is with thee.

Lorn] in Argyll   blinkt] glanced   Easterling] east country
lad

He said he was no Easterling born,
    The child thus answered courteously:
My father is the Lord of Lorn,
    And I his Son perdye.

The Schoolmaster turned round about,
    His angry mood he could not swage;
He marvelled the child could speak so wise,
    He being of so tender age.

He girt the Saddle to the Steed,
    The bridle of the best gold shone;
He took his leave of his fellows all
    And quickly he was gone.

And when he came to his Father dear
    He kneeled down upon his knee:
I am come to you, Father, he said,
    Gods blessing give you me.

Thou art welcome, Son, he said,
    Gods blessing I give thee;
What tidings hast thou brought, my Son,
    Being come so hastily?

I have brought tidings, Father, he said,
    And so liked it may be,
There's never a book in all Scotland
    But I can read it truly.

There's nere a Doctor in all this Realm,
    For all he goes in rich array,
I can write him a Lesson soon
    To learn in seven years day.

perdye] indeed

That is good tidings, said the Lord,
　All in the place where I do stand;
My Son, thou shalt into France go
　To learn the speeches of [that] land.

Who shall go with him? said the Lady;
　Husband, we have no more but he;
Madam, he saith, my head Steward,
　He hath bin true to me.

She cal'd the steward to an account,
　A thousand pound she gave him anon;
Sayes, Good sir steward, be as good to my child
　When he is far from home.

If I be fals unto my young Lord
　Then God be [the] like to me indeed!
And now to France they both are gone,
　And God be their good speed.

They had not been in France Land
　Not three weeks unto an end,
But meat and drink the child got none
　Nor mony in purse to spend.

The child ran to the Rivers side,
　He was fain to drink water then;
And after followed the fals steward
　To put the child therein.

But nay, marry, said the child;
　He asked mercy pittifully:
Good steward, let me have my life
　What ere betide my body.

fain] eager　　　marry] indeed

Now put off thy fair cloathing
   And give it me anon;
So put thee of[f] thy s[i]lken shirt
   With many a golden seam.

But when the child was stript naked,
   His body white as the lilly flower,
He might have bin seen for his body
   A Princes paramour.

He put him in an old kelter coat
   And hose of the same above the knee;
He bid him go to the shepherds house
   To keep sheep on a [lonely lee].

The child did say, What shall be my name?
   Good steward, tell to me.—
Thy name shall be Poor [Disawear],
   That thy name shall be.

The child came to the shepheards house
   And asked mercy pittifully;
Sayes, Good sir shepheard, take me in
   To keep sheep on a [lonely lee].

But when the shepheard saw the child,
   He was so pleasant in his eye:
I have no child, Ile make thee my heir,
   Thou shalt have my goods, perdie.

And then bespake the shepheards wife
   Unto the child so tenderly:
Thou must take the sheep and go to the field,
   And [keep] them on a [lonely lee].

kelter] coarse   lee] pasture   Disawear] ? Sans-aver, Stripped-
of-wealth

Now let us leave talk of the child
   That is keeping sheep on a [lonely lee],
And we'l talk more of the fals steward
   And of his fals treachery.

He bought himself three suits of apparrell
   That any Lord might a' seem[d] to worn;
He went a wooing to the Duke's daughter
   And cal'd himself the Lord of Lorn.

The Duke he welcomed the yong lord
   With three baked stags anon;
If he had wist him the fals steward
   To the Divell he would have gone.

But when they were at Supper set
   With dainty delicates that was there,
The D[uke] said, If thou wilt wed my daughter
   Ile give thee a thousand pound a year.

The Lady would see the red Buck run
   And also for to hunt the Doe;
And with a hundred lusty men
   The Lady did a hunting go.

The Lady is a hunting gon
   Over le[e] and fell that is so high;
There was she ware of a shepherds boy
   With sheep on a [lonely lee].

And ever he sighed and made moan
   And cried out pittifully:
My Father is the Lord of Lorn
   And knows not wha[t]s become of me.

wist] known   moan] complaint

And then bespake the Lady gay
   And to her Maid she spake anon:
Go fetch me hither the shepherds boy;
   Why maketh he all this moan?

[When he came before that lady fair
   He fell down upon his knee;
He had been so well brought up
   He needed not to learn courtesie.]

Where was thou born, thou bonny child?
   For whose sake makst thou all this mone?
My dearest Friend, Lady, he said,
   Is dead many years agon.

Tell thou to me, thou bonny child,
   Tell me the truth and do not lye;
Kno[w]st thou not the yong Lord of Lorn
   Is come a wooing unto me?

Yes, forsooth, then said the child,
   I know the Lord then, veryly;
The young Lord is a valliant Lord
   At home in his own Country.

Wilt leave thy sheep, thou bonny child,
   And come in service unto me?
Yes, forsooth, then said the child,
   At your bidding will I be.

When the steward lookt upon the child
   He bewrail'd him villainously:
Where wast thou born, thou vagabone?
   Or where is thy Country?

Ha' don, ha' don, said the Lady gay;
　　She cal'd the steward then presently:
Without you bear him more good will
　　You get no love of me.

Then bespake the false steward
　　Unto the lady hastily:
At Aberdine beyond the Seas
　　His Father robbed thousands three.

But then bespake the Lady gay
　　Unto her Father courteously;
Saying, I have found a bonny child
　　My chamberlain to be.

Not so, not so, then said the Duke,
　　For so it may not be;
For that young L[ord] of Lorn that comes a wooing
　　Will think somthing of thee and me.

When the Duke had lookt upon the child,
　　He seem'd so pleasant to the eye:
Child, because thou lovst horses well,
　　My groom of stables thou shalt be.

The child plied the horses well
　　A twelve month to an end;
He was so courteous and so true
　　Every man became his fri[e]nd.

He led a fair Gelding to the water
　　Where he might drink, verily;
The great Gelding up with his head
　　And hit the child above the eye.

Wo worth th[ee], horse, then said the child,
  That ere Mare foaled thee;
Thou little knowst what thou hast done;
  Thou hast stricken a Lord of high degree.

The D[uke's] daughter was in her garden green,
  She heard the child make great moan;
She ran to the child all weeping
  And left her Maidens all alone.

Sing on thy Song, thou bonny child,
  I will release thee of thy pain.—
I have made an oath, Lady, he said,
  I dare not tell my tale again.

Tell the horse thy tale, thou bonny child,
  And so thy Oath shall saved be.
But when he told the horse his tale
  The Lady wept full tenderly.

Ile do for thee, my bonny child,
  In faith I will do more for thee;
For I will send thy Father word
  And he shall come and speak with me.

I will do more, my bonny child,
  In faith I will do more for thee;
And for thy sake, my bonny child,
  Ile put my wedding off months three.

The Lady she did write a letter
  Full pittifully with her own hand;
She sent it to the Lord of Lorn
  Whereas he dwelt in fair Scotland.

But when the Lord had read the letter
  His Lady wept most tenderly:
I knew what would become of my child
  In such a far Country.

The old Lord cal'd up his merry men
  And all that he gave cloth and fee,
With seven Lords by his side,
  And into France rides he.

The wind serv'd, and they did saile
  So far into France land;
They were ware of the Lord of Lorn
  With a porters staff in his hand.

The Lords they moved hat and hand,
  The Servingmen fell on their knee;
What folks be yonder, said the steward,
  That makes the porter courtesie?

Thou art a false thief, said the L[ord] of Lorn,
  No longer might I bear with thee;
By the Law of France thou shalt be jugd,
  Whether it be to live or die.

A Quest of Lords there chosen was,
  To Bench they came hastily;
But when the Quest was ended
  The fals steward must dye.

First they did him half hang
  And then they took him down anon,
And then put him in boyling lead;
  And then was sodden, brest and bone.

Quest] inquest

And then bespake the Lord of Lorn
   With many other Lords mo:
Sir Duke, if you be as willing as we,
   We'l have a marriage before we go.

These children both they did rejoyce
   To hear the Lord his tale so ended;
They had rather to day then to morrow,
   So he would not be offended.

But when the wedding ended was
   There was delicious dainty cheer;
Ile tell you how long the wedding did last—
   Full three quarters of a year.

Such a banquet there was wrought,
   The like was never seen;
The king of France brought with him then
   A hundred tun of good red wine.

Five set of Musitians were to be seen
   That never rested night nor day;
Also Italians there did sing
   Full pleasantly with great joy.

Thus have you heard what troubles great
   Unto successive joyes did turn,
And happy news among the rest
   Unto the worthy Lord of Lorn.

Let rebels therefore warned be
   How mischief once they do pretend;
For God may suffer for a time
   But will disclose it in the end.

77. Lady Maisry

THE young lords o' the north country
 Have all a wooing gone
To win the love of Lady Maisry;
 But o' them she wou'd hae none.

O they hae courted Lady Maisry
 Wi' a' kin' kind o' things,
An' they hae sought her Lady Maisry
 Wi' brotches an' wi' rings.

An' they ha' sought her Lady Maisry
 Frae father and frae mother,
An' they ha' sought her Lady Maisry
 Frae sister an' frae brother.

An' they ha' follow'd her Lady Maisry
 Thro' chamber an' thro' ha';
But a' that they cou'd say to her,
 Her answer still was Na.

O had your tongues, young men, she says,
 An' think nae mair o' me;
For I've gien my love to an English lord,
 An' think nae mair o' me.

had] hold

Her father's kitchy boy heard that—
   An ill death may he dee—
An' he is on to her brother
   As fast as gang cou'd hee.

O is my father an' my mother well,
   But an' my brothers three?
Gin my sister Lady Maisry be well
   There 's naething can ail me.

Your father and your mother is well,
   But an' your brothers three;
Your sister Lady Maisry 's well,
   So big wi' bairn gangs she.

Gin this be true you tell to me,
   My mailison light on thee;
But gin it be a lie you tell
   You sal be hangit hie.

He 's done him to his sister's bow'r
   Wi' meikle doole an' care,
An' there he saw her Lady Maisry
   Kembing her yallow hair.

O wha is aught that bairn, he says,
   That ye sae big are wi'?
And gin ye winna own the truth
   This moment ye sall dee.

kitchy] kitchen   gang] go   But an'] and also   Gin] if
mailison] curse   done him] taken himself   doole] sorrow
wha is aught] whose is   winna] won't

She turn'd her right an' roun' about
   An' the kem fell frae her han';
A trembling seiz'd her fair body
   An' her rosy cheek grew wan.

O pardon me, my brother dear,
   An' the truth I'll tell to thee;
My bairn it is to Lord William
   An' he is betroth'd to me.

O cou'd na ye gotten dukes or lords
   Intill your ain country,
That ye draw up wi' an English dog
   To bring this shame on me?

But ye maun gi' up the English lord
   Whan youre young babe is born,
For gin you keep by him an hour langer
   Your life sall be forlorn.

I will gi' up this English blood
   Till my young babe be born,
But the never a day nor hour langer
   Tho' my life should be forlorn.

O whare is a' my merry young men
   Whom I gi' meat and fee,
To pu' the thistle and the thorn
   To burn this wile whore wi'?

kem] comb   gotten] have got   Intill] within   forlorn]
lost, destroyed   fee] wages   wile] vile

O whare will I get a bonny boy
   To help me in my need,
To rin wi' haste to Lord William
   And bid him come wi' speed?

O out it spake a bonny boy
   Stood by her brother's side:
O I would rin your errand, Lady,
   O'er a' the world wide.

Aft have I run your errands, Lady,
   Whan blawn baith win' and weet;
But now I'll rin your errand, Lady,
   Wi' sat tears on my cheek.

O whan he came to broken briggs
   He bent his bow and swam,
And whan he came to the green grass growin
   He slack'd his shoone and ran.

O whan he came to Lord William's yates
   He baed na to chap or ca',
But set his bent bow till his breast
   An' lightly lap the wa';
An' or the porter was at the yate
   The boy was i' the ha'.

O is my biggins broken, boy?
   Or is my towers won?
Or is my Lady lighter yet
   Of a dear daughter or son?

weet] rain	sat] salt	briggs] bridges	slack'd] eased off
yates] gates	baed] stayed	chap] knock	till] to lap]
leapt or] ere	biggins] buildings	won] taken	

Your biggin is na broken, Sir,
  Nor is your towers won;
But the fairest Lady in a' the lan'
  For you this day maun burn.

O saddle me the black, the black,
  Or saddle me the brown;
O saddle me the swiftest steed
  That ever rade frae a town.

Or he was near a mile awa
  She heard his wild horse sneeze:
Mend up the fire, my false brother,
  It 's na come to my knees.

O whan he lighted at the yate
  She heard his bridle ring:
Mend up the fire, my false brother,
  It 's far yet frae my chin.

Mend up the fire to me, brother,
  Mend up the fire to me;
For I see him comin hard an' fast
  Will soon men' 't up to thee.

O gin my hands had been loose, Willy,
  Sae hard as they are boun',
I would have turn'd me frae the gleed
  And casten out your young son.

O I'll gar burn for you, Maisry,
  Your father an' your mother;
An' I'll gar burn for you, Maisry,
  Your sister an' your brother.

gleed] glowing fire   gar] make

An' I'll gar burn for you, Maisry,
  The chief of a' your kin;
An' the last bonfire that I come to
  Mysel I will cast in.

78. *Katherine Jaffray*

THERE lives a maid down under yon brae,
  In a bower biggit wi' stone;
Her name is Katherine Jaffray,
  And she's loved by many a one.

There cam' a lord from Southsea baulks,
  I mean from fair England;
He lichtit at her father's gate,
  And his name's Lord Lamington.

He socht her frae her father and mither,
  And her kinsfolk ane and a';
But he never taul' the lassie hersel'
  Till he set her wedding day.

Then ben it cam' her father dear,
  Just stepping ben the floor:
Prepare, prepare, my own daughter,
  For your wedding prepare.

The day it is on Wednesday,
  The morn's your wedding day;
And it is wi' Lord Lamington,
  And ye daurna say him nay.

brae] hill   biggit] built   baulks] sand bars   lichtit]
alighted   taul'] told   ben] through, within

Then ben it cam' Lord Lamington,
   Just stepping ben the floor:
Prepare, prepare, my own true love,
   For your wedding prepare.

The day it is on Wednesday,
   And the morn 's your wedding day;
And I'm the Lord Lamington,
   And ye daurna say me nay.

Whatever she thocht, and she spak' nocht,
   But a sorry min' had she;
She min't upon her Lochnavare
   When they suner't on the lea.

————

What news, what news, my bonnie boy,
   What news hae ye to me?
Pray, tell me, how is my own true love,
   Sweet Katherine Jaffray?

Ye're bidden horse, and ride richt fast,
   Gin ye set for the may;
Ye're bidden min' upon the nicht
   Ye suner't on the lea.

They rendezvous'd on Calie's banks,
   And ranked on Calie's braes;
Oh, stay ye here a little wee while
   Till I to yon wedding-house gae.

suner't] parted   lea] meadowland   horse] take horse   Gin]
if   set for the may] are resolved to have the girl   min' upon]
recall   Calie] *perh.* Cally; in Kirkcudbright or near Blairgowrie,
Perthshire

I sall go to yon wedding-house,
   And none shall go wi' me;
My love she goes another man's bride,
   And they've played me foul, foul play.

But when ye hear my little horn blaw,
   See that ye be ready a';
Or else your master will be slain,
   And ye winna sain the day.

Then he has gone to yon wedding-house,
   And there he lichtit doon;
And there, there was dinner makin',
   Wi' mirth and great renown.

Oh, are ye come to fight? they said,
   Or for guid companie?
Or are ye come to steal the bride
   On this her wedding day?

I cam' na here to fight, he said,
   But for guid companie,
To drink wi' him that is bridegroom,
   And then bound on my way;
And one word o' your bride, my lord,
   And then to bound my way.

The cups were filled o' guid red wine,
   To be drunk between them twa;
And Lamington called on his bride,
   But she answered nane ava.

sain] bless   ava] at all

But Lochnavare called on her neist,
  And shortly did she draw;
But her maiden stood upon the floor,
  And shortly said she na.

For it 's the maiden's only due,
  And the cat in a' oor lan',
To fee the bride to the bridegroom
  As soon 's the sun goes down.

But one word o' your bride, maiden;
  Oh, wad ye say me na?
Afore her wedding day could a-stan',
  Wi' her I'd spoken twa.

Then he leant owre his saddle bow,
  To kiss her check and chin;
And even-up by the gown breist
  He horsed her him ahin'.

Then he set spurs to his horse sides,
  And they rode up the street;
Ye wadna seen his yellow hair
  For the dust o' his horse's feet.

Then he put his horn to his mouth
  And blew baith loud and shrill;
And a hundred harnessed horse and men
  Cam' Lochnavare until.

---

neist] next   shortly . . . shortly] soon . . . briefly   draw] come
cat] ? game, custom   fee] hire, engage   a- stan'] have taken
place   ahin'] behind

The blood ran down Duncalie's banks,
  And owre Duncalie's brae;
And aye they bade the trumpet sound
  The voice o' foul, foul play.

Turn back, turn back now, Lamington,
  Of me there 's no remeid;
It 's only the killing o' your men,
  And shedding o' their bleed.

Your shoes are on my feet, she said,
  And your gloves are on my han's;
And a' the love-tokens I got frae you
  I'll sen' them back again.

remeid] redress

79. McNaughtan

[*Johnny Scot*]

JOHNNY's into England gane
  Three quarters of a year;
Johnny 's into England gane
  The King's banner to bear.

He had na been in England lang
   But and a little while,
Untill the King[is ae] Daughter
   To Johnny gaes wi' child.

Word is to the Kitchin gane
   And word is to the Ha',
And word is to the King's palace
   Amang the nobles a'.

Word's gane to the King's palace,
   The palace where [he] sat,
That his ae Daughter gaes wi' child
   To Jock the little Scot.

If she be wi' child, he says,
   As I trow well she be,
I'll put her into strang prison
   And hang her till she die.

But up and spak young Johnny,
   And O he spak in time:
Is there never a bony Boy here
   Will rin my errand soon?

That will gae to yon Castle
   And look it round about?
And there he'll see a fair lady
   The window looking out.

Up then spak a bony Boy,
   And a bony Boy was he:
I'll run thy errand, Johnny, he said,
   Untill the day I die.

ae] only   strang] secure

Put on your gown o' silk, Madam,
   And on your hand a glove,
And gang into the good Green-wood
   To Johnny your true love.

The fetters they are on my feet,
   And O but they are cauld;
My bracelets they are sturdy steel
   Instead of beaten gold.

But I will write a lang letter
   And seal it tenderlie,
And I will send to my true love
   Before that I do die.

The first look that Johnny look'd,
   A loud laughter ga'e he;
But the next look that Johnny ga'e,
   The tear blinded his e'e.

He says, I'll into England gae
   Whatever may betide,
And a' to seek a fair woman
   That sud hae been my bride.

But up and speaks his Father,
   And O he spak in time:
If that ye into England gae
   I'm feer'd ye ne'er come hame.

But up then speaks our gude Scotch King,
   And a brisk young man was he:
He 's hae five hunder o' my Life-guard
   To bear him companie.

gang] go   sud] should   feer'd] afraid   's hae] shall have

When Johnny was on Saddle set
  And seemly for to see,
There was not a married man
  Into his companie.

When Johnny sat on Saddle-seat
  And seemly to behold,
The hair that hang on Johnny's head
  Was like the threads o' gold.

When he cam to [fair London]
  He gar'd the Bells a' ring,
Untill the King and a' his Court
  Did marvel at the thing.

Is this the brave Argyle, he said,
  That's landed and come hame?
Is this the brave Argyle, he said,
  Or James, our Scottish King?

It's no the brave Argyle, they said,
  That's landed and come hame;
But it is a brave young Scotch Knight,
  MᶜNaughtan is his name.

If MᶜNaughtan be his name, he says,
  As I trow weel it be,
The fairest Lady in a' my Court
  Gangs wi' child to thee.

If that she be wi' child, he says,
  As I wat weel she be,
I'll mak it Lord o' a' my land
  And her my gay Lady.

gar'd] caused

I have a Champion in my Court
　　Will fight you a' by three:
But up then speaks a brisk young man,
　　And a brisk young man was he:
I will fight to my life's end
　　Before poor Johnny die.

The King but and his Nobles a'
　　Went out into the plain,
The Queen but and her maidens a',
　　To see young Johnny slain.

The first wound that Johnny ga'e the Champion
　　Was a deep wound and [a] sair;
The next wound that he ga'e the Champion
　　He never spak mair.

A priest, a priest, young Johnny cries,
　　To wed me and my love;
A clerk, a clerk, the King he cries,
　　To sign her tocher gude.

I'll hae nane o' your goud, he says,
　　I'll hae nane o' your gear,
But a' I want is my true love
　　For I hae bought her dear.

He took out a little Goat-horn
　　And blew baith loud and shill;
The vict'ry 's into Scotland gane,
　　Tho' sair against their will.

by three] in threes　　　but and] and also　　　ga'e] gave　　　tocher]
marriage settlement　　　goud] gold　　　gear] property　　　shill] shrill

80. *The Bonny Earl of Livingston*

O WE were sisters seven, Maisry,
   And five are dead wi' child;
There is nane but you and I, Maisry,
   And we'll go maidens mild.

She hardly had the word spoken
   And turn'd her round about,
When the bonny Earl of Livingston
   Was calling Maisry out;

Upon a bonny milk-white steed
   That drank out of the Tyne;
And a' was for her Ladie Maisry
   To take her hyne and hyne.

Upon a bonny milk-white steed
   That drank out o' the Tay;
And a' was for her Lady Maisry
   To carry her away.

She had not been at Livingston
   A twelve month and a day
Until she was as big wi' bairn
   As any ladie coud gae.

She call'd upon her little foot-page,
   Says, Ye maun run wi' speed
And bid my mother come to me,
   For of her I'll soon have need.

wi' child] in childbirth   Livingston] in Linlithgow, of which the
Livingstons were earls 1600–1715   hyne and hyne] hence and away
gae] go   maun] must

THE BONNY EARL OF LIVINGSTON

See, there is the brootch frae my hause-bane,
    It is of gowd sae ried;
Gin she winna come when I'm alive
    Bid her come when I am dead.

But ere she wan to Livingston
    As fast as she coud ride,
The gaggs they were in Maisry's mouth
    And the sharp sheers in her side.

Her good lord wrang his milk-white hands
    Till the gowd rings flaw in three:
Let ha's and bowers and a' gae waste,
    My bonny love 's taen frae me!

O hold your tongue, Lord Livingston,
    Let a' your mourning be;
For I bare the bird between my sides
    Yet I maun thole her to die.

Then out it spake her sister dear
    As she sat at her head:
That man is not in Christendoom
    Shall gar me die sicken dead.

O hold your tongue, my ae daughter,
    Let a' your folly be,
For ye shall be married ere this day week
    Tho' the same death you should die.

hause-bane] neck-bone   Gin] if   winna] won't   wan
to] reached   sheers . . . side] i.e. for a Caesarean section   gowd]
gold   flaw] flew, broke   bird] girl   maun thole] must
suffer   gar] make   sicken dead] such a death   ae] only

81. Sir Patrick Spence

THE king sits in Dumferling toune,
   Drinking the blude-reid wine:
O quhar will I get [a] guid sailor,
   To sail this schip of mine?

Up and spak an eldern knicht,
   Sat at the kings richt kne:
Sir Patrick Spence is the best sailor,
   That sails upon the se.

The king has written a braid letter,
   And sign'd it wi' his hand;
And sent it to Sir Patrick Spence,
   Was walking on the sand.

The first line that Sir Patrick red,
   A loud lauch lauched he:
The next line that Sir Patrick red,
   The teir blinded his e'e.

O quha is this has don this deid,
   This ill deid don to me;
To send me out this time o' the yeir,
   To sail upon the se?

eldern] old   braid] broad, long

Mak haste, mak haste, my mirry men all,
   Our guid schip sails the morne.
O say na sae, my master deir,
   For I feir a deadlie storme.

Late, late yestreen I saw the new moone
   Wi' the auld moone in hir arme;
And I feir, I feir, my deir master,
   That we will com to harme.

O our Scots nobles wer richt laith
   To weet their cork-heil'd schoone;
Bot lang owre a' the play wer play'd,
   Thair hats they swam aboone.

O lang, lang may thair ladies sit
   Wi' thair fans into their hand,
Or eir they se Sir Patrick Spence
   Cum sailing to the land.

O lang, lang may the ladies stand
   Wi' thair gold kems in their hair,
Waiting for thair ain deir lords,
   For they'll se thame na mair.

Haf owre, haf owre to Aberdour,
   It 's fiftie fadom deip:
And thair lies guid Sir Patrick Spence,
   Wi' the Scots lords at his feit.

yestreen] last evening   laith] loth   owre] before   aboone] above   Or eir] ere ever   kems] combs   Haf owre] half-way over   Aberdour] on the north shore of the Firth of Forth

82. *Lamkin*

It 's Lamkin was a mason good
  As ever built wi' stane;
He built lord Wearie's castle,
  But payment got he nane.

O pay me, lord Wearie,
  Come, pay me my fee.
I canna pay you, Lamkin,
  For I maun gang o'er the sea.

O pay me now, lord Wearie,
  Come, pay me out o' hand.
I canna pay you, Lamkin,
  Unless I sell my land.

O gin ye winna pay me
  I here sall mak a vow,
Before that ye come hame again,
  Ye sall ha'e cause to rue.

stane] stone   lord Wearie] ? one of the Leslies, earls of Leven and
barons of Balwearie in Fife   maun gang] must go   out o'
hand] at once   gin] if   winna] won't

LAMKIN

Lord Wearie got a bonny ship
 To sail the saut sea faem;
Bade his lady weel the castle keep
 Ay till he should come hame.

But the nourice was a fause limmer
 As e'er hung on a tree;
She laid a plot wi' Lamkin
 Whan her lord was o'er the sea.

She laid a plot wi' Lamkin
 When the servants were awa',
Loot him in at a little shot window
 And brought him to the ha'.

O whare 's a' the men o' this house
 That ca' me Lamkin?
They're at the barnwell thrashing,
 'Twill be lang ere they come in.

And whare 's the women o' this house
 That ca' me Lamkin?
They're at the far well washing,
 'Twill be lang ere they come in.

And whare 's the bairns o' this house
 That ca' me Lamkin?
They're at the school reading,
 'Twill be night or they come hame.

saut] salt   faem] foam   nourice] nurse   limmer] jade
Loot] let   shot window] hinged window, casement

LAMKIN

O whare 's the lady o' this house
   That ca's me Lamkin?
She 's up in her bower sewing,
   But we soon can bring her down.

Then Lamkin 's tane a sharp knife
   That hang down by his gaire,
And he has gi'en the bonny babe
   A deep wound and a sair.

Then Lamkin he rocked
   And the fause nourice sang,
Till frae ilkae bore o' the cradle
   The red blood out sprang.

Then out it spak the lady
   As she stood on the stair:
What ails my bairn, nourice,
   That he 's greeting sae sair?

O still my bairn, nourice,
   O still him wi' the pap.
He winna still, lady,
   For this, nor for that.

O still my bairn, nourice,
   O still him wi' the wand.
He winna still, lady,
   For a' his father's land.

gaire] gown   ilkae bore] each crevice, hole   greeting] crying
wand] staff

O still my bairn, nourice,
   O still him wi' the bell.
He winna still, lady,
   Till ye come down yoursel.

O the firsten step she steppit,
   She steppit on a stane;
But the neisten step she steppit,
   She met him, Lamkin.

O mercy, mercy, Lamkin,
   Ha'e mercy upon me!
Though you've ta'en my young son's life
   Ye may let mysel be.

O sall I kill her, nourice?
   Or sall I let her be?
O kill her, kill her, Lamkin,
   For she ne'er was good to me.

O scour the bason, nourice,
   And mak it fair and clean,
For to keep this lady's heart's blood;
   For she 's come o' noble kin.

There need nae bason, Lamkin,
   Lat it run through the floor;
What better is the heart's blood
   O' the rich than o' the poor?

But ere three months were at an end
   Lord Wearie came again;
But dowie, dowie was his heart
   When first he came hame.

neisten] next   dowie] sorrowful

O wha's blood is this, he says,
   That lies in the châmer?
It is your lady's heart's blood,
   'Tis as clear as the lamer.

And wha's blood is this, he says,
   That lies in my ha'?
It is your young son's heart's blood,
   'Tis the clearest ava.

O sweetly sang the black-bird
   That sat upon the tree;
But sairer grat Lamkin
   When he was condemn'd to die.

And bonny sang the mavis
   Out o' the thorny brake;
But sairer grat the nourice
   When she was tied to the stake.

lamer] amber   ava] of all   grat] wept   mavis] thrush

83. *Hugh of Lincoln*

FOUR AND TWENTY bonny boys
   Were playing at the ba';
And by it came him, sweet sir Hugh,
   And he play'd o'er them a'.

He kick'd the ba' with his right foot
   And catch'd it wi' his knee;
And throuch-and-thro' the Jew's window
   He gar'd the bonny ba' flee.

ba'] football   play'd o'er] surpassed   gar'd ... flee] made ... fly

He 's doen him to the Jew's castell
   And walk'd it round about,
And there he saw the Jew's daughter
   At the window looking out.

Throw down the ba', ye Jew's daughter,
   Throw down the ba' to me.
Never a bit, says the Jew's daughter,
   Till up to me come ye.

How will I come up? How can I come up?
   How can I come to thee?
For as ye did to my auld father,
   The same ye'll do to me.

She 's gane till her father's garden
   And pu'd an apple red and green;
'Twas a' to wyle him, sweet sir Hugh,
   And to entice him in.

She 's led him in through ae dark door,
   And sae has she thro' nine;
She 's laid him on a dressing table
   And stickit him like a swine.

And first came out the thick, thick blood,
   And syne came out the thin;
And syne came out the bonny heart's blood;
   There was nae mair within.

---

doen him] taken himself   stickit] stabbed in the throat

She 's row'd him in a cake o' lead,
    Bade him lie still and sleep;
She 's thrown him in Our Lady's draw well,
    Was fifty fathom deep.

When bells were rung and mass was sung
    And a' the bairns came hame,
When every lady gat hame her son,
    The Lady Maisry gat nane.

She 's ta'en her mantle her about,
    Her coffer by the hand,
And she 's gane out to seek her son
    And wander'd o'er the land.

She 's doen her to the Jew's castell
    Where a' were fast asleep;
Gin ye be there, my sweet sir Hugh,
    I pray you to me speak.

She 's doen her to the Jew's garden,
    Thought he had been gathering fruit;
Gin ye be there, my sweet sir Hugh,
    I pray you to me speak.

She near'd Our Lady's deep draw well
    Was fifty fathom deep;
Whare'er ye be, my sweet sir Hugh,
    I pray you to me speak.

row'd] wrapped   cake] sheet, layer   draw well] well from
which water is drawn in a bucket   coffer] strongbox   Gin] if

Gae hame, gae hame, my mither dear,
    Prepare my winding sheet;
And at the back o' merry Lincoln
    The morn I will you meet.

Now lady Maisry is gane hame,
    Made him a winding sheet;
And at the back o' merry Lincoln
    The dead corpse did her meet.

And a' the bells o' merry Lincoln
    Without men's hands were rung,
And a' the books o' merry Lincoln
    Were read without man's tongue;
And ne'er was such a burial
    Sin Adam's days begun.

The morn] tomorrow   **Sin]** since

84. *Young Waters*

ABOUT Yule, quhen the wind blew cule
  And the round tables began,
A! there is cum to our king's court
  Mony a well-favour'd man.

The queen luikt owre the castle wa',
  Beheld baith dale and down,
And then she saw young Waters
  Cum riding to the town.

His footmen they did rin before,
  His horsemen rade behind,
Ane mantel of the burning gowd
  Did keip him frae the wind.

round tables] gatherings of knights   gowd] gold

Gowden graith'd his horse before
   And siller shod behind,
The horse yo[u]ng Waters rade upon
   Was fleeter than the wind.

But then spake a wylie lord,
   Unto the queen said he:
O tell me quha's the fairest face
   Rides in the company.

I've sene lord and I've sene laird
   And knights of high degree,
Bot a fairer face than young Waters
   Mine eyne did never see.

Out then spack the jealous king
   (And an angry man was he):
O if he had been twice as fair
   You micht have excepted me.

You're neither laird nor lord, she says,
   Bot the king that wears the crown;
Ther is not a knight in fair Scotland
   Bot to thee maun bow down.

For a' that she could do or say
   Appeas'd he wad nae bee;
Bot for the words which she had said
   Young Waters he maun dee.

graith'd] harnessed   laird] gentleman   maun] must

They hae ta'en young Waters and
  Put fetters to his feet;
They hae ta'en young Waters and
  Thrown him in dungeon deep.

Aft I have ridden thro' Stirling town
  In the wind bot and the weit,
Bot I neir rade thro' Stirling town
  Wi' fetters at my feet.

Aft have I ridden thro' Stirling town
  In the wind bot and the rain,
Bot I neir rade thro' Stirling town
  Neir to return again.

They hae ta'en to the heiding-hill
  His young son in his craddle,
And they hae ta'en to the heiding-hill
  His horse bot and his saddle.

They hae ta'en to the heiding-hill
  His lady fair to see,
And for the words the Queen had spoke
  Young Waters he did dee.

Aft] often   bot and] and also   weit] rain   heiding-hill]
hill of execution

85. *Lord Douglas*

I WAS a lady of high renown
    As lived in the north countrie;
I was a lady of high renown
    Whan Earl Douglas loved me.

Whan we came through Glasgow toun
    We war a comely sight to see;
My gude lord in velvet green
    And I mysel in cramasie.

Whan we cam to Douglas toun
    We war a fine sight to behold;
My gude lord in cramasie
    And I mysel in shining gold.

Whan that my auld son was born
    And set upon the nurse's knee,
I was as happy a woman as e'er was born,
    And my gude lord he loved me.

cramasie] crimson cloth   Douglas toun] in Lanarkshire   auld]
eldest

But oh, an my young son was born
   And set upon the nurse's knee,
And I mysel war dead and gane,
   For a maid again I'll never be.

There cam a man into this house
   And Jamie Lockhart was his name;
And it was told to my gude lord
   That I was in the bed wi' him.

There cam anither to this house
   And a bad friend he was to me;
He put Jamie's shoon below my bed-stock,
   And bade my gude lord come and see.

O wae be unto thee, Blackwood,
   And ae an ill death may ye dee;
For ye was the first and the foremost man
   That parted my gude lord and me.

Whan my gude lord cam in my room
   This grit falsehood for to see,
He turn'd about and, wi' a gloom,
   He straucht did tak farewell o' me.

O fare thee well, my once lovely maid,
   O fare thee well, once dear to me;
O fare thee well, my once lovely maid,
   For wi' me again ye sall never be.

---

an] if   shoon] shoes   bed-stock] beam along the front of
a bed   Blackwood] William Lawrie, Douglas's chamberlain
gloom] scowl   straucht] at once

Sit doun, sit doun, Jamie Douglas,
  Sit thee doun and dine wi' me,
And I'll set thee on a chair of gold
  And a silver towel on thy knee.

Whan cockle-shells turn silver bells,
  And mussels they bud on a tree,
Whan frost and snaw turns fire to burn,
  Then I'll sit down and dine wi' thee.

O wae be unto thee, Blackwood,
  And ae an ill death may ye dee;
Ye war the first and the foremost man
  That parted my gude lord and me.

Whan my father he heard word
  That my gude lord had forsaken me,
He sent fifty o' his brisk dragoons
  To fesh me hame to my ain countrie.

That morning before I did go
  My bonny palace for to leave,
I went into my gude lord's room,
  But alas, he wad na speak to me.

Fare thee well, Jamie Douglas,
  Fare thee well, my ever dear to me;
Fare thee well, Jamie Douglas,
  Be kind to the three babes I've born to thee.

———

fesh] fetch

Waly, Waly

O Waly, Waly, up yon Bank,
   And Waly, Waly, down yon Brae;
And Waly by yon River's side
   Where my Love and I was wont to gae.

Waly, Waly, gin Love be bonny,
   A little while when it is new,
But when it's auld it waxes cauld
   And wears away like Morning Dew.

I leant my Back unto an Aik,
   I thought it was a trusty Tree;
But first it bow'd, and sine it brake,
   And sae did my fause Love to me.

When Cockle-shells turn siller Bells,
   And Muscles grow on ev'ry Tree,
When Frost and Snaw shall warm us a',
   Then shall my Love prove true to me.

Now *Arthur-Seat* shall be my Bed,
   The Sheets shall ne'er be fyl'd by me;
Saint *Anton*'s Well shall be my Drink,
   Since my true Love has forsaken me.

O *Martinmas* Wind, when wilt thou blaw
   And shake the green Leaves off the Tree?
O gentle Death, when wilt thou come
   And take a Life that wearies me?

Waly] *exclam. of sorrow*   gin] if, that   Aik] oak   *Arthur-Seat*] hill in Edinburgh   fyl'd] soiled, used   Saint *Anton*'s Well] below Arthur's Seat   *Martinmas*] i.e. November

'Tis not the Frost that freezes fell,
　Nor blawing Snaw's Inclemency,
'Tis not sic Cauld that makes me cry,
　But my Love's Heart grown cauld to me.

When we came in by *Glasgow* Town
　We were a comely Sight to see;
My Love was cled in the black Velvet
　And I my sell in Cramasie.

But had I wist before I kiss'd
　That Love had been sae ill to win,
I'd lock'd my Heart in a Case of Gold
　And pin'd it with a silver Pin.

Oh, oh! if my young Babe were born
　And set upon the Nurse's knee,
And I my sell were dead and gane;
　For a Maid again I'll never be.

86. *Mary Hamilton*

O MARY HAMILTON to the kirk is gane
　Wi' ribbons in her hair;
An' the king thocht mair o' Marie
　Then onie that were there.

thocht] thought　　　onie] any

MARY HAMILTON

Mary Hamilton 's to the preaching gane
   Wi' ribbons on her breast;
An' the king thocht mair o' Marie
   Than he thocht o' the priest.

Syne word is thro' the palace gane,
   I heard it tauld yestreen,
The king loes Mary Hamilton
   Mair than he loes his queen.

A sad tale thro' the town is gaen,
   A sad tale on the morrow:
Oh Mary Hamilton has born a babe
   And slain it in her sorrow.

And down then cam the auld queen,
   Goud tassels tied her hair:
What did ye wi' the wee wee bairn
   That I heard greet sae sair?

There ne'er was a bairn into my room,
   An' as little designs to be;
'T was but a stitch o' my sair side
   Cam owre my fair bodie.

Rise up now, Marie, quo' the queen,
   Rise up, an' come wi' me,
For we maun ride to Holyrood
   A gay wedding to see.

Syne] then   yestreen] last evening   loes] loves   gaen]
gone   Goud] gold   greet] cry   owre] over   maun]
must   Holyrood] royal palace in Edinburgh

The queen was drest in scarlet fine,
    Her maidens all in green;
An' every town that they cam thro'
    Took Marie for the queen.

But little wist Marie Hamilton
    As she rode oure the lea
That she was gaun to Edinbro' town
    Her doom to hear and dree.

When she cam to the Netherbow Port
    She laughed loud laughters three;
But when she reached the gallows-tree
    The tears blinded her e'e.

Yestreen the queen had four Maries,
    The nicht she'll hae but three;
There's Marie Seaton, an' Marie Beaton,
    An' Marie Carmichael, an' me.

Oh aften have I dressed my queen
    An' put gowd in her hair;
The gallows-tree is my reward
    An' shame maun be my share.

Oh aften hae I dressed my queen
    An' saft, saft made her bed;
An' now I've got for my reward
    The gallows-tree to tread.

wist] knew   lea] pasture   gaun] going   dree] suffer
Netherbow Port] gateway at the head of the Canongate leading down to
Holyrood   The nicht] tonight   gowd] gold

There's a health to all gallant sailors
  That sail upon the sea:
Oh never let on to my father and mither
  The death that I maun dee.

An' I charge ye, all ye mariners,
  When ye sail owre the main,
Let neither my father nor mither know
  But that I'm comin hame.

Oh little did my mither ken,
  That day she cradled me,
What lands I was to tread in
  Or what death I should dee.

let on] disclose

87. Clyde's Waters

YOUNG Willie stands in his stable door,
  And combing down his steed;
And looking through his white fingers,
  His nose began to bleed;
And looking through his white fingers,
  His nose began to bleed.

331

Gie corn to my horse, mother,
  And meat unto my man,
For I'm awa to Maggie's bowers;
  I'll win or she lie doon.

Oh bide this nicht wi' me, Willie,
  Oh bide this nicht wi' me;
The besten cock o' a' the reest
  At your supper shall be.

A' your cocks an' a' your reests
  I value nae a prin;
But I'll awa to Maggie's bowers,
  I'll win or she lie doon.

Oh stay at hame, my Willie dear,
  Oh stay at hame wi' me,
And the best fed lamb in a' my flock
  Shall be weel dressed for thee.

A' your sheep an' a' your flocks
  I value nae a prin;
But I'll awa to Maggie's bowers,
  I'll win or she lie doon.

Oh an ye gang to Maggie's bowers
  Sae sair against my will,
The deepest pot in Clyde's waters
  My malison ye'se feel.

win] reach **or]** ere **bide]** stay **reest]** roost **prin]**
pin **an]** if **pot]** pit, pool **malison]** curse **ye'se]** you
shall

332

It's I've a steed in my stable
    Cost me twice twenty pound,
And I'll put trust in his four legs
    To carry me safe to land.

As he rade owre yon high high hill
    And doon yon dreary glen,
The noise that was in Clyde's waters
    Wad feared a thousand men.

Oh spare me, spare me, Clyde's waters,
    Oh spare me as I gang;
Make me your wrack as I come back,
    But spare me as I gang.

Then he is on to Maggie's bowers,
    And tirlin' at the pin:
Oh sleep ye, wauk ye, Maggie dear,
    Oh rise and lat me in.

Oh wha is that at my bower door,
    And tirlin' at the pin?
It's I, it's I, your true love Willie,
    Oh rise and lat me in.

I hae few lovers thereout, thereout,
    As few hae I therein;
The besten love that e'er I had
    He was here just late yestreen.

Wad feared] would have frightened   wrack] wreckage on the
flood   tirlin'] rattling   pin] door-knocker, latch   yestreen]
last evening

The meanest sta' in a' your stable
  For my steed to stand in;
The soberest bed in a' your house
  Myself for to lie in;
For my boots are fu' o' Clyde's water
  And I'm shivering at the chin.

My stables they are fu' o' horse,
  And my barns fu' o' hay;
My bowers are fu' o' gentlemen,
  And they'll nae remove till day.

He turned his horse right round about,
  Wi' the saut tear in his e'e:
I never thocht to come here this nicht,
  And be denied by thee.

Oh fare-ye-weel, ye fause Maggie,
  Since better maunna be;
I've gotten my mither's malison
  This nicht, comin' to thee.

As he rade owre yon high high hill,
  And down yon dreary glen,
The rush that was in Clyde's waters
  Took Willie's cane frae him.

As Willie he sat saddle owre
  To catch the cane again,
The rush that ran in Clyde's waters
  Took Willie's hat frae him.

sta'] stall   **saut]** salt

He leaned him owre his saddle bow
   To catch his hat through force,
But the rush that ran in Clyde's waters
   Took Willie frae his horse.

His brither stood upo' the bank,
   Cries, Willie, will ye droon?
Oh, haud ye to your high horse heid,
   He'll learn ye how to soom.

How can I haud to my horse heid
   And learn how to soom?
I've gotten my mither's malison,
   It's here that I maun droon.

It's up arose his Maggie dear,
   All in a frightful dream:
I dreamt that Willie was here this nicht,
   And ye wadna lat him in.

Go to your bed, my daughter dear,
   Lie doon and tak' your rest;
Sin' your true love was at our yetts
   It's but twa quarters past.

To her chamber she has gane wi' speed,
   And quickly pat she on;
And she is aff to Clyde's waters
   As fast as she can run.

---

droon] drown   soom] swim   Sin'] since   yetts] gates
pat . . . on] dressed

When she came to the water's side
   Right boldly stepped she in;
And loud her true love's name she called,
   But louder blew the win'.

The firsten step that she stept in,
   She steppit to the queet;
Ohon, alas, said that lady,
   This water's wondrous deep.

The nexten step that she wade in,
   She wadit to the knee;
Says she, I would wade further in,
   Gin my love I could see.

The nexten step that she wade in,
   She wadit to the chin;
The deepest pot in Clyde's waters
   She got sweet Willie in.

Ye've had a cruel mither, Willie,
   And I have had anither;
But we shall sleep in Clyde's waters
   Like sister and like brither.

queet] ankle

88. *Young Benjie*

Of a' the maids o' fair Scotland
    The fairest was Marjorie;
And Young Benjie was her ae true love,
    And a dear true love was he.

And wow! but they were lovers dear
    And loved fu' constantlie;
But aye the mair when they fell out
    The sairer was their plea.

And they hae quarrelled on a day
    Till Marjorie's heart grew wae,
And she said she'd chuse another luve
    And let Young Benjie gae.

And he was stout and proud-hearted,
    And thought o't bitterlie,
And he's ga'en by the wan moon-light
    To meet his Marjorie.

O open, open, my true love,
    O open and let me in:
I dare na open, Young Benjie,
    My three brothers are within.

ae] one   stout] haughty

337

Ye lied, ye lied, ye bonny burd,
   Sae loud's I hear ye lie;
As I came by the Lowden banks
   They bade gude e'en to me.

But fare ye weel, my ae fause love,
   That I hae loved sae lang;
It sets ye chuse another love
   And let Young Benjie gang.

Then Marjorie turned her round about,
   The tear blinding her e'e:
I darena, darena let thee in
   But I'll come down to thee.

Then saft she smiled, and said to him,
   O what ill hae I done?
He took her in his armis twa
   And threw her o'er the linn.

The stream was strang, the maid was stout,
   And laith, laith to be dang,
But ere she wan the Lowden banks
   Her fair colour was wan.

Then up bespak her eldest brother,
   O see na ye what I see?
And out then spak her second brother,
   It's our sister Marjorie.

burd] lass   Lowden] ? Loudoun, on the River Irvine, Ayrshire
sets] suits   linn] waterfall   laith] loth   dang] defeated
wan] reached

Out then spak her eldest brother,
   O how shall we her ken?
And out then spak her youngest brother,
   There's a honey mark on her chin.

Then they've taen up the comely corpse
   And laid it on the ground:
O wha has killed our ae sister,
   And how can he be found?

The night it is her low lykewake,
   The morn her burial day,
And we maun watch at mirk midnight
   And hear what she will say.

Wi' doors ajar, and candle light,
   And torches burning clear,
The streikit corpse, till still midnight,
   They waked, but naething hear.

About the middle o' the night
   The cocks began to craw,
And at the dead hour o' the night
   The corpse began to thraw.

O wha has done thee wrang, sister,
   Or dared the deadly sin?
Wha was sae stout, and feared nae dout,
   As thraw ye o'er the linn?

honey mark] birthmark, mole   lykewake] vigil over a corpse
maun] must   streikit] stretched, laid out   thraw] contort
stout] bold   dout] fear

YOUNG BENJIE

Young Benjie was the first ae man
    I laid my love upon;
He was sae stout and proud-hearted,
    He threw me o'er the linn.

Sall we Young Benjie head, sister?
    Sall we Young Benjie hang?
Or sall we pike out his twa gray e'en
    And punish him ere he gang?

Ye mauna Benjie head, brothers,
    Ye mauna Benjie hang;
But ye maun pike out his twa grey e'en
    And punish him ere he gang.

Tie a green gravat round his neck
    And lead him out and in,
And the best ae servant about your house
    To wait Young Benjie on.

And ay at every seven years' end
    Ye'll tak him to the linn,
For that's the penance he maun drie
    To scug his deadly sin.

head] behead   gang] go   mauna] must not   gravat] kerchief
drie] suffer   scug] expiate

89. *Bonnie George Campbell*

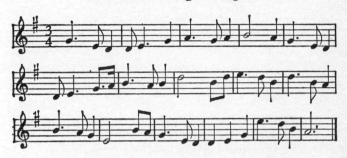

Hie upon Hielands and laigh upon Tay
Bonnie George Campbell rode out on a day;
He saddled, he bridled, and gallant rode he,
And hame cam his guid horse, but never cam he.

Out cam his mother dear greeting fu' sair,
And out cam his bonnie bryde riving her hair;
My meadow lies green and my corn is unshorn,
My barn is to build and my baby's unborn.

Saddled and bridled and booted rode he,
A plume in his helmet, a sword at his knee;
But toom cam his saddle all bloody to see;
Oh hame cam his guid horse, but never cam he.

laigh] low   riving] tearing   toom] empty

90. *The Bailiff's Daughter of Islington*

THERE was a youthe, and a well-beloved youthe,
    And he was a squires son:
He loved the bayliffes daughter deare,
    That lived in Islington.

Yet she was coye and would not believe
    That he did love her soe,
Noe nor at any time would she
    Any countenance to him showe.

But when his friendes did understand
    His fond and foolish minde,
They sent him up to faire London
    An apprentice for to binde.

And when he had been seven long yeares,
    And never his love could see:
Many a teare have I shed for her sake,
    When she little thought of mee.

Then all the maids of Islington
    Went forth to sport and playe,
All but the bayliffes daughter deare;
    She secretly stole awaye.

binde] indenture (him)

She pulled off her gowne of greene,
   And put on ragged attire,
And to faire London she would go
   Her true love to enquire.

And as she went along the high road,
   The weather being hot and drye,
She sat her downe upon a green bank,
   And her true love came riding bye.

She started up, with a colour soe redd,
   Catching hold of his bridle-reine;
One penny, one penny, kind sir, she sayd,
   Will ease me of much paine.

Before I give you one penny, sweet-heart,
   Praye tell me where you were borne.
At Islington, kind sir, sayd shee,
   Where I have had many a scorne.

I prythee, sweet-heart, then tell to mee,
   O tell me, whether you knowe
The bayliffes daughter of Islington:
   She is dead, sir, long agoe.

If she be dead, then take my horse,
   My saddle and bridle also;
For I will into some farr countrye,
   Where noe man shall me knowe.

O staye, O staye, thou goodlye youthe,
   She standeth by thy side;
She is here alive, she is not dead,
   And readye to be thy bride.

O farewell griefe, and welcome joye,
    Ten thousand times therefore;
For nowe I have founde mine owne true love,
    Whom I thought I should never see more.

91. *The Duke o' Athole's Nurse*

As I gaed in by the Duke o' Athole's gates,
    I heard his yule-nurse singin';
And aye as she sang and her bonnie voice rang,
    Till hills and dales were ringin'.

Oh, I am the bonnie Duke o' Athole's nurse,
    And the post it does weel become me;
But I wad gie a' my half-year's fee
    For a kiss and a sicht o' my Johnnie.

He leant him inowre his saddle bow,
    And he has gien her kisses mony;
Says, Keep weel, keep weel your half-year's fee,
    Ye'll get twa sichts o' your Johnnie.

wad gie] would give   inowre] over

But ye hae my heart and another has my hand,
    And what can I do wi' ye?
Gin I hae your heart and another has your hand,
    What the better will I be o' ye?

But ye'll go down to yonder alehouse,
    And drink or the day be a-dawnin',
And spare nae the beer tho' it be dear,
    And the wine keep constantly drawin';
And gin I be a woman, as surely as I am,
    I will come and clear ye o' your lawin'.

Her seven brothers were standin' nearby,
    And they heard them thus talkin',
And they hae said among themselves—
    We'll go and clear his lawin'.

So he went down to yonder alehouse,
    And drank till the day was a-dawnin';
And he spared nae the beer tho' it was dear,
    And the wine he kept constantly drawin'.

But he lookit over the castle-wa',
    To see gin the day was a-dawnin',
And there he spied seven weel-armed men,
    They were comin' wi' their swords weel drawn.

O landlady, O landlady, what shall I do?
    For my life it is nae worth a farthin';
For here they come seven weel-armed men;
    I'll be dead or the day be a-dawnin'.

Gin] if   or] ere   lawin'] reckoning

But she's casten off her petticoat,
  Likewise her goon and her apron;
And she has gien him the mutch frae her heid,
  And she set the young squ[i]re to the bakin'.

Oh, when they came up to the gates,
  Sae loudly as they rappit;
And when they came up to the door,
  Sae loudly as they chappit.

Oh, cam' there a stranger here last nicht,
  To drink or the day was a-dawnin'?
Come, show us the room that the stranger is in,
  For we're come to clear his lawin'.

Oh, there cam' a stranger here last nicht,
  But he went ere the day was a-dawnin',
For he bocht but a pint, and he paid it ere he went,
  So he didna leave ony lawin'.

But they socht him up and they socht him doon,
  And they spared nae the feather beds a-turnin',
And aye as they gaed but, and aye as they gaed ben,
  They said, Bonnie lassie, are ye bakin'?

They socht him up and they socht him doon,
  And spared nae the curtains a-rivin',
And aye as the auld wife gaed but and ben,
  She scolded her maid at the bakin';
And she said, I have had mony a maid,
  But the marrows o' you I ne'er had bakin'.

mutch] linen cap   chappit] knocked   but ... ben] to ... fro
a-rivin'] tearing   marrows] mates, likes

They socht him up and they socht him doon,
    Thro' kitchie and ha' a-rakin',
But for a' that they ca'd, and for a' that they socht,
    They left the young squ[i]re busy bakin'.

kitchie] kitchen   a-rakin'] rampaging

92. *The Lowlands of Holland*

New Holland is a barren place, in it there grows no
  grain,
Nor any habitation wherein for to remain;
But the sugar canes are plenty and the wine draps frae the
  tree,
And the Lowlands of Holland has twin'd my Love and
  me.

has twin'd] have parted

My Love has built a bony ship, and set her on the Sea,
With seven score good Mariners to bear her Company;
There 's threescore is sunk and threescore dead at Sea
And the Lowlands of Holland has twin'd my Love and
    me.

My Love he built another ship and set her on the Main,
And nane but twenty Mariners for to bring her hame;
But the weary wind began to rise and the sea began to
    rout,
My love then and his bonny ship turn'd withershins
    about.

There shall neither Coif come on my head nor Comb
    come on my hair,
There shall neither Coal nor candle light shine in my
    Bower mair,
Nor will I love another one until the day I die,
For I never lov'd a Love but one and he 's drowned in the
    Sea.

O had your tongue my Daughter dear, be still and be con-
    tent,
There are mair Lads in Galloway, ye need nae sair
    lament;
O! there is none in Gallow, there 's none at a' for me,
For I never lov'd a Love but one and he 's drowned in
    the Sea.

rout] roar   withershins] the wrong way, west to east   Coif]
cap

93. *The Trumpeter of Fyvie*

At Fyvie's yetts there grows a flower,
   It grows baith braid and bonny;
There's a daisie in the midst o' it,
   And it's ca'd by Andrew Lammie.

O gin that flower war in my breast
   For the love I bear the laddie,
I wad kiss it and I wad clap it
   And daut it for Andrew Lammie.

The first time me and my love met
   Was in the woods of Fyvie;
He kissed my lips five thousand times
   And ay he ca'd me bonny,
And a' the answer he gat frae me
   Was, My bonny Andrew Lammie!

Fyvie] a castle about 20 miles north-east of Aberdeen   yetts] gates
braid] large   ca'd by] named after   gin] if   clap] stroke
daut] fondle

Love, I maun gang to Edinburgh,
    Love, I maun gang and leave thee.
I sighed right sair and said nae mair
    But, O gin I were wi' ye.

But true and trusty will I be
    As I am Andrew Lammie;
I'll never kiss a woman's mouth
    Till I come back and see thee.

And true and trusty will I be
    As I am Tiftie's Annie;
I'll never kiss a man again
    Till ye come back and see me.

Syne he's come back frae Edinburgh
    To the bonny hows o' Fyvie,
And ay his face to the nor-east
    To look for Tiftie's Annie.

I ha'e a love in Edinburgh,
    Sae ha'e I intill Leith, man;
I ha'e a love intill Montrose,
    Sae ha'e I in Dalkeith, man.

And east and west where'er I go
    My love she's always wi' me;
For east and west where'er I go
    My love she dwells in Fyvie.

My love possesses a' my heart,
    Nae pen can e'er indite her;
She's ay sae stately as she goes
    That I see nae mae like her.

maun gang] must go   Tiftie's] i.e. the miller's   hows] glens

But Tiftie winna gi'e consent
   His dochter me to marry,
Because she has five thousand marks
   And I have not a penny.

Love pines away, love dwines away,
   Love, love decays the body;
For love o' thee, oh I must die:
   Adieu, my bonny Annie!

Her mither raise out o' her bed
   And ca'd on baith her women:
What ails ye, Annie, my dochter dear?
   O Annie, was ye dreamin'?

What dule disturb'd my dochter's sleep,
   O tell to me, my Annie?
She sighed right sair, and said nae mair
   But, O for Andrew Lammie!

Her father beat her cruellie,
   Sae also did her mither;
Her sisters sair did scoff at her,
   But wae betide her brother!

Her brother beat her cruellie,
   Till his straiks they werena canny;
He brak her back and he beat her sides
   For the sake o' Andrew Lammie.

O fie, O fie, my brother dear,
   The gentlemen 'll shame ye;
The laird o' Fyvie he's gaun by
   And he'll come in and see me.

dule] sorrow   straiks] blows   canny] light   gaun] going

And he'll kiss me and he'll clap me
   And he will speer what ails me;
And I will answer him again,
   It's a' for Andrew Lammie.

Her sisters they stood in the door,
   Sair griev'd her wi' their folly;
O sister dear, come to the door,
   Your cow is lowin' on you.

O fie, O fie, my sister dear,
   Grieve me not wi' your folly;
I'd rather hear the trumpet sound
   Than a' the kye o' Fyvie.

Love pines away, love dwines away,
   Love, love decays the body;
For love o' thee now I maun die:
   Adieu to Andrew Lammie!

But Tiftie 's wrote a braid letter
   And sent it into Tyvie
Saying, His daughter was bewitch'd
   By bonny Andrew Lammie.

Now Tiftie, ye maun gi'e consent
   And lat the lassie marry.—
I'll never, never gi'e consent
   To the Trumpeter of Fyvie.

When Fyvie looked the letter on
   He was baith sad and sorry;
Says, The bonniest lass o' the country-side
   Has died for Andrew Lammie.

speer] ask   lowin' on] lowing for   kye] cows   braid] long

O Andrew's gane to the house-top
    O' the bonny house o' Fyvie;
He 's blawn his horn baith loud and shill
    O'er the lawland leas o' Fyvie:

Mony a time ha'e I walk'd a' night
    And never yet was weary;
But now I may walk wae my lane
    For I'll never see my deary.

Love pines away, love dwines away,
    Love, love decays the body;
For the love o' thee now I maun die:
    I come, my bonnie Annie!

leas] meadows   wae my lane] sorrowful by myself

94. *Bonny Barbara Allan*

IT was in and about the Martinmas time,
    When the green leaves were a-falling,
That Sir John Græme in the west country
    Fell in love with Barbara Allan.

He sent his man down through the town,
    To the place where she was dwelling,
O haste, and come to my master dear,
    Gin ye be Barbara Allan.

O hooly, hooly rose she up,
  To the place where he was lying,
And when she drew the curtain by,
  Young man, I think you're dying.

O it 's I'm sick, and very very sick,
  And 'tis a' for Barbara Allan.
O the better for me ye's never be,
  Tho' your heart's blood were a-spilling.

O dinna ye mind, young man, said she,
  When ye was in the tavern a-drinking,
That ye made the healths gae round and round,
  And slighted Barbara Allan?

He turn'd his face unto the wall,
  And death was with him dealing;
Adieu, adieu, my dear friends all,
  And be kind to Barbara Allan.

And slowly, slowly raise she up,
  And slowly, slowly left him;
And sighing, said, she cou'd not stay,
  Since death of life had reft him.

She had not gane a mile but twa,
  When she heard the dead-bell ringing,
And every jow that the dead-bell gied,
  It cry'd, Wo to Barbara Allan.

O mother, mother, make my bed,
  O make it saft and narrow,
Since my love dy'd for me to-day,
  I'll die for him to-morrow.

hooly] gently, softly   dinna ye mind] don't you remember
jow] toll   gied] gave

95. *The Bonny Brown Girl*

I AM as brown as brown can be,
    My Eyes as black as a Sloe;
I am as brisk as a Nightingale,
    And as wilde as any Doe.

My Love has sent me a Love-Letter
    Not far from yonder Town,
That he could not fancy me
    Because I was so brown.

I sent him his Letter back again,
    For his Love I valu'd not,
Whether that he could fancy me,
    Or whether he could not.

He sent me his Letter back again
    That he lay dangerous sick;
That I might then go speedily
    To give him up his Eilk.

Now you shall hear what Love she had
    Then for this Love-sick Man;
She was a whole long Summer's Day
    In a Mile agoing on.

When she came to her Love's Bed-side
    Where he lay dangerous sick,
She could not for Laughing stand
    Upright upon her Feet.

brown] dark-complexioned   Eilk] ? ilk, same (love)

She had a white Wand all in her Hand
And smooth'd it all on his Breast:
In Faith and Troth come pardon me,
I hope your Soul's at Rest.

I'll do as much for my true Love
As other Maidens may;
I'll dance and sing on my Love's Grave
A whole Twelvemonth and a Day.

96. *The Bewick and the Græme*

GUDE Lord Græme is to Carlisle gane,
Sir Robert Bewick there met he;
And arm in arm to the wine they did go
And they drank till they were baith merrie.

Gude Lord Græme has ta'en up the cup:
Sir Robert Bewick, and here's to thee;
And here's to our twa sons at hame;
For they like us best in our ain countrie.

O were your son a lad like mine
   And learn'd some books that he could read,
They might hae been twa brethren bauld
   And they might hae bragg'd the Border side.

But your son 's a lad, and he 's but bad,
   And billie to my son he canna be;
[For my son Bewick can baith write and read,
   And sure I am that cannot he.]

Ye sent him to the schools and he wadna learn,
   Ye bought him books and he wadna read.—
But my blessing shall he never earn
   Till I see how his arm can defend his head.

Gude Lord Græme has a reckoning call'd,
   A reckoning then called he;
And he paid a crown and it went roun'—
   It was all for the gude wine and free.

And he has to the stable gane
   Where there stude thirty steeds and three;
He 's ta'en his ain horse amang them a'
   And hame he rade sae manfullie.

Welcome, my auld father, said Christie Græme,
   But where sae lang frae hame were ye?
It 's I hae been at Carlisle town,
   And a baffled man by thee I be.

bragg'd] challenged, defied   billie] comrade   wadna] would
not   free] fine   baffled] disgraced

I hae been at Carlisle town
   Where Sir Robert Bewick he met me;
He says ye're a lad, and ye are but bad,
   And billie to his son ye canna be.

I sent ye to the schools and ye wadna learn,
   I bought ye books and ye wadna read;
Therefore my blessing ye shall never earn
   Till I see with Bewick thou save thy head.

Now God forbid, my auld father,
   That ever sic a thing suld be;
Billie Bewick was my master and I was his scholar,
   And aye sae weel as he learned me.

O hald thy tongue, thou limmer loon,
   And of thy talking let me be;
If thou disna end me this quarrel soon
   There is my glove, I'll fight wi' thee.

Then Christie Græme he stooped low,
   Unto the ground you shall understand:
O father put on your glove again,
   The wind has blown it from your hand.

What 's that thou says, thou limmer loon,
   How dares thou stand to speak to me?
If thou do not end this quarrel soon,
   There 's my right hand, thou shalt fight with me.

Then Christie Græme 's to his chamber gane
   To consider weel what then should be:
Whether he should fight with his auld father
   Or with his billie Bewick he.

limmer loon] rascally rogue   disna] do not

If I suld kill my billie dear
  God's blessing I shall never win;
But if I strike at my auld father
  I think 'twould be a mortal sin.

But if I kill my billie dear
  It is God's will, so let it be;
But I make a vow ere I gang frae hame
  That I shall be the next man's dee.

Then he's put on his back a gude auld jack
  And on his head a cap of steel,
And sword and buckler by his side;
  O gin he did not become them weel!

We'll leave off talking of Christie Græme
  And talk of him again belyve;
And we will talk of bonnie Bewick
  Where he was teaching his scholars five.

When he had taught them well to fence
  And handle swords without any doubt,
He took his sword under his arm
  And he walk'd his father's close about.

He looked atween him and the sun,
  And a' to see what there might be,
Till he spied a man in armour bright
  Was riding that way most hastilie.

O wha is yon that cam this way,
  Sae hastilie that hither came?
I think it be my brother dear—
  I think it be young Christie Græme.

win] gain   dee] death   jack] short mail coat   buckler]
small round shield   belyve] soon   close] courtyard

Ye're welcome here, my billie dear,
   And thrice ye're welcome unto me.—
But I'm wae to say I've seen the day
   When I am come to fight wi' thee;

My father's gane to Carlisle town,
   Wi' your father Bewick there met he;
He says I'm a lad and I am but bad,
   And a baffled man I trow I be.

He sent me to schools and I wadna learn,
   He gae me books and I wadna read;
Sae my father's blessing I'll never earn
   Till he see how my arm can guard my head.

O God forbid, my billie dear,
   That ever such a thing suld be;
We'll take three men on either side
   And see if we can our fathers agree.

Oh haud thy tongue now, billie Bewick,
   And of thy talking let me be;
But if thou 'rt a man, as I'm sure thou art,
   Come o'er the dyke and fight wi' me.

But I hae nae harness, billie, on my back,
   As weel I see there is on thine.—
But as little harness as is on thy back,
   As little, billie, shall be on mine.

Then he 's thrown off his coat o' mail,
   His cap o' steel awa flung he;
He stuck his spear into the ground
   And he tied his horse unto a tree.

wae] sorry   harness] armour

Then Bewick has thrawn aff his cloak,
   And 's psalter-book frae 's hand flung he;
He laid his hand upon the dyke,
   And ower he lap most manfullie.

O they hae fought for twa lang hours;
   When twa lang hours were come and gane
The sweat drapp'd fast frae aff them baith,
   But a drop o' blude could not be seen.

Till Græme ga'e Bewick an akward stroke,
   An akward stroke strucken sickerlie;
He has hit him under the left breast,
   And dead-wounded to the ground fell he.

Rise up, rise up now, billie dear,
   Arise and speak three words to me;
Whether thou 's gotten thy deadly wound,
   Or if God and good leeching may succour thee?

O horse, O horse now, billie Græme,
   And get thee far from hence with speed,
And get thee out of this country
   That none may know who has done the deed.

O I have slain thee, billie Bewick,
   If this be true thou tellest to me;
But I made a vow ere I came frae hame
   That aye the next man I wad be.

He has pitched his sword in a moodie hill,
   And he has leap'd twenty lang feet and three,
And on his ain sword's point he lap,
   And dead upon the ground fell he.

ower he lap] over he leapt   sickerlie] surely, violently   moodie]
mole

'T was then came up Sir Robert Bewick,
   And his brave son alive saw he.
Rise up, rise up, my son, he said,
   For I think ye hae gotten the victorie.

O haud your tongue, my father dear;
   Of your pridefu' talking let me be;
Ye might hae drunken your wine in peace
   And let me and my billie be.

Gae dig a grave baith wide and deep,
   And a grave to haud baith him and me;
But lay Christie Græme on the sunny side
   For I'm sure he wan the victorie.

Alack, a wae, auld Bewick cried,
   Alack, was I not much to blame?
I'm sure I've lost the liveliest lad
   That e'er was born unto my name.

Alack, a wae, quo' gude Lord Græme,
   I'm sure I hae lost the deeper lack;
I durst hae ridden the Border through
   Had Christie Græme been at my back.

Had I been led through Liddesdale,
   And thirty horsemen guarding me,
And Christie Græme been at my back,
   Sae soon as he had set me free.

I've lost my hopes, I've lost my joy,
   I've lost the key but and the lock;
I durst hae ridden the world around
   Had Christie Græme been at my back.

haud] hold   durst] dared   but and] and also

97. *The Outlaw Murray*

ETRICK Forest is a fair Forest,
  In it grows manie a semelie trie;
The Hart, the Hynd, the Dae, the Rae,
  And of a' [wild] beistis grete plentie.

There 's a Castell biggit with Lime and Stane—
  O gin it stands not pleasantlie;
In the fore front o' that Castell fair
  Twa unicorns are bra' to see.

There 's the picture of a knight and a Ladye bright,
  And the grene Hollin aboon the[ir] brie;
There an *Outlaw* keepes five hundir men,
  He keipis a Royal Companie.

His Merry Men are in liverie clad
  Of the Lincoln grene so fair to see;
He and his Ladie in purple clad—
  O, if they live not royallie!

Word is gane to our Nobil King,
  In Edinburgh where that he lay,
That there was an Outlaw in Eteric forest
  Counted him nought and all his courtry gay.

I mak a Vowe, then the goode King said,
  Unto the Man that dear bought me;
I 'se either be king of Etric forest,
  Or king of Scotland that Outlaw [']s be.

Dae ... Rae] doe ... roe   biggit] built   gin] *expletive*
bra'] fine   Hollin] holly   aboon] above   brie] brow
courtry] court life   'se] shall

Then spak the Erle hight Hamilton,
    And to the Noble King said he:
My Sovereign Prince, sum counsel tak
    First of your Nobles, syne of me.

I redd you send yon bra' outlaw till
    And see gif your Man cum will he;
Desyre him cum and be your Man,
    And hald of you yon forest frie.

And gif he refuses to do that
    We'll conquess both his Lands and he;
Or else we'll throw his Castell down
    And mak a Widow of his gaye Ladie.

The King called on a gentleman,
    James Boyd, Earl of Arran, his brother was he;
When James he came before the King
    He fell before him on his knee.

Welcum, James Boyd, said our Noble King,
    A Message ye man gang for me;
Ye man hie to Etrick forest
    To yon Outlaw where dwelleth he.

Ask him of whom he haldis his Lands,
    Or, Man, wha may his Master be;
Desyre him cum and be my Man
    And hald of me yon forest frie.

To Edinburgh to cum and gang
    His safe Warrand I sall be;
And gif he refuses to do that
    We'll conquess baith his Lands and he.

hight] called   syne] then   redd] advise   gif] if   man] must

Thou may'st vow I'll cast his Castell down
   And mak a Widow of his gay Ladie;
I'll hang his merry men pair by pair
   In ony frith where I may them see.

James Boyd took his leave of the Nobil King,
   To Etrick forest fair came he;
Down Birkendale Brae when that he cam
   He saw the fair forest with his e'e:

Baith Dae and Rae and Hart and Hynd
   And of all wylde beastis grete plentie.
He heard the Bows that bauldly ring,
   And arrows whidderand him near by.

Of the fair Castell he got a sight
   The like he ne'er saw with his e'e;
On the fore front of that Castell
   Twa unicorns were bra' to see;

The picture of a Knight and a Ladye bright,
   And the grene Hollin aboon their bree;
There at he spyed five hundred men
   Shuting with Bows upon the Lee.

They a' were in ae Liverie clad
   Of the Lincoln grene sae fair to see;
The Knight and his Ladye in purple clad—
   O gif they lived right Royallie!
There fore he ken'd he was Master-man,
   And served him in his ain degree.

frith] clearing in a wood   Birkendale Brae] Birkendailly, over-
looking Yarrow   Lee] meadow

God mot thee save, brave Outlaw *Murray*,
    Thy Ladie and a' thy chivalrie!
Marry, thou 's wellcum, gentleman,
    Sum King's Messenger thou seems to be.

The King of Scotland sent me here
    And, gude Outlaw, I'm sent to thee;
I wad wat of whom ye hald your Lands,
    Or, Man, wha may thy Master be.

Thir Lands are mine, the Outlaw said,
    I own nae King in Christentie;
Frae Soudron I this forest wan,
    When the King nor 's knights were not to see.—

He desires you'l come to Edinburgh
    And hald of him this Forest frie;
And gif you refuse to do this,
    He'll conquess both thy Lands and thee.
He has vow'd to cast thy castell down
    And mak a Widow of thy gaye Ladie.

He'll hang thy merry men pair by pair
    In ony frith where he may them finde;
Ay, by my troth, the Outlaw said,
    Then wad I think me far behinde.

Ere the King my fair country get,
    This Land that 's nativest to me,
Mony of his Nobils sall be cauld,
    Their Ladies sall be right wearie.

mot] may   wad wat] want to know   Christentie] Christendom   Soudron] an Englishman

Then spak his Ladie, fair of face;
    She said, Without consent of me
That an outlaw shuld come before the King,
    I am right rad of treasonrie.

Bid him be good to his Lords at hame,
    For Edinburgh my Lord sall never see.—
James took his leave of the Outlaw keene,
    To Edinburgh bound is he.

And when he came before the King
    He fell before him on his knee.
Welcum, James Boyd, said the Nobil King;
    What foreste is Etrick forest free?

Etric forest is the fairest forest
    That ever man saw [w]ith his e'e;
There 's the Dae, the Rae, the Hart, the Hynd,
    And of all wild beastis grete plentee.

There 's a pretty Castell of Lime and Stone—
    O gif it staunds not plesauntlie;
There 's on the foreside of that Castell
    Twa Unicorns sae bra' to see.

There 's the picture of a knight and a Ladye bright,
    And the grene hollin aboon their brie;
There the outlaw keeps five hunder men—
    O gif they lived not royallie!

His merry men in liverie clad
    O' the Lincoln grene is fair to see;
He and his Ladye in purple clad—
    O gi[f] they live not royallie!

rad] afraid   keene] fierce

He says yon forest is his ain,
  He wan it from the Soudronie;
Sae as he won it, sae will he keep it
  Contrair all kings in Christentie.

Gar 'ray my Horse, said the Nobil King,
  To Etrick [forest] hie will I me;
Then he gard graith five thousand men
  And sent them on for the forest frie.

Then word is gane the Outlaw till,
  In Etrick forest where dwelleth he,
That the King was cummand to his cuntrie
  To conquess baith his Lands and he.

I mak a Vow, the Outlaw said,
  I mak a Vow and that truelie;
Were there but three men to tak my part
  Yon King's coming full deir should be.

Then Messengers he called forth
  And bad them haste them speedilie:
Ane of you go to Halliday,
  The Laird of the Corehead is he.

He certain is my Sister's Son;
  Bid him come quick and succour me;
Tell Halliday with thee to cum
  And sha' him a' the veritie.

What news, What news, said Halliday,
  Man, frae thy Master unto me?
Not as ye wad—Seeking your aid;
  The King 's his mortal Enemie.

Soudronie] English   Gar 'ray] get harnessed   graith] get
ready   Corehead] at the head of Moffat water   sha'] show

Aye, by my troth, quoth Halliday,
    Even for that it repenteth me;
For gif he lose fair Etrick forest
    He'll tak fair Moffatdale frae me.

I'll meet him wi' five hundred men,
    And surely mae, if mae may be;
The Outlaw call'd a Messenger
    And bid him hie him speedily.

To Andrew Murray of Cockpool—
    That Man's a deir cousin to me;
Desire him cum and mak me aid
    With all the power that he may be.

The King has vow'd to cast my castell down
    And mak a Widow of my gay Ladye;
He'll hang my merry men pair by pair
    In ony place where he may them see.

It stands me hard, quoth Andrew Murray;
    Judge if it stands not hard with me
To enter against a King with Crown
    And put my Lands in Jeopardie.

Yet gif I cum not on the day
    Surelie at night he sall me see.—
To Sir James Murray, Laird of Traquair,
    A Message came right speedilie.

What news, what news, James Murray said,
    Man, frae thy Master unto me?
What needs I tell, for well ye ken
    The King's his mortal Enemie.

mae] more   Cockpool] near Ruthwell, Dumfriesshire   Traquair]
on the Tweed near Innerleithen

He desires ye'll cum and mak him aid
  With all the powers that ye may be;
And by my troth, James Murray said,
  With that Outlaw I'll live and die.
The King has gifted my Lands lang syne,
  It cannot be nae war with me.

The King was cummand thro' Caddenford,
  And fiftene thousand Men [h]as he;
They saw the forest them before,
  They thought it awsom for to see.

Then spak the Erle hight Hamilton,
  And to the Nobil King said he:
My Sovereign Prince, sum counsel tak
  First at your Nobles, syne at me.

Desire him meet you at Penman's core
  And bring four in his companie;
Five Erles sall gang your sell before,
  Gude cause that you suld honour'd be.

And if he refuses to do that,
  Wi' fire and sword we'll follow thee;
There sall never a Murray after him
  Have Land in Etrick forest free.

The King then called a Gentleman—
  Royal Banner-bearer then was he—
James Hope Pringle of Torsonse by name;
  He cam and knelit upon his knie.

nae war] any worse   Caddenford] on the Tweed, near Yair
Torsonse] on Gala water   Penman's core] Permanscore, between
Tweeddale and Yarrow

Welcum, James Pringle of Torsonse,
   Ye man a Message gae for me;
Ye man gae to yon Outlaw Murray
   Surely where bauldly bideth he.

Bid him meet me at Penman's core
   And bring four of his companie;
Five Erlis sall cum wi' my sell,
   Gude reason I should honour'd be.

And if he refuses to do that,
   Bid him look for nae gude o' me;
There sall never a Murray after him
   Have Land in Etrick forest frie.

James cum before the Outlaw keene
   And served him in his ain degree:
Well cum, James Pringle of Torsonse,
   What tidings frae the King to me?

He bids ye meet him at Penman's core
   And bring four of your companie;
Five Erles will cum with the King,
   Nae mae in Number will he be.

And gif you refuse to do that,
   I freely here upgive with thee
There will never a Murray after thee
   Have Land in Etrick forest frie.

He'll cast your bonny Castell down
   And mak a Widow of your gay Ladie;
He'll hang your Merry Men pair by pair
   In ony place where he may them see.

upgive with] acknowledge to

It stands me hard, the Outlaw said,
   Judge if it stands not hard with me;
I reck not of losing of my sell,
   But all my offspring after me.

Auld Haleday, Young Haleday,
   Ye sall be twa to gang wi' me;
Andrew Murray and Sir James Murray,
   We'll be nae mair in cumpanie.

When that they came before the King
   They fell before him on their knie:
Grant mercy, mercy, royal king,
   E'en for his sake that died on trie.

Sicken like mercy sall ye have,
   On Gallows ye sall hangit be.
God forbid, quo' the Outlaw then,
   I hope your grace will better be.

Thir Lands of Etrick forest fair,
   I wan them frae the enemie;
Like as I wan them, sae will I keep them
   Contrair all Kings in Christentie.

All the Nobilis said, the King about,
   Pitye it were to see him die.—
Yet graunt me mercy, sovereign Prince,
   Extend your favour unto me.

I'll give you the keys of my Castell
   With the blessing of my fair Ladye;
Mak me the Sheriff of the forest
   And all my offspring after me.

Wilt thou give me the Keys of thy Castell
    With the blessing of thy fair Ladye,
I'll mak thee Sheriff of the forest
    Surely while upward grows the trie.
If you be not traytour to the King,
    Forfaulted sall ye never be.

But, Prince, what sall cum o' my men?
    When I gae back, traitour they'l ca' me;
I had rather lose my Life and Land
    E'er ony merry men rebuked me.

Will your merry men amend their lives
    And all their pardouns I grant thee.
Now name thy Lands whe'ere they be,
    And here I render them to thee.

Fair Philiphaugh, Prince, is my awin,
    I biggit it wi' Lime and Stone;
The Tinnies and the Hanginshaw,
    My Leige, are native steeds of mine.
I have mony steeds in the forest shaw
    But them by name I dinna knaw.

The Keys of the Castell he gave the King
    With the blessing of his fair Ladye;
He was made Sheryff of Etrick forest
    Surely while upward grows the trie;
And if he was not traytour to the King
    Forfaulted he suld never be.

Philiphaugh, etc.] in Yarrow and Ettrick   steeds] places   For-
faulted] forfeited

Wha ever heard in ony tymes
    Sicken an Outlaw in his degre
Sic favour get before a King,
    As did the Outlaw Murray of the forest frie?

Sicken] such

98. *Robyn and Gandeleyn*

I HERDE a carpyng of a clerk
    Al at ȝone wodes ende
Of gode Robyn and Gandeleyn;
    Was þer non oþer þynge.
Robynn lyth in grene wode bowndyn.

Stronge theuys wern þo chylderin non
    But bowmen gode and hende,
He wentyn to wode to getyn hem fleych
    If God wold it hem sende.

Al day wentyn þo chylderin too
    And fleych fowndyn he non
Til it were ageyn euyn;
    þe chylderin wold gon hom.

Half an honderid of fat falyf der
    He comyn aȝon,
And alle he wern fayr and fat inow
    But markyd was þer non;
Be dere God, seyde gode Robyn,
    Here of we shul haue on.

carpyng] singing   *clerk*] cleric, scholar   *lyth*] lies   *Stronge*] violent   *wern þo chylderin*] were those fellows   *hende*] gracious *He, hem*] they, them   *fleych*] venison   *ageyn euyn*] towards evening   *falyf*] fallow   *He comyn aȝon*] came against them, in their path   *shul*] shall   *on*] one

Robyn bent his joly bowe,
  þer in he set a flo;
þe fattest der of alle
  þe herte he clef a to.

He hadde not þe der iflawe
  Ne half out of þe hyde,
þere cam a schrewde arwe out of þe west
  þat felde Robertes pryde.

Gandeleyn lokyd hym est and west
  Be euery syde:
Hoo hat myn mayster slayin?
  Ho hat don þis dede?
Shal I neuer out of grene wode go
  Til I se [his] sydis blede.

Gandeleyn lokyd hym est and lokyd west,
  And sowt vnder þe sunne;
He saw a lytil boy
  He clepyn Wrennok of Donne.

A good bowe in his hond,
  A brod arwe þer ine,
And fowre and twenti goode arwys
  Trusyd in a þrumme:
Be war þe, war þe, Gandeleyn,
  Her of þu shalt han summe.

---

flo] arrow   a to] in two   iflawe] flayed   schrewde] sharp
hat] has   sowt] sought   He clepyn] they call   Trusyd]
trussed   þrumme] piece of waste yarn

Be war þe, war þe, Gandeleyn,
  Her of þu gyst plente.
Euer on for an oþer, seyde Gandeleyn;
  Mysaunter haue he shal fle.

Qwer at shal our marke be?
  Seyde Gandeleyn:
Eueryche at oþeris herte,
  Seyde Wrennok ageyn.

Ho shal ȝeue þe ferste schote?
  Seyde Gandeleyn:
And I shal ȝeue þe on be forn,
  Seyde Wrennok ageyn.

Wrennok schette a ful good schote,
  And he schet not to hye;
þrow the sanchoþis of his bryk;
  It towchyd neyþer thye.

Now hast þu ȝouyn me on be forn,
  Al þus to Wrennok seyde he,
And þrow þe myȝt of our lady
  A bettere I shal ȝeue þe.

Gandeleyn bent his goode bowe
  And set þer in a flo;
He schet þrow his grene certyl,
  His herte he clef on too.

gyst] gettest   Mysaunter] misadventure   he shal] he who shall
Qwer] where   Eueryche] each one   ȝeue] give   on be forn]
one before   sanchoþis] fork?   bryk] breeches   certyl] kirtle,
tunic

Now shalt þu neuer ȝelpe, Wrennok,
   At ale ne at wyn,
þat þu hast slawe goode Robyn
   And his knaue Gandeleyn.

Now shalt þu neuer ȝelpe, Wrennok,
   At wyn ne at ale,
þat þu hast slawe goode Robyn
   And Gandeleyn his knaue.
Robyn lyȝth in grene wode bowndyn.

ȝelpe] boast   slawe] slain   knaue] servant

99. *The Birth of Robin Hood*

O WILLIE's large o' limb and lith
   And come o' high degree,
And he is gane to Earl Richard
   To serve for meat and fee.

Earl Richard had but ae daughter
   Fair as a lily flower;
And they made up their love-contract
   Like proper paramour.

It fell upon a simmer's nicht
   Whan the leaves were fair and green,
That Willie met his gay ladie
   Intil the wood alane.

lith] joint within   meat and fee] food and pay   ae] one   Intil]

O narrow is my gown, Willie,
   That wont to be sae wide;
And gane is a' my fair colour
   That wont to be my pride.

But gin my father should get word
   What 's past between us twa,
Before that he should eat or drink
   He'd hang you o'er that wa'.

But ye'll come to my bower, Willie,
   Just as the sun gaes down;
And kep me in your arms twa
   And latna me fa' down.

O whan the sun was now gane down
   He 's doen him till her bower;
And there by the lee licht o' the moon
   Her window she lookit o'er.

Intill a robe o' red scarlet
   She lap, fearless o' harm;
And Willie was large o' lith and limb
   And keppit her in his arm.

And they've gane to the gude green wood;
   And ere the night was deen
She 's born to him a bonny young son
   Amang the leaves sae green.

Whan night was gane and day was come
   And the sun began to peep,
Up and raise the Earl Richard
   Out o' his drowsy sleep.

gin] if   doen him] taken himself   lee] desolate, eerie   deen] done

He 's ca'd upon his merry young men
   By ane, by twa, and by three:
O what 's come o' my daughter dear,
   That she 's nae come to me?

I dreamt a dreary dream last night—
   God grant it come to gude—
I dreamt I saw my daughter dear
   Drown in the saut sea flood.

But gin my daughter be dead or sick,
   Or yet be stown awa,
I mak a vow, and I'll keep it true,
   I'll hang ye ane and a'.

They sought her back, they sought her fore,
   They sought her up and down;
They got her in the gude green wood
   Nursing her bonny young son.

He took the bonny boy in his arms
   And kist him tenderlie;
Says, Though I would your father hang,
   Your mother 's dear to me.

He kist him o'er and o'er again:
   My grandson I thee claim;
And Robin Hood in gude green wood,
   And that shall be your name.

And mony ane sings o' grass, o' grass,
   And mony ane sings o' corn,
And mony ane sings o' Robin Hood
   Kens little whare he was born.

By ane] in ones   stown] stolen

It wasna in the ha', the ha',
  Nor in the painted bower,
But it was in the gude green wood
  Amang the lily flower.

100. *Adam Bel, Clym of the Cloughe, and Wyllyam of Cloudesle*

MERY it was in grene forest
  Amonge the leues grene,
Where that men walke both east and west
  Wyth bowes and arrowes kene

To ryse the dere out of theyr denne;
  Suche sightes as hath ofte bene sene
As by thre yemen of the north countrey—
  By them it is as I meane.

The one of them hight Adam Bel,
  The other Clym of the Clough,
The thyrd was William of Cloudesly,
  An archer good ynough.

They were outlawed for venyson,
  These thre yemen euerechone;
They swore them breth[r]en vpon a day
  To Englysshe-wood for to gone.

---

ryse] rouse   hight] was called   Clym] Clement   Clough]
steep-sided ravine   good ynough] very good   venyson] poaching
deer   Englysshe-wood] Inglewood, near Carlisle

Now lith and lysten, gentylmen,
    And that of myrthes loueth to here:
Two of them were single men,
    The third had a wedded fere.

Wyllyam was the wedded man,
    Muche more then was hys care.
He sayde to hys breth[r]en vpon a day
    To Carelel he would fare

For to speke with fayre Al[y]se hys wife
    And with hys chyldren thre:
By my trouth, sayde Adam Bel,
    Not by the counsell of me.

For if ye go to Caerlel, brother,
    And from thys wylde wode wende,
If the justice mai you take
    Your lyfe were at an ende.

If that I come not to morowe, brother,
    By pryme to you agayne,
Truste not els but that I am take
    Or else that I am slayne.

He toke hys leaue of hys breth[r]en two
    And to Carlel he is gone;
There he knocked at hys owne wyndowe
    Shortlye and anone.

Wher be you, fayre Alyce my wyfe,
    And my chyldren three?
Lyghtly let in thyne husbande
    Wyllyam of Cloudesle.

lith] hearken   fere] companion   justice] magistrate   pryme]
six, sunrise

Alas, then sayde fayre Alyce,
   And syghed wonderous sore,
Thys place hath ben besette for you
   Thys halfe yere and more.

Now am I here, sayde Cloudesle,
   I woulde that I in were;
Now feche vs meate and drynke ynoughe,
   And let vs make good chere.

She feched him meat and drynke plenty
   Lyke a true wedded wyfe,
And pleased hym with that she had
   Whome she loued as her lyfe.

There lay an old wyfe in that place
   A lytle besyde the fyre,
Whych Wyllyam had found of cherytye
   More then seuen yere.

Up she rose and walked full styll—
   Euel mote she spede therefoore—
For she had not set no fote on ground
   In seuen yere before.

She went vnto the justice hall
   As fast as she could hye:
Thys nyght is come vn to thys town
   Wyllyam of Cloudesle.

---

besette for] surrounded, besieged because of   found of] main-
tained out of   styll] secretly   Euel mote] evilly may   spede]
fare

Thereof the iustice was full fayne
    And so was the shirife also:
Thou shalt not trauaile hether, dame, for nought;
    Thy meed thou shalt haue or thou go.

They gaue to her a ryght good goune,
    Of scarlat it was, as I heard sayne;
She toke the gyft and home she wente
    And couched her doune agayne.

They rysed the towne of mery Carlel
    In all the hast that they can,
And came thronging to Wyllyames house
    As fast as they might gone.

Theyr they besette that good yeman
    Round about on euery syde;
Wyllyam hearde great noyse of folkes
    That heytherward they hyed.

Alyce opened a shot-wyndow
    And loked all about;
She was ware of the justice and the shrife bothe
    Wyth a full great route.

Alas, treason, cryed Alyce,
    Euer wo may thou be!
Go into my chambre, my husband, she sayd,
    Swete Wyllyam of Cloudesle.

He toke hys sweard and hys bucler,
    Hys bow and hys chyldren thre,
And wente into hys strongest chamber
    Where he thought surest to be.

fayne] glad   meed] reward   shot-wyndow] hinged window,
casement   bucler] small round shield

Fayre Alice folowed him as a louer true
   With a pollaxe in her hande:
He shalbe deade that here cometh in
   Thys dore whyle I may stand.

Cloudesle bent a wel good bowe
   That was of trusty tre,
He smot the justise on the brest
   That hys arrowe brest in thre.

God's curse on his hartt, saide William,
   Thys day thy cote dyd on;
If it had ben no better then myne
   It had gone nere thy bone.

Yelde the, Cloudesle, sayd the justise,
   And thy bowe and thy arrowes the fro:
Gods curse on hys hart, sayde fair Al[y]ce,
   That my husband councelleth so.

Set fyre on the house, saide the sherife,
   Syth it wyll no better be,
And brenne we therin William, he saide,
   Hys wyfe and chyldren thre.

They fyred the house in many a place,
   The fyre flew vpon hye;
Alas, than cryed fayr Alice,
   I se we shall here dy.

William openyd hys backe wyndow
   That was in hys chambre on hye,
And wyth shetes let hys wyfe downe
   And hys chyldren thre.

tre] wood   brest] burst   dyd] put   Syth] since

Haue here my treasure, sayde William,
  My wyfe and my chyldren thre;
For Christes loue do them no harme
  But wreke you all on me.

Wyllyam shot so wonderous well
  Tylls hys arrowes were all go,
And the fyre so fast vpon hym fell
  That hys bow stryng brent in two.

The spercles brent and fell hym on,
  Good Wyllyam of Cloudesle;
But than was he a wofull man, and sayde,
  Thys is a cowardes death to me.

Leuer I had, sayde Wyllyam,
  With my sworde in the route to renne,
Then here among myne ennemyes wode
  Thus cruelly to bren.

He toke hys sweard and hys buckler
  And among them all he ran;
Where the people were most in prece
  He smot downe many a man.

There myght no man stand hys stroke,
  So fersly on them he ran;
Then they threw wyndowes and dores on him
  And so toke that good yeman.

There they hym bounde both hand and fote
  And in depe dongeon hym cast:
Now, Cloudesle, sayde the hye justice,
  Thou shalt be hanged in hast.

wreke] take vengeance   Leuer] rather   ˌwode] mad   bren]
burn

385

One vow shal I make, sayde the sherife,
 A payre of new galowes shall I for the make,
And al the gates of Caerlel shalbe shutte,
 There shall no man come in therat.

Then shall not helpe Clim of the Cloughe
 Nor yet Adam Bell,
Though they came with a thousand mo
 Nor all the deuels in hell.

Early in the mornyng the justice vprose,
 To the gates fast gan he gon,
And commaunded to be shut full cloce
 Lightile euerychone.

Then went he to the market-place
 As fast as he coulde hye;
A payre of new gallous there dyd he vp set
 Besyde the pyllory.

A lytle boy stod them amonge
 And asked what meaned that gallow-tre;
They sayde, To hange a good yeaman
 Called Wyllyam of Cloudesle.

That lytle boye was the towne swyne-heard
 And kept fayre Alyce swyne;
Full oft he had sene Cloudesle in the wodde
 And geuen hym there to dyne.

He went out of a creues in the wall
 And lightly to the woode dyd gone;
There met he with these wyght yonge men
 Shortly and anone.

Lightile] quickly geuen] given creues] crevice wyght]
sturdy

Alas, then sayde that lytle boye,
    Ye tary here all to longe;
Cloudesle is taken and dampned to death
    All readye for to honge.

Alas, then sayde good Adam Bell,
    That euer we see thys daye;
He myght her with vs haue dwelled
    So ofte as we dyd him praye.

He myght haue taryed in grene foreste
    Under the shadowes sheene,
And haue kepte both hym and vs in reaste
    Out of trouble and teene.

Adam bent a ryght good bow,
    A great hart sone had he slayne:
Take that, chylde, he sayde, to thy dynner,
    And bryng me myne arrowe agayne.

Now go we hence, sayed these wight yong men,
    Tary we no lenger here;
We shall hym borowe, by Gods grace,
    Though we bye it full dere.

To Caerlel went these good yemen
    In a mery mornyng of Maye.
Her is a fyt of Cloudesli;
    And another is for to saye.

---

dampned] condemned   sheene] lovely   teene] malice,
vexation   borowe] ransom   fyt] canto

AND when they came to mery Caerlell
  In a fayre mornyng-tyde
They founde the gates shut them vntyll,
  Round about on euery syde.

Alas, than sayd good Adam Bell,
  That euer we were made men:
These gates be shyt so wonderly well
  That we may not come here in.

Than spake Clymme of the Cloughe:
  With a wyle we wyll vs in brynge;
Let vs say we be messengers
  Streyght comen from oure kynge.

Adam sayd, I haue a lettre wryten wele,
  Now let vs wysely werke;
We wyll say we haue the kynges seale,
  I holde the porter no clerke.

Than Adam Bell bete on the gate
  With strokes greate and stronge;
The porter herde suche a noyse therate
  And to the gate faste he thronge.

Who is there nowe, sayd the porter,
  That maketh all this knockynge?
We be two messengers, sayd Clymme of the
    Cloughe,
  Be comen streyght frome oure kynge.

We haue a lettre, sayd Adam Bell,
  To the justyce we must it brynge;
Let vs in, oure message to do,
  That we were agayne to our kynge.

vntyll] against   clerke] scholar   thronge] hastened

388

Here cometh no man in, sayd the porter,
　　By hym that dyed on a tre,
Tyll a false thefe be hanged
　　Called Wyllyam of Clowdysle.

Than spake that good yeman Clym of the Cloughe,
　　And swore by Mary fre;
If that we stande long wythout
　　Lyke a thefe hanged shalt thou be.

Lo here we haue got the kynges seale;
　　What, lordane, arte thou wode?
The porter had wende it had been so
　　And lyghtly dyd of his hode.

Welcome be my lordes seale, sayd he,
　　For that shall ye come in:
He opened the gate ryght shortly—
　　An euyll openynge for hym!

Nowe we are in, sayd Adam Bell,
　　Therof we are full fayne;
But Cryst knoweth, that herowed hell,
　　How we shall come oute agayne.

Had we the keys, sayd Clym of the Clowgh,
　　Ryght well than sholde we spede;
Than myght we come out well ynough
　　Whan we se tyme and nede.

fre] gracious　　　　lordane] dolt　　　wode] mad　　　wende]
thought　　　dyd] put off　　　fayne] glad　　　herowed] harried,
dispoiled

They called the porter to a councell
   And wronge hys necke in two,
And kest hym in a depe dongeon
   And toke the keys hym fro.

Now am I porter, sayd Adam Bell;
   Se, broder, the keys haue we here;
The worste porter to mery Carlell
   That ye had this hondreth yere.

Now wyll we oure bowes bende,
   Into the towne wyll we go
For to delyuer our dere broder
   Where he lyeth in care and wo.

Then they bent theyr good yew bowes
   And loked theyr stringes were round;
The market-place of mery Carlyll
   They beset in that stounde.

And as they loked them besyde
   A payre of newe galowes there they se,
And the iustyce, with a quest of swerers,
   That had iuged Clowdysle there hanged to be.

And Clowdysle hymselfe lay redy in a carte
   Fast bounde bothe fote and hande,
And a strong rope aboute his necke,
   All redy for to be hangde.

The iustyce called to hym a ladde:
   Clowdysles clothes sholde he haue
To take the mesure of that good yoman
   And therafter to make his graue.

round] in good shape   stounde] time   quest] inquest
swerers] jurors

I haue sene as greate a merueyll, sayd Clowdesle,
  As bytwene this and pryme,
He that maketh thys graue for me
  Hymselfe may lye therin.

Thou spekest proudely, sayd the iustyce;
  I shall hange the with my hande.
Full well that herde his bretheren two
  There styll as they did stande.

Than Clowdysle cast hys eyen asyde
  And saw hys bretheren stande
At a corner of the market-place,
Redy the iustyce for to chase,
  With theyr good bowes bent in theyr hand.

I se good comforte, sayd Clowdysle,
  Yet hope I well to fare;
If I myght haue my handes at wyll
  Ryght lytell wolde I care.

Than bespake good Adam Bell
  To Clymme of the Clowgh so fre:
Broder, se ye marke the iustyce well;
  Lo, yonder ye may him se.

And at the sheryf shote I wyll
  Strongly with an arowe kene;
A better shotte in mery Carlyll
  Thys seuen yere was not sene.

They loused theyr arowes bothe at ones,
  Of no man had they drede;
The one hyt the iustyce, the other the sheryf,
  That bothe theyr sydes gan blede.

at wyll] free

391

All men voyded that them stode nye
    Whan the iustyce fell to the grounde
And the sheryf fell nyghe hym by;
    Eyther had his dethes wounde.

All the cytezeyns fast gan fle,
    They durste no lenger abyde;
There lyghtly they loused Clowdysle
    Where he with ropes lay tyde.

Wyllyam sterte to an offycer of the towne,
    Hys axe out his hande he wronge;
On eche syde he smote them downe,
    Hym thought he had taryed to longe.

Wyllyam sayd to his bretheren two:
    Thys daye let vs togyder lyue and deye;
If euer you haue nede as I haue nowe,
    The same shall ye fynde by me.

They shyt so well in that tyde
    For theyr strynges were of sylke full sure
That they kepte the stretes on euery syde;
    That batayll dyd longe endure.

They fought togyder as bretheren true
    Lyke hardy men and bolde;
Many a man to the grounde they threwe
    And made many an herte colde.

But whan theyr arowes were all gone
    Men presyd on them full fast;
They drewe theyr swerdes than anone
    And theyr bowes from them caste.

voyded] gave room   Eyther] each of the two   gan] did
lyghtly] quickly

They wente lyghtly on theyr waye
    With swerdes and buckelers rounde;
By that it was the myddes of the daye
    They had made many a wounde.

There was many an oute-horne in Carlyll blowen
    And the belles backwarde dyd they rynge;
Many a woman sayd alas,
    And many theyr handes dyd wrynge.

The mayre of Carlyll forth come was
    And with hym a full grete route;
These thre yomen dredde hym full sore
    For theyr lyues stode in doubte.

The mayre came armed, a full greate pace,
    With a polaxe in his hande;
Many a stronge man with hym was
    There in that stoure to stande.

The mayre smote at Clowdysle with his byll,
    His buckeler he brast in two;
Full many a yoman with grete yll,
    Alas, treason, they cryed for wo;
Kepe we the gates fast, they bad,
    That these traytours theroute not go.

But all for nought was that they wrought,
    For so fast they downe were layde
Tyll they all thre that so manfully fought
    Were goten without at a brayde.

oute-horne] horn blown to summon lieges in pursuit of a criminal
stoure] press, battle   byll] halberd   brayde] sudden onset

Haue here your keys, sayd Adam Bell,
   Myne offyce I here forsake;
Yf ye do by my councell
   A newe porter ye make.

He threwe the keys there at theyr hedes
   And bad them evyll to thryue,
And all that letteth ony good yoman
   To come and comforte his wyue. .

Thus be these good yomen gone to the wode
   As lyght as lefe on lynde;
They laughe and be mery in theyr mode,
   Theyr enemyes were farre behynde.

Whan they came to Inglyswode
   Under theyr trysty-tre,
There they founde bowes full gode
   And arowes great plente.

So helpe me God, sayd Adam Bell,
   And Clymme of the Clowgh so fre,
I wolde we were nowe in mery Carlell
   Before that fayre meyne.

They set them downe and made good chere
   And eate and dranke full well.
Here is a fytte of these wyght yongemen,
   And another I shall you tell.

---

letteth] hinders   lynde] linden   mode] spirit   trysty-tre]
tree where they assembled   meyne] company

As they sat in Inglyswode
   Under theyr trysty-tre,
Them thought they herde a woman wepe,
   But her they myght not se.

Sore syghed there fayre Alyce, and sayd,
   Alas that euer I se this daye;
For now is my dere husbonde slayne,
   Alas and welawaye!

Myght I haue spoken wyth hys dere bretheren,
   With eyther of them twayne,
To shew to them what him befell,
   My herte were out of payne.

Clowdysle walked a lytell besyde
   And loked vnder the grene wodde lynde;
He was ware of his wyfe and his chyldren thre
   Full wo in herte and mynde.

Welcome, wyfe, than sayd Wyllyam,
   Unto this trysty-tre;
I had wende yesterdaye, by swete Saint John,
   Thou sholde me neuer haue se.

Now wele is me, she sayd, that ye be here,
   My herte is out of wo:
Dame, he sayd, be mery and glad
   And thanke my bretheren two.

Here of to speke, sayd Adam Bell,
   I-wys it is no bote;
The meat that we must supp withall
   It runneth yet fast on fote.

wende] thought   I-wys] indeed   bote] help, use

Then went they down into a launde,
   These noble archares all thre;
Eche of them slewe a harte of grece,
   The best they coude there se.

Haue here the best, Alyce my wyfe,
   Sayde Wyllyam of Clowdysle,
By cause ye so boldely stode me by
   Whan I was slayne full nye.

Than they wente to theyr souper
   Wyth suche mete as they had,
And thanked God of theyr fortune;
   They were bothe mery and glad.

And whan they had souped well,
   Certayne withouten leace,
Clowdysle sayde, We wyll to oure kynge
   To get vs a chartre of peace.

Alyce shal be at soiournynge
   In a nunry here besyde;
My tow sonnes shall with her go
   And ther they shall abyde.

Myne eldest sone shall go with me,
   For hym haue I no care,
And he shall breng you worde agayne
   How that we do fare.

Thus be these wight men to London gone
   As fast as they maye hye,
Tyll they came to the kynges palays
   There they woulde nedes be.

launde] glade   of grece] fat, ready for killing   leace] lying
at soiournynge] in temporary lodging

And whan they came to the kynges courte,
   Unto the pallace gate,
Of no man wold they aske leue
   But boldly went in therat.

They preced prestly into the hall,
   Of no man had they dreade;
The porter came after and dyd them call
   And with them began to chyde.

The vssher sayd, Yemen, what wolde ye haue?
   I praye you tell[e] me;
Ye myght thus make offycers shent:
   Good syrs, of whens be ye?

Syr, we be outlawes of the forest,
   Certayne withouten leace,
And hyther we be come to oure kynge
   To get vs a charter of peace.

And whan they came before oure kynge,
   As it was the lawe of the lande,
They kneled downe without lettynge
   And eche helde vp his hande.

They sayd, Lorde, we beseche you here
   That ye wyll graunte vs grace,
For we haue slayne your fatte falowe dere
   In many a sondry place.

What is your names? than sayd our kynge,
   Anone that you tell me.
They sayd, Adam Bell, Clym of the Clough,
   And Wyllyam of Clowdesle.

preced prestly] pressed quickly   shent] ruined   lettynge] delay

Be ye those theues, than sayd our kynge,
   That men haue tolde of to me?
Here to God I make a vowe
   Ye shall be hanged all thre.

Ye shall be dead without mercy,
   As I am kynge of this lande.
He commanded his officers euerichone
   Fast on them to lay hand.

There they toke these good yemen
   And arested them al thre:
So may I thryue, sayd Adam Bell,
   Thys game lyketh not me.

But, good lorde, we beseche you nowe,
   That ye wyll graunte vs grace
In so moche as we be to you commen;
   Or elles that we may fro you passe

With suche weapons as we haue here
   Tyll we be out of your place;
And yf we lyue this hondred yere
   We wyll aske you no grace.

Ye speke proudly, sayd the kynge,
   Ye shall be hanged all thre.
That were great pity, sayd the quene,
   If any grace myght be.

My lorde, whan I came fyrst in to this lande
   To be your wedded wyfe,
The fyrst bone that I wolde aske,
   Ye wolde graunte me belyfe.

belyfe] directly

And I asked you neuer none tyll nowe,
  Therfore, good lorde, graunte it me:
Nowe aske it, madame, sayd the kynge,
  And graunted shall it be.

Than, good lorde, I you beseche,
  The yemen graunte you me:
Madame, ye myght haue asked a bone
  That sholde haue ben worthe them thre.

Ye myght haue asked towres and townes,
  Parkes and forestes plentie:
None so pleasaunt to mi pay, she said,
  Nor none so lefe to me.

Madame, sith it is your desyre,
  Your askyng graunted shalbe;
But I had leuer haue geuen you
  Good market-townes thre.

The quene was a glad woman
  And sayd, Lord, gramarcy;
I dare vndertake for them
  That true men shall they be.

But, good lord, speke som mery word
  That comfort they may se:
I graunt you grace, then said our king;
  Wasshe, felo[w]s, and to meate go ye.

They had not setten but a whyle,
  Certayne without lesynge,
There came messengers out of the north
  With letters to our kyng.

pay] liking, satisfaction   lefe] dear   sith] since   leuer]
rather   gramarcy] thank you   lesynge] lying

And whan the[y] came before the kynge
    The[y] kneled downe vpon theyr kne,
And sayd, Lord, your offycers grete you wel
    Of Caerlel in the north cuntre.

How fareth my justice, sayd the kyng,
    And my sherife also?
Syr, they be slayne, without leasynge,
    And many an officer mo.

Who hath them slayne? sayd the kyng,
    Anone thou tell[e] me:
Adam Bel and Clime of the Clough
    And Wyllyam of Cloudesle.

Alas for rewth, then sayd our kynge,
    My hart is wonderous sore;
I had leuer than a thousand pounde
    I had knowne of thys before.

For I haue y-graunted them grace,
    And that forthynketh me;
But had I knowne all thys before
    They had ben hanged all thre.

The kyng opened the letter anone,
    Hym selfe he red it tho,
And founde how these thre outlawes had slaine
    Thre hundred men and mo.

Fyrst the justice and the sheryfe
    And the mayre of Caerlel towne;
Of all the constables and catchipolles
    Alyue were left not one.

forthynketh me] I repent of   tho] then

The baylyes and the bedyls both,
 And the sergeauntes of the law,
And forty fosters of the fe
 These outlawes had y-slaw;

And broken his parks and slaine his dere—
 Ouer all they chose the best;
So perelous outlawes as they were
 Walked not by easte nor west.

When the kynge this letter had red
 In hys harte he syghed sore:
Take vp the table, anone he bad,
 For I may eate no more.

The kyng called hys best archars
 To the buttes with hym to go:
I wyll se these felowes shote, he sayd,
 That in the north haue wrought this wo.

The kynges bowmen buske them blyue,
 And the quenes archers also,
So dyd these thre wyght yemen,
 Wyth them they thought to go.

There twyse or thryse they shote about
 For to assay theyr hande;
There was no shote these thre yemen shot
 That any prycke might them stand.

baylyes] sheriff's officers   bedyls] warrant officers   fosters . . .
fe] foresters of the (feudal) estate   y-slaw] slain   So] as
buttes] targets   buske them] made ready   blyue] at once
prycke] mark

Then spake Wyllyam of Cloudesle:
    By God that for me dyed,
I hold hym neuer no good archar
    That shuteth at buttes so wyde.

Wherat? then sayd our kyng,
    I pray thee tell[e] me:
At suche a but, syr, he sayd,
    As men vse in my countree.

Wyllyam wente into a fyeld,
    And his t[w]o brothren with him;
There they set vp t[w]o hasell roddes
    Twenty score paces betwene.

I hold him an archar, said Cloudesle,
    That yonder wande cleueth in two:
Here is none suche, sayd the kyng,
    Nor none that can so do.

I shall assaye, syr, sayd Cloudesle,
    Or that I farther go:
Cloudesle, with a bearyng arow,
    Claue the wand in t[w]o.

Thou art the best archer, then said the king,
    Forsothe that euer I se:
And yet for your loue, sayd Wylliam,
    I wyll do more maystry.

I haue a sonne is seuen yere olde,
    He is to me full deare;
I wyll hym tye to a stake,
    All shall se that be here;

Or] ere   bearyng arow] tapered, long-range arrow   do . . .
maystry] show . . . superior skill

And lay an apple vpon hys head
   And go syxe score paces hym fro,
And I my selfe, with a brode arow,
   Shal cleue the apple in two.

Now haste the, then sayd the kyng;
   By him that dyed on a tre,
But yf thou do not as thou hest sayde
   Hanged shalt thou be.

And thou touche his head or gowne
   In syght that men may se,
By all the sayntes that be in heaven
   I shall hange you all thre.

That I haue promised, said William,
   I wyl it neuer forsake.
And there euen before the kynge
   In the earth he droue a stake;

And bound therto his eldest sonne
   And bad hym stande styll therat,
And turned the childes face fro him
   Because he shuld not sterte.

An apple vpon his head he set
   And then his bowe he bent;
Syxe score paces they were outmet,
   And thether Cloudesle went.

There he drew out a fayr brode arrowe,
   Hys bowe was great and longe;
He set that arowe in his bowe
   That was both styffe and stronge.

And thou] if thou   outmet] measured out

He prayed the people that was there
   That they would styll[e] stande:
For he that shooteth for such a wager
   Behoueth a stedfast hand.

Muche people prayed for Cloudesle
   That hys lyfe saued myght be,
And whan he made hym redy to shote
   There was many a wepynge eye.

Thus Clowdesle clefte the apple in two
   That many a man it se:
Ouer Goddes forbode, sayd the kynge,
   That thou sholdest shote at me!

I giue the .xviii. pens a daye,
   And my bowe shalte thou bere,
And ouer all the north countree
   I make the chefe rydere.

And I gyue the .xii. pens a day, sayd the quene,
   By God and by my faye;
Come fetche thy payment whan thou wylt,
   No man shall say the naye.

Wyllyam, I make the gentylman
   Of clothynge and of fee,
And thy two brethren yemen of my chambre,
   For they are so semely to se.

Youre sone, for he is tendre of age,
   Of my wyne-seller shall he be,
And whan he commeth to mannes state
   Better auaunced shall he be.

rydere] ranger   faye] faith   fee] wages   -seller] cellar

And, Wylliam, brynge me your wyfe, sayd the
 quene,
 Me longeth sore her to se;
She shall be my chefe gentylwoman
 And gouerne my nursery.

The yemen thanked them full courteysly
 And sayd, To Rome streyght wyll we wende,
Of all the synnes that we haue done
 To be assoyled of his hand.

So forthe be gone these good yemen
 As fast as they myght hye,
And after came and dwelled with the kynge
 And dyed good men all thre.

Thus endeth the lyues of these good yemen,
 God sende them eternall blysse,
And all that with hande-bowe shoteth,
 That of heuen they may neuer mysse!

assoyled] absolved

101. *Robyn Hode and the Munke*

IN somer, when þe shawes be sheyne
 And leves be large and long,
Hit is full mery in feyre foreste
 To here þe foulys song;

shawes] small woods in hollow places sheyne] lovely foulys]
birds'

To se þe dere draw to þe dale
  And leve þe hilles hee,
And shadow hem in þe leves grene
  Vnder þe grene-wode tre.

Hit befel on Whitsontide,
  Erly in a May mornyng,
The son vp feyre can shyne
  And the briddis mery can syng.

This is a mery mornyng, seid Litull John,
  Be hym þat dyed on tre;
A more mery man þen I am one
  Lyves not in Cristiante.

Pluk vp þi hert, my dere mayster,
  Litull John can sey,
And thynk hit is a full fayre tyme
  In a mornyng of May.

3e, on thyng greves me, seid Robyn,
  And does my hert mych woo—
þat I may not no solem day
  To mas nor matyns goo.

Hit is a fourtnet and more, seid he,
  Syn I my sauyour see;
To day wil I to Notyngham, seid Robyn,
  With þe myght of mylde Marye.

hee] high   hem] them   can] did   hym . . . tre] Christ
on] one   solem day] holy, feast day

Than spake Moche, þe mylner s[o]n,
   Euer more wel hym betyde:
Take twelue of þi wyght ȝemen,
   Well weppynd, be þi side.
Such on wolde þi selfe slon,
   þat twelue dar not abyde.

Of all my mery men, seid Robyn,
   Be my feith I wil non haue,
But Litull John shall beyre my bow
   Til þat me list to drawe.

þou shall beyre þin own, seid Litull Jon,
   Maister, and I wyl beyre myne,
And we well shete a peny, seid Litull Jon,
   Vnder þe grene-wode lyne.

I wil not shete a peny, seyd Robyn Hode,
   In feith, Litull John, with the,
But euer for on as þou shetis, seide Robyn,
   In feith I holde þe thre.

Thus shet þei forth, þese ȝemen t[w]o,
   Bothe at buske and brome,
Til Litull John wan of his maister
   Fiue shillings to hose and shone.

A ferly strife fel þem betwene
   As they went bi the wey:
Litull John seid he had won fiue shillings,
   And Robyn Hode seid schortly, nay.

---

mylner] miller's   wyght] sturdy   ȝemen] yeomen   weppynd] armed   slon] slay   abyde] withstand   me list to drawe] I am disposed to draw (it)   shete] shoot (for)   lyne] linden   holde] wager   buske and brome] bush and broom   ferly] wondrous

With þat Robyn Hode lyed Litul Jon
   And smote hym with his hande;
Litul Jon waxed wroth þerwith
   And pulled out his bright bronde.

Were þou not my maister, seid Litull John,
   þou shuldis b[e] hit ful sore;
Get þe a man wher þou wilt,
   For þou getis me no more.

þen Robyn goes to Notyngham
   Hym selfe mo[u]rnyng allone,
And Litull John to mery Scherwode—
   The pathes he knew ilkone.

Whan Robyn came to Notyngham,
   Sertenly withouten layn,
He prayed to God and myld Mary
   To bryng hym out saue agayn.

He gos in to Seynt Mary chirch
   And kneled down before the rode;
Alle þat euer were þe church within
   Beheld wel Robyn Hode.

Beside hym stod a gret-hedid munke,
   I pray to God woo he be!
Fful sone he knew gode Robyn
   As sone as he hym se.

Out at þe durre he ran
   Fful sone and anon;
Alle the ȝatis of Notyngham
   He made to be sparred euerychon.

lyed] called . . . a liar   bronde] sword   mournyng] sorrowing
ilkone] every one   layn] disguise   saue] safe   rode] cross
ȝatis] gates   sparred] barred   euerychon] every one

Rise vp, he seid, þou prowde schereff,
    Buske þe and make þe bowne;
I haue spyed þe kynggis felon
    Ffor sothe he is in þis town.

I haue spyed þe false felon
    As he stondis at his masse;
Hit is long of þe, seide the munke,
    And euer he fro vs passe.

þis traytur name is Robyn Hode,
    Vnder the grene-wode lynde;
He robbyt me onys of a hundred pound,
    Hit shalle neuer out of my mynde.

Vp then rose þis prowde shereff
    And radly made hym ȝare;
Many was þe moder son
    To þe kyrk with hym can fare.

In at the durres þei throly thrast
    With staves ful gode wone:
Alas, alas, seid Robyn Hode,
    Now mysse I Litull John.

But Robyn toke out a t[w]o-hond sworde
    þat hangit down be his kne;
þer as þe schereff and his men stode thyckust,
    Thedurwarde wolde he.

Buske þe] dress yourself   bowne] ready   Hit is . . . þe . . .
And] It is your fault . . . if   onys] once   radly] quickly
ȝare] ready   throly] right through   thrast] pushed   gode
wone] plenty

409

Thryes thorowout þem he ran þen,
    For soþe as I yow sey,
And woundyt mony a moder son,
    And twelue he slew þat day.

His sworde vpon þe schireff hed
    Sertanly he brake in t[w]o;
Þe smyth þat þe made, seid Robyn,
    I pray to God wyrke hym woo!

Ffor now am I weppynlesse, seid Robyn,
    Alasse, agayn my wylle;
But if I may fle þese traytors fro,
    I wot þei wil me kyll.

Robyn in to the churche ran
    Throout hem euerilkon. . . .

[*News of his capture reaches his men.*]

Sum fel in swonyng as þei were dede,
    And lay stil as any stone;
Non of theym were in her mynde
    But only Litull Jon.

Let be your rule, seid Litull Jon,
    Ffor his luf þat dyed on tre,
Ʒe þat shulde be duʒty men—
    Het is gret shame to se.

But if] unless   wot] believe   euerilkon] every one, all   were
. . . mynde] kept their heads   rule] disorderly behaviour   duʒty]
valiant   Het] it

Oure maister has bene hard bystode
    And ȝet scapyd away;
Pluk vp your hertis, and leve this mone,
    And harkyn what I shal say.

He has seruyd Oure Lady many a day
    And ȝet wil, securly;
þerfor I trust in hir specialy
    No wyckud deth shal he dye.

þerfor be glad, seid Litul John,
    And let this mournyng be;
And I shal be þe munkis gyde
    With þe myght of mylde Mary.

[Than spake Moche, the mylner son:]
    We will go, but we t[w]o;
And I mete hym, seid Litul John,
    [I trust to wyrke hym woo.]

Loke þat ȝe kepe wel owre tristil-tre
    Vnder þe levys smale,
And spare non of this venyson
    That gose in thys vale.

Fforþe þen went these ȝemen t[w]o,
    Litul John and Moche on fere,
And lokid on Moch emys hows—
    þe hye way lay full nere.

bystode] beset, assailed   mone] moaning   securly] assuredly
be . . . gyde] take care of   And] if   tristil-tre] tree for assembling
at, rendezvous   smale] small   on fere] together   Moch
emys hows] Much's uncle's house

Litul John stode at a wyndow in þe mornyng
    And lokid forþ at a stage;
He was war wher þe munke came ridyng,
    And with hym a litul page.

Be my feith, seid Litul John to Moch,
    I can þe tel tithyngus gode:
I se wher þe munke cumys rydyng,
    I know hym be his wyde hode.

They went in to the way, þese ʒemen boþe,
    As curtes men and hende;
þei spyrred tithyngus at þe munke
    As they hade bene his frende.

Ffro whens come ʒe? seid Litull Jon,
    Tel vs tithyngus, I yow pray,
Off a false owtlay callid Robyn Hode
    Was takyn ʒisterday.

He robbyt me and my felowes boþe
    Of twenti marke, in serten;
If þat false owtlay be takyn,
    Ffor soþe we wolde be fayn.

So did he me, seid þe munke,
    Of a hundred pound and more;
I layde furst hande hym apon,
    ʒe may thonke me þerfore.

I pray God thanke you, seid Litull John,
    And we wil when we may;
We wil go with you, with your leve,
    And bryng yow on your way.

at a stage] from an upper room   tithyngus] tidings   hende]
gracious, civil   spyrred] asked   in serten] truly   fayn] glad

Ffor Robyn Hode hase many a wilde felow,
    I tell you in certen;
If þei wist ȝe rode þis way
    In feith ȝe shulde be slayn.

As þei went talking be þe way,
    The munke and Litull John,
John toke þe munkis horse be þe hede
    Fful sone and anon.

Johne toke þe munkis horse be þe hed,
    Ffor soþe as I yow say;
So did Much þe litull page,
    Ffor he shulde not scape away.

Be þe golett of þe hode
    John pulled þe munke down;
John was nothyng of hym agast,
    He lete hym falle on his crown.

Litull John was sore agrevyd
    And drew owt his swerde in hye;
This munke saw he shulde be ded,
    Lowd mercy can he crye.

He was my maister, seid Litull John,
    þat þou hase browȝt in bale;
Shalle þou neuer cum at our kyng
    Ffor to telle hym tale.

John smote of þe munkis hed,
    No longer wolde he dwell;
So did Moch þe litull page
    Ffor ferd lest he wolde tell.

Ffor he] so that he   golett] neck   of hym agast] concerned about
him   hye] haste   can] did   bale] harm   dwell] wait   ferd] fear

þer þei beryed hem boþe
  In nouþer mosse nor lyng,
And Litull John and Much infere
  Bare þe letturs to oure kyng.

[Whan John came unto the kyng]
  He knelid down vpon his kne:
God 30w saue, my lege lorde,
  Ihesus yow saue and se!

God yow saue, my lege kyng!
  To speke John was full bolde;
He gaf hym þe letturs in his hond,
  The kyng did hit vnfold.

þe kyng red þe letturs anon
  And seid, So mot I the,
þer was neuer 30man in mery Inglond
  I longut so sore to se.

Wher is þe munke þat þese shuld haue brou3t?
  Oure kyng can say:
Be my trouth, seid Litull John,
  He dyed after þe way.

þe kyng gaf Moch and Litul John
  Twenti pound in sertan,
And made þeim 3emen of þe crown
  And bade þeim go agayn.

nouþer mosse nor lyng] neither bog nor heath   infere] in
company   lege] feudal   mot I the] may I thrive   after]
back on

414

He gaf John þe seel in hand
    The sheref for to bere,
To bryng Robyn hym to
    And no man do hym dere.

John toke his leve at oure kyng,
    þe sothe as I yow say;
þe next way to Notyngham
    To take, he ȝede þe way.

Whan John came to Notyngham
    The ȝatis were sparred ychon;
John callid vp þe porter,
    He answerid sone anon.

What is þe cause, seid Litul John,
    þou sparris þe ȝates so fast?
Because of Robyn Hode, seid þe porter,
    In depe prison is cast.

John and Moch and Wyll Scathlok,
    Ffor sothe as I yow say,
þei slew oure men vpon our wallis
    And sawten vs euery day.

Litull John spyrred after þe schereff,
    And sone he hym fonde;
He oppyned þe kyngus priue seell
    And gaf hym in his honde.

bere] carry to   dere] injury   next] nearest   ȝede] went
ȝatis] gates   sparred] barred   ychon] all   sawten] assaulted

Whan þe scheref saw þe kyngus seell
   He did of his hode anon:
Wher is þe munke þat bare þe letturs?
   He seid to Litull John.

He is so fayn of hym, seid Litul John,
   Ffor soþe as I yow say,
He has made hym abot of Westmynster,
   A lorde of þat abbay.

The scheref made John gode chere
   And gaf hym wyne of the best;
At nyȝt þei went to her bedde
   And euery man to his rest.

When þe scheref was on slepe,
   Dronken of wyne and ale,
Litul John and Moch for soþe
   Toke þe way vnto þe jale.

Litul John callid vp þe jayler
   And bade hym rise anon;
He seyd Robyn Hode had brokyn prison
   And out of hit was gon.

The porter rose anon sertan
   As sone as he herd John calle;
Litul John was redy with a swerd
   And bare hym to þe walle.

Now wil I be porter, seid Litul John,
   And take þe keyes in honde.
He toke þe way to Robyn Hode
   And sone he hym vnbounde.

did of] threw off   fayn of] pleased with   her] their   bare]
bore, drove

He gaf hym a gode swerde in his hond,
  His hed therwith for to kepe,
And ther as þe walle was lowyst
  Anon down can þei lepe.

Be þat þe cok began to crow
  The day began to spryng;
The scheref fond þe jaylier ded,
  The comyn bell made he ryng.

He made a crye thoroout al þe town,
  Wheder he be ȝoman or knave
þat cowþe bryng hym Robyn Hode,
  His warison he shuld haue.

Ffor I dar neuer, said þe scheref,
  Cum before oure kyng;
Ffor if I do, I wot serten
  Ffor soþe he wil me heng.

The scheref made to seke Notyngham
  Bothe be strete and stye,
And Robyn was in mery Scherwode
  As liȝt as lef on lynde.

Then bespake gode Litull John,
  To Robyn Hode can he say:
I haue done þe a gode turne for an euyll,
  Quyte þe whan þou may.

ther as] where   comyn] public, town   crye] proclamation
knave] servant, serf   cowþe] could   warison] reward   made
... Notyngham] had Nottingham searched   stye] alley   liȝt]
light, carefree   Quyte] requite, repay

I haue done þe a gode turne, seid Litull John,
    Ffor sothe as I yow say;
I haue brouȝht þe vnder grene-wode lyne;
    Ffare wel, and haue gode day.

Nay, be my trouth, seid Robyn Hode,
    So shall hit neuer be;
I make þe maister, seid Robyn Hode,
    Of alle my men and me.

Nay, be my trouth, seid Litull John,
    So shalle hit neuer be;
But lat me be a felow, seid Litull John,
    No noder kepe I be.

Thus John gate Robyn Hode out of prison,
    Sertan withoutyn layn;
Whan his men saw hym hol and sounde,
    Ffor sothe they were full fayne.

They filled in wyne and made hem glad
    Vnder þe levys smale,
And ȝete pastes of venyson
    þat gode was with ale.

Than worde came to oure kyng
    How Robyn Hode was gon,
And how þe scheref of Notyngham
    Durst neuer loke hym vpon.

Then bespake oure cumly kyng
    In an angur hye:
Litull John hase begyled þe schereff,
    In faith so hase he me.

lyne] linden   felow] comrade   No . . . be] nothing else do
I care to be   gate] got   layn] disguise   ȝete] ate

Litul John has begyled vs bothe,
  And þat full wel I se;
Or ellis þe schereff of Notyngham
  Hye hongut shulde he be.

I made hem ȝemen of þe crowne
  And gaf hem fee with my hond;
I gaf hem grith, seid oure kyng,
  Thorowout all mery Inglond.

I gaf theym grith, þen seid oure kyng;
  I say, so mot I the,
Ffor sothe soch a ȝeman as he is on
  In all Inglond ar not thre.

He is trew to his maister, seid our kyng;
  I sey, be swete Seynt John,
He louys better Robyn Hode
  Then he dose vs ychon.

Robyn Hode is euer bond to hym
  Bothe in strete and stalle;
Speke no more of this mater, seid oure kyng,
  But John has begyled vs alle.

Thus endys the talkyng of the munke
  And Robyn Hode i-wysse;
God þat is euer a crowned kyng
  Bryng vs all to his blisse!

gaf] gave   fee] reward   grith] safe conduct, pardon   mot
I the] may I prosper   on] one   Bothe . . . stalle] everywhere
i-wysse] indeed

419

102. *A Gest of Robyn Hode*

LYTHE and listin, gentilmen,
    That be of frebore blode;
I shall you tel of a gode yeman,
    His name was Robyn Hode.

Robyn was a p[ro]ude outlaw
    [Whyles he walked on grounde;
So curteyse an outlawe] as he was one
    Was neuer non founde.

Robyn stode in Bernesdale
    And lenyd hym to a tre;
And bi hym stode Litell Johnn,
    A gode yeman was he.

And alsoo dyd go[d]e Scarlok
    And Much, the mil[l]er's son;
There was none ynch of his bodi
    But it was worth a grome.

Than bespake Lytell Johnn
    All vntoo Robyn Hode:
Maister, and ye wolde dyne betyme
    It wolde doo you moche gode.

Than bespake hym gode Robyn:
    To dyne haue I noo lust,
Till that I haue som bolde baron
    Or som vnkout[h] gest;

Gest] romance
the earth
grome] man
known, strange
Lythe] hear
Bernesdale] forest between Doncaster and Pontefract
and ye] if you
frebore] free-born
lust] desire
grounde]

vnkouth] un-

420

[Till that I haue som ryche abbot]
  That may pay for the best,
Or som knyght or [som] squyer
  That dwelleth here bi west.

A gode maner than had Robyn;
  In londe where that he were,
Euery day or he wold dyne
  Thre messis wolde he here:

The one in the worship of the Fader,
  And another of the Holy Gost,
The thirde of Our dere Lady
  That he loued all ther moste.

Robyn loued Our dere Lady;
  For dout of dydly synne
Wolde he neuer do compani harme
  That any woman was in.

Maistar, than sayde Lytil Johnn,
  And we our borde shal sprede,
Tell vs wheder that we shal go
  And what life that we shall lede.

Where we shall take, where we shall leue,
  Where we shall abide behynde,
Where we shall robbe, where we shal reue,
  Where we shal bete and bynde.

bi] towards	maner] habit	were] might be	or] ere
messis] masses	all ther moste] most of all	dout] fear	And
we] if we	reue] reive, plunder		

Therof no force, than sayde Robyn,
　　We shall do well inowe;
But loke ye do no husbonde harme
　　That tillet[h] with his ploughe.

No more ye shall no gode yeman
　　That walketh by grene wode shawe,
Ne no knyght ne no squyer
　　That wol be a gode felawe.

These bisshoppes and these archebishoppes,
　　Ye shall them bete and bynde;
The hye sherif of Notyingham,
　　Hym holde ye in your myn[d]e.

This worde shalbe holde, sayde Lytell Johnn,
　　And this lesson we shall lere;
It is fer dayes; God sende vs a gest,
　　That we were at oure dynere!

Take thy gode bowe in thy honde, sayde Robyn;
　　Late Much wende with the,
And so shal Willyam Scarlok,
　　And no man abyde with me.

And walke vp to the Saylis
　　And so to Watlinge Stret[e],
And wayte after some vnknuth gest;
　　Vp chaunce ye may them mete.

force] matter　　　　inowe] enough　　　　husbonde] husbandman
shawe] little wood in a hollow　　　holde] kept　　　　lere] learn
fer dayes] late in the day　　　Saylis] a tenancy of Pontefract manor
Watlinge Strete] the North Road　　　wayte] wait and watch　　Vp
chaunce] perchance

Be he erle or ani baron,
   Abbot or ani knyght,
Bringhe hym to lodge to me;
   His dyner shall be dight.

They wente vp to the Saylis,
   These yeman all thre;
They loked est, they loke[d] weest;
   They myght no man see.

But as they loked in to Bernysdale
   Bi a derne strete
Than came a knyght ridinghe;
   Full sone they gan hym mete.

All dreri was his semblaunce
   And lytell was his pryde;
His one fote in the styrop stode,
   That othere wauyd beside.

His hode hanged in his iy[e]n two,
   He rode in symple aray;
A soriar man than he was, one
   Rode neuer in somer day.

Litell Johnn was full curteyes
   And sette hym on his kne:
Welcom be ye, gentyll knyght,
   Welcom ar ye to me.

Welcom be thou to grene wode,
   Hende knyght and fre;
My maister hath abiden you fastinge,
   Syr, al these oures thre.

dight] got ready   derne strete] hidden road   gan] did
semblaunce] appearance   wauyd] dangled   sette hym] knelt
down   Hende] gracious   fre] noble   abiden] waited for

Who is thy maister? sayde the knyght;
   Johnn sayde, Robyn Hode.
He is [a] gode yoman, sayde the knyght,
   Of hym I haue herde moche gode.

I graunte, he sayde, with you to wende,
   My bretherne, all in fere;
My purpos was to haue dyned to day
   At Blith or Dancastere.

Furth than went this gentyl knight
   With a carefull chere;
The teris oute of his iyen ran
   And fell downe by his lere.

They brought hym to the lodge dore;
   Whan Robyn hym gan see,
Full curtesly dyd of his hode
   And sette hym on his knee.

Welcome, sir knight, than sayde Robyn,
   Welcome art thou to me;
I haue abyden you fastinge, sir,
   All these ouris thre.

Than answered the gentyll knight
   With wordes fayre and fre:
God the saue, goode Robyn,
   And all thy fayre meyne.

in fere] in company, together   Blith] near Retford   carefull
chere] woeful countenance   lere] cheek   lodge] hut in the
forest   dyd of] threw off   sette hym] knelt   fre] gracious
meyne] company

They wasshed togeder and wyped bothe
    And sette to theyr dynere;
Brede and wyne they had right ynough[e]
    And noumbles of the dere.

Swannes and fe[s]sauntes they had full gode,
    And foules of the ryuere;
There fayled none so litell a birde
    That euer was bred on bryre.

Do gladly, sir knight, sayde Robyn;
    Gramarcy, sir, sayde he:
Suche a dinere had I nat
    Of all these wekys thre.

If I come ageyne, Robyn,
    Here by thys contre,
As gode a dyner I shall the make
    As that thou haest made to me.

Gramarcy, knyght, sayde Robyn;
    My dyner whan that I it haue,
I was neuer so gredy, bi dere worthy God,
    My dyner for to craue.

But pay or ye wende, sayde Robyn;
    Me thynketh it is gode ryght;
It was neuer the maner, by dere worthi God,
    A yoman to pay for a kny[g]ht.

I haue nought in my coffers, saide the knyght,
    That I may profer for shame:
[Litell] Johnn, go loke, sayde Robyn,
    Ne let nat for no blame.

sette] sat down   noumbles] innards   bryre] briar   Do
gladly] help yourself   Gramarcy] thank you   dere worthy]
glorious   let] desist

Tel me truth, than saide Robyn,
  So God [haue] parte of [th]e:
I haue no more but [ten] shelynges, sayde the
    knyght,
  So God haue parte of me.

If thou hast no more, sayde Robyn,
  I woll nat one peny;
And yf thou haue nede of any more,
  More shall I lend the.

Go nowe furth, Littell Johnn,
  The truth tell thou me;
If there be no more but [ten] shelinges,
  No peny that I se.

Lyttell Johnn sprede downe hys mantell
  Full fayre vpon the grounde,
And there he fonde in the knyghtes cofer
  But euen halfe [a] pounde.

Littell Johnn let it lye full styll
  And went to hys maysteer lowe.
What tidynges, Johnn? sayde Robyn;
  Sir, the knyght is true inowe.

Fyll of the best wine, sayde Robyn,
  The knyght shall begynne;
Moche wonder thinketh me
  Thy clot[h]ynge is so thin[n]e.

Tell me [one] worde, sayde Robyn,
  And counsel shal it be;
I trow thou warte made a knyght of force
  Or ellys of yemanry.

Or ellys thou has bene a sori husbande
  And lyued in stro[k]e and stryfe;
An okerer, or ellis a lechoure, sayde Robyn,
  Wyth wronge hast led thy lyfe.

I am none of those, sayde the knyght,
  By God that made me;
An hundred wynter here before
  Myn auncetres knyghtes haue [be].

But oft it hath befal, Robyn,
  A man hath be disgrate;
But God that sitteth in heuen aboue
  May amende his state.

Withyn this two yere, Robyne, he sayde,
  My neghbours well it knowe,
Foure hundred pounde of gode money
  Ful well than myght I spende.

Nowe haue I no gode, saide the knyght—
  God had shaped such an ende—
But my chyldren and my wyfe,
  Tyll God yt may amende.

counsel] in confidence   of force] by force (in consequence of hold-
ing an estate worth £20 a year)   of yemanry] from the yeoman class
sori husbande] bad manager   stroke] lawless violence   okerer]
usurer   disgrate] unfortunate   Withyn . . . yere] less than two
years ago

In what maner, than sayde Robyn,
   Hast thou lorne thy rychesse?
For my greate foly, he sayde,
   And for my kynd[e]nesse.

I hade a sone, forsoth, Robyn,
   That shulde hau[e] ben myn ayre,
Whanne he was twenty wynter olde
   In felde wolde iust full fayre.

He slewe a knyght of Lancaster
   And a squyer bolde;
For to saue hym in his ryght
   My godes both sette and solde.

My londes both sette to wedde, Robyn,
   Vntyll a certayn day,
To a ryche abbot here besyde
   Of Seynt Mari Abbey.

What is the som? sayde Robyn;
   Trouth than tell thou me:
Sir, he sayde, foure hundred pounde;
   The abbot told it to me.

Nowe and thou lese thy lond, sayde Robyn,
   What woll fall of the?
Hastely I wol me buske, sayd the knyght,
   Ouer the salte see,

lorne] lost   For] through   iust] joust   sette] priced
sette to wedde] mortgaged   told] counted   Nowe and] now if
fall of the] befall thee   buske] get ready (to go)

And se w[h]ere Criste was quyke and dede
    On the mount of Caluere;
Fare wel, frende, and haue gode day,
    It ma no better be.

Teris fell out of hys iyen two;
    He wolde haue gone hys way:
Farewel, frende, and haue gode day,
    I ne haue no more to pay.

Where be thy frendes? sayde Robyn:
    Syr, neuer one wol me knowe;
While I was ryche ynowe at home
    Great boste than wolde they blowe.

And nowe they renne away fro me
    As bestis on a rowe;
They take no more hede of me
    Thanne they had me neuer sawe.

For ruthe thanne wept Litell Johnn,
    Scarlok and Muche in fere;
Fyl of the best wyne, sayde Robyn,
    For here is a symple chere.

Hast thou any frende, sayde Robyn,
    Thy borowe that wolde be?
I haue none, than sayde the knyght,
    But God that dyed on tree.

---

quyke] living   boste] clamour (of friendship)   ruthe] pity
in fere] together   symple chere] sincere feast   borowe] surety

Do away thy iapis, than sayde Robyn,
  Thereof wol I right none;
Wenest thou I wolde haue God to borowe,
  Peter, Poule, or Johnn?

Nay, by hym that me made
  And shope both sonne and mone,
Fynde me a better borowe, sayde Robyn,
  Or money getest thou none.

I haue none other, sayde the knyght,
  The sothe for to say,
But yf yt be Our dere Lady—
  She fayled me neuer or thys day.

By dere worthy God, sayde Robyn,
  To seche all Englonde thorowe,
Yet fonde I neuer to my pay
  A moche better borowe.

Come nowe furth, Litell Johnn,
  And go to my tresoure,
And bringe me foure hundered pound[e],
  And loke well tolde it be.

Furth than went Litell Johnn
  And Scarlok went before;
He tolde oute foure hundred pounde
  [By eight and twenty] score.

Do . . . iapis] away with your jests   Wenest] do you think
to] for a   shope] created   But yf] unless   dere worthy]
glorious   seche] search   pay] satisfaction   tolde]
counted

Is thys well tolde? sayde [litell] Much;
    Johnn sayde, What gre[ue]th the?
It is almus to helpe a gentyll knyght
    That is fal in pouerte.

Master, than sayde Lityll John,
    His clothinge is full thynne;
Ye must gyue the knight a lyueray
    To [lap]pe his body therin.

For ye haue scarlet and grene, mayster,
    And man[y] a riche aray;
Ther is no marchaunt in mery Englond
    So ryche, I dare well say.

Take hym thre yerdes of euery colour
    And loke well mete that it be;
Lytell Johnn toke none other mesure
    But his bowe tree.

And at euery handfull that he met
    He leped footes three;
What deuylles drapar, sayid litell Muche,
    Thynkest thou for to be?

Scarlok stode full stil and loughe,
    And sayd, By God Almyght,
Johnn may gyue hym gode mesure
    For it costeth hym but lyght.

Mayster, than said Litell Johnn
    To gentill Robyn Hode:
Ye must giue the knig[h]t a hors
    To lede home this gode.

almus] alms   lappe] wrap   mete] measured   bowe tree]
wooden bow

Take hym a gray coursar, sayde Robyn,
  And a saydle newe;
He is Oure Ladye's messangere,
  God grant that he be true.

And a gode palfray, sayde lytell Much,
  To mayntene hym in his right;
And a peyre of botes, sayde Scarlok,
  For he is a gentyll knight.

What shalt thou gyue hym, Litell John? said
    Robyn;
  Sir, a peyre of gilt sporis clene,
To pray for all this company;
  God bringe hym oute of tene.

Whan shal mi day be, said the knight,
  Sir, and your wyll be?
This day twelue moneth, saide Robyn,
  Vnder this grene wode tre.

It were greate shame, sayde Robyn,
  A knight alone to ryde,
Withoute squyre, yeman or page
  To walke by his syde.

I shall the lende Litell John, my man,
  For he shalbe thy knaue;
In a yema[n]'s stede he may the stande
  If thou greate nede haue.

palfray] saddle-horse   clene] clear   tene] trouble   knaue]
servant

432

The Seconde Fytte

Now is the knight gone on his way;
   This game hym thought full gode;
Whanne he loked on Berne[sd]ale
   He blessyd Robyn Hode.

And whanne he thought on Bernysdale,
   On Scarlok, Much, and Johnn,
He blyssyd them for the best company
   That euer he in come.

Then spake that gentyll knyght,
   To Lytel Johan gan he saye:
To-morrowe I must to Yorke toune
   To Saynt Mary abbay.

And to the abbot of that place
   Foure hondred pounde I must pay;
And but I be there vpon this nyght
   My londe is lost for ay.

The abbot sayd to his couent,
   There he stode on grounde:
This day twelfe moneth came there a knyght
   And borowed foure hondred pounde.

[He borowed foure hondred pounde]
   Upon all his londe fre;
But he come this ylke day
   Dysheryte shall he be.

Fytte] canto   in come] came into   but] unless   couent]
community (of monks)   ylke] same

It is full erely, sayd the pryoure,
  The day is not yet ferre gone;
I had leuer to pay an hondred pounde
  And lay downe anone.

The knyght is ferre beyonde the see,
  In Englonde [is his] right,
And suffreth honger and colde
  And many a sory nyght.

It were grete pyte, said the pryoure,
  So to haue his londe;
An ye be so lyght of your consyence
  Ye do to hym moch wronge.

Thou art euer in my berde, sayd the abbot,
  By God and Saynt Rycharde!
With that cam in a fat-heded monke,
  The heygh selerer.

He is dede or hanged, sayd the monke,
  By God that bought me dere;
And we shall haue to spende in this place
  Foure hondred pounde by yere.

The abbot and the hy selerer
  Sterte forthe full bolde;
The [hye] iustyce of Englonde
  The abbot there dyde holde.

The hye iustyce and many mo
  Had take in to they[r] honde
Holy all the knyghtes det,
  To put that knyght to wronge.

leuer] rather   An] if   in my berde] thwarting me
selerer] cellarer   holde] retain as counsel   mo] more

They demed the knyght wonder sore,
   The abbot and his meyne:
But he come this ylke day
   Dysheryte shall he be.

He wyll not come yet, sayd the iustyce,
   I dare well vndertake;
But in sorowe tyme for them all
   The knyght came to the gate.

Than bespake that gentyll knyght
   Untyll his meyne:
Now put on your symple wedes
   That ye brought fro the see.

[They put on their symple wedes,]
   They came to the gates anone;
The porter was redy hymselfe
   And welcomed them euerychone.

Welcome, syr knyght, sayd the porter:
   My lorde to mete is he,
And so is many a gentyll man
   For the loue of the.

The porter swore a full grete othe:
   By God that made me,
Here be the best coresed hors
   That euer yet sawe I me.

demed] judged   wonder sore] very severely   meyne] company
But] unless   Untyll] to   euerychone] everyone   to mete]
at dinner   coresed] bartered

Lede them in to the stable, he sayd,
 That eased myght they be;
They shall not come therin, sayd the knyght,
 By God that dyed on a tre.

Lordes were to mete isette
 In that abbotes hall;
The knyght went forth and kneled downe,
 And salued them grete and small.

Do gladly, syr abbot, sayd the knyght,
 I am come to holde my day:
The fyrst word the abbot spake,
 Has thou brought my pay?

Not one peny, sayd the knyght,
 By God that maked me.
Thou art a shrewed dettour, sayd the abbot;
 Syr iustyce, drynke to me.

What doost thou here, sayd the abbot,
 But thou haddest brought thy pay?
For God, than sayd the knyght,
 To pray of a lenger daye.

Thy daye is broke, sayd the iustyce,
 Londe getest thou none.
Now, good syr iustyce, be my frende,
 And fende me of my fone!

mete] dinner salued] hailed holde] keep shrewed]
cursed But] if not of a . . . daye] for a . . . term fende
. . . fone] defend me from my foes

I am holde with the abbot, sayd the iustyce,
  Both with cloth and fee.
Now, good syr sheryf, be my frende!
  Nay, for God, sayd he.

Now, good syr abbot, be my frende
  For thy curteyse,
And holde my londes in thy honde
  Tyll I haue made the gree!

And I wyll be thy true seruaunte
  And trewely serue the[e]
Tyl ye haue foure hondred pounde
  Of money good and free.

The abbot sware a full grete othe:
  By God that dyed on a tre,
Get the londe where thou may
  For thou getest none of me.

By dere worthy God, then sayd the knyght,
  That all this worlde wrought,
But I haue my londe agayne
  Full dere it shall be bought.

God that was of a mayden borne
  Leue vs well to spede!
For it is good to assay a frende
  Or that a man haue nede.

holde with] retained by   cloth and fee] clothing and payment
for] before   the gree] thee satisfaction   But] unless   spede]
prosper   Or that] before

The abbot lothely on hym gan loke,
   And vylaynesly hym gan [call]:
Out, he sayd, thou false knyght,
   Spede the out of my hall!

Thou lyest, then sayd the gentyll knyght,
   Abbot, in thy hal;
False knyght was I neuer,
   By God that made vs all.

Vp then stode that gentyll knyght,
   To the abbot sayd he:
To suffre a knyght to knele so longe
   Thou canst no curteysye.

In ioustes and in tournement
   Full ferre than haue I be,
And put my selfe as ferre in prees
   As ony that euer I se.

What wyll ye gyue more, sayd the iustyce,
   And the knyght sall make a releyse?
And elles dare I safly swere
   Ye holde neuer your londe in pees.

An hondred pounde, sayd the abbot;
   The justice sayd, Gyue hym two;
Nay, be God, sayd the knyght,
   Yit gete ye it not so.

lothely] contemptuously   canst] knowest   ferre] far
prees] in the conflict   And . . . releyse] if . . . quittance   elles]
else

Though ye wolde gyue a thousand more,
    Yet were ye neuer the nere;
Shall there neuer be myn heyre
    Abbot, iustice, ne frere.

He stert hym to a borde anone,
    Tyll a table rounde,
And there he shoke oute of a bagge
    Euen four hondred pound.

Haue here thi golde, sir abbot, saide the knight,
    Which that thou lentest me;
Had thou ben curtes at my comynge
    Rewarded shuldest thou haue be.

The abbot sat styll and ete no more,
    For all his ryall fare;
He cast his hede on his shulder
    And fast began to stare.

Take me my golde agayne, saide the abbot,
    Sir iustice, that I toke the.
Not a peni, said the iustice,
    Bi Go[d, that dy]ed on tree.

Sir [abbot, and ye me]n of lawe,
    Now haue I holde my daye;
Now shall I haue my londe agayne
    For ought that you can saye.

The knyght stert out of the dore,
    Awaye was all his care,
And on he put his good clothynge,
    The other he lefte there.

nere] nearer   stert hym] moved   borde] table   Take] give

He wente hym forth full mery syngynge
   As men haue tolde in tale;
His lady met hym at the gate
   At home in Verysdale.

Welcome, my lorde, sayd his lady:
   Syr, lost is all your good?
Be mery, dame, sayd the knyght,
   And pray for Robyn Hode,

That euer his soule be in blysse:
   He holpe me [out of] tene;
Ne had be his kyndenesse,
   Beggers had we bene.

The abbot and I accorded ben,
   He is serued of his pay;
The god yoman lent it me
   As I cam by the way.

This knight than dwelled fayre at home,
   The sothe for to saye,
Tyll he had gete four hundred pound
   Al redy for to pay.

He purueyed him an hundred bowes,
   The strynges well ydyght,
An hundred shefe of aro[wes] gode,
   The hedys burneshed full bryght;

Verysdale] ? Wyresdale, south of Lancaster   tene] trouble   Ne
had be] if it had not been for   ydyght] furnished, adjusted

And euery arowe an [e]lle longe,
    With pecok wel idyght,
[Ynocked] all with whyte siluer;
    It was a semely syght.

He purueyed hym an [hondreth men]
    Well harness[ed in that stede],
And hym selfe in that same sete
    And clothed in whyte and rede.

He bare a launsgay in his honde,
    And a man ledde his male,
And reden with a lyght songe
    Vnto Bernysdale.

But as he went at a brydge ther was a wraste-
        lyng,
    And there taryed was he,
And there was all the best yemen
    Of all the west countree.

A full fayre game there was vp set,
    A whyte bulle vp i-pyght,
A grete courser, with sadle and brydil,
    With golde burnyssht full bryght.

A payre of gloues, a rede golde rynge,
    A pype of wyne, in fay;
What man that bereth hym best i-wys
    The pryce shall bere away.

---

elle] 45 inches   pecok] peacock feathers   Ynocked] notched
to take the bowstring   stede] place   sete] company   launsgay]
lance   ledde] carried on a horse   male] bag   reden] they
rode   i-pyght] fixed, placed   pype] cylinder   fay] faith
i-wys] indeed   pryce] prize

There was a yoman in that place,
   And best worthy was he,
And for he was ferre and frembde bested,
   Slayne he shulde haue be.

The knight had ruthe of this yoman
   In place where he stode;
He sayde that yoman shulde haue no harme,
   For loue of Robyn Hode.

The knyght presed in to the place,
   An hundreth folowed hym [fre],
With bowes bent and arowes sharpe
   For to shende that companye.

They shulderd all and made hym rome
   To wete what he wolde say;
He toke the yeman bi the hande
   And gaue hym al the play.

He gaue hym fyue marke for his wyne,
   There it lay on the molde,
And bad it shulde be set a broche,
   Drynke who so wolde.

Thus longe taried this gentyll knyght
   Tyll that play was done;
So longe abode Robyn fastinge
   Thre houres after the none.

ferre . . . bested] in the plight of a stranger from far   ruthe] pity
shende] put to shame, confusion   shulderd] shouldered, shoved
wete] know   molde] ground   a broche] abroach

The Thirde Fytte

LYTH and lystyn, gentilmen,
  All that nowe be here;
Of Litell Johnn, that was the knightes man,
  Goode myrth ye shall here.

It was vpon a mery day
  That yonge men wolde go shete;
Lytell Johnn fet his bowe anone
  And sayde he wolde them mete.

Thre tymes Litell John shet aboute
  And alwey he slet the wande;
The proude sherif of Notingham
  By the markes can stande.

The sherif swore a full greate othe:
  By hym that dyede on a tre,
This man is the best arschere
  That euer yet sawe I [me].

Say me nowe, wight yonge man,
  What is nowe thy name?
In what countre were thou borne,
  And where is thy wonynge wane?

In Holdernes, sir, I was borne,
  Iwys al of my dame;
Men cal me Reynolde Grenelef
  Whan I am at home.

Fytte] canto   lyth] hear   shete] shoot   fet] fetched
slet] slit, split   wande] branch, target   hym . . . tre] Christ
wight] sturdy   wonynge wane] dwelling-place   Holdernes]
in south-east Yorkshire   Iwys] assuredly

Sey me, Reyno[l]de Grenelefe,
  Wolde thou dwell with me?
And euery yere I woll the gyue
  Twenty marke to thy fee.

I haue a maister, sayde Litell Johnn,
  A curteys knight is he;
May ye leue get of hym
  The better may it be.

The sherif gate Litell John
  Twelue monethes of the knight;
Therfore he gaue him right anone
  A gode hors and a wight.

Nowe is Litell John the sherifes man—
  God lende vs well to spede!
But alwey thought Lytell John
  To quyte hym wele his mede.

Nowe so God me helpe, sayde Litell John,
  And by my true leutye,
I shall be the worst seruaunt to hym
  That euer yet had he.

It fell vpon a Wednesday
  The sherif on huntynge was gone,
And Litel Iohn lay in his bed
  And was foriete at home.

Therfore he was fastinge
  Til it was past the none:
Gode sir stuarde, I pray to the,
  Gyue me my dynere, saide Litell John.

gate] got   lende] grant   quyte] requite   mede] reward
leutye] loyalty   foriete] forgotten

It is longe for Grenelefe
  Fastinge thus for to be ;
Therfor I pray the, sir stuarde,
  Mi dyner gif me.

Shalt thou neuer ete ne drynke, saide the stuarde,
  Tyll my lorde be come to towne;
I make myn auowe to God, saide Litell John,
  I had leuer to crake thy crowne.

The boteler was full vncurteys
  There he stode on flore;
He start to the botery
  And shet fast the dore.

Lytell Johnn gaue the boteler suche a tap
  His backe went nere in two;
Thoug[h] he liued an hundred ier
  The wors shuld he be go.

He sporned the dore with his fote,
  It went open wel and fyne;
And therfore he made large lyueray
  Bothe of ale and of wyne.

Sith ye wol nat dyne, sayde Litell John,
  I shall gyue you to drinke;
And though ye lyue an hundred wynter
  On Lytel Johnn ye shall thinke.

Litell John ete and Litel John drank
  The while that he wolde;
The sherife had in his kechyn a coke,
  A stoute man and a bolde.

leuer] rather   start] dashed   ier] years   go] gone
lyueray] allowance, ration   Sith] since   kechyn] kitchen
stoute] stalwart

I make myn auowe to God, saide the coke,
  Thou arte a shrewde hyne
In ani hous for to dwel
  For to aske thus to dyne.

And there he lent Litell John
  God[e] strokis thre;
I make myn auowe to God, sayde Lytell John,
  These strokis lyked well me.

Thou arte a bold man and hardy,
  And so thinketh me;
And or I pas fro this place
  Assayed better shalt thou be.

Lytell Johnn drew a ful gode sworde,
  The coke toke another in hande;
They thought no thynge for to fle,
  But stifly for to stande.

There they faught sore togedere
  Two myle way and well more;
Myght neyther other harme done,
  The mountnaunce of an owre.

I make myn auowe to God, sayde Litell Johnn,
  And by my true lewte,
Thou art one of the best sworde men
  That euer yit sawe I [me].

Cowdest thou shote as well in a bowe,
  To grene wode thou shuldest with me;
And two times in the yere thy clothinge
  Chaunged shulde be;

hyne] hind, servant   lent] gave   or] ere   Assayed] tried,
proved   other] the other   mountnaunce] space, duration
Cowdest] couldest

And euery yere of Robyn Hode
    Twenty merke to thy fe.
Put vp thy swerde, saide the coke,
    And felowes woll we be.

Thanne he fet to Lytell Johnn
    The nowmbles of a do,
Gode brede, and full gode wyne;
    They ete and drank theretoo.

And when they had dronkyn well
    Theyre trouthes togeder they plight,
That they wo[l]de be with Robyn
    That ylke same nyght.

They dyd them to the tresoure hows
    As fast as they myght gone;
The lokkis, that were of full gode stele,
    They brake them euerichone.

They toke away the siluer vessell
    And all that thei mig[h]t get;
Pecis, [m]asars, ne sponis
    Wolde thei not forget.

Also [they] toke the gode pens,
    Thre hundred pounde and more,
And did them st[r]eyte to Robyn Hode
    Under the grene wode hore.

merke] marks (13s. 4d.)   fe] wage   fet] brought   nowmbles]
innards   trouthes] pledges   ylke] very   dyd them] took
themselves   euerichone] every one   Pecis] vessels   masars]
maplewood bowls   hore] grey, because wanting foliage

God the saue, my dere mayster,
   And Criste the saue and se!
And thanne sayde Robyn to Litell Johnn,
   Welcome myght thou be;

Also be that fayre yeman
   Thou bryngest there with the;
What tydynges fro Noty[n]gham?
   Lytill Johnn, tell thou me.

Well the gretith the proude sheryf,
   And sen[t]e the here by me
His coke and his siluer vessell
   And thre hundred pounde and thre.

I make myn auowe to God, sayde Robyn,
   And to the Trenyte,
It was neuer by his gode wyll
   This gode is come to me.

Lytyll Johnn there hym bethought
   On a shrewde wyle;
Fyue myle in the forest he ran,
   Hym happed all his wyll.

Than he met the proude sheref
   Hyntynge with houndes and horne;
Lytell Johnn coude of curtesye,
   And knelyd hym beforne.

God the saue, my dere mayster,
   And Criste the saue and se!
Reynolde Grenelefe, sayde the shyref,
   Where hast thou nowe be?

gretith] greets   Hym . . . wyll] all that he wanted came about
coude of] knew about

I haue be in this forest;
  A fayre syght can I se;
It was one of the fayrest syghtes
  That euer yet sawe I me.

Yonder I sawe a ryght fayre harte,
  His coloure is of grene;
Seuen score of dere vpon a herde
  Be with hym all bydene.

Their tyndes are so sharpe, maister,
  Of sexty and well mo,
That I durst not shote for drede
  Lest they wolde me slo.

I make myn auowe to God, sayde the shyre[f],
  That syght wolde I fayne se.
Buske you thyderwarde, my dere mayster,
  Anone, and wende with me.

The sherif rode, and Litell Johnn
  Of fote he was full smerte,
And whane they came before Robyn,
  Lo, sir, here is the mayster-herte.

Still stode the proude sherief,
  A sory man was he:
Wo the worthe, Raynolde Grenelefe,
  Thou hast betrayed nowe me.

I make myn auowe to God, sayde Litell Johnn,
  Mayster, ye be to blame;
I was mysserued of my dynere
  Whan I was with you at home.

bydene] together   tyndes] branches of antlers   slo] slay
fayne] gladly   Buske] make ready   Wo the worthe] Woe come
to you

Sone he was to souper sette
   And serued well with siluer white,
And whan the sherif sawe his vessell
   For sorowe he myght nat ete.

Make glad chere, sayde Robyn Hode,
   Sherif, for charite,
And for the loue of Litill Johnn
   Thy lyfe I graunt to the.

Whan they had souped well
   The day was al gone;
Robyn commaunde[d] Litell Johnn
   To drawe of his hosen and his shone,

His kirtell, and his cote of pie
   That was fured well and fine,
And to[ke] hym a grene mantel
   To lap his body therin.

Robyn commaundyd his wight yonge men
   Vnder the grene wode tree,
They shulde lye in that same sute
   That the sherife myght them see.

All nyght lay the proude sherif
   In his breche and in his [s]chert;
No wonder it was in grene wode
   Though his sydes gan to smerte.

Make glade chere, sayde Robyn Hode,
   Sheref, for charite;
For this is our ordre iwys
   Vnder the grene wode tree.

shone] shoes   kirtell] tunic   cote of pie] courtepy, short cloak
lap] wrap   breche] breeches   gan] began   smerte] hurt
ordre] habit, rule   iwys] indeed

This is harder order, sayde the sherief,
    Than any ankir or frere;
For all the golde in mery Englonde
    I wolde nat longe dwell her[e].

All this twelue monthes, sayde Robyn,
    Thou shalt dwell with me;
I shall the teche, proude sherif,
    An outlawe for to be.

Or I be here another nyght, sayde the sherif,
    Robyn, nowe pray I the,
Smyte of mijn hede rather to-morowe
    And I forgyue it the.

Lat me go, than sayde the sherif,
    For saynte charite,
And I woll be the best frende
    That euer yet had ye.

Thou shalt swere me an othe, sayde Robyn,
    On my bright bronde:
Shalt thou neuer awayte me scade
    By water ne by lande.

And if thou fynde any of my men
    By nyght or [by] day,
Vpon thyn othe thou shalt swere
    To helpe them tha[t] thou may.

Nowe hathe the sherif sworne his othe,
    And home he began to gone;
He was as full of grene wode
    As euer was hepe of stone.

ankir or frere] hermit or friar	Or] ere	saynte] blessed
bronde] sword awayte] plot	scade] harm	hepe] (rose) hip

The Fourth Fytte

THE sherif dwelled in Notingham,
  He was fayne he was agone;
And Robyn and his mery men
  Went to wode anone.

Go we to dyner, sayde Littell Johnn;
  Robyn Hode sayde, Nay;
For I drede Our Lady be wroth with me,
  For she sent me nat my pay.

Haue no doute, maister, sayde Litell Johnn,
  Yet is nat the sonne at rest;
For I dare say and sauely swere
  The knight is true and truste.

Take thy bowe in thy hande, sayde Robyn,
  Late Much wende with the,
And so shal Wyllyam Scarlok,
  And no man abyde with me.

And walke vp vnder the Sayles
  And to Watlynge-strete,
And wayte after some vnketh gest;
  Vp-chaunce ye may them mete.

Whether he be messengere
  Or a man that myrthes can,
Of my good he shall haue some
  Yf he be a pore man.

Fytte] canto   fayne] glad   pay] reward   sauely] safely
truste] trustworthy   the Sayles] a tenancy of Pontefract manor
Watlynge-strete] the North Road   wayte] wait and watch   vnketh]
strange   Vp-chaunce] perchance   myrthes can] can make jokes

Forth then stert Lytel Johan
    Half in tray and tene,
And gyrde hym with a full good swerde
    Under a mantel of grene.

They went vp to the Sayles,
    These yemen all thre;
They loked est, they loked west,
    They myght no man se.

But as [they] loked in Bernysdale
    By the hye waye,
Than were they ware of two blacke monkes
    Eche on a good palferay.

Then bespake Lytell Johan,
    To Much he gan say:
I dare lay my lyfe to wedde
    That [these] monkes haue brought our pay.

Make glad chere, sayd Lytell Johan,
    And frese your bowes of ewe,
And loke your hertes be seker and sad,
    Your strynges trusty and trewe.

The monke hath two and fifty [men]
    And seuen somers full stronge;
There rydeth no bysshop in this londe
    So ryally, I vnderstond.

stert] started   tray and tene] vexation and trouble   gyrde hym] girded himself   Bernysdale] forest between Doncaster and Pontefract   blacke monkes] Benedictines   palferay] saddle-horse   to wedde] in wager   frese] ? prepare   seker and sad] sure and firm   somers] sumpter-, pack-horses

Brethern, sayd Lytell Johan,
    Here are no more but we thre;
But we brynge them to dyner,
    Our mayster dare we not se.

Bende your bowes, sayd Lytell Johan,
    Make all yon prese to stonde;
The formost monke, his lyfe and his deth
    Is closed in my honde.

Abyde, chorle monke, sayd Lytell Johan,
    No ferther that thou gone;
Yf thou doost, by dere worthy God,
    Thy deth is in my honde.

And euyll thryfte on thy hede, sayd Lytell Johan,
    Ryght vnder thy hattes bonde;
For thou hast made our mayster wroth
    He is fastynge so longe.

Who is your mayster? sayd the monke;
    Lytell Johan sayd, Robyn Hode;
He is a stronge thefe, sayd the monke,
    Of hym herd I neuer good.

Thou lyest, than sayd Lytell Johan,
    And that shall rewe the;
He is a yeman of the forest,
    To dyne he hath bode the.

But] unless   prese] crowd   dere worthy] glorious   thryfte]
luck   stronge] violent   rewe] repent   bode the] bidden
thee

Much was redy with a bolte,
　Redly and anone,
He set the monke to-fore the brest
　To the grounde that he can gone.

Of two and fyfty wyght yonge yemen
　There abode not one,
Saf a lytell page and a grome,
　To lede the somers with Lytel Johan.

They brought the monke to the lodge-dore
　Whether he were loth or lefe,
For to speke with Robyn Hode,
　Maugre in [his] tethe.

Robyn dyde adowne his hode
　The monke whan that he se;
The monk was not so curteyse,
　His hode then let he be.

He is a chorle, mayster, by dere worthy God,
　Than sayd Lytell Johan;
Thereof no force, sayd Robyn,
　For curteysy can he none.

How many men, sayd Robyn,
　Had this monke, Johan?
Fyfty and two whan that we met,
　But many of them be gone.

bolte] short blunt arrow　　Redly] quickly　　set ... to-fore]
hit ... upon　　can gone] did go　　Saf] except　　lodge-] hut
in the forest　　loth or lefe] reluctant or glad　　Maugre ... tethe]
in spite of his resistance　　dyde adowne] threw back　　force]
matter　　can] knows

Let blowe a horne, sayd Robyn,
    That felaushyp may vs knowe.
Seuen score of wyght yemen
    Came pryckynge on a rowe.

And euerych of them a good mantell
    Of scarlet and of raye;
All they came to good Robyn
    To wyte what he wolde say.

They made the monke to wasshe and wype
    And syt at his denere;
Robyn Hode and Lytell Johan
    They serued him both in-fere.

Do gladly, monke, sayd Robyn,
    Gramercy, syr, sayde he.
Where is your abbay, whan ye are at home,
    And who is your avowe?

Saynt Mary abbay, sayd the monke,
    Though I be symple here.
In what offyce? sayd Robyn:
    Syr, the hye selerer.

Ye be the more welcome, sayd Robyn,
    So euer mote I the;
Fyll of the best wyne, sayd Robyn,
    This monke shall drynke to me.

felaushyp] the company (of outlaws)   pryckynge] spurring   on
a rowe] in file   euerych] each   raye] striped cloth   wyte]
know   in-fere] together   Do gladly] help yourself   Gra-
mercy] thank you   avowe] patron   symple] of humble rank
selerer] cellarer   mote I the] may I prosper

But I haue grete meruayle, sayd Robyn,
   Of all this longe day;
I drede Our Lady be wroth with me,
   She sent me not my pay.

Haue no doute, mayster, sayd Lytell Johan,
   Ye haue no nede, I saye;
This monke it hath brought, I dare well swere,
   For he is of her abbay.

And she was a borowe, sayd Robyn,
   Betwene a knyght and me,
Of a lytell money that I hym lent
   Under the grene wode tree.

And yf thou hast that syluer ibrought,
   I pray the let me se;
And I shall helpe the eftsones
   Yf thou haue nede to me.

The monke swere a full grete othe
   With a sory chere:
Of the borowehode thou spekest to me
   Herde I neuer ere.

I make myn avowe to God, sayd Robyn,
   Monke, thou art to blame;
For God is holde a ryghtwys man
   And so is his dame.

haue ... meruayle] have had ... wonder   borowe] surety
the eftsones] you soon   chere] countenance   borowehode]
suretyship   holde] held to be   dame] mother

Thou toldest with thyn owne tonge,
   Thou may not say nay,
How thou arte her seruaunt
   And seruest her euery day.

And thou art made her messengere
   My money for to pay;
Therefore I cun the more thanke
   Thou arte come at thy day.

What is in your cofers? sayd Robyn,
   Trewe than tell thou me.
Syr, he sayd, twenty marke,
   Al so mote I the.

Yf there be no more, sayd Robyn,
   I wyll not one peny;
Yf thou hast myster of ony more
   Syr, more I shall lende to the.

And yf I fynde [more, sayd] Robyn,
   I-wys thou shalte it forgone;
For of thy spendynge-syluer, monke,
   Thereof wyll I ryght none.

Go nowe forthe, Lytell Johan,
   And the trouth tell thou me;
If there be no more but twenty marke,
   No peny that I se.

Lytell Johan spred his mantell downe
   As he had done before,
And he tolde out of the monkes male
   Eyght [hondred] pounde and more.

(thy) day] day of reckoning	marke] marks (13s. 4d.)	wyll not]
won't (take) myster] need	I-wys] certainly	male] coffer

Lytell Johan let it lye full styll
　　And went to his mayster in hast:
Syr, he sayd, the monke is trewe ynowe,
　　Our Lady hath doubled your cast.

I make myn avowe to God, sayd Robyn—
　　Monke, what tolde I the?—
Our Lady is the trewest woman
　　That euer yet founde I me.

By dere worthy God, sayd Robyn,
　　To seche all Englond thorowe,
Yet founde I neuer to my pay
　　A moche better borowe.

Fyll of the best wyne and do hym drynke, sayd
　　　　Robyn,
　　And grete well thy lady hende,
And yf she haue nede to Robyn Hode
　　A frende she shall hym fynde.

And yf she nedeth ony more syluer
　　Come thou agayne to me
And, by this token she hath me sent,
　　She shall haue such thre.

The monke was goynge to London ward,
　　There to holde grete mote,
The knyght that rode so hye on hors,
　　To brynge hym vnder fote.

ynowe] enough　　　　　cast] throw (as of dice)　　　seche] search
hende] gracious　　　　such thre] three times as much　　　mote]
meeting

459

Whether be ye away? sayd Robyn:
    Syr, to maners in this londe,
To reken with our reues
    That haue done moch wronge.

Come now forth, Lytell Johan,
    And harken to my tale;
A better yem[a]n I knowe none
    To seke a monkes male.

How moch is in yonder other corser? sayd
    Robyn,
    The soth must we see.
By Our Lady, than sayd the monke,
    That were no curteysye

To bydde a man to dyner,
    And syth hym bete and bynde!
It is our olde maner, sayd Robyn,
    To leue but lytell behynde.

The monke toke the hors with spore,
    No lenger wolde he abyde;
Aske to drynke, than sayd Robyn,
    Or that ye forther ryde.

Nay, for God, than sayd the monke,
    Me reweth I cam so nere;
For better chepe I myght haue dyned
    In Blythe or in Dankestere.

maners] manors   reues] reeves   seke] search   male] bag
corser] ? coffer   syth] then   maner] habit   toke] took to
spore] spur   for God] before God   Me reweth] I repent
For better chepe] more cheaply

Grete well your abbot, sayd Robyn,
   And your pryour, I you pray,
And byd hym sende me such a monke
   To dyner euery day.

Now lete we that monke be styll
   And speke we of that knyght;
Yet he came to holde his day
   Whyle that it was lyght.

He dyde him streyt to Bernysdale
   Under the grene-wode tre,
And he founde there Robyn Hode
   And all his mery meyne.

The knyght lyght doune of his good palfray,
   Robyn whan he gan see;
So curteysly he dyde adoune his hode
   And set hym on his knee.

God the saue, Robyn Hode,
   And all this company!
Welcome be thou, gentyll knyght,
   And ryght welcome to me.

Than bespake hym Robyn Hode
   To that knyght so fre:
What nede dryueth the to grene wode?
   I praye the, syr knyght, tell me.

And welcome be thou, ge[n]tyll knyght,
   Why hast thou be so longe?
For the abbot and the hye iustyce
   Wolde haue had my londe.

holde] keep	dyde him] took himself	meyne] company
dyde adoune] threw back	set hym] knelt	fre] gracious

461

Hast thou thy londe [a]gayne? sayd Robyn;
  Treuth than tell thou me.
Ye, for God, sayd the knyght,
  And that thanke I God and the.

But take not a grefe, sayd the knyght, that I
    haue be so longe;
  I came by a wrastelynge,
And there I holpe a pore yeman
  With wronge was put behynde.

Nay, for God, sayd Robyn,
  Syr knyght, that thanke I the;
What man that helpeth a good yeman
  His frende than wyll I be.

Haue here foure hondred pounde, than sayd the
    knyght,
  The whiche ye lent to me;
And here is also twenty marke
  For your curteysy.

Nay, for God, than sayd Robyn,
  Thou broke it well for ay;
For Our Lady by her selerer
  Hath sent to me my pay;

And yf I toke it i-twyse
  A shame it were to me:
But trewely, gentyll knyght,
  Welcom arte thou to me.

wrastelynge] wrestling-match   holpe] helped   put behynde]
held back, penalized   broke] hold, use

Whan Robyn had tolde his tale
  He leugh and had good chere;
By my trouthe, then sayd the knyght,
  Your money is redy here.

Broke it well, sayd Robyn,
  Thou gentyll knyght so fre;
And welcome be thou, ge[n]tyll knyght,
  Under my trystell-tre.

But what shall these bowes do? sayd Robyn,
  And these arowes ifedred fre?
By God, than sayd the knyght,
  A pore present to the.

Come now forth, Lytell Johan,
  And go to my treasure,
And brynge me there foure hondred pounde;
  The monke ouer-tolde it me.

Haue here foure hondred pounde,
  Thou gentyll knyght and trewe,
And bye hors and harnes good
  And gylte thy spores all newe.

And yf thou fayle ony spendynge
  Com to Robyn Hode,
And by my trouth thou shalt none fayle
  The whyles I haue any good.

And broke well thy foure hondred pound
  Whiche I lent to the,
And make thy selfe no more so bare
  By the counsell of me.

trystell-tre] tree for meeting at, rendezvous   ifedred fre] finely
feathered   ouer-tolde] counted over   gylte] gild   fayle] lack

Thus than holpe hym good Robyn,
    The knyght all of his care:
God that syt in heuen hye
    Graunte vs well to fare!

The Fyfth Fytte

Now hath the knyght his leue i-take
    And wente hym on his way;
Robyn Hode and his mery men
    Dwelled styll full many a day.

Lyth and lysten, gentil men,
    And herken what I shall say—
How the proud sheryfe of Notyngham
    Dyde crye a full fayre play;

That all the best archers of the north
    Sholde come vpon a day,
And [he] that shoteth allther best
    The game shall bere a way.

He that shoteth allther best,
    Furthest, fayre and lowe,
At a payre of fynly buttes
    Under the grene-wode shawe,

A ryght good arowe he shall haue,
    The shaft of syluer whyte,
The hede and the feders of ryche rede golde;
    In Englond is none lyke.

syt] sits   Fytte] canto   crye] proclaim   allther best] best
of all   fynly] fine   buttes] targets   shawe] little wood

This than herde good Robyn
    Under his trystell-tre:
Make you redy, ye wyght yonge men;
    That shotynge wyll I se.

Buske you, my mery yonge men,
    Ye shall go with me;
And I wyll wete the shryues fayth,
    Trewe and yf he be.

Whan they had theyr bowes i-bent,
    Theyr takles fedred fre,
Seuen score of wyght yonge men
    Stode by Robyns kne.

Whan they cam to Notyngham
    The buttes were fayre and longe;
Many was the bolde archere
    That shoted with bowes stronge:

There shall but syx shote with me,
    The other shal kepe my he[ue]de
And stand with good bowes bent
    That I be not desceyued.

The fourth outlawe his bowe gan bende,
    And that was Robyn Hode;
And that behelde the proud sheryfe,
    All by the but he stode.

Thryes Robyn shot about
    And alway he slist the wand,
And so dyde good Gylberte
    Wyth the whyte hande.

Buske you] get ready   wete] know   shryues fayth] sheriff's
good faith   takles] arrows   fre] fine   other] others
heuede] head, life   desceyued] deceived   slist] split

Lytell Johan and good Scatheloke
　　Were archers good and fre;
Lytell Much and good Reynolde,
　　The worste wolde they not be.

Whan they had shot aboute,
　　These archours fayre and good,
Euermore was the best,
　　For soth, Robyn Hode.

Hym was delyuered the good arowe,
　　For best worthy was he;
He toke the yeft so curteysly,
　　To grene wode wolde he.

They cryed out on Robyn Hode
　　And grete hornes gan they blowe:
Wo worth the, treason! sayd Robyn,
　　Full euyl thou art to knowe.

And wo be thou, thou proude sheryf,
　　Thus gladdynge thy gest;
Other wyse thou behote me
　　In yonder wylde forest.

But had I the in grene wode
　　Under my trystell-tre,
Thou sholdest leue me a better wedde
　　Than thy trewe lewte.

Full many a bowe there was bent,
　　And arowes let they glyde;
Many a kyrtell there was rent
　　And hurt many a syde.

The outlawes shot was so stronge
　　That no man myght them dryue,
And the proud sheryfes men
　　They fled away full blyue.

Robyn sawe the busshement to-broke,
　　In grene wode he wolde haue be;
Many an arowe there was shot
　　Amonge that company.

Lytell Johan was hurte full sore
　　With an arowe in his kne
That he myght neyther go nor ryde;
　　It was full grete pyte.

Mayster, then sayd Lytell Johan,
　　If euer thou louest me,
And for that ylke lordes loue
　　That dyed vpon a tre,

And for the medes of my seruyce
　　That I haue serued the,
Lete neuer the proude sheryf
　　Alyue now fynde me.

But take out thy browne swerde
　　And smyte all of my hede,
And gyue me woundes depe and wyde;
　　No lyfe on me be lefte.

I wolde not that, sayd Robyn,
　　Johan, that thou were slawe,
For all the golde in mery Englonde
　　Though it lay now on a rawe.

dryue] drive away　　　blyue] quickly　　　　busshement] ambush
to-broke] utterly broken　　ylke] same　　medes] wages　　browne]
burnished　　　slawe] slain　　rawe] row, line

God forbede, sayd Lytell Much,
　　That dyed on a tre,
That thou sholdest, Lytell Johan,
　　Parte our company.

Up he toke hym on his backe
　　And bare hym well a myle;
Many a tyme he layd hym downe,
　　And shot another whyle.

Then was there a fayre castell
　　A lytell within the wode;
Double-dyched it was about
　　And walled, by the rode.

And there dwelled that gentyll knyght
　　Syr Rychard at the Lee,
That Robyn had lent his good
　　Under the grene-wode tree.

In he toke good Robyn
　　And all his company:
Welcome be thou, Robyn Hode,
　　Welcome arte thou to me;

And moche [I] thanke the of thy comfort
　　And of thy curteysye
And of thy grete kyndenesse
　　Under the grene-wode tre.

I loue no man in all this worlde
　　So much as I do the;
For all the proud sheryf of Notyngham
　　Ryght here shalt thou be.

rode] Cross　　　　　good] goods, equipment　　　　　For all] despite

Shyt the gates and drawe the brydge
   And let no man come in,
And arme you well and make you redy,
   And to the walles ye wynne.

For one thynge, Robyn, I the behote;
   I swere by Saynt Quyntyne,
These forty dayes thou wonnest with me,
   To soupe, ete, and dyne.

Bordes were layde and clothes were spredde,
   Redely and anone;
Robyn Hode and his mery men
   To mete can they gone.

The Sixth Fytte

LYTHE and lysten, gentylmen,
   And herkyn to your songe:
Howe the proude shyref of Notyngham
   And men of armys stronge

Full fast cam to the hye shyref
   The contre vp to route,
And they besette the knyghtes castell,
   The walles all aboute.

The proude shyref loude gan cry,
   And sayde, Thou traytour knight,
Thou kepest here the kynges enemys
   Agaynst the lawe and right.

wynne] get, go   behote] promise   wonnest] dwellest   Redely]
quickly   Fytte] canto   Lythe] hear   vp to route] to stir up, call
to arms

Syr, I wyll auowe that I haue done
　　The dedys that here be dyght
Vpon all the landes that I haue,
　　As I am a trewe knyght.

Wende furth, sirs, on your way,
　　And do no more to me
Tyll ye wyt oure kynges wille,
　　What he wyll say to the.

The shyref thus had his answere
　　Without any lesynge;
[Fu]rth he yede to London towne
　　All for to tel our kinge.

Ther he telde him of that knight
　　And eke of Robyn Hode,
And also of the bolde archars
　　That were so noble and gode.

He wyll auowe that he hath done
　　To mayntene the outlawes stronge;
He wyll be lorde and set you at nought
　　In all the northe londe.

I wyl be at Notyngham, saide our kynge,
　　Within this fourteenyght,
And take I wyll Robyn Hode,
　　And so I wyll that knight.

Go nowe home, shyref, sayde our kynge,
　　And do as I byd the;
And ordeyn gode archers ynowe
　　Of all the wyde contre.

auowe] admit, answer for　　dyght] done　　wyt] know　　lesynge]
lying　　　yede] went　　　auowe that] admit what　　stronge]
violent　　fourteenyght] fortnight　　ynowe] enough

The shyref had his leue itake
  And went hym on his way,
And Robyn Hode to grene wode
  Vpon a certen day.

And Lytel John was hole of the arowe
  That shote was in his kne,
And dyd hym streyght to Robyn Hode
  Vnder the grene wode tree.

Robyn Hode walked in the forest
  Vnder the leuys grene;
The proude shyref of Notyngham
  Thereof he had grete tene.

The shyref there fayled of Robyn Hode,
  He myght not haue his pray;
Than he awayted this gentyll knyght
  Bothe by nyght and day.

Euer he wayted the gentyll knyght
  Syr Richarde at the Lee,
As he went on haukynge by the ryuer syde
  And lete [his] haukes flee.

Toke he there this gentyll knight
  With men of armys stronge,
And led hym to Notyngham warde
  Bounde bothe fote and hande.

The sheref sware a full grete othe
  Bi hym that dyed on rode,
He had leuer than an hundred [pound]
  That he had Robyn Hode.

hole] healed   tene] vexation   awayted] waited and watched
for

This harde the knyghtes wyfe,
    A fayr lady and a free;
She set hir on a gode palfrey,
    To grene wode anone rode she.

Whanne she cam in the forest
    Vnder the grene wode tree,
Fonde she there Robyn Hode
    And al his fayre mene.

God the saue, gode Robyn,
    And all thy company;
For Our dere Ladyes sake
    A bone graunte thou me.

Late neuer my wedded lorde
    Shamefully slayne be;
He is fast bowne to Notingham warde
    For the loue of the.

Anone than saide goode Robyn
    To that lady so fre:
What man hath your lorde [i]take?
    [The proude shyref, than saide she.]

[The proude shyref hath hym i-take]
    For soth as I the say;
He is nat yet thre myeles
    Passed on his way.

Vp than sterte gode Robyn
    As man that had ben wode:
Buske you, my mery men,
    For hym that dyed on rode.

harde] heard   free] gracious   set hir] mounted   mene]
company   Late] let   bowne] bound, going   itake] captured
wode] mad, furious   Buske you] get ready

And he that this sorowe forsaketh,
   By hym that dyed on tre,
Shall he neuer in grene wode
   No lenger dwel with me.

Sone there were gode bowes bent
   Mo than seuen score;
Hedge ne dyche spared they none
   That was them before.

I make myn auowe to God, sayde Robyn,
   The sherif wolde I fayne see;
And if I may hym take,
   Iquyte shall it be.

And whan they came to Notingham
   They walked in the strete;
And with the proude sherif iwys
   Sone can they mete.

Abyde, thou proude sherif, he sayde,
   Abyde and speke with me;
Of some tidinges of oure kinge
   I wolde fayne here of the.

This seuen yere, by dere worthy God,
   Ne yede I this fast on fote;
I make myn auowe to God, thou proude sherif,
   It is nat for thy gode.

Robyn bent a full goode bowe,
   An arrowe he drowe at wyll;
He hit so the proude sherife
   Vpon the grounde he lay full still.

fayne] gladly   Iquyte . . . be] our account shall be squared
yede] went

473

And or he myght vp aryse
  On his fete to stonde,
He smote of the sherifs hede
  With his bright bronde.

Lye thou there, thou proude sherife,
  Euyll mote thou cheue!
There myght no man to the[e] truste
  The whyles thou were a lyue.

His men drewe out theyr bryght swerdes
  That were so sharpe and kene,
And layde on the sheryues men
  And dryued them downe bydene.

Robyn stert to that knyght
  And cut a two his [bonde],
And toke hym in his hand a bowe
  And bad hym by hym stonde.

Leue thy hors the behynde
  And lerne for to renne;
Thou shalt with me to grene wode
  Through myre, mosse, and fenne.

Thou shalt with me to grene wode,
  Without any leasynge,
Tyll that I haue gete vs grace
  Of Edwarde our comly kynge.

or] ere   bronde] sword   mote . . . cheue] may . . . end   by-
dene] together   stert] ran   toke] gave   mosse] bog
leasynge] lying

A GEST OF ROBYN HODE

The Seuenth Fytte

THE kynge came to Notynghame
  With knyghtes in grete araye,
For to take that gentyll knyght
  And Robyn Hode, yf he may.

He asked men of that countre
  After Robyn Hode,
And after that gentyll knyght
  That was so bolde and stout.

Whan they had tolde hym the case,
  Our kynge vnderstode ther tale
And seased in his honde
  The knyghtes londes all.

All the passe of Lancasshyre
  He went both ferre and nere
Tyll he came to Plomton Parke;
  He fayled many of his dere.

Ther our kynge was wont to se
  Herdes many one,
He coud vnneth fynde one dere
  That bare ony good horne.

The kynge was wonder wroth withall
  And swore by the Trynyte:
I wolde I had Robyn Hode,
  With eyen I myght hym se.

Fytte] canto   stout] stalwart   passe] extent   Plomton]
Plumpton, near Knaresborough, west of York   fayled] missed
Ther] where   vnneth] scarcely

And he that wolde smyte of the knyghtes hede
  And brynge it to me,
He shall haue the kynghtes londes,
  Syr Rycharde at the Le.

I gyue it hym with my charter,
  And sele it [with] my honde,
To haue and holde for euer more
  In all mery Englonde.

Than bespake a fayre olde knyght
  That was treue in his fay:
A, my leege lorde the kynge,
  One worde I shall you say.

There is no man in this countre
  May haue the knyghtes londes
Whyle Robyn Hode may ryde or gone
  And bere a bowe in his hondes,

That he ne shall lese his hede
  That is the best ball in his hode;
Giue it no man, my lorde the kynge,
  That ye wyll any good.

Half a yere dwelled our comly kynge
  In Notyngham, and well more;
Coude he not here of Robyn Hode,
  In what countre that he were.

But alway went good Robyn
  By halke and eke by hyll,
And alway slewe the kynges dere
  And welt them at his wyll.

fay] faith   gone] go about   That ye wyll] to whom you wish
halke] corner, hiding-place   welt] disposed of

Than bespake a proude fostere
   That stode by our kynges kne:
Yf ye wyll se good Robyn,
   Ye must do after me.

Take fyue of the best knyghtes
   That be in your lede,
And [walke] downe by yon abbay
   And gete you monkes wede.

And I wyll be your ledes-man
   And lede you the way,
And or ye come to Notyngham
   My hede then dare I lay

That ye shall mete with good Robyn,
   On lyue yf that he be;
Or ye come to Notyngham
   With eyen ye shall hym se.

Full hast[e]ly our kynge was dyght,
   So were his knyghtes fyue,
Euerych of them in monkes wede,
   And hasted them thyder bly[u]e.

Our kynge was grete aboue his cole,
   A brode hat on his crowne;
Ryght as he were abbot-lyke
   They rode up in-to the towne.

fostere] forester   lede] company   wede] habit   ledes-man] guide   or] ere   On lyue] alive   dyght] ready   blyue] at once   cole] monastic habit with a hood

Styf botes our kynge had on,
  Forsoth as I you say;
He rode syngynge to grene wode;
  The couent was clothed in graye.

His male-hors and his grete somers
  Folowed our kynge behynde
Tyll they came to grene wode,
  A myle vnder the lynde.

There they met with good Robyn
  Stondynge on the waye,
And so dyde many a bold archere,
  For soth as I you say.

Robyn toke the kynges hors
  Hastely in that stede,
And sayd, Syr abbot, by your leue,
  A whyle ye must abyde.

We be yemen of this foreste
  Vnder the grene-wode tre;
We lyue by our kynges dere,
  [Other shyft haue not wee.]

And ye haue chyrches and rentes both,
  And gold full grete plente;
Gyue vs some of your spendynge
  For saynt[e] charyte.

Than bespake our cumly kynge,
  Anone than sayde he:
I brought no more to grene wode
  But forty pounde with me.

couent] company of 'monks'   male-hors] horse carrying money-
bags   somers] pack-horses   lynde] linden, lime tree   stede]
place   shyft] expedient, means   saynte] blessed

I haue layne at Notyngham
  This fourtynyght with our kynge,
And spent I haue full moche good
  On many a grete lordynge.

And I haue but forty pounde,
  No more than haue I me;
But yf I had an hondred pounde
  I wolde vouch it safe on the.

Robyn toke the forty pounde
  And departed it in two partye;
Halfendell he gaue his mery men
  And bad them mery to be.

Full curteysly Robyn gan say:
  Syr, haue this for your spendyng,
We shall mete another day.
  Gramercy, than sayd our kynge:

But well the greteth Edwarde our kynge,
  And sent to the his seale,
And byddeth the com to Notyngham
  Both to mete and mele.

He toke out the brode targe
  And sone he lete hym se;
Robyn coud his courteysy
  And set hym on his kne.

I loue no man in all the worlde
  Se well as I do my kynge;
Welcome is my lordes seale,
  And monke, for thy tydynge—

good] money   vouch it safe] bestow it   departed] divided
partye] parts   Halfendell] half   the greteth] greets you   targe]
i.e. seal   coud] knew

Syr abbot, for thy tydynges
    To day thou shalt dyne with me
For the loue of my kynge
    Under my trystell-tre.

Forth he lad our comly kynge
    Full fayre by the honde;
Many a dere there was slayne,
    And full fast dyghtande.

Robyn toke a full grete horne
    And loude he gan blowe;
Seuen score of wyght yonge men
    Came redy on a rowe.

All they kneled on theyr kne
    Full fayre before Robyn;
The kynge sayd hym selfe vntyll
    And swore by Saynt Austyn:

Here is a wonder semely syght;
    Me thynketh, by Goddes pyne,
His men are more at his byddynge
    Then my men be at myn.

Full hast[e]ly was theyr dyner idyght
    And therto gan they gone;
They serued our kynge with al theyr myght,
    Both Robyn and Lytell Johan.

Anone before our kynge was set
    The fatte venyson,
The good whyte brede, the good rede wyne,
    And therto the fyne ale and browne.

trystell-tre] trysting-tree   lad] led   dyghtande] prepared
rowe] line   vntyll] to   Austyn] Augustine   pyne]
agony, passion   gan . . . gone] went

Make good chere, said Robyn,
    Abbot, for charyte;
And for this ylke tydynge
    Blyssed mote thou be.

Now shalte thou se what lyfe we lede
    Or thou hens wende,
Than thou may enfourme our kynge
    Whan ye togyder lende.

Up they sterte all in hast,
    Theyr bowes were smartly bent;
Our kynge was neuer so sore agast,
    He wende to haue be shente.

Two yerdes there were vp set,
    Thereto gan they gange;
By fyfty pase, our kynge sayd,
    The merkes were to longe.

On euery syde a rose-garlonde,
    They shot vnder the lyne:
Who so fayleth of the rose-garlonde, sayd
    Robyn,
    His takyll he shall tyne

And yelde it to his mayster,
    Be it neuer so fyne;
For no man wyll I spare,
    So drynke I ale or wyne;

ylke] same   mote] may   Or] ere   lende] come
wende . . . shente] thought he would be disgraced   yerdes] rods
gan . . . gange] went   longe] far apart   vnder the lyne] in
array (a tag)   takyll] weapons   fyne] forfeit

And bere a buffet on his hede
   [I-]wys ryght all bare.
And all that fell in Robyns lote,
   He smote them wonder sare.

Twyse Robyn shot aboute
   And euer he cleued the wande,
And so dyde good Gylberte
   With the Whyte Hande.

Lytell Johan and good Scathelocke,
   For nothynge wolde they spare;
When they fayled of the garlonde
   Robyn smote them full sore.

At the last shot that Robyn shot
   For all his frendes fare
Yet he fayled of the garlonde
   Thre fyngers and mare.

Than bespake good Gylberte,
   And thus he gan say:
Mayster, he sayd, your takyll is lost,
   Stande forth and take your pay.

If it be so, sayd Robyn,
   That may no better be;
Syr abbot, I delyuer the myn arowe;
   I pray the, syr, serue thou me.

It falleth not for myn ordre, sayd our kynge,
   Robyn, by thy leue,
For to smyte no good yeman,
   For doute I sholde hym greue.

I-wys] certainly   aboute] in his turn   cleued the wande]
split the mark   fare] fortune   pay] deserts   falleth] is
proper   doute] fear   greue] harm

Smyte on boldely, sayd Robyn,
  I giue the large leue.
Anone our kynge, with that worde,
  He folde vp his sleue;

And sych a buffet he gaue Robyn,
  To grounde he yede full nere;
I make myn avowe to God, sayd Robyn,
  Thou arte a stalworthe frere.

There is pith in thyn arme, sayd Robyn,
  I trowe thou canst well shote.
Thus our kynge and Robyn Hode
  Togeder than they met[e].

Robyn behelde our comly kynge
  Wystly in the face;
So dyde Syr Rycharde at the Le,
  And kneled downe in that place.

And so dyde all the wylde outlawes
  Whan they se them knele:
My lorde the kynge of Englonde,
  Now I knowe you well.

Mercy then, Robyn, sayd our kynge,
  Vnder your trystyll-tre,
Of thy goodnesse and thy grace,
  For my men and me.

Yes, for God, sayd Robyn,
  And also God me saue,
I aske mercy, my lorde the kynge,
  And for my men I craue.

large] unreserved   yede] went   frere] friar   Wystly]
intently   for God] before God

Yes, for God, than sayd our kynge,
　And therto sent I me,
With that thou leue the grene wode,
　And all thy company;

And come home, syr, to my courte,
　And there dwell with me.
I make myn avowe to God, sayd Robyn,
　And ryght so shall it be.

I wyll come to your courte,
　Your seruyse for to se,
And brynge with me of my men
　Seuen score and thre.

But me lyke well your seruyse
　I come agayne full soone,
And shote at the donne dere
　As I am wonte to done.

<small>With that thou] so that you should　　But me] unless I　　donne] dun</small>

The Eighth Fytte

HASTE thou ony grene cloth, sayd our kynge,
　That thou wylte sell nowe to me?
Ye, for God, sayd Robyn,
　Thyrty yerdes and thre.

Robyn, sayd our kynge,
　Now pray I the,
Sell me some of that cloth
　To me and my meyne.

<small>Fytte] canto　　meyne] company</small>

Yes, for God, then sayd Robyn,
    Or elles I were a fole;
Another day ye wyll me clothe,
    I trowe, ayenst the Yole.

The kynge kest of his cole then,
    A grene garment he dyde on;
And euery knyght also, i-wys,
    Another had full sone.

Whan they were clothed in Lyncolne grene
    They keste away theyr graye;
Now we shall to Notyngham,
    All thus our kynge gan say.

Theyr bowes bente, and forth they went
    Shotynge all in-fere
Towarde the towne of Notyngham,
    Outlawes as they were.

Our kynge and Robyn rode togyder,
    For soth as I you say,
And they shote plucke-buffet
    As they went by the way.

And many a buffet our kynge wan
    Of Robyn Hode that day;
And nothynge spared good Robyn
    Our kynge in his pay.

for God] before God   ayenst] ready for   Yole] Christmas
kest] cast   cole] habit   dyde] put   in-fere] in company
plucke-buffet] contest in which the archer who missed 'caught' a buffet
from his opponent   pay] deserts

So God me helpe, sayd our kynge,
    Thy game is nought to lere;
I sholde not get a shote of the
    Though I shote all this yere.

All the people of Notyngham
    They stode and behelde;
They sawe nothynge but mantels of grene
    That couered all the felde.

Than euery man to other gan say:
    I drede our kynge be slone;
Come Robyn Hode to the towne, i-wys
    On lyue he lefte neuer one.

Full hast[e]ly they began to fle,
    Both yemen and knaues,
And olde wyues that myght euyll goo,
    They hypped on theyr staues.

The kynge l[o]ughe full fast
    And commaunded theym agayne;
When they se our comly kynge
    I-wys they were full fayne.

They ete and dranke and made them glad,
    And sange with notes hye;
Than bespake our comly kynge
    To Syr Rycharde at the Lee.

He gaue hym there his londe agayne,
    A good man he bad hym be;
Robyn thanked our comly kynge
    And set hym on his kne.

lere] learn	On lyue] alive	knaues] serfs	hypped]
hobbled	agayne] back	I-wys] indeed	fayne] pleased
hye] loud			

Had Robyn dwelled in the kynges courte
    But twelue monethes and thre,
That [he had] spent an hondred pounde
    And all his mennes fe.

In euery place where Robyn came
    Euer more he layde downe,
Both for knyghtes and for squyres,
    To gete hym grete renowne.

By than the yere was all agone
    He had no man but twayne,
Lytell Johan and good Scathelocke
    With hym all for to gone.

Robyn sawe yonge men shote
    Full ferre vpon a day:
Alas, than sayd good Robyn,
    My welthe is went away.

Somtyme I was an archere good,
    A styffe and eke a stronge;
I was com[pt]ed the best archere
    That was in mery Englonde.

Alas, then sayd good Robyn,
    Alas and well a woo;
Yf I dwele lenger with the kynge
    Sorowe wyll me sloo.

Forth than went Robyn Hode
    Tyll he came to our kynge:
My lorde the kynge of Englonde,
    Graunte me myn askynge.

fe] wages   layde downe] paid out   By than] by the time that
ferre] far   styffe] staunch   compted] accounted   sloo] slay

487

I made a chapell in Bernysda[l]e
    That semely is to se,
It is of Mary Magdaleyne,
    And thereto wolde I be.

I myght neuer in this seuen nyght
    No tyme slepe ne wynke,
Nother all these seuen dayes
    Nother ete ne drynke.

Me longeth sore to Bernysdale,
    I may not be therfro;
Barefote and wolwarde I haue hyght
    Thyder for to go.

Yf it be so, than sayd our kynge,
    It may no better be;
Seuen nyght I gyue the leue,
    No lengre, to dwell fro me.

Gramercy, lorde, then sayd Robyn,
    And set hym on his kne;
He toke his leue full courteysly,
    To grene wode then went he.

Whan he came to grene wode
    In a mery mornynge,
There he herde the notes small
    Of byrdes mery syngynge.

It is ferre gone, sayd Robyn,
    That I was last here;
Me lyste a lytell for to shote
    At the donne dere.

Nother] neither   therfro] turned from it   wolwarde] wearing
wool next the skin, in penance   hyght] promised   Gramercy]
thank you   Me lyste] it pleases me   donne] dun

488

Robyn slewe a full grete harte;
   His horne than gan he blow,
That all the outlawes of that forest
   That horne coud they knowe,

And gadred them togyder
   In a lytell throwe.
Seuen score of wyght yonge men
   Came redy on a rowe,

And fayre dyde of theyr hodes
   And set them on theyr kne:
Welcome, they sayd, our mayster,
   Under this grene-wode tre.

Robyn dwelled in grene wode
   Twenty yere and two;
For all drede of Edwarde our kynge
   Agayne wolde he not goo.

Yet he was begyled, i-wys,
   Through a wicked woman,
The pryoresse of Kyrkesly,
   That nye was of hys kynne;

For the loue of a knyght,
   Syr Roger of Donkesly,
That was her owne speciall:
   Full euyll mote they the!

throwe] space of time   dyde of] put off   set them] got
Agayne] back   Kyrkesly] Kirklees, near Mirfield in Yorkshire
Donkesly] Doncaster   speciall] lover   mote they the] may they
fare

489

They toke togyder theyr counsell
  Robyn Hode for to sle,
And how they myght best do that dede
  His banis for to be.

Than bespake good Robyn
  In place where as he stode:
To morow I muste to Kyrke[s]ly
  Craftely to be leten blode.

Syr Roger of Donkestere
  By the pryoresse he lay,
And there they betrayed good Robyn Hode
  Through theyr false playe.

Cryst haue mercy on his soule
  That dyed on the rode;
For he was a good outlawe
  And dyde pore men moch god[e].

banis] murderers   Craftely] skilfully   rode] cross

103. *Battle of Otterbourne*

IT fell about the Lammas tide
 When the muir-men win their hay,
The doughty Douglas bound him to ride
 Into England, to drive a prey.

He chose the Gordons and the Græmes,
 With them the Lindesays light and gay;
But the Jardines wald not with him ride
 And they rue it to this day.

And he has burn'd the dales of Tyne
 And part of Bambrough shire;
And three good towers on Reidswire fells,
 He left them all on fire.

And he march'd up to Newcastle
 And rode it round about:
O wha 's the lord of this castle,
 Or wha 's the lady o 't?

But up spake proud Lord Percy then,
 And O but he spake hie:
I am the lord of this castle,
 My wife 's the lady gay.

Lammas tide] 1 August   win] take in   bound him] got
ready   Bambrough shire] south of Berwick   Reidswire] on the
border near Carter Bar

If thou 'rt the lord of this castle
   Sae weel it pleases me;
For ere I cross the Border fells
   The tane of us shall die.

He took a lang spear in his hand,
   Shod with the metal free,
And for to meet the Douglas there
   He rode right furiouslie.

But O how pale his lady look'd
   Frae aff the castle wa',
When down before the Scottish spear
   She saw proud Percy fa'.

Had we twa been upon the green,
   And never an eye to see,
I wad hae had you, flesh and fell;
   But your sword sall gae wi' me.

But gae ye up to Otterbourne
   And wait there dayis three,
And if I come not ere three dayis end
   A fause knight ca' ye me.

The Otterbourne 's a bonnie burn,
   'Tis pleasant there to be;
But there is nought at Otterbourne
   To feed my men and me.

The deer rins wild on hill and dale,
   The birds fly wild from tree to tree,
But there is neither bread nor kale
   To fend my men and me.

tane] one   free] fine   fell] skin   sall gae] shall go
kale] borecole, green kale   fend] provide for

Yet I will stay at Otterbourne
  Where you shall welcome be,
And if ye come not at three dayis end
  A fause lord I'll ca' thee.

Thither will I come, proud Percy said,
  By the might of our Ladie:
There will I bide thee, said the Douglas,
  My troth I plight to thee.

They lighted high on Otterbourne
  Upon the bent sae brown;
They lighted high on Otterbourne
  And threw their pallions down.

And he that had a bonnie boy
  Sent out his horse to grass;
And he that had not a bonnie boy,
  His ain servant he was.

But up then spake a little page
  Before the peep of dawn:
O waken ye, waken ye, my good lord,
  For Percy 's hard at hand.

Ye lie, ye lie, ye liar loud,
  Sae loud I hear ye lie;
For Percy had not men yestreen
  To dight my men and me.

But I have dream'd a dreary dream
  Beyond the Isle of Sky;
I saw a dead man win a fight,
  And I think that man was I.

lighted] dismounted   bent] moor covered with bent-grass   pal-
lions] pavilions, tents   yestreen] last evening   dight] chastise, beat

He belted on his guid braid sword
   And to the field he ran;
But he forgot the helmet good
   That should have kept his brain.

When Percy wi' the Douglas met
   I wat he was fu' fain:
They swakked their swords till sair they swat,
   And the blood ran down like rain.

But Percy with his good broad sword
   That could so sharply wound
Has wounded Douglas on the brow
   Till he fell to the ground.

Then he call'd on his little foot-page
   And said, Run speedilie,
And fetch my ain dear sister's son
   Sir Hugh Montgomery.

My nephew good, the Douglas said,
   What recks the death of ane:
Last night I dream'd a dreary dream
   And I ken the day 's thy ain.

My wound is deep, I fain would sleep;
   Take thou the vanguard of the three,
And hide me by the braken bush
   That grows on yonder lilye lee.

O bury me by the braken bush,
   Beneath the blooming brier;
Let never living mortal ken
   That ere a kindly Scot lies here.

kept] protected   wat] know   fu' fain] overjoyed   swakked]
brandished   swat] sweated   Sir Hugh] *Percy was captured by Sir*
John Montgomery of Eglisham   lilye] lovely

He lifted up that noble lord
    Wi' the saut tear in his e'e;
He hid him in the braken bush
    That his merrie men might not see.

The moon was clear, the day drew near,
    The spears in flinders flew,
But mony a gallant Englishman
    Ere day the Scotsmen slew.

The Gordons good, in English blood
    They steep'd their hose and shoon;
The Lindsays flew like fire about
    Till all the fray was done.

The Percy and Montgomery met
    That either of other were fain;
They swapped swords, and they twa swat,
    And aye the blood ran down between.

Now yield thee, yield thee, Percy, he said,
    Or else I vow I'll lay thee low:
To whom must I yield, quoth Earl Percy,
    Now that I see it must be so?

Thou shalt not yield to lord nor loun
    Nor shalt thou yield to me;
But yield thee to the braken bush
    That grows upon yon lilye lee.

I will not yield to a braken bush
    Nor yet will I yield to a brier;
But I would yield to Earl Douglas,
    Or Sir Hugh the Montgomery, if he were here.

flinders] smithereens   fain] eager   swapped] struck   loun]
peasant

As soon as he knew it was Montgomery
 He struck his sword's point in the gronde;
The Montgomery was a courteous knight
 And quickly took him by the honde.

This deed was done at the Otterbourne
 About the breaking of the day;
Earl Douglas was buried at the braken bush
 And the Percy led captive away.

104. *Chevy Chase*

THE Perse owt off Northombarlonde,
 And avowe to God mayd he
That he wold hunte in the mowntayns
 Off Chyviat within days thre,
In the magg[re] of doughte Dogl[a]s,
 And all that euer with him be.

The fattiste hartes in all Cheviat
 He sayd he wold kyll, and cary them away:
Be my feth, sayd the dougheti Doglas agayn,
 I wyll let that hontyng yf that I may.

The[n] the Perse owt off Banborowe cam,
 With him a myghtee meany,
With fifteen hondrith archares bold off blood and
  bone;
 The[y] wear chosen owt of shyars thre.

And avowe] a vow   In the maggre] in spite   let] hinder
Banborowe] on the Northumberland coast   meany] company
shyars thre] ? Bamborough, Norham, Lindisfarne

This begane on a Monday at morn,
　　In Cheviat the hillys so he;
The chylde may rue that ys vn-born,
　　It wos the mor pitte.

The dryvars thorowe the woodes went
　　For to reas the dear;
Bomen byckarte vppone the bent
　　With ther browd aros cleare.

Then the wyld thorowe the woodes went
　　On euery syde shear;
Greahondes thorowe the grevis glent
　　For to kyll thear dear.

Th[i]s begane in Chyviat the hyls abone
　　Yerly on a Monnyn-day;
Be that it drewe to the oware off none
　　A hondrith fat hartes ded ther lay.

The[y] blewe a mo[r]t vppone the bent,
　　The[y] semblyde on sydis shear;
To the quyrry then the Perse went
　　To se the bryttlynge off the deare.

He sayd, It was the Duglas promys
　　This day to met me hear;
But I wyste he wolde faylle, verament;
　　A great oth the Perse swear.

he] high　　　　reas] rouse　　　　Bomen byckarte] bowmen attacked
bent] moor covered with bent-grass　　　aros] arrows　　　wyld] deer
shear] several　　　Greahondes] greyhounds　　　grevis] groves
glent] darted　　　abone] above　　　Yerly] early　　　Be that] by
the time that　　　oware] hour　　　mort] blast to celebrate the kill
semblyde] assembled　　　quyrry] dead game　　　bryttlynge] cutting up
wyste] knew

At the laste a squyar off Northomberlonde
  Lokyde at his hand full ny;
He was war a the doughetie Doglas commynge,
  With him a myghtte meany.

Both with spear, [bylle,] and brande,
  Yt was a myghtti sight to se;
Hardyar men both off hart not hande
  Wear not in Cristiante.

The[y] wear twenti hondrith spear-men good
  Withoute any feale;
The[y] wear borne along be the watter a Twyde
  Yth bowndes of Tividale.

Leave of the brytlyng of the dear, he sayd,
  And to your bo[w]ys lock ye tayk good hede;
For neuer sithe ye wear on your mothars borne
  Had ye neuer so mickle nede.

The dougheti Dogglas on a stede
  He rode alle his men beforne;
His armor glytteryde as dyd a glede;
  A boldar barne was neuer born.

Tell me whos men ye ar, he says,
  Or whos men that ye be;
Who gave youe leave to hunte in this Chyviat
    chays
  In the spyt of myn and of me?

at his hand] close by him   war a] aware of   myghtte meany]
mighty company   bylle] halberd   brande] sword   Cris-
tiante] Christendom   feale] fail   a Twyde] of Tweed   Yth
bowndes of Tividale] within the limits of Teviotdale   lock] look
sithe] since   glede] glowing coal   chays] hunting-ground

The first mane that euer him an answear mayd,
   Yt was the good lord Perse:
We wyll not tell the whoys men we ar, he says,
   Nor whos men that we be;
But we wyll hounte hear in this chays
   In the spyt of thyne and of the.

The fattiste hartes in all Chyviat
   We haue kyld, and cast to carry them away.
Be my troth, sayd the doughete Dogglas agay[n],
   Therfor the ton of vs shall de this day.

Then sayd the doughte Doglas
   Unto the lord Perse:
To kyll alle thes giltles men,
   Alas, it wear great pitee:

But Perse, thowe art a lord of lande,
   I am a yerle callyd within my contre;
Let all our men vppone a parti stande,
   And do the battell off the and of me.

Nowe Cristes cors on his crowne, sayd the lorde
     Perse,
   Who-so-euer ther-to says nay;
Be my troth, doughtte Doglas, he says,
   Thow shalt neuer se that day.

Nethar in Ynglonde, Skottlonde, nar France,
   Nor for no man of a woman born,
But, and fortune be my chance,
   I dar met him, on man for on.

cast] reckon, intend   ton] one   de] die   yerle] earl
vppone a parti] aside   do] (let us do)   cors] curse   and
fortune] if fortune   on man for on] man to man

Then bespayke a squyar off Northombarlonde,
  Richard Wytharyngton was his nam:
It shall neuer be told in Sothe-Ynglonde, he says,
  To Kyng Herry the Fourth for sham.

I wat youe byn great lordes twaw,
  I am a poor squyar of lande;
I wylle neuer se my captayne fyght on a fylde
  And stande my selffe and loocke on,
But whylle I may my weppone welde
  I wylle not [fayle], both hart and hande.

That day, that day, that dredfull day!
  The first fit here I fynde;
And youe wyll here any mor a the hountynge a
    the Chyviat,
  Yet ys ther mor behynde.

———

The Yngglyshe men hade ther bowys yebent,
  Ther hartes wer good yenoughe;
The first off arros that the[y] shote off,
  Seven skore spear-men the[y] sloughe.

Yet byddys the yerle Doglas vppon the bent,
  A captayne good yenoughe,
And that was sene verament
  For he wrought hom both woo and wouche.

wat] know	byn] are	fit] canto	fynde] end	And] if
a] of	yebent] bent	sloughe] slew		byddys] stays
good yenoughe] excellent		hom] them		wouche] harm

The Dogglas partyd his ost in thre
　　Lyk a cheffe cheften off pryde;
With suar spears off myghtte tre
　　The[y] cum in on euery syde;

Thrughe our Yngglyshe archery
　　Gave many a wounde fulle wyde;
Many a doughete the[y] garde to dy,
　　Which ganyde them no pryde.

The Ynglyshe men let thear bo[w]ys be
　　And pulde owt brandes that wer brighte;
It was a hevy syght to se
　　Bryght swordes on basnites lyghte.

Thorowe ryche male and myneyeple
　　Many sterne the[y] strocke done streght;
Many a freyke that was fulle fre
　　Ther vndar foot dyd lyght.

At last the Duglas and the Perse met
　　Lyk to captayns of myght and of mayne;
The[y] swapte togethar tylle the[y] both swat
　　With swordes that wear of fyn myllan.

Thes worthe freckys for to fyght
　　Ther-to the[y] wear fulle fayne,
Tylle the bloode owte off thear basnetes sprente
　　As euer dyd heal or ra[y]n.

off pryde] proud　　　suar] sure, trusty　　　tre] wood　　　　Gave]
(they) gave　　　doughete] doughty (fellow)　　　　garde] made
ganyde] gained　　　let . . . be] abandoned　　　brandes] swords
basnites] steel caps　　male] mail.　　myneyeple] *obscure.* ? manople,
gauntlet (*O. French*; *Skeat*)　　　sterne] warriors　　　done] down
freyke] man　　fre] noble　　　swapte] smote　　swat] sweated
myllan] Milan steel　　fayne] eager　　sprente] spurted　　heal] hail

Yelde the, Perse, sayde the Doglas,
　And i' feth I shalle the brynge
Wher thowe shalte haue a yerls wagis
　Of Jamy our Skottish kynge.

Thoue shalte haue thy ransom fre,
　I hight the hear this thinge;
For the manfullyste man yet art thowe [he]
　That euer I conqueryd in filde fighttynge.

Nay, sayd the lord Perse,
　I tolde it the beforne,
That I wolde neuer yeldyde be
　To no man of a woman born.

With that ther cam an arrowe hastely
　Forthe off a myghtte wane;
Hit hathe strekene the yerle Duglas
　In at the brest-bane.

Thorowe lyvar and longes bathe
　The sharpe arrowe ys gane,
That neuer after in all his lyffe-days
　He spayke mo wordes but ane:
That was, Fyghte ye, my myrry men, whyllys ye
　　may,
　For my lyff-days ben gan.

The Perse leanyde on his brande
　And sawe the Duglas de;
He tooke the dede mane by the hande
　And sayd, Wo ys me for the!

yerls] earl's　　　hight] promise　　　the beforne] to you before
off . . . wane] out of . . . multitude (?)　　　lyvar and longes] liver and
lungs　　　bathe] both　　　gan] gone

To haue savyde thy lyffe, I wolde haue partyde
    with
  My landes for years thre;
For a better man of hart nare of hande
  Was nat in all the north contre.

Off all that se a Skottishe knyght
  Was callyd Ser Hewe the Mon[t]gombyrry;
He sawe the Duglas to the deth was dyght,
  He spendyd a spear, a trusti tre.

He rod vppone a corsiare
  Throughe a hondrith archery;
He neuer stynttyde, nar neuer blane,
  Tylle he cam to the good lord Perse.

He set vppone the lorde Perse
  A dynte that was full soare;
With a suar spear of a myghtte tre
  Clean thorow the body he the Perse ber;

A the tothar syde that a man myght se
  A large cloth-yard and mare:
Towe bettar captayns wear not in Cristiante
  Then that day slan wear ther.

An archar of Northomberlonde
  Sa[w] slean was the lord Perse;
He bar a bende bowe in his hand
  Was made off trusti tre.

nare] nor   dyght] done   spendyd] grasped   corsiare] charger
stynttyde] stayed   blane] stopped   dynte] blow   suar] sure,
trusty   ber] bore   A the tothar] on the other   cloth-yard]
by which cloth was measured   Towe] two

An arow that a cloth-yarde was lang
  To the harde stele halyde he;
A dynt that was both sad and soar
  He sat on Ser Hewe the Mon[t]gombyrry.

The dynt yt was both sad and soar
  That he of Mon[t]gomberry sete;
The swane-fethars that his arrowe bar
  With his hart-blood the[y] wear wete.

Ther was neuer a freake wone foot wolde fle
  But still in stour dyd stand,
Heawyng on yche othar, whylle the[y] myghte
    dre,
  With many a balfull brande.

This battell begane in Chyviat
  An owar before the none,
And when [the] even-songe bell was rang
  The battell was nat half done.

The[y] tocke [a stande] on ethar hande
  Be the lyght off the mone;
Many had no strength for to stande
  In Chyviat the hillys abon.

Of fifteen hondrith archars of Ynglonde
  Went away but seuenti and thre;
Of twenti hondrith spear-men of Skotlonde
  But even five and fifti.

---

stele] steel head   halyde] hauled   sad] grave   sat] set
freake] warrior   wone] one   stour] press of battle   myghte
dre] hold out   balfull] deadly   even-songe] vespers   abon]
above

But all wear slayne Cheviat within,
  The[y] hade no streng[th]e to stand on hy;
The chylde may rue that ys vnborne,
  It was the mor pitte.

Thear was slayne withe the lord Perse
  Ser Johan of Agerstone,
Ser Rogar, the hinde Hartly,
  Ser Wyllyam, the bolde Hearone.

Ser Jorg[e], the worthe Loumle,
  A knyghte of great renowen,
Ser Raff, the ryche Rugbe,
  With dyntes wear beaten dowene.

For Wetharryngton my harte was wo
  That euer he slayne shulde be;
For when both his leggis wear hewyne in t[w]o
  Yet he knyled and fought on hys kny.

Ther was slayne with the dougheti Duglas
  Ser Hewe the Mon[t]gombyrry,
Ser Dauy Lwdale that worthe was,
  His sistars son was he;

Ser Charls a Murre in that place
  That neuer a foot wolde fle;
Ser Hewe Maxwelle a lorde he was,
  With the Doglas dyd he dey.

Agerstone] ? Haggerston Castle, opposite Lindisfarne   hinde]
gentle   Hartly] near Whitley Bay   Hearone] Heron of Ford,
near Haggerston   Loumle] Lumley   Ser Raff . . . Rugbe]
? Ralph Neville of Raby Castle, son of Earl of Westmorland (Skeat)
Wetharryngton] ? Widrington, north of Morpeth   Dauy Lwdale]
obscure. David Lambwell *in later version*

So on the morrowe the[y] mayde them byears
   Off birch and hasell so g[r]ay;
Many wedous with wepyng tears
   Cam to fache ther makys away.

Tivydale may carpe off care,
   Northombarlond may mayk great mon,
For towe such captayns as slayne wear thear
   On the March-parti shall neuer be non.

Word ys commen to Eddenburrowe
   To Jamy the Skottishe kynge,
That dougheti Duglas, lyff-tenant of the Marches,
   He lay slean Chyviat within.

His handdes dyd he weal and wryng,
   He sayd, Alas, and woe ys me;
Such an other captayn Skotland within,
   He sayd, ye-feth shuld neuer be.

Worde ys commyn to lovly Londone
   Till the fourth Harry our kynge,
That lord Perse, [ly]ff-tenante of the Marches,
   He lay slayne Chyviat within.

God haue merci on his solle, sayde Kyng Harry,
   Good lord, yf thy will it be;
I haue a hondrith captayns in Ynglonde, he sayd,
   As good as euer was he;
But Perse, and I brook my lyffe,
   Thy deth well quyte shall be.

byears] biers   wedous] widows   fache ther makys] fetch their mates   carpe] sing   mon] lamentation   March-parti] Borderland   Jamy] James I (king 1406-37)   weal] mark with weals   ye-feth] i' faith, indeed   the fourth Harry] (king 1399-1413)   and . . . lyffe] if I live   quyte] requited

As our noble kynge mayde his avowe
   Lyke a noble prince of renowen,
For the deth of the lord Perse
   He dyde the battell of Hombyll-down;

Wher syx and thritte Skottishe knyghtes
   On a day wear beaten down;
Glendale glytteryde on ther armor bryght
   Over castille, towar, and town.

This was the hontynge off the Cheviat
   That [ther] begane this spurn;
Old men that knowen the grownde well yenoughe
   Call it the battell of Otterburn.

At Otterburn begane this spurne
   Vppone a Monnynday;
Ther was the doughte Doglas slean,
   The Perse went neuer away.

Ther was neuer a tym on the Marche-partes
   Sen the Doglas and the Perse met,
But yt ys mervele and the rede blude ronne not
   As the reane doys in the stret.

Ihesue Crist our balys bete
   And to the blys vs brynge;
Thus was the hountynge of the Chivyat:
   God send vs alle good endyng!

Hombyll-down] Homildon, near Wooler (1402; in reign of Henry IV
and Robert III)   Glendale] beyond Wooler   spurn] fray
mervele and] a wonder if   our balys bete] remedy our misfortunes

105. *Sir Andrew Bartton*

As itt beffell in Midsumer time
    When burds singe sweetlye on euery tree,
Our noble King, King Henery the eighth,
    Ouer the riuer of Thames past hee.

Hee was no sooner ouer the riuer,
    Downe in a fforrest to take the ayre,
But eighty merchants of London cittye
    Came kneeling before King Henery there.

O yee are welcome, rich merchants,
    [Good saylors, welcome vnto me.]
They swore by the rood they were saylers good
    But rich merchants they cold not bee.

To France nor Flanders dare we nott passe
    Nor Burdeaux voyage wee dare not ffare,
And all ffor a ffalse robber that lyes on the seas
    And robb[s] vs of our merchants ware.

King Henery was stout, and he turned him about
    And swore by the Lord that was mickle of might:
I thought he had not beene in the world throughout
    That durst haue wrought England such vnright.

But euer they sighed and said alas
    Vnto King Harry this answere againe:
He is a proud Scott that will robb vs all
    If wee were twenty shipps and hee but one.

rood] cross   stout] furious

The King looket ouer his left shoulder
    Amongst his Lords and Barrons soe ffree:
Haue I neuer Lord in all my realme
    Will ffeitch yond traitor vnto mee?

Yes, that dare I, sayes my Lord Chareles Howard,
    Neere to the King wheras hee did stand:
If that your grace will giue me leaue
    My selfe wilbe the only man.

Thou shalt haue six hundred men, saith our King,
    And chuse them out of my realme soe ffree;
Besids Marriners and boyes
    To guide the great shipp on the sea.

Ile goe speake with Sir Andrew, sais Charles my Lord
        Haward,
    Upon the sea, if hee be there;
I will bring him and his shipp to shore
    Or before my prince I will neuer come neere.

The ffirst of all my Lord did call,
    A noble gunner hee was one;
This man was sixty yeeres and ten
    And Peeter Simon was his name.

Peeter, sais hee, I must sayle to the sea
    To seeke out an enemye; God be my speed:
Before all others I haue chosen thee,
    Of a hundred guners thoust be my head.

My Lord, sais hee, if you haue chosen mee
    Of a hundred gunners to be the head,
Hange me att your maine-mast tree
    If I misse my marke past three pence bread.

ffree] noble   thoust] you must   three pence bread] the width
of a threepenny piece

The next of all my Lord he did call,
    A noble bowman hee was one;
In Yorekeshire was this gentleman borne,
    And William Horsley was his name.

Horsley, sayes hee, I must sayle to the sea
    To seeke out an enemye; God be my speede:
Before all others I haue chosen thee,
    Of a hundred boweman thoust be my head.

My Lord, sais hee, if you haue chosen mee
    Of a hundred bowemen to be the head,
Hang me att your mainemast tree
    If I misse my marke past twelue pence bread.

With pikes, and gunnes, and bowemen bold
    This Noble Howard is gone to the sea
On the day before Midsummer euen,
    And out att Thames mouth sayled they.

They had not sayled dayes three
    Upon their Iourney they tooke in hand,
But there they mett with a noble shipp
    And stoutely made itt both stay and stand.

Thou must tell me thy name, sais Charles my Lord
    Haward,
    Or who thou art, or ffrom whence thou came,
Yea, and where thy dwelling is,
    To whom and where thy shipp does belong.

My name, sayes hee, is Henery Hunt,
    With a pure hart and a penitent mind;
I and my shipp they doe belong
    Vnto the New castle that stands vpon Tine.

stoutely] boldly

Now thou must tell me, Harry Hunt,
    As thou hast sayled by day and by night,
Hast thou not heard of a stout robber?
    Men calls him Sir Andrew Bartton, Knight.

But euer he sighed and sayd Alas,
    Full well, my Lord, I know that wight:
He robd me of my merchants ware
    And I was his prisoner but yesternight.

As I was sayling vppon the sea,
    And Burdeaux voyage as I did ffare,
He clasped me to his archborde
    And robd me of all my merchants ware;

And I am a man both poore and bare,
    And euery man will haue his owne of me,
And I am bound towards London to ffare,
    To complaine to my Prince Henerye.

That shall not need, sais my Lord Haward,
    If thou canst lett me this robber see;
For euery peny he hath taken thee ffroe
    Thou shalt be rewarded a shilling, quoth hee.

Now God ffore-fend, saies Henery Hunt,
    My Lord, you shold worke soe farr amisse;
God keepe you out of that Traitors hands,
    For you wott ffull litle what a man hee is.

Hee is brasse within, and steele without,
    And beanes hee beares in his topcastle stronge;
His shipp hath ordinance cleane round about;
    Besids, my Lord, hee is verry well mand.

archborde] a part of the stern   wott] know   beanes] ? beans,
? missiles   topcastle] embattled platform at mainmast-head   cleane]
right

He hath a pinnace is deerlye dight,
   Saint Andrews crosse, that is his guide;
His pinnace beares nine score men and more
   Besids fifteen cannons on euery side.

If you were twenty shippes, and he but one,
   Either in charke-bord or in hall,
He wold ouercome you euerye one
   And if his beanes they doe downe fall.

This is cold comfort, sais my Lord Haward,
   To wellcome a stranger thus to the sea;
Ile bring him and his shipp to shore
   Or else into Scottland hee shall carrye mee.

Then you must gett a noble gunner, my Lord,
   That can sett well with his eye
And sinke his pinnace into the sea,
   And soone then ouercome will hee bee.

And when that you haue done this,
   If you chance Sir Andrew for to bord,
Lett no man to his topcastle goe;
   And I will giue you a glasse, my Lord,

And then you need to [feare] no Scott
   Whether you sayle by day or by night;
And to-morrow by seuen of the clocke
   You shall meete with Sir Andrew Bartton, Knight.

I was his prisoner but yester night
   And he hath taken mee sworne, quoth hee;
I trust my Lord God will me forgiue
   And if that oath then broken bee.

deerlye dight] richly ornamented   guide] guidon, pennant
charke-bord] ? = *archbord*   hall] hull   glasse] lantern to follow
sworne] bound by oath

You must lend me sixe peeces, my Lord, quoth hee,
   Into my shipp to sayle the sea,
And to-morrow by nine of the clocke
   Your honour againe then will I see.

        *   *   *   *   *

And the hache-bord where Sir Andrew lay
   Is hached with gold deerlye dight;
Now by my ffaith, sais Charles my Lord Haward,
   Then yonder Scott is a worthye wight!

Take in your ancyents and your standards,
   Yea, that no man shall them see,
And put me fforth a white willow wand
   As Merchants vse to sayle the sea.

But they stirred neither top nor mast
   But Sir Andrew they passed by.
Whatt English are yonder, said Sir Andrew,
   That can so litle curtesye?

I haue beene Admirall ouer the sea
   More then these yeeres three;
There is neuer an English dog nor Portingall
   Can passe this way without leaue of mee.

But now yonder pedlers they are past,
   Which is no litle greffe to me;
Feich them backe, sayes Sir Andrew Bartton,
   They shall all hang att my maine-mast tree.

hache-bord] ? stern   hached] inlaid   ancyents] colours
wand] staff   can] know   Portingall] Portuguese

With that the pinnace itt shott of,
   That my Lord Haward might itt well ken,
Itt stroke downe my Lords fforemast
   And killed fourteen of my Lord his men.

Come hither, Simon, sayes my Lord Haward,
   Looke that thy words be true thou sayd;
Ile hang thee att my maine-mast tree
   If thou miss thy marke past twelue pence bread.

Simon was old, but his hart itt was bold,
   Hee tooke downe a peece and layd itt ffull lowe;
He put in chaine yeards nine
   Besids other great shott lesse and more.

With that he lett his gun shott goe;
   Soe well hee settled itt with his eye
The ffirst sight that Sir Andrew sawe
   Hee see his pinnace sunke in the sea.

When hee saw his pin[n]ace sunke
   Lord, in his hart hee was not well:
Cutt my ropes, it is time to be gon;
   Ile goe ffeitch yond pedlers backe my selfe!

When my Lord Haward saw Sir Andrew loose
   Lord, in his hart that hee was ffaine:
Strike on your drummes, spread out your ancyents!
   Sound out your trumpetts, sound out amaine!

Fight on, my men, sais Sir Andrew Bartton,
   Weate, howsoeuer this geere will sway,
Itt is my Lord Adm[i]rall of England
   Is come to seeke mee on the sea.

| peece] gun | chaine] chain-shot | ffaine] eager | Weate] |
| know | geere] business, battle | sway] turn out | |

Simon had a sonne, with shott of a gunn
   (Well Sir Andrew might itt ken),
He shott itt in att a priuye place
   And killed sixty more of Sir Andrews men.

Harry Hunt came in att the other syde
   And att Sir Andrew hee shott then;
He droue downe his fformost tree
   And killed eighty more of Sir Andirwes men.

I haue done a good turne, sayes Harry Hunt,
   Sir Andrew is not our Kings ffreind;
He hoped to haue vndone me yesternight
   But I hope I haue quitt him well in the end.

Euer alas, sayd Sir Andrew Barton,
   What shold a man either thinke or say?
Yonder ffalse theeffe is my strongest Enemye
   Who was my prisoner but yesterday.

Come hither to me, thou Gourden good,
   And be thou readye att my call;
And I will giue thee three hundred pound
   If thou wilt lett my beanes downe ffall.

With that hee swarued the maine-mast tree,
   Soe did he itt with might and maine:
Horseley with a bearing arrow
   Stroke the Gourden through the braine;

And he ffell into the haches againe
   And sore of this wound that he did bleed;
Then word went throug[h] Sir Andrews men
   That the Gourden hee was dead.

tree] mast   quitt] requited   Gourden] Gordon   swarued]
climbed up   bearing] long-distance

Come hither to me, James Hambliton,
  Thou art my sisters sonne, I haue no more;
I will giue [thee] six hundred pound
  If thou will lett my beanes downe ffall.

With that he swarued the maine-mast tree,
  Soe did hee itt with might and maine:
Horseley with an-other broad Arrow
  Strake the yeaman through the braine,

That hee ffell downe to the haches againe,
  Sore of his wound that hee did bleed.
Itt is verry true, as the Welchman sayd,
  Couetousness getts no gaine.

But when hee saw his sisters sonne slaine
  Lord, in his heart hee was not well:
Goe ffeitch me downe my armour of proue
  For I will to the topcastle my-selfe.

Goe ffeitch me downe my armour of prooffe
  For itt is guilded with gold soe cleere;
God be with my brother, Iohn of Bartton,
  Amongst the Portingalls hee did itt weare.

But when hee had his armour of prooffe
  And on his body hee had itt on,
Euery man that looked att him
  Sayd, Gunn nor arrow hee neede ffeare none!

Come hither, Horsley, sayes my Lord Haward,
  And looke your shaft that itt goe right;
Shoot a good shoote in the time of need
  And ffor thy shooting thoust be made a Knight.

as the Welchman said] the proverb, Covetousness brings nothing home
proue] tried strength   cleere] bright

Ile doe my best, sayes Horslay then,
  Your honour shall see beffore I goe;
If I shold be hanged att your mainemast,
  I haue in my shipp but arrowes tow.

But att Sir Andrew hee shott then,
  Hee made sure to hitt his marke;
Under the spole of his right arme
  Hee smote Sir Andrew quite throw the hart.

Yett ffrom the tree hee wold not start,
  But hee clinged to itt with might and maine.
Under the coller then of his Iacke
  He stroke Sir Andrew thorrow the braine.

Fight on, my men, sayes Sir Andrew Bartton,
  I am hurt but I am not slaine;
Ile lay mee downe and bleed a-while
  And then Ile rise and ffight againe.

Fight on, my men, sayes Sir Andrew Bartton,
  These English doggs they bite soe lowe;
Fight on for Scottland and Saint Andrew
  Till you heare my whistle blowe.

But when they cold not heare his whistle blow
  Sayes Harry Hunt, Ile lay my head
You may bord yonder noble shipp, my Lord,
  For I know Sir Andrew hee is dead.

With that they borded this noble shipp
  Soe did they itt with might and maine;
They ffound eighteen score Scotts aliue,
  Besids the rest were maimed and slaine.

tow] two   spole] spauld, shoulder   tree] mast   start]
move   Iacke] coat of mail   lay] wager

My Lord Haward tooke a sword in his hand
   And smote of Sir Andrews head.
The Scotts stood by, did weepe and mourne,
   But neuer a word durst speake or say.

He caused his body to be taken downe
   And ouer the hatch-bord cast into the sea,
And about his middle three hundred crownes:
   Wheresoeuer thou lands, itt will bury thee.

With his head they sayled into England againe
   With right good will, and fforce and m[aine]
And the day beffore Newyeeres euen
   And into Thames mouth againe they came.

My Lord Haward wrote to King Heneryes grace
   With all the newes hee cold him bring:
Such a newyeeres gifft I haue brought to your grace
   As neuer did subiect to any King.

For Merchandyes and Manhood
   The like is nott to be ffound;
The sight of these wold doe you good
   For you haue not the like in your English ground.

But when hee heard tell that they were come
   Full royally hee welcomed them home:
Sir Andrews shipp was the Kings Newyeeres guifft,
   A brauer shipp you neuer saw none.

Now hath England Sir Andrews shipp
   Besett with pearles and precyous stones;
Now hath England two shipps of war,
   Two shipps of warr, before but one.

Who holpe to this? sayes King Henerye,
   That I may reward him ffor his paine.
Harry Hunt and Peter Simon,
   William Horseleay, and I the same.

Harry Hunt shall haue his whistle and chaine
   And all his Iewells, whatsoeuer they bee,
And other rich giffts that I will not name,
   For his good service he hath done mee.

Horslay, right thoust be a Knight,
   Lands and liuings thou shalt haue store.
Howard shalbe Erle of Nottingham,
   And soe was neuer Haward before.

Now Peeter Simon, thou art old,
   I will maintaine thee and thy sonne;
Thou shalt haue fiue hundred pound all in gold
   For the good service that thou hast done.

Then King Henerye shiffted his roome,
   In came the Queene and ladyes bright;
Other arrands they had none
   But to see Sir Andrew Bartton, Knight.

But when they see his deadly fface,
   His eyes were hollow in his head,
I wold giue a hundred pound, sais King Henerye,
   The man were aliue as hee is dead:

Yett ffor the manfull part that hee hath playd
   Both heere and beyond the sea
His men shall haue halfe a crowne a day
   To bring them to my brother King Iamye.

holpe] helped   liuings] property   shiffted his roome] made way

106. Johnie Armstrang

SUM speiks of Lords, sum speiks of Lairds,
  And siclyke Men of hie Degrie,
Of a Gentleman I sing a Sang,
  Sumtyme calld Laird of *Gilnockie*.

Lairds] gentlemen   siclyke] such   *Gilnockie*] south of Langholm,
Dumfries, on the Esk

JOHNIE ARMSTRANG

The King he wrytes a luving Letter
  With his ain Hand sae tenderly,
And he hath sent it to *Johny Armstrang*,
  To cum and speik with him speidily.

The *Eliots* and *Armstrangs* did convene;
  They were a gallant Company:
Weill ryde and meit our lawful King,
  And bring him safe to *Gilnockie*.
Make Kinnen and Capon ready then,
  And Venison in great Plenty,
Weill welcome Hame our Royal King,
  I hope heill dyne at *Gilnockie*.

They ran their Horse on the *Langum Howm*,
  And brake their Speirs with mekle main;
The Ladys lukit frae their loft Windows,
  GOD *bring our Men weil back again.*
Quhen *Johny* came before the King,
  With all his Men sae brave to see,
The King he movit his Bonnet to him,
  He weind he was a King as well as He.

May I find Grace, my Sovereign Liege,
  Grace for my loyal Men and me;
For my Name it is *Johny Armstrang*,
  And Subject of yours, my Liege, said he.
Away, away, thou Traytor Strang,
  Out of my Sicht thou mayst sune be,
I grantit nevir a Traytors Lyfe,
  And now I'll not begin with thee.

Kinnen] rabbit   *Langum Howm*] grassland by the river at **Lang-holm**   mekle main] great strength   weind] thought   **Strang**] violent

521

Grant me my Lyfe, my Liege, my King,
    And a bony Gift I will give to thee,
Full Four and twenty Milk whyt Steids,
    Were a' foald in a Yeir to me.
I'll gie thee all these Milk whyt Steids,
    That prance and nicher at a Speir,
With as mekle gude *Inglis* Gilt,
    As four of their braid Backs dow beir.
Away, away, thou Traytor, &c.

Grant me my Lyfe, my Liege, my King,
    And a bony Gift I'll gie to thee,
Gude Four and twenty ganging Mills,
    That gang throw a' the Yeir to me.
These Four and twenty Mills complete,
    Sall gang for thee throw all the Yeir,
And as mekle of gude reid Quheit,
    As all thair Happers dow to bear.
Away, away, thou Traytor, &c.

Grant me my Lyfe, my Liege, my King,
    And a great Gift I'll gie to thee,
Bauld Four and twenty Sisters Sons,
    Sall for thee fecht tho all sould flee.
Away, away, thou Traytor, &c.

Grant me my Life, my Liege, my King,
    And a brave Gift I'll gie to thee;
All betwene heir and *Newcastle* Town,
    Sall pay thair yeirly Rent to thee.
Away, away, thou Traytor, &c.

nicher] whinny   Gilt] gold   dow] can   ganging] going,
working   Happers] hoppers   reid Quheit] red wheat

JOHNIE ARMSTRANG

Ye leid, ye leid now, King, he says,
  Althocht a King and Prince ye be;
For I luid naithing in all my Lyfe,
  I dare well sayit, but Honesty:
But a fat Horse and a fair Woman,
  Twa bony Dogs to kill a Deir;
But *Ingland* suld haif found me Meil and Malt,
  Gif I had livd this hundred Yeir.

Scho suld haif found me Meil and Malt,
  And Beif and Mutton in all Plentie;
But neir a *Scots* Wyfe could haif said,
  That eir I skaithd her a pure Flie.
To seik het Water beneath cauld Yce,
  Surely it is a great Folie;
I haif asked Grace at a graceless Face,
  But there is nane for my Men and me.

But had I kend or I came frae Hame,
  How thou unkynd wadst bene to me,
I wad haif kept the Border-syde,
  In spyte of all thy Force and thee.
Wist *Englands* King that I was tane,
  O gin a blyth Man wald he be;
For anes I slew his Sisters Son,
  And on his Breist-bane brak a Tree.

John wore a Girdle about his Midle,
  Imbroiderd owre with burning Gold,
Bespangled with the same Mettle,
  Maist beautifull was to behold.

leid] lied	luid] loved	haif] have	Gif] if	skaithd] harmed,
wronged	pure] poor	het] hot	at] from	kend]
known	Wist] knew	gin] *here expletive*		anes] once
Breist-bane] breast-bone		Tree] staff		

523

Ther hang nine Targats at *Johnys* Hat,
   And ilk an worth Three hundred Pound,
What wants that Knave that a King suld haif,
   But the Sword of Honour and the Crown.

O quhair gat thou these Targats, Johnie,
   That blink sae brawly abune thy Brie?
I gat them in the Field fechting,
   Quher, cruel King, thou durst not be.
Had I my Horse and my Harness gude,
   And Ryding as I wont to be,
It sould haif bene tald this hundred Yeir,
   The Meiting of my King and me.

GOD be withee, *Kirsty,* my Brither,
   Lang live thou Laird of *Mangertoun;*
Lang mayst thou dwell on the Border-syde,
   Or thou se thy Brither ryde up and doun.
And GOD be withee, *Kirsty,* my Son,
   Quhair thou sits on thy Nurses Knee;
But and thou live this Hundred Yeir,
   Thy Fathers better thoult never be.

Farweil, my bonny *Gilnockhall,*
   Quhair on *Esk* syde thou standest stout,
Gif I had lived but seven Yeirs mair,
   I wald haif gilt thee round about.—
John murdred was at *Carlinrigg,*
   And all his galant Companie;
But *Scotlands* Heart was never sae wae,
   To see sae mony brave Men die.

Targats] shield-shaped ornaments   ilk an] each one   *quhair*]
where   *blink*] glint   *brawly*] finely   *abune*] above   *Brie*]
brow   *Kirsty*] Christopher   *Mangertoun*] near Newcastleton
in Liddisdale   But and] if   stout] strong   *Carlinrigg*]
Caerlanrig, on the Teviot, south of Hawick   wae] sorrowful

Because they savd their Country deir
　　Frae *Englishmen*; nane were sae bauld,
Quhyle *Johnie* livd on the Border-syde,
　　Nane of them durst cum neir his Hald.

Hald] dwelling, keep

107. *The Lament of the Border Widow*

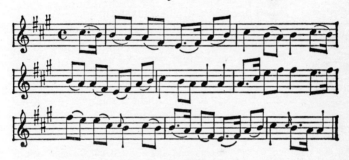

My Love he built me a bonny bower
And clad it a' wi' lilye flour;
A brawer bower ye ne'er did see
Than my true love he built for me.

There came a man by middle day,
He spied his sport and went away,
And brought the king, that very night,
Who brake my bower and slew my knight.

He slew my knight to me sae dear,
He slew my knight and poin'd his gear;
My servants all for life did flee
And left me in extremitie.

brawer] finer　　　poin'd] seized and sold　　　gear] possessions

I sew'd his sheet, making my mane,
I watched the corpse myself alane,
I watched his body night and day;
No living creature came that way.

I took his body on my back,
And whiles I gaed, and whiles I sate;
I digg'd a grave and laid him in,
And happ'd him with the sod sae green.

But think na ye my heart was sair
When I laid the moul on his yellow hair?
O think na ye my heart was wae
When I turn'd about, away to gae?

Nae living man I'll love again
Since that my lovely knight is slain;
Wi ae lock of his yellow hair
I'll chain my heart for evermair.

sheet] shroud	mane] complaint	gaed] went, walked
happ'd] covered up	moul] earth	ae] one

108. *Northumberland betrayd by Dowglas*

Now list and lithe you gentlemen
  And Ist tell you the veretye,
How they haue delt with a banished man
  Driuen out of his countrye.

When as hee came on Scottish ground,
  As woe and wonder be them amonge,
Full much was there traitorye
  They wrought the Erle of Northumberland.

lithe] hearken   Ist] I'll

When they were att the supper sett,
    Beffore many goodly gentlemen
They ffell a fflouting and mocking both,
    And said to the Erle of Northumberland:

What makes you be soe sad, my Lord,
    And in your mind soe sorrowffullye?
In the North of Scottland to-morrow theres a
        shooting,
    And thither thoust goe, my Lord Percye.

The buttes are sett, and the shooting is made,
    And there is like to be great royaltye,
And I am sworne into my bill
    Thither to bring my Lord Pearcy.

Ile giue thee my land, Douglas, he sayes,
    And be the faith in my bodye,
If that thou wilt ryde to the worlds end
    Ile ryde in thy companye.

And then bespake the good Ladye,
    Mary a Douglas was her name,
You shall byde here, good English Lord;
    My brother is a traiterous man.

He is a traitor stout and stronge,
    As Ist tell you the veretye,
For he hath tane liuerance of the Erle
    And into England he will liuor thee.

fflouting] jeering, insulting   into my bill] in writing   be] by
stout] bold   tane liuerance] taken possession   liuor] deliver,
hand over

Now hold thy tounge, thou goodlye Ladye,
    And let all this talking bee;
For all the gold thats in Loug[h] Leuen
    William wold not liuor mee.

It wold breake truce betweene England and Scott-
    land,
    And freinds againe they wold neuer bee
If he shold liuor a bani[s]ht Erle
    Was driuen out of his owne countrye.

Hold your tounge, my Lord, shee sayes,
    There is much ffalsehood them amonge;
When you are dead then they are done,
    Soone they will part them freinds againe.

If you will giue me any trust, my Lord,
    Ile tell you how you best may bee;
Youst lett my brother ryde his wayes
    And tell those English Lords trulye

How that you cannot with them ryde
    Because you are in an Ile of the sea;
Then ere my Brother come againe
    To Edenborrow castle Ile carry thee;

Ile liuor you vnto the Lord Hume,
    And you know a trew Scot[ts] Lord is hee,
For he hath lost both Land and goods
    In ayding of your good bodye.

Marry, I am woe, woman, he sayes,
    That any freind fares worse for mee;
For where one saith it is a true tale,
    Then two will say it is a Lye.

Youst] you must   an Ile] on loch Leven (which is fresh water)
Hume] Alexander, fifth Lord Hume

When I was att home in my [realme]
    Amonge my tennants all trulye,
In my time of losse, wherin my need stoode,
    They came to ayd me honestlye.

Therfore I left many a child ffatherlese
    And many a widdow to looke wanne;
And therfore blame nothing, Ladye,
    But the woeffull warres which I began.

If you will giue me noe trust, my Lord,
    Nor noe credence you will giue mee,
And youle come hither to my right hand
    Indeed, my Lord, Ile lett you see.

Saies, I neuer loued noe witchcraft
    Nor neuer dealt with treacherye
But euermore held the hye way;
    Alas, that may be seene by mee.

If you will not come your selfe, my Lord,
    Youle lett your chamberlaine goe with mee,
Three words that I may to him speake;
    And soone he shall come againe to thee.

When Iames Swynard came that Lady before,
    Shee let him see thorrow the weme of her ring
How many there was of English lords
    To wayte there for his Master and him.

And youle] if you will   weme] (belly), cavity   wayte] wait
in ambush

But who beene yonder, my good Ladye,
   That walkes soe royallye on yonder greene?
Yonder is Lord Hunsden, Iamye, she say[d],
   Alas, heele doe you both tree and teene.

And who beene yonder, thou gay Ladye,
   That walkes soe royallye him beside?
Yond is Sir William Drurye, Iamy, shee sayd,
   And a keene Captain hee is, and tryde.

How many miles is itt, thou good Ladye,
   Betwixt yond English Lord and mee?
Marry, thryse fifty mile, shee sayd,
   And euen to s[ai]le and by the sea.

I neuer was on English ground
   Nor neuer see itt with mine eye,
But as my witt and wisedome serues
   And as [the] booke it telleth mee.

My mother, shee was a witch woman
   And part of itt shee learned mee;
Shee wold let me see out of Lough Leuen
   What they dyd in London Cytye.

But who is yond, thou good Ladye,
   That comes yonder with an Osterne face?
Yonds Sir Iohn Forster, Iamye, shee sayd;
   Methinks thou sholdest better know him then I.
Euen soe I doe, my goodlye Ladye,
   And euer alas, soe woe am I.

Lord Hunsden] Henry Carey, Queen Elizabeth's cousin and Sussex's
lieutenant in the north in 1570   tree and teene] injury and grief
Sir William Drurye] Elizabeth's general on the Border   Marry]
(by Mary), to be sure   Osterne] austere, stern   Sir Iohn Forster]
Elizabeth's emissary; harrier of Teviotdale in 1570

He pulled his hatt ouer his eyes
   And Lord, he wept soe tenderlye;
He is gone to his Master againe
   And euen to tell him the veretye.

Now hast thou beene with Mary, Iamy, he sayd,
   Euen as thy tounge will tell to me;
But if thou trust in any womans words
   Thou must refraine good companye.

It is noe words, my Lord, he sayes,
   Yonder the men shee letts me see,
How many English Lords there is
   Is wayting there for you and mee.

Yonder I see the Lord Hunsden,
   And hee and you is of the third degree;
A greater enemye indeed, my Lord,
   In England none haue yee.

And I haue beene in Lough Leuen
   The most part of these yeeres three,
Yett had I neuer noe out-rake
   Nor good games that I cold see;

And I am thus bidden to yonder shooting
   By William Douglas all trulye;
Therfore speake neuer a word out of thy mouth
   That thou thinkes will hinder mee.

Then he writhe the gold ring of his ffingar
   And gaue itt to that Ladye gay;
Sayes, That was a legacye left vnto mee
   In Harley woods where I cold bee.

of . . . degree] third cousins   out-rake] out-ride, expedition,
holiday   writhe . . . of] twisted . . . off

Then ffarewell hart and ffarewell hand,
   And ffarwell all good companye;
That woman shall neuer beare a sonne
   Shall know soe much of your priuitye.

Now hold thy tounge, Ladye, hee sayde,
   And make not all this dole for mee,
For I may well drinke but Ist neuer eate
   Till againe in Lough Leuen I bee.

He tooke his boate att the Lough Leuen
   For to sayle now ouer the sea,
And he hath cast vpp a siluer wand,
   Saies, Fare thou well, my good Ladye;
The Ladye looked ouer her left shoulder,
   In a dead swoone there fell shee.

Goe backe againe, Douglas, he sayd,
   And I will goe in thy companye,
For sudden sicknesse yonder Ladye has tane
   And euer alas shee will but dye;

If ought come to yonder Ladye but good
   Then blamed fore that I shall bee,
Because a banished man I am
   And driuen out of my owne countrye.

Come on, come on, my Lord, he sayes,
   And lett all such talking bee;
Theres Ladyes enow in Lough Leuen
   And for to cheere yonder gay Ladye.

dole] lamentation   Ist] I shall   fore] for   enow] enough

And you will not goe your selfe, my lord,
    You will lett my chamberlaine goe with me;
Wee shall now take our boate againe
    And soone wee shall ouertake thee.

Come on, come on, my Lord, he sayes,
    And lett now all this talking bee;
For my sister is craftye enoughe
    For to beguile thousands such as you and mee.

When they had sayled fifty myle,
    Now fifty mile vpon the sea,
Hee had fforgotten a message that hee
    Shold doe in Lough Leuen trulye:
Hee asked how farr it was to that shooting
    That William Douglas promised mee.

Now faire words makes fooles faine,
    And that may be seene by thy Master and thee;
For you may happen think itt soone enoughe
    When-euer you that shooting see.

Iamye pulled his hatt now ouer his browe,
    I wott the teares fell in his eye;
And he is to his Master againe
    And ffor to tell him the veretye:

He sayes, fayre words makes fooles faine,
    And that may be seene by you and mee;
For wee may happen thinke itt soone enoughe
    When-euer wee that shooting see.

And you] if you   faine] pleased

Hold vpp thy head, Iamye, the Erle sayd,
  And neuer lett thy hart fayle thee;
He did itt but to proue thee with
  And see how thow wold take with death trulye.

When they had sayled other fifty mile,
  Other fifty mile vpon the sea.
Lord Peercy called to him, himselfe,
  And sayd, Douglas, what wilt thou doe with
    mee?

Looke that your brydle be wight, my Lord,
  That you may goe as a shipp att sea;
Looke that your spurres be bright and sharpe
  That you may pricke her while sheele awaye.

What needeth this, Douglas, he sayth,
  That thou needest to ffloute mee?
For I was counted a horsseman good
  Before that euer I mett with thee.

A ffalse Hector hath my horsse,
  And euer an euill death may hee dye;
And Willye Armestronge hath my spurres
  And all the geere belongs to mee.

When they had sayled other fifty mile,
  Other fifty mile vpon the sea,
They landed low by Barwicke side;
  [There Douglas] landed Lord Percye.

proue] try, test   wight] strong   sheele] she will   Hector]
braggart   Willye Armestronge] i.e. of Liddisdale

109. *Johnie o' Cocklesmuir*

JOHNIE rose up in a May morning,
　Call'd for water to wash his hands,
And he has call'd for his gud gray hunds
　That lay bund in iron bands, bands,
　That lay bund in iron bands.

Ye'll busk, ye'll busk my noble dogs,
　Ye'll busk and mak them boun,
For I'm gaing to the Broadspear-hill
　To ding the dun deer doun.

Whan Johnie's mither heard o' this
　She til her son has gane:
Ye'll win your mither's benison
　Gin ye wad stay at hame.

Your meat sall be o' the very, very best
　And your drink o' the finest wine,
And ye will win your mither's benison
　Gin ye wad stay at hame.

busk] prepare　　　　boun] ready　　　ding] strike　　　til] to
Gin] if

535

His mither's counsel he wad na tak
    Nor wad he stay at hame,
But he's on to the Broadspear hill
    To ding the dun deer doun.

Johnie lookit east, and Johnie lookit west,
    And a little below the sun,
And there he spied the dun deer lying sleeping
    Aneath a buss o' brume.

Johnie shot, and the dun deer lap,
    And he has woundit him in the side,
And atween the water and the wud
    He laid the dun deer's pride.

They ate sae meikle o' the venison
    And drank sae meikle o' the blude
That Johnie and his twa gray hunds
    Fell asleep in yonder wud.

By there cam a silly auld man,
    A silly auld man was he,
And he's aff to the proud foresters
    To tell what he did see.

What news, what news, my silly auld man,
    What news? Come tell to me;
Na news, na news, said the silly auld man,
    But what mine e'en did see.

As I cam in by yon greenwud
    And doun amang the scrogs,
The bonniest youth that ere I saw
    Lay sleeping atween twa dogs.

buss o' brume] broom bush   lap] leapt   wud] wood   sae
meikle] so much   scrogs] stunted bushes

The sark that he had on his back
    Was o' the Holland sma',
And the coat that he had on his back
    Was laced wi' gowd fu' braw.

Up bespak the first forester,
    The first forester ava:
An this be Johnie o' Cocklesmuir
    It 's time we war awa.

Up bespak the niest forester,
    The niest forester ava:
An this be Johnie o' Cocklesmuir
    To him we winna draw.

The first shot that they did shoot
    They wounded him on the thie;
Up bespak the uncle's son:
    The niest will gar him die.

Stand stout, stand stout, my noble dogs,
    Stand stout and dinna flee;
Stand fast, stand fast, my gude gray hunds,
    And we will mak them dee.

He has killed six o' the proud foresters
    And he has woundit the seventh sair;
He laid his leg out oure his steed,
    Says, I will kill na mair.

sark] shirt   Holland sma'] fine-textured Dutch linen   gowd]
gold   braw] splendid   ava] of all   An] if   winna
draw] won't approach   thie] thigh   gar] make

[Oh wae befa' thee, silly auld man,
An ill death may thee dee;
Upon thy head be a' this blude,
For mine, I ween, is free.]

110. *Dick o' the Cow*

Now Liddisdale has lain long in,
Lal de ral, lal de ral, lal de ral, la lal de;
There is no rideing there at a',
Lal de ral, lal de ral, lal de ral, la dal de;
Their horse is growing so lidder and fatt
That are lazie in the sta'.
Lal lal de ridle la di, fal lal de ridle la di,
Fal lal di lal la, fal lal di ridle la.

rideing] i.e. on forays   lidder] idle

Then Johne Armstrang to Willie can say,
  Billie, a rideing then will we;
England and us has been long at a feed,
  Perhaps we may hitt off some bootie.

Then they'r com'd on to Hutton Hall,
  They rade that proper place about;
But the laird he was the wiser man,
  For he had left nae gear without.

Then he had left nae gear to steal
  Except six sheep upon a lee;
Says Johnie, I'de rather in England die
  Before th[i]r six sheep good to Liddisdale with me.

But how cal'd they the man we last with mett,
  Billie, as we came over the know?
That same he is an innocent fool
  And some men calls him Dick o' the Cow.

That fool has three as good kyne of his own
  As is in a' Cumberland, billie, quoth he;
Betide my life, betide my death,
  These three kyne shal go to Liddisdaile with me.

Then they're com'd on to the poor fool's house,
  And they have broken his wals so wide;
They have loos'd out Dick o' the Cow's kyne three
  And tane three co'erlets off his wife's bed.

Billie] brother   feed] feud   Hutton Hall] Hutton-in-the-Forest at
the southern end of Inglewood Forest   gear] livestock   lee] pasture
good] went   know] knoll

Then on the morn when the day grew light
　　The shouts and crys rose loud and high:
Hold thy tongue, my wife, he says,
　　And of thy crying let me bee.

Hald thy tongue, my wife, he says,
　　And of thy crying let me bee,
And ay that where thou wants a kow,
　　Good sooth that I shal bring the[e] three.

Then Dick 's com'd on to lord and master,
　　And I wat[e] a drerie fool [was] he:
Hald thy tongue, my fool, he says,
　　For I may not stand to jest with thee.

Shame speed a' your jesting, my lord, quo' Dickie,
　　For nae such jesting grees with me;
Liddesdaile has been in my house this last night
　　And they have tane my three kyne from me.

But I may nae langer in Cumberland dwel,
　　To be your poor fool and your leel,
Unless ye give me leave, my lord,
　　To go to Liddisdale and steal.

To give thee leave, my fool, he says,
　　Thou speaks against mine honour and me;
Unless thou give me thy trouth and thy right hand
　　Thou'l steal frae nane but them that sta' from thee.

There is my trouth and my right hand;
　　My head shal hing on Hairibie,
I'le never crose Carlele sands again
　　If I steal frae a man but them that sta' frae me.

wate] know　　trouth] pledge　　sta'] stole　　Hairibie] place
of execution at Carlisle

Dickie has tane leave at lord and master,
   And I wate a merrie fool was he;
He has brought a bridle and a pair of new spurs,
   And has packed them up in his breek-thigh.

Then Dickie 's come on for Puddinburn
   Even as fast as he may drie;
Dickie 's come on for Puddinburn
   Where there was thirty Armstrongs and three.

What 's this com'd on me, quo' Dickie,
   What meakle wae 's this happen'd on me, quo' he,
When here is but ae innocent fool
   And there is thirty Armstrongs and three!

Yet he 's com'd up to the hall among them all,
   So wel he became his courtisie:
Well may ye be, my good Laird's Jock,
   But the deil bless all your companie.

I'm come to plain of your man Fair Johnie Armstrong
   And syne his billie Willie, quo' he;
How they have been in my house this last night
   And they have tane my three ky frae me.

Quo' Johnie Armstrong, We'll him hang;
   Nay, thain quo' Willie, we'll him slae;
But up bespake another young man, We'le nit him
     in a four-nooked sheet,
   Give him his burden of batts, and lett him gae.

breek-thigh] thigh of (his) breeches   Puddinburn] an Armstrong
house in Liddisdale   drie] manage   meakle] great   the
Laird's Jock] John, son of Thomas Armstrong of Mangerton   plain]
complain   syne] then   ky] cows   batts] blows, beating

Then up bespake the good Laird's Jock,
  The best falla in the companie:
[S]itt thy way down a little while, Dicke,
  And a peice of thine own cow's hough I'l give to
    thee.

But Dicki[e]'s heart it grew so great
  That never a bitt of it he dought to eat;
But Dickie was warr of ane auld peat-house
  Where there al the night he thought for to sleep.

Then Dickie was warr of that auld peat-house
  Where there al the night he thought for to ly;
And a' the prayers the poor fool pray'd was,
  I wish I had a mense for my own three kye!

Then it was the use of Puddinburn,
  And the house of Mangertoun, all haile,
These that came not at the first call
  They gott no more meat till the next meall.

The lads, that hungry and aevery was,
  Above the door-head they flang the key;
Dickie took good notice to that,
  Says, There's a bootie younder for me.

Then Dickie's gane into the stable
  Where there stood thirty horse and three;
He has ty'd them a' with St Mary knot,
  All these horse but barely three.

falla] fellow   warr] aware   mense] mends, recompense
use] custom   Mangertoun] the house of the Armstrong chief, near
Newcastleton in Liddisdale   aevery] eager for food   ty'd . . .
knot] hamstrung (to prevent pursuit)

He has ty'd them a' with St Mary knott,
    All these horse but barely three;
He has loupen on one, taken another in his hand,
    And out at the door and gane is Dickie.

Then on the morn when the day grew light
    The shouts and cryes rose loud and high:
What 's that theife? quo' the good Laird's Jock;
    Tel me the truth and the verity.

What 's that theife? quo' the good Laird's Jock;
    See unto me ye do not lie.
Dick o' the Cow has been in the stable this last night
    And has my brother's horse and mine frae me.

Ye wad never be told it, quo' the Laird's Jock;
    Have ye not found my tales fu' leel?
Ye wade never out of England bide
    Till crooked and blind and a' wad steal.

But will thou lend me thy bay? Fair Johne Armstrong
      can say;
    There 's nae mae horse loose in the stable but he;
And I'le either bring ye Dick o' the Kow again
    Or the day is come that he must die.

To lend thee my bay, the Laird's Jock can say,
    He 's both worth gold and good monie;
Dick o' the Kow has away twa horse,
    I wish no thou should no make him three.

loupen] leapt   taken another] *and left the Laird's Jock's as a reward*
for his protection   teld it] told, warned   leel] true   wad(e)]
would   bide] stay   nae mae] no more, other

He has tane the Laird's jack on his back,
The twa-handed sword that hang lieugh by his
thigh;
He has tane the steel cap on his head
And on is he to follow Dickie.

Then Dickie was not a mile off the town,
I wate a mile but barely three,
Till John Armstrang has o'ertane Dick o' the Kow
Hand for hand on Cannobei lee.

Abide th[ee], bide now, Dickie than,
The day is come that thow must die.
Dickie looked o'er his left shoulder:
Johnie, has thow any mo in thy company?

There is a preacher in owr chapell,
And a' the lee-lang day teaches he;
When day is gane and night is come,
There's never a word I mark but three.

The first and second's Faith and Conscience,
The third is, Johnie, Take head of thee;
But what faith and conscience had thow, traitor,
When thou took my three kye frae me?

And when thou had tane my three kye
Thou thought in thy heart thou was no wel sped;
But thou sent thi billie Willie o'er the know
And he took three co'erlets of my wife's bed.

jack] mail coat   lieugh] low   off the town] away from the
farm   Hand for hand] abreast   Cannobei] above Longtown,
on the Scots side of the Border   lee-lang day] whole day through
head] heed   sped] fared

Then Johne lett a spear fa' leaugh by his thigh,
   Thought well to run the innocent through;
But the powers above was more than his,
   He ran but the poor fool's jerkin through.

Together they ran or ever they blan—
   This was Dickie, the fool, and hee—
Dickie could not win to him with the blade of the
     sword
   But he feld [him] with the plummet under the eye.

Now Dickie has [feld] Fair Johne Armstrong,
   The prettiest man in the south countrey;
Gramercie, then can Dickie say,
   I had twa horse, thou has made me three.

He has tane the laird's jack off his back,
   The twa-handed sword that hang leiugh by his thigh;
He has tane the steel cap off his head:
   Johnie, I'le tel my master I met with thee.

When Johne waken'd out of his dream
   I wate a dreiry man was he:
Is thou gane now, Dickie, than?
   The shame gae in thy company.

Is thou gane now, Dickie, than?
   The shame go in thy companie;
For if I should live this hundred year
   I shal never fight with a fool after thee.

---

or . . . blan] ere . . . checked   win to] reach   plummet] pommel
on a sword-hilt   Gramercie] thank you   wate] know, think

Then Dickie comed home to lord and master
   Even as fast as he may driee:
Now Dickie, I shal neither eat meat nor drink
   Till high hanged that thou shall be!

The shame speed the liars, my lord, quo' Dickie,
   That was no the promise ye made to me;
For I'd never gane to Liddesdale to steal
   Till that I sought my leave at thee.

But what gart thow steal the Laird's-Jock's horse?
   And, limmer, what gart thou steal [him? quo' he];
For lang might thow in Cumberland dwelt
   Or the Laird's Jock had stoln ought frae thee.

Indeed I wate ye leed, my lord,
   And even so loud as I hear ye lie;
I wan him frae his man, Fair Johne Armstrong,
   Hand for hand on Cannobie lee.

There 's the jack was on his back,
   The twa-handed sword that hang lewgh by his
     thigh;
There 's the steel cap was on his head;
   I have a' these takens to lett you see.

If that be true thou to me tels—
   I trow thou dare not tel a lie—
I'le give thee twenty pound for the good horse,
   Wel teld in thy clok-lap shall be.

driee] manage   gart] made   teld] counted   clok-lap]
skirts of a cloak

And I'le give thee one of my best milk-kye
  To maintain thy wife and children three;
[And that may be as good, I think,
  As ony twa o' thine might be.]

The shame speed the liars, my lord, quo' Dicke,
  Trow ye ay to make a fool of me?
I'le either have thirty pound for the good horse,
  Or else he 's gae to Mattan fair wi' me.

Then he has given him thirty pound for the good
    horse,
  All in gold and good monie;
He has given him one of his best milk-kye
  To maintain his wife and children three.

Then Dickie 's come down through Carlile town
  Even as fast as he may drie;
The first of men that he with mett
  Was my lord's brother, Bailife Glazenberrie.

Well may ye be, my good Ralph Scrupe!
  Welcome, my brother's fool! quo' he;
Where did thou gett Fair Johnie Armstrong's horse?
  Where did I get him but steall him, quo' he.

But will thou sell me Fair Johnie Armstrong['s]
    horse?
  And, billie, will thou sel him to me? quo' he;
Ay, and tel me the monie on my cloke-lap
  For there 's not one farthing I'le trust thee.

he 's gae] he is to go

547

I'le give thee fifteen pound for the good horse,
    Wel teld on thy cloke-lap shal be;
And I'le give [thee] one of my best milk-kye
    To maintain thy wife and thy children three.

The shame speed the liars, my lord, quo' Dicke,
    Trow ye ay to make a fool of me? quo' he;
I'le either have thirty pound for the good horse
    Or else he's to Mattan Fair with me.

He has given him thirty pound for the good horse,
    All in gold and good monie;
He has given him one of his best milk-kye
    To maintain his wife and children three.

Then Dickie lap a loup on high,
    And I wate a loud laughter leugh he:
I wish the neck of the third horse were browken,
    For I have a better of my own, and onie better can
      be.

Then Dickie com'd hame to his wife again—
    Judge ye how the poor fool he sped;
He has given her three score of English pounds
    For the three auld co'erlets was tane of her bed.

Hae, take thee there twa as good kye,
    I trow, as al thy three might be;
And yet here is a white-footed naigg,
    I think he'le carry booth thee and me.

lap a loup] leapt a leap   and onie] if any

But I may no langer in Cumberland dwell,
The Armstrongs the[y]'ll hang me high;
But Dickie has tane leave at lord and master,
And Burgh under Stanemuir there dwels Dickie.

Burgh under Stanemuir] in Cumbria

111. *Jamie Telfer of the Fair Dodhead*

It fell about the Martinmas tyde
Whan our Border steeds get corn and hay,
The Captain of Bewcastle hath bound him to ryde
And he's ower to Tividale to drive a prey.

The first ae guide that they met wi'
It was high up in Hardhaughswire;
The second guide that they met wi'
It was laigh down in Borthwick water.

What tidings, what tidings, my trusty guide?
Nae tidings, nae tidings I hae to thee;
But gin ye'll gae to the Fair Dodhead
Mony a cow's cauf I'll let thee see.

And whan they cam to the Fair Dodhead
Right hastily they clam the peel;
They loosed the kye out, ane and a',
And ranshakled the house right weel.

Martinmas] 11 November   Captain of Bewcastle] Thomas Mus-
grave   ower] over   Hardhaughswire] the pass between Liddesdale and Teviotdale   laigh] low, far   Borthwick water] tributary of the Teviot west of Hawick   hae to] have for   gin] if
Fair Dodhead] a tower on Ettrick Water   peel] palisade, keep
ranshakled] ransacked

Now Jamie Telfer's heart was sair,
　　The tear aye rowing in his ee;
He pled wi' the Captain to hae his gear
　　Or else revenged he wad be.

The Captain turned him round and leugh,
　　Said, Man, there's naething in thy house
But ae auld sword without a sheath
　　That hardly now wad fell a mouse.

The sun was na up but the moon was down,
　　It was the gryming of a new fa'n snaw;
Jamie Telfer has run ten myles a-foot
　　Between the Dodhead and the Stobs's Ha'.

And whan he cam to the fair tower yate
　　He shouted loud and cried weel hie,
Till out bespak auld Gibby Elliot:
　　Whae's this that brings the fray to me?

It's I, Jamie Telfer o' the Fair Dodhead,
　　And a harried man I think I be;
There's naething left at the Fair Dodhead
　　But a waefu' wife and bairnies three.

Gae seek your succour at Branksome Ha'
　　For succour ye 'se get nane frae me;
Gae seek your succour where ye paid black-mail
　　For, man, ye ne'er paid money to me.

---

rowing] rolling　　gear] cattle　　ae] one　　gryming] sprinkling
Stobs's Ha'] south of Hawick　　　　yate] gate　　　weel hie] loudly
fray] alarm, outcry　　　harried] plundered　　　black-mail] protection money

Jamie has turned him round about,
   I wat the tear blinded his e'e:
I'll ne'er pay mail to Elliot again,
   And the Fair Dodhead I'll never see.

My hounds may a' rin masterless,
   My hawks may fly frae tree to tree,
My lord may grip my vassal lands
   For there again maun I never be.

He has turned him to the Tiviot side
   E'en as fast as he could drie,
Till he cam to the Coultart Cleugh,
   And there he shouted baith loud and hie.

Then up bespak him auld Jock Grieve:
   Whae's this that brings the fray to me?
It's I, Jamie Telfer o' the Fair Dodhead,
   A harried man I trow I be.

There's naething left in the Fair Dodhead
   But a greeting wife and bairnies three;
And sax poor ca's stand in the sta'
   A' routing loud for their minnie.

Alack a wae! quo' auld Jock Grieve,
   Alack, my heart is sair for thee;
For I was married on the elder sister
   And you on the youngest of a' the three.

wat] believe   maun] must   drie] endure   Coultart
Cleugh] on the road south-west from Hawick   greeting] weeping
ca's] calves   sta'] stall   routing] lowing   minnie] mother

Then he has ta'en out a bonny black,
  Was right weel fed wi' corn and hay,
And he 's set Jamie Telfer on his back
  To the Catslockhill to tak the fray.

And whan he cam to the Catslockhill
  He shouted loud and cried weel hie,
Till out and spak him William's Wat:
  O whae 's this brings the fray to me?

It 's I, Jamie Telfer o' the Fair Dodhead,
  A harried man I think I be;
The Captain o' Bewcastle has driven my gear;
  For God's sake rise and succour me.

Alas for wae! quo' William's Wat,
  Alack, for thee my heart is sair;
I never cam by the Fair Dodhead
  That ever I fand thy basket bare.

He 's set his twa sons on coal-black steeds,
  Himsel upon a freckled gray,
And they are on wi' Jamie Telfer
  To Branksome Ha' to tak the fray.

And whan they cam to Branksome Ha'
  They shouted a' baith loud and hie,
Till up and spak him auld Buccleuch:
  Said, Whae 's this brings the fray to me?

It 's I, Jamie Telfer o' the Fair Dodhead,
  And a harried man I think I be;
There 's nought left in the Fair Dodhead
  But a greeting wife and bairnies three.

Branksome Ha'] Branxholm Hall, home of Scott of Buccleuch, near
Hawick

Alack for wae! quo' the gude auld lord,
   And ever my heart is wae for thee;
But fye, gar cry on Willie my son,
   And see that he cum to me speedilie.

Gar warn the water, braid and wide;
   Gar warn it sune and hastilie:
They that winna ride for Telfer's kye,
   Let them never look in the face o' me.

Warn Wat o' Harden and his sons,
   Wi' them will Borthwick water ride;
Warn Gaudilands and Allanhaugh
   And Gilmanscleugh and Commonside;

Ride by the gate at Priesthaughswire
   And warn the Currors o' the Lee;
As ye cum down the Hermitage Slack
   Warn doughty Willie o' Gorrinberry.

The Scotts they rade, the Scotts they ran,
   Sae starkly and sae steadilie,
And aye the ower-word o' the thrang
   Was, Rise for Branksome readilie!

The gear was driven the Frostylee up,
   Frae the Frostylee unto the plain,
Whan Willie has look'd his men before
   And saw the kye right fast driving.

Gar warn the water] get the riverside farmers warned. *The names which
follow are of Scotts living by the waters of Borthwick and Ettrick*   gate]
road   starkly] strongly   ower-word] refrain   thrang] company
Frostylee] a tributary of the Teviot above Liddesdale

Whae drives thir kye, can Willie say,
   To make an outspeckle o' me?
It 's I, the Captain o' Bewcastle, Willie;
   I winna layne my name for thee.

O will ye let Telfer's kye gae back?
   Or will ye do aught for regard o' me?
Or by the faith of my body, quo' Willie Scott,
   I 'se ware my dame's cauf's skin on thee.

I winna let the kye gae back
   Neither for thy love nor yet thy fear;
But I will drive Jamie Telfer's kye
   In spite of every Scott that 's here.

Set on them, lads, quo' Willie than;
   Fye, lads, set on them cruellie;
For ere they win to the Ritterford
   Mony a toom saddle there sall be!

Then till 't they gaed wi' heart and hand,
   The blows fell thick as bickering hail;
And mony a horse ran masterless
   And mony a comely cheek was pale.

But Willie was stricken ower the head
   And through the knapscap the sword has gane;
And Harden grat for very rage
   Whan Willie on the grund lay slane.

thir] these   outspeckle] laughing-stock   winna layne] won't falsify   aught] anything   ware] lay out, use   dame's cauf's skin] mother's calfskin whip   win to] reach   Ritterford] on the Liddel   toom] empty   till] to   bickering] rushing knapscap] headpiece   grat] wept

But he 's ta'en aff his gude steel cap
   And thrice he 's waved it in the air;
The Dinlay snaw was ne'er mair white
   Nor the lyart locks of Harden's hair.

Revenge, revenge, auld Wat can cry:
   Fye, lads, lay on them cruellie;
We'll ne'er see Tiviot side again
   Or Willie's death revenged sall be.

O mony a horse ran masterless,
   The splintered lances flew on hie;
But or they wan to the Kershope ford
   The Scotts had gotten the victory.

John o' Brigham there was slane
   And John o' Barlow, as I hear say,
And thirty mae o' the Captain's men
   Lay bleeding on the grund that day.

The Captain was run through the thick of the thigh
   And broken was his right leg-bane;
If he had lived this hundred years
   He had never been loved by woman again.

Hae back thy kye, the Captain said;
   Dear kye, I trow, to some they be;
For gin I suld live a hundred years
   There will ne'er fair lady smile on me.

Then word is gane to the Captain's bride
   Even in the bower where that she lay,
That her lord was prisoner in enemy's land
   Since into Tividale he had led the way.

Dinlay] mountain in Liddesdale   lyart] grizzled   mae] more
gin I suld] if I should

I wad lourd have had a winding-sheet
   And helped to put it ower his head,
Ere he had been disgraced by the border Scot
   Whan he ower Liddel his men did lead.

There was a wild gallant amang us a',
   His name was Watty wi' the Wudspurs,
Cried, On for his house in Stanegirthside
   If ony man will ride with us!

Whan they cam to the Stanegirthside
   They dang wi' trees and burst the door;
They loosed out a' the Captain's kye
   And set them forth our lads before.

There was an auld wyfe ayont the fire,
   A wee bit o' the Captain's kin:
Whae dar loose out the Captain's kye,
   Or answer to him and his men?

It's I, Watty Wudspurs, loose the kye,
   I winna layne my name frae thee;
And I will loose out the Captain's kye
   In scorn of a' his men and he.

Whan they cam to the Fair Dodhead
   They were a wellcum sight to see;
For instead of his ain ten milk-kye
   Jamie Telfer has gotten thirty and three.

And he has paid the rescue shot
   Baith wi' gowd and white monie;
And at the burial o' Willie Scott
   I wat was mony a weeping e'e.

wad lourd] would rather   Stanegirthside] on the English side of
the Liddel   dang] smote   ayont] beyond   rescue shot] cost
of the rescue   gowd] gold   white monie] silver

112. *Geordie*

THERE was a battle in the north,
    And nobles there was many,
And they hae kill'd Sir Charlie Hay,
    And they laid the wyte on Geordie.

O he has written a lang letter,
    He sent it to his lady;
Ye maun cum up to Enbrugh town
    To see what words o' Geordie.

When first she look'd the letter on,
    She was baith red and rosy;
But she had na read a word but twa,
    Till she wallow't like a lily.

Gar get to me my gude grey steed,
    My menzie a' gae wi' me;
For I shall neither eat nor drink,
    Till Enbrugh town shall see me.

wyte] blame   maun] must   Enbrugh] Edinburgh
wallow't] grew pale, withered   Gar get] cause to be got   menzie]
company

And she has mountit her gude grey steed,
  Her menzie a' gaed wi' her;
And she did neither eat nor drink
  Till Enbrugh town did see her.

And first appear'd the fatal block,
  And syne the aix to head him;
And Geordie cumin down the stair,
  And bands o' airn upon him.

But tho' he was chain'd in fetters strang,
  O' airn and steel sae heavy,
There was na ane in a' the court,
  Sae bra' a man as Geordie.

O she's down on her bended knee,
  I wat she's pale and weary,
O pardon, pardon, noble king,
  And gie me back my Dearie!

I hae born seven sons to my Geordie dear,
  The seventh ne'er saw his daddie:
O pardon, pardon, noble king,
  Pity a waefu' lady!

Gar bid the headin-man mak haste!
  Our king reply'd fu' lordly:
O noble king, tak a' that's mine,
  But gie me back my Geordie.

The Gordons cam and the Gordons ran,
  And they were stark and steady;
And ay the word amang them a'
  Was, Gordons keep you ready.

syne] then   head] behead   airn] iron   bra'] splendid
wat] am sure   headin-man] executioner   stark] strong

An aged lord at the king's right hand
    Says, noble king, but hear me;
Gar her tell down five thousand pound
    And gie her back her Dearie.

Some gae her marks, some gae her crowns,
    Some gae her dollars many;
And she's tell'd down five thousand pound,
    And she's gotten again her Dearie.

She blinkit blythe in her Geordie's face,
    Says, dear I've bought thee, Geordie:
But there sud been bluidy bouks on the green,
    Or I had tint my laddie.

He claspit her by the middle sma',
    And he kist her lips sae rosy:
The fairest flower o' woman-kind
    Is my sweet, bonie Lady!

tell] count   gae] gave   blinkit] glanced   sud] should (have)
bouks] carcasses   Or] before   tint] lost   sma'] slender

113. *Kinmont Willie*

O HAVE ye na heard o' the fause Sakelde?
    O have ye na heard o' the keen Lord Scroope?
How they hae ta'en bauld Kinmont Willie,
    On Haribee to hang him up?

Sakelde] deputy to Lord Scrope of Bolton, warden of the west Marches
for Queen Elizabeth   Kinmont Willie] William Armstrong of
Kinmonth, a notorious reiver   Haribee] the place of execution at
Carlisle

Had Willie had but twenty men,
    But twenty men as stout as he,
Fause Sakelde had never the Kinmont ta'en
    Wi' eight score in his cumpanie.

They band his legs beneath the steed,
    They tied his hands behind his back;
They guarded him, fivesome on each side,
    And they brought him ower the Liddel-rack.

They led him thro' the Liddel-rack
    And also thro' the Carlisle sands;
They brought him to Carlisle castell
    To be at my Lord Scroope's commands.

My hands are tied but my tongue is free,
    And whae will dare this deed avow?
Or answer by the border law?
    Or answer to the bauld Buccleuch?

Now haud thy tongue, thou rank reiver,
    There's never a Scot shall set ye free;
Before ye cross my castle yate
    I trow ye shall take farewell o' me.

Fear na ye that, my lord, quo' Willie;
    By the faith o' my bodie, Lord Scroope, he said,
I never yet lodged in a hostelrie
    But I paid my lawing before I gaed.

Now word is gane to the bauld Keeper
    In Branksome Ha' where that he lay,
That Lord Scroope has ta'en the Kinmont Willie
    Between the hours of night and day.

the Liddel-rack] a ford on the Liddel   Buccleuch] Sir Walter Scott
of Buccleuch   yate] gate   lawing] reckoning   gaed] went
Branksome Ha'] Branxholm Hall, near Hawick

He has ta'en the table wi' his hand,
   He garr'd the red wine spring on hie:
Now Christ's curse on my head, he said,
   But avenged of Lord Scroope I'll be:

O is my basnet a widow's curch?
   Or my lance a wand of the willow-tree?
Or my arm a ladye's lilye hand?
   That an English lord should lightly me.

And have they ta'en him, Kinmont Willie,
   Against the truce of Border tide,
And forgotten that the bauld Buccleuch
   Is Keeper here on the Scottish side?

And have they e'en ta'en him, Kinmont Willie,
   Withouten either dread or fear,
And forgotten that the bauld Buccleuch
   Can back a steed or shake a spear?

O were there war between the lands,
   As well I wot that there is none,
I would slight Carlisle castell high
   Tho' it were builded of marble stone.

I would set that castell in a low
   And sloken it with English blood;
There 's nevir a man in Cumberland
   Should ken where Carlisle castell stood.

But since nae war's between the lands
   And there is peace, and peace should be,
I'll neither harm English lad or lass
   And yet the Kinmont freed shall be.

garr'd] made   basnet] steel headpiece   curch] kerchief
wand] branch   lightly] slight   slight] level, raze   low]
blaze   sloken] quench

KINMONT WILLIE

He has call'd him forty marchmen bauld,
 I trow they were of his ain name
Except Sir Gilbert Elliot, call'd
 The Laird of Stobs, I mean the same.

He has call'd him forty marchmen bauld,
 Were kinsmen to the bauld Buccleuch,
With spur on heel, and splent on spauld,
 And gleuves of green, and feathers blue.

There were five and five before them a'
 Wi' hunting horns and bugles bright;
And five and five came wi' Buccleuch
 Like Warden's men, arrayed for fight.

And five and five like a mason gang
 That carried the ladders lang and hie,
And five and five like broken men;
 And so they reached the Woodhouselee.

And as we cross'd the Bateable Land,
 When to the English side we held,
The first o' men that we met wi',
 Whae sould it be but fause Sakelde!

Where be ye gaun, ye hunters keen,
 Quo' fause Sakelde, Come tell to me:
We go to hunt an English stag,
 Has trespassed on the Scots countrie.

Stobs] near Hawick   splent on spauld] armour on shoulder
gleuves] gloves   broken] under sentence of outlawry   the
Bateable Land] east of the Solway, claimed by Scotland and England
gaun] going

562

Where be ye gaun, ye marshal men,
   Quo' fause Sakelde, Come tell me true:
We go to catch a rank reiver,
   Has broken faith wi' the bauld Buccleuch.

Where are ye gaun, ye mason lads,
   Wi' a' your ladders lang and hie?
We gang to herry a corbie's nest
   That wons not far frae Woodhouselee.

Where be ye gaun, ye broken men,
   Quo' fause Sakelde, Come tell to me:
Now Dickie of Dryhope led that band,
   And the nevir a word o' lear had he.

Why trespass ye on the English side?
   Row-footed outlaws, stand, quo' he;
The nevir a word had Dickie to say,
   Sae he thrust the lance thro' his fause bodie.

Then on we held for Carlisle toun
   And at Staneshaw-bank the Eden we cross'd;
The water was great and meikle of spait,
   But the nevir a horse nor man we lost.

And when we reach'd the Staneshaw-bank
   The wind was rising loud and hie;
And there the laird garr'd leave our steeds
   For fear that they should stamp and nie.

marshal] martial   herry] plunder   corbie] raven   wons]
dwells   Woodhouselee] near the junction of the Esk and the Liddel
Dryhope] a Scott peel-tower by St. Mary's Loch   lear] learning
Row-footed] rough-shod, in shoes of undressed hide   the Eden] north
of Carlisle   garr'd] made us

And when we left the Staneshaw-bank
   The wind began full loud to blaw,
But 'twas wind and weet and fire and sleet
   When we came beneath the castel wa'.

We crept on knees and held our breath
   Till we placed the ladders against the wa',
And sae ready was Buccleuch himsell
   To mount the first before us a'.

He has ta'en the watchman by the throat,
   He flung him down upon the lead:
Had there not been peace between our lands
   Upon the other side thou hadst gaed.

Now sound out, trumpets, quo' Buccleuch,
   Let 's waken Lord Scroope right merrilie!
Then loud the Warden's trumpet[s] blew,
   O whae dare meddle wi' me?

Then speedilie to wark we gaed
   And raised the slogan ane and a',
And cut a hole thro' a sheet of lead,
   And so we wan to the castel ha'.

They thought King James and a' his men
   Had won the house wi' bow and speir;
It was but twenty Scots and ten
   That put a thousand in sic a stear.

Wi' coulters and wi' forehammers
   We garr'd the bars bang merrilie,
Untill we cam to the inner prison
   Where Willie o' Kinmont he did lie.

weet] rain   slogan] battle-cry (*Gaelic*)   wan to] gained
sic a stear] such a commotion   coulters] ploughshares   fore-
hammers] sledge-hammers

And when we cam to the lower prison
    Where Willie o' Kinmont he did lie:
O sleep ye, wake ye, Kinmont Willie,
    Upon the morn that thou 's to die?

O I sleep saft and I wake aft,
    It 's lang since sleeping was fley'd frae me;
Gie my service back to my wyfe and bairns
    And a' gude fellows that speer for me.

Then Red Rowan has hente him up,
    The starkest man in Teviotdale;
Abide, abide now, Red Rowan,
    Till of my Lord Scroope I take farewell.

Farewell, farewell, my gude Lord Scroope;
    My gude Lord Scroope, farewell, he cried:
I'll pay you for my lodging maill
    When first we meet on the border side.

Then shoulder high with shout and cry
    We bore him down the ladder lang;
At every stride Red Rowan made
    I wot the Kinmont's airns play'd clang.

O mony a time, quo' Kinmont Willie,
    I have ridden horse baith wild and wood;
But a rougher beast than Red Rowan
    I ween my legs have ne'er bestrode.

---

fley'd] scared away   speer] ask   hente] taken   starkest]
strongest   maill] rent   airns] irons   wood] mad

And mony a time, quo' Kinmont Willie,
  I've pricked a horse out oure the furs:
But since the day I backed a steed
  I nevir wore sic cumbrous spurs.

We scarce had won the Staneshaw-bank
  When a' the Carlisle bells were rung,
And a thousand men in horse and foot
  Cam wi' the keen Lord Scroope along.

Buccleuch has turned to Eden Water
  Even where it flow'd frae bank to brim,
And he has plunged in wi' a' his band
  And safely swam them thro' the stream.

He turned him on the other side
  And at Lord Scroope his glove flung he:
If ye like na my visit in merry England,
  In fair Scotland come visit me!

All sore astonished stood Lord Scroope,
  He stood as still as rock of stane;
He scarcely dared to trew his eyes
  When thro' the water they had gane:

He is either himsell a devil frae hell,
  Or else his mother a witch maun be;
I wad na have ridden that wan water
  For a' the gowd in Christentie.

pricked] spurred   oure the furs] over the furrows   gowd]
gold   Christentie] Christendom

114. *Jock o' the Side*

Now Liddesdale has ridden a raid,
  Wi' my fa ding diddle, lal low dow diddle:
But I wat they had better hae staid at hame;
For Michael o' Winfield he is dead
  And Jock o' the Side is prisoner ta'en.
    Wi' my fa ding diddle, lal low dow diddle.

For Mangerton house Lady Downie has gane,
  Her coats she has kilted up to her knee;
And down the water wi' speed she rins
  While tears in spaits fa' fast frae her e'e.

Then up and spoke our gude auld Lord:
  What news? what news, sister Downie, to me?
Bad news, bad news, my Lord Mangerton;
  Michael is killed and they hae ta'en my son
    Johnie.

the Side] on the bank of the Liddel. *Jock was nephew to Armstrong, the laird of Mangerton*   spaits] floods

Ne'er fear, sister Downie, quo' Mangerton:
  I have yokes of ousen eighty and three;
My barns, my byres, and my faulds a' weil fill'd,
  And I'll part wi' them a' ere Johnie shall die.

Three men I'll send to set him free,
  A' harneist wi' the best o' steil;
The English louns may hear and drie
  The weight o' their braid swords to feel.

Lord Mangerton then orders gave:
  Your horses the wrang [way] maun be shod;
Like gentlemen ye mauna seim,
  But look like corn caugers ga'en the road.

Your armour gude you mauna shaw,
  Nor yet appear like men o' weir;
As country lads be a' array'd,
  Wi' branks and brecham on each mare.

Sae now their horses are the wrang way shod,
  And Hobbie has mounted his grey sae fine;
Jock's on his lively bay, Wat's on his white horse,
    behind,
  And on they rode for the water of Tyne.

At the Cholerford they all light down
  And there, wi' the help of the light o' the moon,
A tree they cut wi' fifteen nogs on each side
  To climb up the wa' of Newcastle toun.

ousen] oxen   louns] peasants, rogues   drie] suffer
maun(a)] must (not)   caugers ga'en] hucksters travelling   weir]
war   branks and brecham] halter and straw collar   the Choler-
ford] on the Tyne where it meets the Roman Wall 5 miles above Hexham
nogs] projecting pegs

But when they cam to Newcastle toun
 And were alighted at the wa',
They fand their tree three ells ower laigh,
 They fand their stick baith short and sma'.

Then up and spak the Laird's ain Jock:
 There 's naithing for 't, the gates we maun force.
But when they cam the gate untill,
 A proud porter withstood baith men and horse.

His neck in twa the Armstrangs wrang,
 Wi' fute or hand he ne'er play'd pa!
His life and his keys at anes they hae ta'en,
 And cast the body ahind the wa'.

Now sune they reach Newcastle jail
 And to the prisoner thus they call:
Sleeps thou, wakes thou, Jock o' the Side,
 Or art thou weary of thy thrall?

Jock answers thus, wi' dulefu' tone:
 Aft, aft I wake, I seldom sleep;
But whae 's this kens my name sae weil
 And thus to mese my waes does seik?

Then out and spak the gude Laird's Jock:
 Now fear ye na, my billie, quo' he;
For here are the Laird's Jock, the Laird's Wat,
 And Hobbie Noble, come to set thee free.

three ells] over 9 feet ower laigh] too short the Laird's ain
Jock] Jock, son of Armstrong of Mangerton play'd pa] made a
move anes] once thrall] imprisonment dulefu'] sorrowful
mese] alleviate billie] comrade

Now haud thy tongue, my gude Laird's Jock,
    For ever, alas, this canna be;
For if a' Liddesdale was here the night
    The morn 's the day that I maun die.

Full fifteen stane o' Spanish iron
    They hae laid a' right sair on me;
Wi' locks and keys I am fast bound
    Into this dungeon dark and dreirie.

Fear ye na' that, quo' the Laird's Jock,
    A faint heart ne'er wan a fair ladie;
Work thou within, we'll work without,
    And I'll be sworn we'll set thee free.

The first strong door that they cam at,
    They loosed it without a key;
The next chain'd door that they cam at,
    They garr'd it a' to flinders flee.

The prisoner now upon his back
    The Laird's Jock has gotten up fu' hie;
And down the stair, him, irons, and a',
    Wi' nae sma' speid and joy brings he.

Sae out at the gates they a' are gane,
    The prisoner 's set on horseback hie;
And now wi' speid they've ta'en the gate
    While ilk ane jokes fu' wantonlie:

O Jock, sae winsomely 's ye ride,
    Wi' baith your feet upon ae side;
Sae well ye 're harniest and sae trigg,
    In troth ye sit like ony bride!

haud] hold   the night] tonight   garr'd] made   flinders]
smithereens   ilk] each   trigg] trim

The night, tho' wat, they did na mind,
   But hied them on fu' merrilie,
Until they cam to Cholerford brae
   Where the water ran like mountains hie.

But when they cam to Cholerford
   There they met with an auld man;
Says, Honest man, will the water ride?
   Tell us in haste if that ye can.

I wat weel no, quo' the gude auld man;
   I hae lived here threty years and thrie,
And I ne'er yet saw the Tyne sae big
   Nor running anes sae like a sea.

Then out and spak the Laird's saft Wat,
   The greatest coward in the cumpanie:
Now halt, now halt, we needna try 't;
   The day is come we a' maun die!

Puir faint-hearted thief, cried the Laird's ain Jock,
   There'll nae man die but him that 's fie;
I'll guide thee a' right safely thro';
   Lift ye the pris'ner on ahint me.

Wi' that the water they hae ta'en,
   By ane's and twa's they a' swam thro';
Here are we a' safe, quo' the Laird's Jock,
   And puir faint Wat, what think ye now?

They scarce the other brae had won
   When twenty men they saw pursue;
Frae Newcastle toun they had been sent,
   A' English lads baith stout and true.

wat] wet	ride] take a rider	wat weel no] know well, not
anes] once	saft] stupid Puir] poor	fie] fey, doomed
ahint] behind	stout] stalwart	

But when the Land-serjeant the water saw,
  It winna ride, my lads, says he;
Then cried aloud: The prisoner take,
  But leave the fetters, I pray, to me.

I wat weil no, quo' the Laird's Jock;
  I'll keep them a', shoon to my mare they'll be;
My gude bay mare—for I am sure
  She has bought them a' right dear frae thee.

Sae now they are on to Liddesdale,
  E'en as fast as they could them hie;
The prisoner is brought to 's ain fire-side,
  And there o 's airns they mak him free.

Now Jock, my billie, quo' a' the three,
  The day is com'd thou was to die;
But thou 's as weil at thy ain ingle side
  Now sitting, I think, 'twixt thee and me!

Land-serjeant] officer of the Border watch   winna] won't
shoon] shoes   ingle] fire burning on a hearth

115. *Hobie Noble*

FOUL fa' the breast first treason bred in:
  That Liddisdale may safely say,
For in it there was baith meat and drink
  And corn unto our geldings gay.
    Fala la diddle, &c.

We were stout hearted men and true,
    As England it did often say;
But now we may turn our backs and fly
    Since brave Noble is sel'd away.

Now Hobie he was an English man
    And born into Bewcastle dale,
But his misdeeds they were sae great
    They banish'd him to Liddisdale.

At Kershope foot* the tryst was set,
    Kershope of the lily lee;
And there was traitour Sim o' the Mains†,
    With him a private companie.

Then Hobie has graith'd his body weel,
    I wat it was wi' baith good iron and steel;
And he has pull'd out his fringed grey,
    And there brave Noble he rade him weel.

Then Hobie is down the water gane
    E'en as fast as he may drie;
Tho' they shou'd a brusten and broken their
      hearts,
    Frae that tryst Noble he would not be.

---

  * At the joining of the Rivers of Kershope and Liddal, where there is still some remains of an old tower to be seen [1784].

  † The Mains is a farm house about six hundred yards above the Castle-toun Church, on the north side of Liddal.

---

sel'd] sold   tryst] meeting   lily lee] lovely meadows   Sim]
Syme   graith'd] armed   fringed] long-haired at the fetlocks
drie] manage   a brusten] have burst

Weel may ye be, my feiries five!
   And aye, what is your wills wi' me?
Then they cry'd a' wi' ae consent,
   Thou'rt welcome here, brave Noble, to me.

Wilt thou with us in England ride?
   And thy safe warrand we will be,
If we get a horse worth a hundred punds,
   Upon his back that thou shalt be.

I dare not with you into England ride,
   The land-sergeant has me at feid;
I know not what evil may betide,
   For Peter of Whitfield his brother is dead.

And Anton Shiel he loves not me,
   For I gat twa drifts of his sheep;
The great Earl of Whitfield loves me not,
   For nae gear frae me he e'er cou'd keep.

But will ye stay till the day gae down,
   Until the night come o'er the grund,
And I'll be a guide worth ony twa
   That may in Liddisdale be fund.

Tho' dark the night as pick and tar,
   I'll lead ye o'er yon hills fu' hie,
And bring ye a' in safety back
   If you'll be true and follow me.

feiries] comrades   land-sergeant] officer of the Border watch
feid] feud   drifts] flocks   gear] livestock   gae] goes
pick] pitch

He 's guided them o'er moss and muir,
   O'er hill and houp and mony ae down,
Till they came to the Foul-bog-shiel;
   And there brave Noble he lighted down.

Then word is gane to the land-sergeant
   In Askirtoun where that he lay:
The deer that ye hae hunted lang
   Is seen into the Waste this day.

Then Hobie Noble is that deer,
   I wat he carries the style fu' hie;
Aft has he beat your slough-hounds back
   And set yourselves at little [e'e].

Gar warn the bows of Hartlie-Burn,
   See they sha[ft] their arrows on the wa';
Warn Willeva and Spear Edom
   And see the morn they meet me a'.

Gar meet me on the Rodrie-haugh,
   And see it be by break o' day;
And we will on to Conscowthart Green,
   And there, I think, we'll get our prey.

Then Hobie Noble has dream'd a dream
   In the Foul-bog-shiel where that he lay;
He thought his horse was 'neath him shot
   And he himself got hard away.

moss] bog   houp] upland valley   Foul-bog-shiel . . . Askirtoun]
*these and other names are of the places in the Waste of Bewcastle, south of
Liddesdale in Cumberland*   slough-hounds] bloodhounds   e'e]
? regard   Gar warn] have warned   bows] bowmen
the morn] tomorrow

The cocks could cr[a]w and the day could da[w],
　　And I wat so even down fell the rain;
If Hobie had no waken'd at that time
　　In the Foul-bog-shiel he had been tane or slain.

Get up, get up, my feiries five,
　　For I wat here makes a fu' ill day;
And the warst clock of this companie
　　I hope shall cross the Waste this day.

Now Hobie thought the gates were clear
　　But, ever alas, it was not sae;
They were beset wi' cruel men and keen
　　That away brave Noble could not gae.

Yet follow me, my feiries five,
　　And see of me ye keep good ray,
And the worst clock of this companie
　　I hope shall cross the Waste this day.

There was heaps of men now Hobie before,
　　And other heaps was him behind,
That had he been as wight as Wallace was
　　Away brave Noble he could not win.

Then Hobie he had but a laddie's sword,
　　But he did more than a laddie's deed;
In the midst of Conscowthart Green
　　He brake it o'er Jersawigham's head.

clock] limper, hobbler　　　gates] ways　　　wight] strong

Now they have tane brave Hobie Noble,
  Wi' his ain bow-string they band him sae;
And I wat his heart was ne'er sae sair
  As when his ain five band him on the brae.

They have tane him [on] for West Carlisle,
  They ask'd him if he knew the way;
Whate'er he thought, yet little he said;
  He knew the way as well as they.

They hae tane him up the Ricker-gate;
  The wives they cast their windows wide,
And ilka wife to anither can say,
  That 's the man loos'd Jock o' the Side.

Fy on ye, women; why ca' ye me man?
  For it 's nae man that I'm us'd like;
I'm but like a forfoughen hound
  Has been fighting in a dirty syke.

Then they hae tane him up thro' Carlisle town
  And set him by the chimney fire;
They gave brave Noble a wheat loaf to eat,
  And that was little his desire.

Then they gave him a wheat loaf to eat,
  And after that a can o' beer;
Then they cried a' wi' ae consent,
  Eat, brave Noble, and make good cheer!

band] bound   brae] hillside   ilka] every   loos'd] freed
forfoughen] worn out   syke] ditch

Confess my lord's horse, Hobie, they say,
    And the morn in Carlisle thou 's no die;
How shall I confess them? Hobie says,
    For I never saw them with mine eye.

Then Hobie has sworn a fu' great aith,
    By the day that he was gotten or born,
He never had ony thing o' my lord's
    That either eat him grass or corn.

Now fare thee weel, sweet Mangerton,
    For I think again I'll ne'er the[e] see;
I wad betray nae lad alive
    For a' the goud in Christentie.

And fare thee weel now, Liddisdale,
    Baith the hie land and the law;
Keep ye weel frae traitor Mains,
    For goud and gear he'll sell ye a'.

I'd rather be ca'd Hobie Noble
    In Carlisle where he suffers for his faut,
Before I were ca'd traitor Mains
    That eats and drinks of meal and maut.
      Fala, &c.

Confess] i.e. to stealing   goud] gold   Christentie] Christendom

116. *Hughie Graham*

OUR lords are to the mountains gane,
  A hunting o' the fallow deer;
And they hae gripet Hughie Graham
  For stealing o' the bishop's mare.—

And they hae tied him hand and foot,
  And led him up thro' Stirling town;
The lads and lasses met him there,
  Cried, Hughie Graham thou art a loun.—

O lowse my right hand free, he says,
  And put my braid sword in the same;
He's no in Stirling town this day,
  Daur tell the tale to Hughie Graham.—

gripet] apprehended   loun] rogue   lowse] loose   Daur]
dare

Up then bespake the brave Whitefoord,
  As he sat by the bishop's knee;
Five hundred white stots I'll gie you,
  If ye'll let Hughie Graham gae free.—

O haud your tongue, the bishop says,
  And wi' your pleading let me be;
For tho' ten Grahams were in his coat,
  Hughie Graham this day shall die.—

Up then bespake the fair Whitefoord,
  As she sat by the bishop's knee;
Five hundred white pence I'll gie you,
  If ye'll gie Hughie Graham to me.—

O haud your tongue now lady fair,
  And wi' your pleading let me be;
Altho' ten Grahams were in his coat,
  Its for my honor he maun die.—

They've taen him to the gallows knowe,
  He looked to the gallows tree,
Yet never color left his cheek,
  Nor ever did he blin' his e'e.—

At length he looked round about,
  To see whatever he could spy;
And there he saw his auld father,
  And he was weeping bitterly.—

stots] young bullocks   haud] hold   white] silver   maun]
must   knowe] hillock

O haud your tongue, my father dear,
  And wi' your weeping let it be;
Thy weeping 's sairer on my heart,
  Than a' that they can do to me.—

And ye may gie my brother John
  My sword that 's bent in the middle clear,
And let him come at twelve o'clock
  And see me pay the bishop's mare.—

And ye may gie my brother James
  My sword that 's bent in the middle brown;
And bid him come at four o'clock,
  And see his brother Hugh cut down.—

Remember me to Maggy my wife,
  The niest time ye gang o'er the moor;
Tell her, she staw the bishop's mare,
  Tell her, she was the bishop's whore.

And ye may tell my kith and kin,
  I never did disgrace their blood;
And when they meet the bishop's cloak,
  To mak it shorter by the hood.—

bent] curved   brown] burnished   niest] next   staw] stole

117. *The Lochmaben Harper*

O HEARD ye of a silly Harper,
   Liv'd long in Lochmaben town,
How he did gang to fair England
   To steal King Henry's wanton brown,
How he did gang to fair England
   To steal King Henry's wanton brown.

But first he gaed to his gudewife
   Wi' a' the speed that he cou'd thole:
This wark, quo' he, will never work,
   Without a mare that has a foal.

Quo' she, thou has a gude grey mare,
   That'll rin o'er hills baith low and hie;
Gae tak' the grey mare in thy hand,
   And leave the foal at hame wi' me.

Lochmaben] in Dumfriesshire   gang] go   wanton brown] a
mare   gudewife] wife   thole] manage

And tak' a halter in thy hose,
    And o' thy purpose dinna fail;
But wap it o'er the wanton's nose;
    And tie her to the grey mare's tail.

Syne ca' her out at yon back yeate,
    O'er moss and muir and ilka dale,
For she'll ne'er let the wanton bite
    Till she come hame to her ain foal.

So he is up to England gane,
    Even as fast as he can hie,
Till he came to King Henry's yeate;
    And wha was there but King Henry?

Come in, quo' he, thou silly blind Harper;
    And of thy harping let me hear.
O! by my sooth, quo' the silly blind Harper,
    I'd rather hae stabling for my mare.

The King looks o'er his left shoulder,
    And says unto his stable groom,
Gae tak the silly poor Harper's mare
    And tie her 'side my wanton brown.

And ay he harpit, and ay he carpit,
    Till a' the Lords gaed through the floor;
They thought the music was sae sweet,
    That they forgat the stable door.

dinna] don't   wap] wrap   Syne] then   yeate] gate
moss] bog   ilka] every   carpit] sang

And ay he harpit, and ay he carpit,
　　Till a' the nobles were sound asleep;
Then quietly he took aff his shoon,
　　And saftly down the stair did creep.

Syne to the stable door he hies,
　　Wi' tread as light as light cou'd be;
And whan he open'd and gaed in,
　　There he fand thirty good steeds and three.

He took the halter frae his hose,
　　And of his purpose did na' fail;
He slipt it o'er the wanton's nose,
　　And tied it to his grey mare's tail.

He ca'd her out at yon back yeate,
　　O'er moss and muir and ilka dale,
And she loot ne'er the wanton bite,
　　But held her still gaun at her tail.

The grey mare was right swift o' fit,
　　And did na fail to find the way;
For she was at Lochmaben yeate
　　Fu' lang three hours ere it was day.

When she came to the Harper's door,
　　There she gae mony a nicher and snear;
Rise, quo' the wife, thou lazy lass,
　　Let in thy master and his mare.

shoon] shoes　　　　gaun] going　　　fit] foot　　　nicher] whinny
snear] snort

Then up she raise, pat on her claes,
    And lookit but through the lock-hole;
O! by my sooth then, quoth the lass,
    Our mare has gotten a braw big foal.

Come haud thy peace then, foolish lass,
    The moon's but glancing in thy e'e;
I'll wad my haill fee 'gainst a groat,
    It's bigger than e'er our foal will be.

The neighbours too that heard the noise
    Cried to the wife to put her in;
By my sooth, then quoth the wife,
    She's better than ever he rade on.

But on the morn at fair day light,
    When they had ended a' their chear,
King Henry's wanton brown was stawn,
    And eke the poor old Harper's mare.

Alace! alace! says the silly blind Harper,
    Alace! alace! that I came here;
In Scotland I've tint a braw cowte foal,
    In England they've stawn my guid grey mare.

Come had thy tongue, thou silly blind harper,
    And of thy alacing let me be;
For thou shall get a better mare,
    And weel paid shall thy cowte foal be;
For thou shall get a better mare,
    And weel paid shall thy cowte foal be.

pat] put	claes] clothes	wad] wager	haill fee] whole wages
stawn] stolen	tint] lost	braw] fine	cowte] colt

118. Parcy Reed

O PARCY REED has Crozer ta'en
    And has deliver'd him to the law;
But Crozer says he'll do warse than that
    For he'll gar the tower of the Troughend fa'.

And Crozer says he will do warse,
    He will do warse if warse can be;
For he'll make the bairns a' fatherless,
    And then the land it may lie lea.

O Parcy Reed has ridden a raid,
    But he had better have staid at hame;
For the three fause Ha's of Girsenfield
    Alang with him he has them ta'en.

He 's hunted up and he 's hunted down,
    He 's hunted a' the water of Reed,
Till wearydness has on him ta'en,
    I' the Baitinghope he 's fa'en asleep.

Parcy Reed] laird of Troughend in Redesdale, Northumberland
Crozer] leader of a band of moss-troopers   gar] make   lea]
fallow   Ha's of Girsenfield] neighbours of Reed's   Baitinghope]
a glen off Redesdale

. . . . . .
. . . . . .

And the fause, fause Ha's o' Girsenfield,
   They'll never be trowed nor trusted again.

They've ta'en frae him his powther-bag
   And they've put water i' his lang gun;
They've put the sword into the sheathe
   That out again it'll never come.

Awaken ye, awaken ye, Parcy Reed,
   For I do fear ye've slept owre lang;
For yonder are the five Crozers
   A coming owre by the hinging-stane.

If they be five and we be four,
   If that ye will stand true to me,
If every man ye will take one,
   Ye surely will leave two to me.

O turn, O turn, O Johny Ha',
   O turn now, man, and fight wi' me;
If ever ye come to Troughend again
   A good black nag I will gie to thee;
He cost me twenty pounds o' gowd
   Atween my brother John and me.

I winna turn, I canna turn,
   I darena turn and fight wi' thee,
For they will find out Parcy Reed
   And then they'll kill baith thee and me.

owre] over   hinging-stane] ? a stone marking a gibbet?   gowd]
gold   winna] won't

O turn, O turn now, Willie Ha',
  O turn [now,] man, and fight wi' me,
And if ever ye come to the Troughend again
  A yoke of owsen I will gie thee.

I winna turn, I canna turn,
  I darena turn and fight wi' thee,
For they will find out Parcy Reed
  And they will kill baith thee and me.

O turn, O turn, O Thommy Ha',
  O turn now, man, and fight wi' me,
If ever ye come to the Troughend again
  My daughter Jean I'll gie to thee.

I winna turn, I darena turn,
  I winna turn and fight with thee,
For they will find out Parcy Reed
  And then they'll kill baith thee and me.

O woe be to ye, traitors a',
  I wish England ye may never win;
Ye've left me in the field to stand,
  And in my hand an uncharged gun.

Ye've ta'en frae me my powther-bag,
  And ye've put water i' my lang gun;
Ye've put the sword into the sheath
  That out again it'll never come.

owsen] oxen   win] reach

O fare ye weel, my married wife,
    And fare ye weel, my brother John,
That sits into the Troughend ha'
    Wi' heart as black as any stone.

O fare ye weel, my married wife,
    And fare ye weel now, my sons five;
For had ye been wi' me this day
    I surely had been man alive.

O fare ye weel, my married wife,
    And fare ye weel now, my sons five;
And fare ye weel, my daughter Jean,
    I loved ye best ye were born alive.

O some do ca' me Parcy Reed
    And some do ca' me Laird Troughend;
But it 's nae matter what they ca' me,
    My faes have made me ill to ken.

The laird o' Clennel wears my bow,
    The laird o' Brandon wears my brand;
Whae ever rides i' the Border side
    Will mind the laird o' the Troughend.

brand] sword   mind] remember

119. *The Braes of Yarrow*

I DREAMED a dreary dream this night
    That fills my heart wi' sorrow;
I dreamed I was pouing the heather green
    Upon the braes of Yarrow;

O true-luve mine, stay still and dine
    As ye ha' done before, O.—
O I'll be hame by hour[i]s nine,
    And frae the braes of Yarrow.

I dreamed a dreary dream this night
    That fills my heart wi' sorrow;
I dreamed my luve came headless hame
    O frae the braes of Yarrow;

O true-love mine, stay still and dine
    As ye ha' done before, O.—
O I'll be hame by hour[i]s nine,
    And frae the braes of Yarrow.

pouing] pulling   braes] hills, slopes

O are ye going to hawke, she says,
    As ye ha' done before, O?
Or are ye going to weild your brand
    Upon the braes of Yarrow?

O I am not going to hawke, he says,
    As I have done before, O,
But for to meet your brother Jhon
    Upon the braes of Yarrow.

As he gaed down yon dowy glen
    Sorrow went him before, O;
Nine well-wight men lay waiting him
    Upon the braes of Yarrow.

I have your sister to my wife,
    Ye think me an unmeet marrow;
But yet one foot will I never flee
    Now frae the braes of Yarrow.

Than four he kill'd and five did wound,
    That was an unmeet marrow;
And he had weel nigh wan the day
    Upon the braes of Yarrow.

Bot a cowardly loon came him behind—
    Our Lady lend him sorrow—
And wi' a rappier pierced his heart
    And laid him low on Yarrow.

brand] sword   dowy] dismal   well-wight] very strong
marrow] mate   loon] knave

Now Douglas to his sister's gane
   Wi' meikle dule and sorrow:
Gae to your luve, sister, he says,
   He's sleeping sound on Yarrow.

As she went down yon dowy glen
   Sorrow went her before, O;
She saw her true-love lying slain
   Upon the braes of Yarrow.

She swoon'd thrice upon his breist
   That was her dearest marrow;
Said, Ever alace and wae the day
   Thou wentst frae me to Yarrow!

She kist his mouth, she kaimed his hair,
   As she had done before, O;
She wiped the blood that trickled doun
   Upon the braes of Yarrow.

Her hair it was three quarters lang,
   It hang baith side and yellow;
She tied it round her white hause-bane
   And tint her life on Yarrow.

meikle dule] much grief   side] long   hause-bane] neck-bone
tint] lost

120. *Rare Willy*

WILLY's rare, and *Willy*'s fair,
  And *Willy*'s wond'rous bony;
And *Willy* heght to marry me,
  Gin e'er he marry'd ony;
    [O gin e'er he marry'd ony.]

Yestreen I made my Bed fu' brade,
  The Night I'll make it narrow;
For a' the live-long Winter's Night
  I lie twin'd of my Marrow.

O came you by yon Water-side,
  Pu'd you the Rose or Lilly;
Or came you by yon Meadow green,
  Or saw you my sweet *Willy*?

She sought him East, she sought him West,
  She sought him brade and narrow;
Sine in the clifting of a Craig
  She found him drown'd in *Yarrow*.

heght] promised   Gin] if   live-long ... Night] whole ... night
through   twin'd] parted   Marrow] mate, lover   clifting] cleft

121. *The Bonny Earl of Murray*

A

YE *Highlands* and ye *Lawlands*,
  Oh! where ha'e ye been:
They ha'e slain the Earl of *Murray*,
  And they laid him on the Green:
[They ha'e slain the Earl of *Murray*,
  And they laid him on the Green.]

Now wae be to thee *Huntly*,
  And wherefore did ye sae;
I bad you bring him wi' you,
  But forbad you him to slae.

He was a braw Gallant,
  And he rid at the Ring;
And the bonny Earl of *Murray*,
  Oh! he might have been a King.

rid] rode   Ring] metal ring on a post, to be carried off on the
rider's lance

He was a braw Gallant,
   And he play'd at the Ba',
And the bonny Earl of *Murray*
   Was the Flower amang them a'.

He was a braw Gallant,
   And he play'd at the Glove,
And the bonny Earl of *Murray*,
   Oh! he was the Queen's Love.

Oh! lang will his Lady
   Look o'er the Castle-*Down*,
E'er she see the Earl of *Murray*
   Come sounding through the Town.

B

OPEN the gates
   And let him come in;
He is my brother Huntly,
   He'll do him nae harm.

The gates they were opent,
   They let him come in;
But fause traitor Huntly,
   He did him great harm.

He 's ben and ben,
   And ben to his bed,
And with a sharp rapier
   He stabbed him dead.

Ba'] hand or football   Glove] *set up for a target, like the* Ring
Town] village   ben and ben] further and further into the house

The lady came down the stair
   Wringing her hands:
He has slain the Earl o' Murray,
   The flower o' Scotland.

But Huntly lap on his horse,
   Rade to the king:
Ye're welcome hame, Huntly,
   And whare hae ye been?

Whare hae ye been,
   And how hae ye sped?
I've killed the Earl o' Murray
   Dead in his bed.

Foul fa' you, Huntly,
   And why did ye so?
You might hae ta'en the Earl o' Murray,
   And saved his life too.

Her bread it's to bake,
   Her yill is to brew;
My sister's a widow,
   And sair do I rue.

Her corn grows ripe,
   Her meadows grow green,
But in bonny Dinnibristle
   I darena be seen.

---

lap] leapt   sped] fared   yill] ale   Dinnibristle] Doni-
bristle, Moray's estate in Fife on the Firth of Forth

122. *Burning of Auchindown* [1592]

TURN, Willie Macintosh,
    Turn, I bid you;
Gin ye burn Auchindown
    Huntly will head you.

Head me or hang me,
    That canna fley me;
I'll burn Auchendown
    Ere the life lea' me.

Coming down Deeside
    In a clear morning,
Auchindown was in flame
    Ere the cock crawing.

But coming o'er Cairn Croom
    And looking down, man,
I saw Willie Macintosh
    Burn Auchindown, man.

Bonny Willie Macintosh,
    Whare left ye your men?
I left them in the Stapler,
    But they'll never come hame.

Bonny Willie Macintosh,
    Whare now is your men?
I left them in the Stapler,
    Sleeping in their sheen.

Gin] if   head] behead   canna fley] cannot frighten   Cairn Croom] ? Cairngorm, Inverness-shire, about 30 miles south-west of Auchindown   the Stapler] a hill on Huntly's lands of Cabrach, Aberdeenshire   sheen] shoes

123. *Edom o' Gordon*

IT fell about the Martinmas
    Quhen the wind blew schrile and cauld,
Said Edom o' Gordon to his men:
    We maun draw to a hald.

And [qu]hatan a hald sall we draw to,
    My merry men and me?
We will gae to the house of the Rhodes
    To see that fair lady.

She had nae sooner busket her sell
    Nor putten on her gown,
Till Edom o' Gordon and his men
    Were round about the town.

They had nae sooner sitten down
    Nor sooner said the grace,
Till Edom o' Gordon and his men
    Were closed about the place.

Martinmas] 11 November   maun draw] must move   hald]
place of shelter   quhatan] what sort of   Rhodes] near Duns,
Berwickshire. *The historical scene of the ballad was Towie, Aberdeenshire*
busket] dressed   town] homestead

The lady ran up to her tower head
  As fast as she could drie,
To see if by her fair speeches
  She could with him agree.

As soon [as] he saw the lady fair,
  And hir yates all locked fast,
He fell into a rage of wrath
  And his heart was aghast.

Cum down to me, ye lady fair,
  Cum down to me; let 's see;
This night ye 's ly by my ain side,
  The morn my bride sall be.

I winnae cum down, ye fals Gordon,
  I winnae cum down to thee;
I winnae forsake my ane dear lord
  That is sae far frae me.

Gi' up your house, ye fair lady,
  Gi' up your house to me,
Or I will burn yoursel therein,
  Bot and your babies three.

I winnae gie up, you fals Gordon,
  To nae sik traitor as thee,
Tho' you should burn mysel therein,
  Bot and my babies three.

Set fire to the house, quoth fals Gordon,
  Sin' better may nae bee;
And I will burn hersel therein,
  Bot and her babies three.

could drie] was able   yates] gates   ye 's] you shall   ain]
own   winnae] won't   ane] one   Gi'] give   Bot and]
and also   nae sik] no such   Sin'] since

And e'in wae worth ye, Jock my man,
   I paid ye weil your fee;
[Qu]hy pow ye out my ground-wa' stane,
   Lets in the reek to me?

And e'in wae worth ye, Jock my man,
   For I paid you weil your hire;
[Qu]hy pow ye out my ground-wa' stane,
   To me lets in the fire?

Ye paid me weil my hire, lady,
   Ye paid me weil my fee;
But now I'm Edom of Gordon's man,
   Maun either do or die.

O then bespake her youngest son,
   Sat on the nurse's knee:
Dear mother, gie owre your house, he says,
   For the reek it worries me.

I winnae gie up my house, my dear,
   To nae sik traitor as he;
Cum weil, cum wae, my jewels fair,
   Ye maun tak share wi' me.

O then bespake her dochter dear,
   She was baith jimp and sma':
O row me in a pair o' shiets
   And tow me owre the wa'.

e'in] just, simply   wae worth] woe be to   fee] wages
Quhy pow] why pull   ground-wa' stane] ground-level course in the
building   reek] smoke   jimp and sma'] graceful and slender
tow] wrap   tow] let down by a rope

They row'd her in a pair of shiets
   And tow'd her owre the wa',
But on the point of Edom's speir
   She gat a deadly fa'.

O bonny, bonny was hir mouth,
   And chirry were hir cheiks,
And clear, clear was hir yellow hair
   Whereon the reid bluid dreips.

Then wi' his speir he turn'd hir owr—
   O gin hir face was wan;
He said, You are the first that e'er
   I wist alive again.

He turned hir owr and owr again—
   O gin hir skin was [qu]hyte;
He said, I might ha' spar'd thy life
   To been some man's delyte.

Busk and boon, my merry men all,
   For ill dooms I do guess;
I cannae luik in that bonny face
   As it lyes on the grass.

Them luiks to freits, my master deir,
   Then freits will follow them;
Let it neir be said brave Edom o' Gordon
   Was daunted with a dame.

---

gin] *here expletive*   wist] wished   Busk and boon] make
ready to go   cannae] cannot   Them luiks to freits] Those who
look for ill omens   daunted with] cast down, subdued by

O then he spied hir ain deir lord
 As he came owr the lee;
He saw his castle in a fire
 As far as he could see.

Put on, put on, my mighty men,
 As fast as ye can drie;
For he that 's hindmost of my men
 Sall ne'ir get guid o' me.

And some they raid, and some they ran,
 Fu' fast out owr the plain,
But lang, lang e'er he coud get up
 They were a' deid and slain.

But mony were the mudie men
 Lay gasping on the grien,
For o' fifty men that Edom brought out
 There were but five ged heme.

And mony were the mudie men
 Lay gasping on the grien,
And mony were the fair ladys
 Lay lemanless at heme.

And round and round the wa[']s he went
 Their ashes for to view;
At last into the flames he flew
 And bad the world adieu.

hir . . . lord] Alexander Forbes lee] meadow drie] endure,
manage mudie] bold lemanless] loverless

124. *The Death of Lord Warriston*

My mother was an ill woman,
    In fifteen years she married me;
I hadna wit to guide a man,
    Alas, ill counsell guided me.

O Warriston, O Warriston,
    I wish that ye may sink for sin;
I was but bare fifteen years auld
    Whan first I enter'd your yates within.

I hadna been a month married
    Till my gude lord went to the sea;
I bare a bairn ere he came hame
    And set it on the nourice' knee.

But it fell ance upon a day
    That my gude lord return'd from sea;
Then I did dress in the best array
    As blythe as ony bird on tree.

I took my young son in my arms,
    Likewise my nourice me forebye,
And I went down to yon shore side,
    My gude lord's vessel I might spy.

My lord he stood upon the deck,
    I wyte he hail'd me courteouslie:
Ye are thrice welcome, my lady gay;
    Whase aught that bairn on your knee?

married me] married me off   Warriston] John Kincaid of Warriston (d. 1600)   yates] gates   nourice] nurse   forebye] beside
wyte] believe   Whase aught] whose is

She turn'd her right and round about,
    Says, Why take ye sic dreads o' me?
Alas, I was too young married
    To love another man but thee.

Now hold your tongue, my lady gay,
    Nae mair falsehoods ye'll tell to me;
This bonny bairn is not mine,
    You've lov'd another while I was on sea.

In discontent then hame she went,
    And aye the tear did blin' her e'e;
Says, Of this wretch I'll be revenged
    For these harsh words he 's said to me.

She 's counsell'd wi' her father's steward
    What way she cou'd revenged be;
Bad was the counsel then he gave,
    It was to gar her gude lord dee.

The nourice took the deed in hand,
    I wat she was well paid her fee;
She kiest the knot, and the loop she ran,
    Which soon did gar this young lord dee.

His brother lay in a room hard by,
    Alas, that night he slept too soun';
But then he waken'd wi' a cry:
    I fear my brother 's putten down;

O get me coal and candle light,
    And get me some gude companie.
But before the light was brought
    Warriston he was gart dee.

sic] such   gar . . . dee] cause . . . to die   wat] know   kiest]
cast

They've ta'en the lady and fause nourice,
   In prison strong they ha'e them boun';
The nourice she was hard o' heart,
   But the bonny lady fell in swoon.

In it came her brother dear,
   And aye a sorry man was he:
I wou'd gie a' the lands I heir,
   O bonny Jean, to borrow thee.

O borrow me, brother, borrow me?
   O borrow'd shall I never be;
For I gart kill my ain gude lord
   And life is nae pleasure to me.

In it came her mother dear,
   I wyte a sorry woman was she:
I wou'd gie my white monie and gowd,
   O bonny Jean, to borrow thee.

Borrow me, mother, borrow me?
   O borrow'd shall I never be;
For I gart kill my ain gude lord
   And life 's now nae pleasure to me.

Then in it came her father dear,
   I wyte a sorry man was he;
Says, Ohon, alas, my bonny Jean,
   If I had you at hame wi' me!

Seven daughters I ha'e left at hame,
   As fair women as fair can be;
But I would gi'e them ane by ane,
   O bonny Jean, to borrow thee.

boun'] bound   borrow] ransom   white monie] silver
gowd] gold   Ohon] alas (*Gaelic*)

THE DEATH OF LORD WARRISTON

O borrow me, father, borrow me?
  O borrow'd shall I never be;
I that is worthy o' the death,
  It is but right that I shou'd dee.

Then out it speaks the king himsell,
  And aye as he steps in the fleer;
Says, I grant you your life, lady,
  Because you are of tender year.

A boon, a boon, my liege the king,
  The boon I ask, ye'll grant to me.
Ask on, ask on, my bonny Jean,
  Whate'er ye ask it 's granted be.

Cause take me out at night, at night,
  Lat not the sun upon me shine,
And take me to yon heading hill,
  Strike aff this dowie head o' mine.

Ye'll take me out at night, at night,
  When there are nane to gaze and see,
And ha'e me to yon heading hill,
  And ye'll gar head me speedilie.

They've ta'en her out at nine at night,
  Loot not the sun upon her shine,
And had her to yon heading hill,
  And headed her baith neat and fine.

fleer] floor   heading] beheading   dowie] sad

Then out it speaks the king himsell,
    I wyte a sorry man was he:
I've travell'd east, I've travell'd west,
    And sail[e]d far beyond the sea,
But I never saw a woman's face
    I was sae sorry to see dee.

But Warriston was sair to blame
    For slighting o' his lady so;
He had the wyte o' his ain death
    And bonny lady's overthrow.

wyte] blame

125. *Lord Maxwell's Last Goodnight*

GOOD lord of the land, will you stay thane
    About my faither's house,
And walk into these gardines green?
    In my arms I'll thee embraice;

Ten thousand times I'll kiss thy face;
    Make sport, and let 's be mery.
I thank you, lady, fore your kindness;
    Trust me, I may not stay with the.

thane] then

For I have kil'd the laird Johnston;
  I vallow not the feed;
My wiked heart did still incline,
  He was my faither's dead.

Both night and day I did proceed
  And a' on him revainged to be;
But now have I gotten what I long sowght,
  Trust me, I may not stay with the.

Adue, Dumfriese, that proper place;
  Fair well, Carlaurike faire;
Adue the castle of the Trive,
  And all my buldings there.

Adue, Lochmaben gaits so faire,
  And the Langhm shank where birks bobs
    bony;
Adue, my leady and only joy;
  Trust me, I may not stay with the.

Adue, fair Eskdale, up and doun,
  Wher my poor frends do duell;
The bangisters will beat them doun
  And will them sore compell.

I'll reveinge the cause mysell
  Again when I come over the sea;
Adue, my leady and only joy;
  Fore, trust me, I may not stay with the.

the laird Johnston] Sir James Johnstone, shot in 1608 by John, ninth Lord
Maxwell, avenging his father   vallow] do not care (about the feud
that will follow)   dead] death   Carlaurike] Caerlaverock,
Maxwell's castle near Dumfries   gaits] ways   Langhm] Langholm
shank] ridge   birks] birches   bangisters] violent folk

Adue, Dumlanark, fals was ay,
  And Closburn, in a band;
The laird of the Lag from my faither fled
  When the Jhohnstones struek of his head.

They wer three brethren in a band;
  I pray they may never be merry;
Adue, my leady and only joy;
  Trust me, I may not stay with the.

Adue, madam my mother dear,
  But and my sister[s] two;
Fair well, Robin in the Orchet,
  Fore the my heart is wo.

Adue the lillie, and fair well rose,
  And the primros, spreads fair and bony;
Adue, my leady and only joy;
  Fore, trust me, I may not stay with thee.

He took out a good gold ring
  Where at hang sygnets three:
Take thou that, my own kind thing,
  And ay have mind of me.

Do not mary another lord
  Agan or I come over the sea;
Adue, my leady and only joy;
  For, trust me, I may not stay with the.

Dumlanark] Douglas of Drumlanrig   Closburn] Kirkpatrick of
Closeburn   The laird] Grierson of Lag   Robin in the Orchet]
Sir Robert Maxwell of Orchardton, Lord Maxwell's cousin (here taken for
his brother)

The wind was fair and the ship was clare,
  And the good lord went away;
The most part of his frends was there
  Giving him a fair convoy.

They drank the wine, they did not spare,
  Presentting in that good lord's sight;
Now he is over the floods so gray;
  Lord Maxwell has te'n his last good-night.

clare] clear, ready to sail

126. *The Fire of Frendraught*

THE eighteenth of October,
  A dismal tale to hear,
How good Lord John and Rothiemay
  Was both burnt in the fire.

When steeds was saddled and well bridled
  And ready for to ride
Then out it came her, false Frendraught,
  Inviting them to bide.

false Frendraught] the wife of James Crichton of Frendraught in Forgue, Aberdeenshire

Said, Stay this night untill we sup,
    The morn untill we dine;
'Twill be a token of good 'greement
    'Twixt your good Lord and mine.

We'll turn again, said good Lord John,
    But no, said Rothiemay;
My steed's trapan'd, my bridle's broken,
    I fear the day I'm fey.

When mass was sung and bells was rung
    And all men bound for bed,
Then good Lord John and Rothiemay
    In one chamber was laid.

They had not long cast off their cloaths
    And were but now asleep,
When the weary smoke began to rise,
    Likewise the scorching heat.

O waken, waken, Rothiemay,
    O waken, brother dear,
And turn you to our Saviour;
    There is strong treason here.

When they were dressed in their cloaths
    And ready for to boun,
The doors and windows was all secur'd,
    The roof tree burning down.

He did him to the wire-window
    As fast as he could gang;
Says, Wae to the hands put in the stancheons,
    For out we'll never win.

the day] today   fey] doomed   bound] ready   boun] go
tree] main beam   wire-window] barred window for defence   win]
reach

When he stood at the wire-window
  Most doleful to be seen,
He did espy her, Lady Frendraught,
  Who stood upon the green.

Cried, Mercy, mercy, Lady Frendraught,
  Will ye not sink with sin?
For first your husband killed my father
  And now you burn his son.

O then out spoke her, Lady Frendraught,
  And loudly did she cry:
It were great pity for good Lord John
  But none for Rothiemay;
But the keys are casten in the deep draw well,
  Ye cannot get away.

While he stood in this dreadful plight
  Most piteous to be seen,
There called out his servant Gordon
  As he had frantic been.

O loup, O loup, my dear master,
  O loup and come to me;
I'll catch you in my arms two,
  One foot I will not flee.

O loup, O loup, my dear master,
  O loup and come away;
I'll catch you in my arms two,
  But Rothiemay may lie.

draw well] well from which water is raised in a bucket   Gordon]
Robert Gordon   loup] jump

The fish shall never swim in the flood
  Nor corn grow through the clay,
Nor the fiercest fire that ever was kindled
  Twin me and Rothiemay.

But I cannot loup, I cannot come,
  I cannot win to thee;
My head's fast in the wire-window,
  My feet burning from me.

My eyes are seething in my head,
  My flesh roasting also,
My bowels are boiling with my blood;
  Is not that a woeful woe?

Take here the rings from my white fingers
  That are so long and small,
And give them to my Lady fair
  Where she sits in her hall.

So I cannot loup, I cannot come,
  I cannot loup to thee;
My earthly part is all consumed,
  My spirit but speaks to thee.

Wringing her hands, tearing her hair,
  His Lady she was seen,
And thus addressed his servant Gordon
  Where he stood on the green:

O wae be to you, George Gordon,
  An ill death may you die,
So safe and sound as you stand here
  And my Lord bereaved from me.

Twin] part

I bad him loup, I bad him come,
 I bad him loup to me;
I'd catch him in my arms two,
 A foot I should not flee.

He threw me the rings from his white fingers
 Which were so long and small,
To give to you, his Lady fair,
 Where you sat in your hall.

Sophia Hay, Sophia Hay,
 O bonny Sophia was her name:
Her waiting maid put on her cloaths
 But I wat she tore them off again;

And aft she cried, Ohon! alas, alas,
 A sair heart's ill to win;
I wan a sair heart when I married him,
 And the day it's well return'd again.

Sophia Hay] daughter of the Earl of Errol and wife of Viscount Melgum
wat] know Ohon] alas (*Gaelic*)

127. *The Bonnie House o' Airlie*

IT fell upon a bonny simmer day,
 When the corn grew green and the barley,
That there fell oot a great dispute
 Atween Argyle and Airlie.

Argyle he has chosen a hundred o' his men,
 He marched them out right early;
He led them doon by the back o' Dunkeld
 To plunder the bonnie house o' Airlie.

The Lady looked owre her window sae hie,
 And oh but she grat sairly
To see Argyle and a' his men
 Come to plunder the bonnie house o' Airlie.

Come doon, come doon, Lady Ogilvie, he cried,
 Come doon and kiss me fairly,
Or I swear by the hilt o' my good broad sword
 That I winna leave a stanin' stane in Airlie.

I winna come down, ye cruel Argyle,
 I winna kiss ye fairly;
I wadna kiss ye, fause Argyle,
 Tho' ye sudna leave a stanin' stane in Airlie.

Come tell me where your dowry is hid,
 Come tell it to me fairly,
Come tell me where your dowry is hid
 Or I winna leave a stanin' stane in Airlie.

I winna tell ye, fause Argyle,
 I winna tell ye fairly,
I winna tell ye where my dowry is hid
 Tho' ye sudna leave a stanin' stane in Airlie

house o' Airlie] west of Forfar grat] wept winna] won't
stanin'] standing

They sought up, and they sought down,
 I wat they sought it sairly,
And it was below the bowling green
 They found the dowry of Airlie.

Gin my good lord had been at hame,
 As he's awa' wi' Charlie,
There durstna a Campbell o' a' Argyle
 Set a fit on the bonnie green o' Airlie.

Eleven bairns hae I born,
 And the twelfth ne'er saw his daddy;
But though I had gotten as mony again
 They sud a' gang to fecht for Charlie.

But since it's so, tak' ye my hand,
 And see ye lead me fairly;
Ye lead me doon to yonder glen,
 That I mayna see the burnin' o' Airlie.

He's ta'en her by the milkwhite hand,
 But he didna lead her fairly;
He led her up to the tap o' the hill,
 Where she saw the burnin' o' Airlie.

The smoke and the flames they rose sae hie
 The walls were blackened fairly,
And the Lady laid her down on the green to die
 When she saw the burnin' o' Airlie.

wat] know Gin] if Charlie] Charles I

128. Bessy Bell and Mary Gray

O BESSIE BELL and Mary Gray
   They war twa bonnie lasses;
They bigget a bower on yon burn brae
   And theekit it o'er wi' rashes.

They theekit it o'er wi' rashes green,
   They theekit it o'er wi' heather;
But the pest cam frae the burrows town
   And slew them baith thegither.

They thought to lye in Methven kirk-yard
   Amang their noble kin;
But they maun lye in Stronach haugh
   To biek forenent the sin.

bigget] built   burn brae] hill above a stream   theekit]
thatched   pest] plague   burrows] borough   Methven]
between Perth and Crieff   Stronach] *properly* Dranoch   haugh]
land by a river   biek . . . sin] bask facing the sun

And Bessy Bell and Mary Gray
 They war twa bonnie lasses;
They bigget a bower on yon burn brae
 And theekit it o'er wi' rashes.

129. *The Baron of Braikley*

DOON Deeside cam Inverey
 A-whistlin and singin,
And lighted at Braikley's yetts
 When the day was dawin.
O braw Lord Braikley,
 O are ye within—
There 's sharp swords at your yett
 Will gar your bluid spin.

Inverey] John Farquharson of Inverey, Braemar, whose cattle were
impounded by John Gordon of Brackley (1666) yetts] gates

THE BARON OF BRAIKLEY

Now rise up, my Baron,
  And turn back your kye,
For the lads o' Drumwharron
  Are driving them by.
O how can I rise up
  And how can I gang,
For when I hae ae man
  I wat they hae ten.

Now rise up, my lassies,
  Tak your rocks in your hands
And turn back the kye—
  I hae you at command.
Gin I had a husband
  As it seems I hae nane,
He wadnae lie in bed
  And see his kye ta'en.

Now kiss me, my lady,
  Nor think I'm to blame;
I well may rin oot
  But I'll never win hame.
When Braikley was buskit
  And leapt on his horse,
A bonnier Baron
  Ne'er rade o'er a close.

There came wi' Inverey
  Full thirty and three,
But wi' Braikley was nane
  But his brither and he.

gang] go out   wat] know   rocks] distaffs   Gin] if
win] reach   buskit] dressed   close] courtyard

Two gallanter Gordons
   Did never sword draw,
But against four and thirty
   Wae 's me, what is twa?

Wi' sword and wi' dirk
   They did him surround,
And they pierced bonny Braikley
   Wi' mony a wound.
From the head o' the Dee
   To the banks o' the Spey
The Gordons may mourn him
   And curse Inverey.

O cam ye by Braikley yetts,
   Or went ye in there?
And saw ye his lady
   A-rivin her hair?
O I cam by Braikley yetts
   And I went in there,
And I saw his lady
   A-making good cheer.

She leuch wi' them and drank wi' them
   And welcomed them ben;
She showed them the way
   Where they wouldna be ta'en.
O there 's wae in the kitchen
   And mirth in the ha',
But the Baron o' Braikley
   Is dead and awa'.

dirk] short Highland dagger   A-rivin] tearing   leuch] laughed
ben] inside

130. *The Battle of Bothwell Bridge*

O BILLIE, billie, bonny billie,
    Will ye go to the wood wi' me?
We'll ca' our horse hame masterless
    An' gar them trow slain men are we.

O no, O no, says Earlstoun,
    For that's the thing that mauna be;
For I am sworn to Bothwell Hill
    Where I maun either gae or die.

So Earlstoun rose in the morning
    An' mounted by the break o' day,
An' he has join'd our Scottish lads
    As they were marching out the way.

billie] comrade   ca'] drive   horse] horses   gar . . . trow]
make . . . believe   Earlstoun] William Gordon of Earlston, a
Covenanter   Bothwell Hill] in Lanarkshire

Now farewell, father, and farewell, mother,
  An' fare ye weel, my sisters three;
An' fare ye weel, my Earlstoun,
  For thee again I'll never see.

So they're awa' to Bothwell Hill
  An' waly, they rode bonnily;
When the Duke o' Monmouth saw them comin
  He went to view their company.

'Ye're welcome, lads, then Monmouth said,
  Ye're welcome, brave Scots lads, to me;
And sae are you, brave Earlstoun,
  The foremost o' your company.

But yield your weapons ane an' a',
  O yield your weapons, lads, to me;
For gin ye'll yield your weapons up
  Ye 'se a' gae hame to your country.

Out up then spak a Lennox lad
  And waly, but he spoke bonnily;
I winna yield my weapons up
  To you nor nae man that I see.

Then he set up the flag o' red
  A' set about wi' bonny blue:
Since ye'll no cease, and be at peace,
  See that ye stand by ither true.

They stell'd their cannons on the height
   And showr'd their shot down in the how,
An' beat our Scots lads even down;
   Thick they lay slain on every know.

As e'er you saw the rain down fa'
   Or yet the arrow frae the bow,
Sae our Scottish lads fell even down;
   An' they lay slain on every know.

O hold your hand, then Monmouth cry'd,
   Gie quarters to yon men for me;
But wicked Claverhouse swore an oath
   His cornet's death reveng'd sud be.

O hold your hand, then Monmouth cry'd,
   If ony thing you'll do for me,
Hold up your hand, you cursed Græme,
   Else a rebel to our king ye'll be.

Then wicked Claverhouse turn'd about,
   I wot an angry man was he,
And he has lifted up his hat
   And cry'd, God bless his Majesty!

Than he 's awa' to London town
   Ay e'en as fast as he can dree;
Fause witnesses he has wi' him ta'en,
   An' ta'en Monmouth's head frae his body.

Alang the brae beyond the brig
   Mony brave man lies cauld and still;
But lang we'll mind and sair we'll rue
   The bloody battle of Bothwell Hill.

stell'd] posted, set   how] valley   even down] right down,
utterly   know] hillock   His cornet] Robert Graham, killed
at Drumclog a month earlier   can dree] is able   mind] recall

131. *The Jolly Beggar*

THERE was a jolly beggar, and a begging he was bound,
And he took up his quarters into a land'art town.
    And we'll gang nae mair a roving
      Sae late into the night,
    And we'll gang nae mair a roving
      Let the moon shine ne'er sae bright,
    And we'll gang nae mair a roving.

He wad neither ly in barn, nor yet wad he in byre,
But in ahint the ha' door, or else afore the fire.
    And we'll gang nae mair, &c.

The beggar's bed was made at e'en wi' good clean straw
    and hay,
And in ahint the ha' door, and there the beggar lay.

Up raise the goodman's dochter, and for to bar the door,
And there she saw the beggar standin i' the floor.

land'art] country   gang nae mair] go no more   ahint] behind

624

He took the lassie in his arms, and to the bed he ran,
O hooly, hooly wi' me, Sir, ye'll waken our goodman.

The beggar was a cunnin' loon, and ne'er a word he
    spake,
Until he got his turn done, syne he began to crack.

Is there ony dogs into this town, Maiden, tell me true;
And what wad ye do wi' them, my hinny and my dow?

They'll rive a' my mealpocks, and do me meikle wrang.
O dool for the doing o't, are ye the poor man.

Then she took up the mealpocks and flang them o'er the
    wa',
The d——l gae wi' the mealpocks, my maidenhead and a'.

I took ye for some gentleman, at least the Laird o' Brodie;
O dool for the doing o't! are ye the poor bodie.

He took the lassie in his arms, and gae her kisses three,
And four-and-twenty hunder mark to pay the nurice-fee.

He took a horn frae his side, and blew baith loud and shrill,
And four-and-twenty belted knights came skipping o'er
    the hill.

And he took out his little knife, loot a' his duddies fa',
And he was the brawest gentleman that was amang them
    a'.

The beggar was a cliver loon, and he lap shoulder height:
O ay for sicken quarters as I gat yesternight.
    And we'll gang nae mair, &c.

hooly] gently	loon] rogue	syne] then	crack] chat
hinny] honey	dow] dove	rive] tear open	mealpocks]
meal-bags	meikle] much	dool] sorrow	bodie] fellow
nurice-] nurse's	belted] wearing the cincture of knighthood		loot]
let	duddies] rags	brawest] finest	lap] leapt	sicken] such

132. *The Gaberlunzie-Man*

THE pawky auld Carle came o'er the Lee,
Wi' many good E'ens and Days to me,
Saying, Good-wife, for your Courtisie,
   Will ye lodge a silly poor Man?
The Night was cauld, the Carle was wat,
And down ayont the Ingle he sat;

pawky] crafty   Carle] old man   Lee] meadow   wat]
wet   Ingle] fire burning on a hearth

My Daughter's shoulders he 'gan to clap,
  And cadgily ranted and sang.

O wow! quo' he, were I as free,
As first when I saw this Country,
How blyth and merry wad I be!
  And I wad never think lang.
He grew canty, and she grew fain;
But little did her auld Minny ken
What thir slee twa togither were say'n,
  When wooing they were sae thrang.

And O! quo' he, ann ye were as black,
As e'er the Crown of my Dady's Hat,
Tis I wad lay thee by my Back,
  And awa' wi' me thou shou'd gang.
And O! quo' she, ann I were as white
As e'er the Snaw lay on the Dike,
I'd clead me braw, and lady-like,
  And awa' with thee I'd gang.

Between the twa was made a Plot;
They raise a wee before the Cock,
And wylily they shot the Lock,
  And fast to the Bent are they gane.
Up in the Morn the auld Wife raise,
And at her Leisure pat on her Claise;
Syne to the Servant's Bed she gaes,
  To speer for the silly poor Man.

clap] caress   cadgily] cheerfully   ranted] made merry   think
lang] grow bored   canty] lively   fain] eager   Minny]
mother   thir slee twa] these cunning two   thrang] closely en-
gaged   ann] if   clead] clothe   braw] fine   Bent] moor
covered with bent-grass   pat] put   Claise] clothes   Syne]
then   speer] ask

She gaed to the Bed where the Beggar lay,
The Strae was cauld, he was away,
She clapt her hands, cry'd, Waladay,
   For some of our Gear will be gane.
Some ran to Coffers, and some to Kists,
But nought was stown that cou'd be mist,
She danc'd her lane, cry'd, Praise be blest,
   I have lodg'd a leal poor Man.

Since nathing 's awa', as we can learn,
The Kirns to Kirn, and Milk to Earn,
Gae butt the House, Lass, and waken my Bairn,
   And bid her come quickly ben.
The Servant gade where the Daughter lay,
The Sheets was cauld, she was away,
And fast to her good Wife can say,
   She 's aff with the Gaberlunzie-Man.

O fy gar ride, and fy gar rin,
And haste ye find these Traitors again;
For she 's be burnt, and he 's be slain,
   The wearifu' Gaberlunzie-Man.
Some rade upo' Horse, same ran a fit,
The Wife was wood, and out o' her Wit:
She cou'd na' gang, nor yet cou'd she sit,
   But ay she curs'd and she ban'd.

Strae] straw   Gear] goods   Kists] chests   stown] stolen
her lane] by herself   leal] true   Kirns] churns   Earn]
curdle   butt] through   ben] through, within   Gaber-
lunzie-Man] licensed beggar   gar . . . rin] get (folk) to . . . run
wearifu'] trying, maddening   a fit] on foot   wood] furious
ban'd] swore

Mean time far hind out o'er the Lee,
Fu' snug in a Glen, where nane cou'd see,
The twa, with kindly Sport and Glee,
   Cut frae a new Cheese a whang:
The Priving was good, it pleas'd them baith,
To lo'e her for ay, he ga'e her his aith;
Quo' she, to leave thee I will be laith,
   My winsome Gaberlunzie-Man.

O ken'd my Minny I were wi' you,
Ill-fardly wad she crook her mou,
Sic a poor Man she'd never trow,
   After the Gaberlunzie-Man.
My Dear, quo' he, ye're yet o'er young,
And ha' na' learn'd the Beggars Tongue,
To follow me frae Town to Town,
   And carry the Gaberlunzie on.

Wi' cauk and keel I'll win your Bread,
And Spindles and Whorles for them wha' need,
Whilk is a gentle Trade indeed,
   To carry the Gaberlunzie-O.
I'll bow my Leg, and crook my Knee,
And draw a black Clout o'er my Eye,
A Cripple or Blind they will ca' me,
   While we shall be merry, and sing.

---

hind] behind   whang] thick slice   Priving] testing, kissing
aith] oath   laith] loath   Ill-fardly] uglily   mou] mouth
Gaberlunzie] beggar's pack   cauk and keel] chalk and ruddle;
sketching   Whorles] pulleys for spinning-wheels   Whilk] which
gentle] civil   Clout] cloth

133. *Johnie Blunt*

THERE liv'd a man in yonder glen,
  And John Blunt was his name, O;
He maks gude maut, and he brews gude ale,
  And he bears a wondrous fame, O.

The wind blew in the hallan ae night,
  Fu' snell out o'er the moor, O;
Rise up, rise up, auld Luckie, he says,
  Rise up and bar the door, O.

They made a paction tween them twa,
  They made it firm and sure, O,
Whae'er sud speak the foremost word
  Should rise and bar the door, O.

Three travellers that had tint their gate,
  As thro' the hills they foor, O,
They airted by the line o' light
  Fu' straught to Johnie Blunt's door, O.

Blunt] Fool   maut] malt, barley for brewing   hallan]
partition between cottage door and fireplace   snell] bitter, keen
Luckie] wife   tint . . . gate] lost . . . way   foor] fared
airted] took their direction

They haurl'd auld Luckie out o' her bed,
  And laid her on the floor, O;
But never a word auld Luckie wad say,
  For barrin o' the door, O.

Ye've eaten my bread, ye hae druken my ale,
  And ye'll mak my auld wife a whore, O:
Aha, Johnie Blunt! ye hae spoke the first word,
  Get up and bar the door, O.

134. *The Cunning Clerk*

As I gaed down to Collistown
  Some white fish for to buy,
The cunning clerk he followed me,
  And he followed me speedily;
    [And he followed me, followed me,
    Followed me speedily.]

Collistown] a fishing village in Slains, Aberdeenshire

Says, Faur ye gaun, my dearest dear?
  O faur ye gaun, my dow?
There 's naebody comes to my bedside,
  And naebody wins to you.

Your brother is a gallant square wright,
  A gallant square wright is he;
Ye'll gar him make a lang ladder
  Wi' thirty steps and three.

And gar him big a deep, deep creel,
  A deep creel and a string,
And ye'll come up to my bedside
  And come bonnily linken in.

The auld gudeman and auld gudewife,
  To bed they went to sleep;
But wae mat worth the auld gudewife,
  A wink she cou'dna get.

I dream'd a dreary dream this night,
  I wish it binna true,
That the rottens had come thro' the wa'
  And cutted the coverin' blue.

Then up it raise the auld gudeman,
  To see gin it was true;
And he 's gane to his daughter dear,
  Says, What are ye doing, my dow?

Faur ye gaun] where are you going   dow] dove   wins to]
reaches   square wright] carpenter   gar him] get . . . him to
big] build, make   creel] basket   linken] tripping   gude-
man] master of the house   mat worth] may be   rottens] rats

What are ye doing, my daughter dear?
    What are ye doing, my dow?
The prayer book 's in my hand, father,
    Praying for my auld minnie and you.

The auld gudeman and auld gudewife,
    To bed they went to sleep;
But wae mat worth the auld gudewife,
    But aye she waken'd yet.

I dream'd a dreary dream this night,
    I wish it binna true,
That the cunning clerk and your ae daughter
    Were aneath the coverin' blue.

O rise yoursell, gudewife, he says,
    The diel may had you fast;
Atween you and your ae daughter
    I canna get ae night's rest.

Up then raise the auld gudewife
    To see gin it was true,
And she fell arselins in the creel
    And up the string they drew.

Win up, win up, gudeman, she says,
    Win up and help me now;
For he that ye ga'e me to last night,
    I think he 's catch'd me now.

Gin Auld Nick he has catch'd you now
    I wish he may had you fast;
As for you and your ae daughter,
    I never get kindly rest.

ae] only   diel] Devil   had] hold   gin] if   arselins)
arse first   Win] get   Auld Nick] the Devil

They howded her and they showded her
Till the auld wife gat a fa',
And three ribs o' the auld wife's side
Gaed knip knap ower in twa.

howded . . . showded] bumped up and down

135. *Kellyburnbraes*

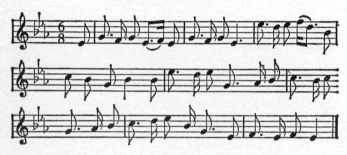

THERE lived a carl in Kellyburnbraes,
Hey and the rue grows bonie wi' thyme;
And he had a wife was the plague o' his days,
And the thyme it is wither'd and rue is in prime;
And he had a wife was the plague o' his days,
And the thyme it is wither'd and rue is in prime.

Ae day as the carl gaed up the lang-glen,
He met wi' the d–v–l, says, how do ye fen?

I've got a bad wife, Sir, that's a' my complaint,
For, saving your presence, to her ye're a saint.

carl] old fellow   Ae] one   fen] shift, do

634

It 's neither your stot nor your staig I shall crave,
But gie me your wife, man, for her I must have.

O, welcome most kindly! the blythe carl said;
But if ye can match her—ye're waur than ye're ca'd.

The d–v–l has got the auld wife on his back,
And like a poor pedlar he 's carried his pack.

He 's carried her hame to his ain hallan–door,
Syne bade her gae in for a b——ch and a wh——.

Then straight he makes fifty, the pick o' his band,
Turn out on her guard in the clap of a hand.

The carlin gaed thro' them like onie wud bear,
Whae'er she gat hands on, cam near her nae mair.

A reekit, wee devil looks over the wa':
O help, Master, help! or she'll ruin us a'.
    And &c.

The d–v–l he swore by the edge o' his knife,
He pitied the man that was ty'd to a wife.

The d–v–l he swore by the kirk and the bell,
He was not in wedlock, thank Heaven, but in h——.

Then Satan has travell'd again wi' his pack,
And to her auld husband he 's carried her back.
    And &c.

stot] young bullock   staig] young horse   waur] worse
hallan-] partition between cottage door and fireplace   carlin] old wife
wud] mad   reekit] smoky

I hae been a d–v–l the feck o' my life,
   Hey and the rue grows bonie wi' thyme;
But ne'er was in h–ll till I met wi' a wife,
   An' the thyme it is wither'd and rue is in prime.
But ne'er was in h–ll till I met wi' a wife,
   An' the thyme it is wither'd and rue is in prime.

136. *Room for a Jovial Tinker:*
Old Brass to Mend

Here is a Tinker full of mettle,
The which can mend pot, pan, or Kettle;
For stopping of holes is his delight,
His work goes forward day and night.
If there be any women brave
Whose Coldrons need of mending have,
Send for this Tinker, nere deny him,
He'l do your work well if you try him.
A proof of him I'le forthwith show.
'Cause you his workmanship may know.

IT was a Lady of the North she lov'd a Gentleman,
And knew not well what course to take, to use him now
   and than.
Wherefore she writ a Letter, and seal'd it with her hand,
And bid him be a Tinker, to mend both pot and pan.
With a hey ho, hey, derry derry down; with hey trey, down,
   down, derry.

And when the merry Gentleman the Letter he did read,
He got a budget on his back, and Apron, with all speed,

budget] wallet, bag

His pretty shears and pincers, so well they did agree;
With a long pike staff upon his back came tripping o're
    the Lee.

When he came to the Ladye's house he knocked at the
    gate;
Then answered this Lady gay, Who knocketh there so late?
'Tis I, Madam, the Tinker said, I work for gold and fee;
If you have any broken pots or pans, come bring them all
    to me.

I am the bravest Tinker that lives beneath the Sun;
If you have any work to do, you shall have it well done;
I have brasse within my budget, and punching under my
    Apron;
I'm come unto your Ladyship and means to mend your
    Coldron.

I prethee, said the Lady gay, bring now thy budget in;
I have store of work for thee to do if thou wilt once
    begin.
Now when the Tinker he came in, that did the budget
    bear,
God blesse, quoth he, your Ladyship! God save you,
    Madam fair.

But when the Lady knew his face she then began to wink;
Hast, lusty Butler! then quoth she, to fetch the man some
    drink.
Give him such meat as we do eat, and drink as we do use,
It is not for a Tinker's Trad[e] good liquor to refuse.

Lee] pasture

But when that he had eat and drunk, the truth of all is so,
The Lady took him by the sleeve, her work to him to
show:
Let up thy Tools, Tinker, quoth she, and see there be
none lost;
And mend my Kettle handsomely, what ere it doth me
cost.

Your work, Madam, shall be well done, if you will pay
me for 't;
For every nayl that I do drive, you shall give me a mark.
If I do not drive the nayl to th' head, I'le have nothing
for my pain;
And what I do receive of you shall be return'd again.

At last being come into the Room where he the work
should do,
The Lady lay down on the bed, so did the Tinker too;
Although the Tinker knockt amain, the Lady was not
offended;
But before that she rose from the bed her Coldron was
well mended.

But when his work was at an end, which he did in the
dark,
She put her hand into her purse and gave him twenty
mark;
Here's mony for thy work, said she, and I thank thee for
thy pain,
And when my Coldron mending lacks I'le send for thee
again.

The Tinker he was well content for that which he had
    done,
So took his budget on his back and quickly he was gone.
Then the Lady to her husband went; O my dear Lord,
    quoth she,
I have set the bravest Tinker at work that ever you did
    see.

No fault at all this Tinker hath, but he takes dear for his
    work,
That little time that he wrought here it cost me twenty
    mark.
If you had been so wise, quoth he, for to have held your
    own,
Before you set him to this work the price you might have
    known.

Pray hold your peace, my Lord, quoth she, and think it
    not too dear;
If you cou'd doo 't so well 'twould save you forty pound
    a year.
With that the Lord most lovingly, to make all things
    amends,
He kindly kist his Lady gay, and so they both were friends.

You merry Tinkers, every one, that hear this new-made
    Sonnet,
When as you do a Lady's work be sure you think upon it;
Drive home your nayls to the very head, and do your
    work profoundly,
And then no doubt your Mistresses will pay you for it
    soundly.
*With hey ho, hey, derry derry down; with hey trey, down
    down, derry.*

137. *The Merchant and the Fidler's Wife*

IT was a Rich Merchant Man
   That had both Ship and all;
And he would cross the salt Seas
   Tho' his cunning it was but small.

The Fidler and his Wife,
   They being nigh at hand,
Would needs go sail along with him
   From *Dover* unto *Scotland*.

The Fidler's Wife look'd brisk,
   Which made the Merchant smile;
He made no doubt to bring it about
   The Fidler to beguile.

Is this thy Wife, the Merchant said,
   She looks like an honest Spouse;
Ay that she is, the Fidler said,
   That ever trod on Shoes.

They Confidence is very great,
   The Merchant then did say;
If thou a Wager darest to bet
   I'll tell thee what I will lay.

I'll lay my Ship against thy Fiddle,
   And all my Venture too,
So *Peggy* may gang along with me
   My Cabin for to View.

If she continues one Hour with me
   Thy true and constant Wife,
Then shalt thou have my Ship and be
   A Merchant all thy Life.

The Fidler was content,
   He Danc'd and Leap'd for joy;
And twang'd his Fiddle in merriment,
   For *Peggy* he thought was Coy.

Then *Peggy* she went along
   His Cabin for to View,
And after her the Merchant-Man
   Did follow, we found it true.

When they were once together
   The Fidler was afraid;
For he crep'd near in pitious fear,
   And thus to *Peggy* he said:

Hold out, sweet *Peggy*, hold out,
   For the space of two half Hours;
If thou hold out, I make no doubt
   But the Ship and Goods are ours.

In troth, sweet *Robin*, I cannot,
   He hath got me about the Middle;
He 's lusty and strong and hath laid me along—
   O Robin, thou 'st lost thy Fiddle.

641

If I have lost my Fiddle
   Then am I a Man undone;
My Fiddle whereon I so often play'd—
   Away I needs must run.

O stay, the Merchant said,
   And thou shalt keep thy place;
And thou shalt have thy Fiddle again
   But *Peggy* shall carry the Case.

Poor *Robin*, hearing that,
   He look'd with a Merry-chear;
His wife she was pleas'd, and the Merchant
     was eas'd,
   And jolly and brisk they were.

The Fidler he was mad,
   But valu'd it not a Fig;
Then *Peggy* unto her Husband said,
   Kind *Robin*, play us a Jigg.

Then he took up his Fiddle,
   And merrily he did play
The *Scottish Jigg* and the *Horn pipe*
   And eke the *Irish Hey*.

It was but in vain to grieve,
   The Deed it was done and past;
Poor *Robin* was born to carry the Horn
   For *Peggy* could not be Chast.

Then Fidlers all beware,
   Your Wives are kind you see;
And he that's made for the Fidling Trade
   Must never a Merchant be.

For *Peggy* she knew right well,
   Although she was but a Woman,
That Gamesters Drink, and Fidlers Wives
   They are ever Free and Common.

138. *The Unfortunate Miller; Or, The Country
    Lasses witty Invention. Shewing*

How he would have Layn with A Maid in his own house;
As also the manner of the Cheat put upon him, By which
meanes his man *Lawrence* grafted a large pair of *horns* upon
      his Masters Head.

ALL you that desire to he[a]r of a jest,
Come listen a while and it shall be exprest;
It is of a Miller that liv'd very near
(The like of this ditty you never did he[a]r).
A handsome young Damsel she came to his Mill
To have her Corn Ground with a Ready good Will.
As soon as he s[aw] her fair beauty so bright
He caused this young Damosel to tarry all night.

Said he, My dear Jewel, it will be ne'r Morn
Before my man Lawrence can grind my Dears Corn;
And therefore if thou wilt be ruled by me,
At home in my Parlour thy Lodging shall be.
For I am inflam'd with thy Amorous Charms,
And therefore this Night thou shalt sleep in my arms.
I swear it, and therefore it needs must be so,
It is but in vain for to answer me no.

At this the young Damsel she blushing did stand,
But strait ways the Master took her by the hand;
And leading her home to young *Gillian* his wife,
Said he, My sweet honey, the joy of my Life,
Be kind to this Maid, for her Father I know,
And let her lye here in the Parlour below;
Stout Lawrence my servant and I, we shall stay
All night in the Mill till the dawning of Day.

To what he desir'd she straitways agreed,
And then to the Mill he did hasten with speed.
He ready was then to leap out of his skin
To think of the Bed which he meant to lye in.
Now when he was gone, the Maid told his intent
To *Gillian*, and they a new Project invent
By which they well fitted this Crafty young blade;
The Miller by Lawrence a Cuckold was made.

The Maid and his Wife they chang'd Bed for that
    night,
So that when the Miller came for his delight
Strait way to the Parlour Bed he did Repair:
Instead of the Damsel, wife *Gillian* was there,
Which he did Imagin had been the young Lass.
When after some hours in pleasure they past
He ris, and return'd to the Mill like one wild,
For fear he had Got the young Damsel with child.

Then to his man Lawrence the miller did say:
I have a young damsel both bony and Gay;
Her Eyes are like diamonds, her cheeks sweet and
    fair,
They may with the Rose and the Lilly Compare;

Her lips they are like the rich coral for Red,
This Lass is at home in my Parlour a Bed;
And if you go home you may freely enjoy
With her the sweet pleasure, for she is not Coy.

His masters kind Proffer he did not refuse,
But was brisk and Airy, and pleased with the News;
But said, To your self much beholding I am,
And for a Requital I'le give you my Ram.
This done, lusty Lawrence away home he goes
And stript of his Coat, Breeches, likewise shooes and
    hose,
And went into Bed to *Gillian* his dame,
Yet Lawrence for this was not worthy of blame.

He little Imagen'd his Dame was in bed,
And therefore his heart was the freer from dread;
The minutes in Pastime and pleasure they spent,
Unknown to them both she injoy'd true content.
Now after a while he his dame had Imbrac'd,
He Rose and Return'd to the mill in all hast,
Telling his master of all the delight
Which he had injoy'd with that damsel this Night.

Next morning the maid to the mill did Repair;
The miller and Lawrence his servant was there.
His master then whisper'd this word in her Ear:
How like you to lye with a miller, my dear?
At this the young damsel then laughing out Right,
And said, I chang'd Beds with young *Gillian* last
    Night;
If you injoy'd any it was your sweet wife,
For my part I ne'r lay with man in my Life.

At this he began for to Rave, stamp and stare,
Both scratching his Elbows and Hauling his hair;
And like one distracted about he did run,
And oftentimes Crying, Ha! what have I done?
Was ever poor miller so finely betray'd?
By Lawrence my man I a Cuckold am made.
The damsel she laught, and was pleas'd in her mind,
And said he was very well serv'd in his kind.

139. *The Crafty Miss of London; or, The Fryar well Fitted*

A FRYAR was walking in Exeter-street
Drest up in his Garb like a Gentleman neat;
He there with a wanton young Lady did meet
And freely did offer and earnestly proffer
    to give her a Bottle of Wine.

Love, let us not stand to Discourse in the Cold,
My amorous Jewel I prithee behold;
Then straight he pull'd out a whole handful of Gold
And said, My dear honey, here 's plenty of Money;
    I'll give thee a Guinny or two.

The glittering Guinnies soon dazel'd her eyes,
That privately straight she began to devise
By what means she might get this rich Golden prize:
Two is but a trifle, his pockets I'll rifle;
    I [hope] to have all now or none.

She seemingly Bashful, disputing did stand
And said, I dare not to the Tavern with Man;
But this was to bring him more eagerly on
So that the Old Fryar did burn with desire
     and she to his humour did yield.

Away to the Tavern they went in all haste,
A glass of Canary resolving to taste,
And there the Old Fryar he freely Embrac'd
This Lady of pleasure; she aim'd at his Treasure
     which constantly run in her mind.

The Drawer supply'd them with Liquor good store,
And when all was out still they called for more;
Her Amorous Charms he did dearly adore,
And as they sat drinking she paid it with thinking
     how she might his Guinnies obtain.

The Fryar to Court her he thus did begin:
Sweet Madam, step out of these Robes you are in,
That I may behold thy white delicate Skin
The which will inflame me; sweet creature, don't
     blame me,
     I'll give you three Guinnies the more.

This Lady of pleasure, she thus did reply:
That Civil Request, Sir, I will not deny
If that you'll strip Naked now as well as I.
To which he consented; both being contented
     they scamper'd a while round the Room.

While naked they danc'd at this Frolicksome rate
His Wigg did flye off, and she see his bald Pate;
I have an Old Fryar, thought she, for my Mate;
I' faith I will fit him, if that I can get him
     to change his Apparel with me.

Then straight with a Smile to the Fryar she goes,
And said, Worthy Sir, here 's one thing I propose;
Let us in this Frolick now change our Cloaths.
He grants her desire, they change their Attire,
     she like a Town-Bully appear'd.

The Fryar immediately sets himself down,
He puts on her Smicket, her Top-Knot and Gown,
And look'd like a Hag-ridden Bawd of the Town
In Ribbons and Laces; but she had her Paces
     and fitted the Fryar at last.

His Cloaths with his Watch and his Guinnies she got,
Then made an excuse to go down to the Vault;
Yet ne'r came again, but left him all the Shot
To pay without Money; his Amorous Honey
     did leave the Old Rogue in the Lurch.

He found she had left him the Dog for to hold;
Then calling the Drawer his Grief to unfold,
He had not a penny of Silver nor Gold;
Then counting his Losses, his Beads and his Crosses,
     he ne'r was so Riffl'd before.

The Drawer he told him the Shot must be pay'd;
The Fryar stood quaking, but little he said;
They stript off the Gown in which he was array'd,
His Ribbons and Laces; he made sower Faces
     to see his most desperate Doom.

They found that he was of the Jesuit breed,
And one that had been a great Rascal indeed;
Now therefore they sent him to *Newgate* with speed.
A woful Disaster, he says Pater-Noster
     but has neither Money nor Cloaths.

Smicket] smock, chemise   Shot] reckoning   Riffl'd] plundered

140. *The Fair Lass of Islington*

THERE was a Lass of *Islington*,
  As I have heard many tell;
And she would to Fair *London* go
  Fine Apples and Pears to sell;
And as along the Streets she flung
  With her basket on her Arm,
Her Pears to sell, you may know it right well,
  This fair Maid meant no harm.

But as she tript along the Street
  Her pleasant Fruit to sell,
A Vintner did with her meet
  Who lik'd this Maid full well.
Quoth he, Fair Maid, what have you there
  In Basket decked brave?
Fine Pears, quoth she, and if it please ye
  A taste, Sir, you shall have.

The Vintner he took a Taste
  And lik'd it well, for why;
This Maid he thought of all the rest
  Most pleasing to his Eye;
Quoth he, Fair Maid, I have a Suit
  That you to me must grant;
Which if I find you be so kind,
  Nothing that you shall want.

Thy beauty doth so please my Eye
  And dazles so my sight,
That now of all my Liberty
  I am deprived quite;
Then prithee now consent to me,
  And do not put me by;
It is but one small courtesie—
  All Night with you to lie.

Sir, if you lie with me one Night,
  As you propound to me,
I do expect that you should prove
  Both courteous, kind, and free;
And for to tell you all in short,
  It will cost you Five Pound.
A Match, a Match, the Vintner said,
  And so let this go round.

When he had lain with her all Night
  Her Money she did crave;
O stay, quoth he, the other Night,
  And thy Money thou shalt have.
I cannot stay, nor I will not stay,
  I needs must now be gone.
Why then, thou may'st thy Money go look,
  For Money I'll pay thee none.

This Maid she made no more ado
  But to a Justice went,
And unto him she made her moan,
  Who did her Case lament;
She said she had a Cellar let out
  To a Vintner in the Town,
And how that he did then agree
  Five Pound to pay her down.

But now, quoth she, the Case is thus,
  No Rent that he will pay;
Therefore your Worship I beseech
  To send for him this Day;
Then strait the Justice for him sent
  And asked the Reason why
That he would pay this Maid no Rent?
  To which he did Reply:

Although I hired a Cellar of her
  And the Possession was mine,
I ne'er put any thing into it
  But one poor Pipe of Wine;
Therefore my Bargain it was hard,
  As you may plainly see;
I from my Freedom was Debarr'd—
  Then, good Sir, favour me.

This Fair Maid being ripe of Wit,
  She strait Reply'd again:
There were two Butts more at the Door,
  Why did you not roul them in?
You had your Freedom and your Will,
  As is to you well known;
Therefore I do desire still
  For to receive my own.

The Justice hearing of their Case
  Did then give Order strait,
That he the Money should pay down,
  She should no longer wait.
Withal he told the Vintner plain,
  If he a Tennant be,
He must expect to pay the same
  For he could not sit Rent-free.

But when the Money she had got
   She put it in her Purse,
And clapt her Hand on the Cellar Door
   And said it was never the worse;
Which caused the People all to Laugh,
   To see this Vintner Fine
Out-witted by a Country Girl
   About his Pipe of Wine.

141. *Squire and Milkmaid; or, Blackberry Fold*

It 's of a rich squire in Bristol doth dwell,
There are ladies of honour that love him well;
But all was in vain, in vain was said,
For he was in love with a charming milkmaid.

As the squire and his sister did sit in the hall,
And as they were talking to one and to all,
And as they were singing each other a song,
Pretty Betsy the milkmaid came tripping along.

Do you want any milk? pretty Betsy did say;
O yes, said the squire; Step in, pretty maid;
It is you, fair body, that I do adore,
Was there ever a body so wounded before?

O hold your tongue, squire, and let me go free,
Do not make your game on my poverty;
There are ladies of honour more fitter for you
Then I, a poor milkmaid, brought up from the cows.

A ring from his finger he instantly drew
And right in the middle he broke it in two;
And half he gave to her, as I have been told,
And they both went a walking to Blackberry Fold.

O Betsy, O Betsy, let me have my will,
So constant a squire I'll prove to you still;
And if you deny me in this open field,
Why, the first time I'll force and make you to yield.

With hugging and struggling poor Betsy got free,
Saying, You never shall have your will of me,
I'll protect my own virtue as I would my life;
And drew from her bosom a large dagger knife.

Then with her own weapon she run him quite
    through,
And home to her master like lightning she flew,
Saying, O my dear master, with tears in her eyes,
I have wounded the squire and I'm afraid dead he
    lies.

The coach was got ready, the squire brought home,
The doctor was sent for to heal up the wound;
Poor Betsy was sent for, the gay maiden fair,
Who wounded the squire, drove his heart in a snare.

The parson was sent for, this couple to wed,
And she did enjoy the sweet marriage bed;
It's better to be honest if ever so poor,
For he's made her his lady instead of his whore.

142. *Verses on Daniel Good*

(Who was executed this morning May [18]42, for the
Murder of Jane Jones)

Of all the wild deeds upon murder's black list
Sure none is so barbarous and cruel as this
Which in these few lines unto you I'll unfold;
The recital's enough to turn your blood cold.

In the great town of London near Manchester square,
Jane Jones kept a mangle in South street we hear;
A gentleman's coachman oft visiting came,
A cold-blooded monster, Dan Good was his name.

As a single man un[to] her he made love,
And in course of time she pregnant did prove;
Then with false pretences he took her from home
To murder his victim and the babe in her womb.

To his master's stables in Putney Park Lane
They went, but she never returned again;
Prepare for your end, then the monster did cry,
You[r] time it is come for this night you must die.

Then with a sharp hatchet her head [he] did cleave,
She begged for mercy but none he would give;
Have mercy, dear Daniel, my wretched life spare
For the sake of your own child which you know I
    bear.

No mercy, he cried, then repeated the blow;
Alive from this stable you never shall go;
Neither you nor your brat shall e'er trouble me
    more.
Then lifeless his victim he struck to the floor.

And when she was dead, this sad deed to hide,
The limbs from her body he straight did divide;
Her bowels ript open and dripping with gore
The child from the womb this black monster he tore.

He made a large fire in the harness room,
Her head, arms, and legs in the fire did consume;
But e'er his intentions were fulfilled quite
This dark deed by Providence was brought to light.

To a pawn-shop the coachman he did go one day,
A boy said some trowsers he did take away;
A policeman followed unto Putney Lane
The coachman and trouwsers to bring back again.

When in searching the stable the body he spied
Without head, legs or arms, and ript open beside,
Then a cry of murder he quickly did raise,
And the coachman was taken within a few days.

And when he was tried, most shocking to state,
The evidence proved what I now relate:
That Daniel Good murdered his victim [Jane] Jones
Then cut up and burnt her flesh and [her] bones.

He soon was found guilty and sentenced to die
The death of a murderer on the gallows high;
The blood of the murder'd must not cry [in] vain,
An' we hope that his like we shall ne'er see again.

143. *Bristowe Tragedie*

Or the Dethe of Syr Charles Bawdin

THE featherd songster chaunticleer
　　Han wounde hys bugle horne,
And tolde the earlie villager
　　The commynge of the morne:

Kynge EDWARDE sawe the ruddie streakes
　　Of lyghte eclypse the greie;
And herde the raven's crokynge throte
　　Proclayme the fated daie.

Thou 'rt right, quod hee, for, by the Godde
　　That syttes enthron'd on hyghe!
CHARLES BAWDIN, and hys fellowes twaine,
　　To-daie shall surelie die.

Thenne wythe a jugge of nappy ale
　　Hys Knyghtes dydd onne hymm waite;
Goe tell the traytour, thatt to-daie
　　Hee leaves thys mortall state.

Syr CANTERLONE thenne bendedd lowe,
　　Wythe harte brymm-fulle of woe;
Hee journey'd to the castle-gate,
　　And to Syr CHARLES dydd goe.

Butt whenne hee came, hys children twaine,
　　And eke hys lovynge wyfe,
Wythe brinie tears dydd wett the floore,
　　For goode Syr CHARLESES lyfe.

Han] hath

656

O goode Syr CHARLES! sayd CANTERLONE,
    Badde tydyngs I doe brynge.
Speke boldlie, manne, sayd brave Syr CHARLES,
    Whatte says thie traytor kynge?

I greeve to telle, before yonne sonne
    Does fromme the welkinn flye,
Hee hath uponne hys honour sworne,
    Thatt thou shalt surelie die.

Wee all must die, quod brave Syr CHARLES;
    Of thatte I'm not affearde;
Whatte bootes to lyve a little space?
    Thanke JESU, I'm prepar'd:

Butt telle thye kynge, for myne hee's not,
    I'de sooner die to-daie
Thanne lyve hys slave, as manie are,
    Tho' I shoulde lyve for aie.

Thenne CANTERLONE hee dydd goe out,
    To telle the maior straite
To gett all thynges ynne reddyness
    For goode Syr CHARLESES fate.

Thenne Maisterr CANYNGE saughte the kynge,
    And felle down onne hys knee;
I'm come, quod hee, unto your grace
    To move your clemencye.

Thenne quod the kynge, Youre tale speke out,
    You have been much oure friende;
Whatever youre request may bee,
    Wee wylle to ytte attende.

welkinn] heaven

657

My nobil leige! alle my request
    Ys for a nobile knyghte,
Who, tho' may hap hee has donne wronge,
    He thoghte ytte stylle was ryghte:

Hee has a spouse and children twaine,
    Alle rewyn'd are for aie;
Yff thatt you are resolv'd to lett
    CHARLES BAWDIN die to-daie.

Speke nott of such a traytour vile,
    The kynge ynne furie sayde;
Before the evening starre doth sheene,
    BAWDIN shall loose hys hedde:

Justice does loudlie for hym calle,
    And hee shalle have hys meede:
Speke, Maister CANYNGE! Whatte thynge else
    Att present doe you neede?

My nobile leige! goode CANYNGE sayde,
    Leave justice to our Godde,
And laye the yronne rule asyde;
    Be thyne the olyve rodde.

Was Godde to serche our hertes and reines,
    The best were synners grete;
CHRIST's vycarr only knowes ne synne,
    Ynne alle thys mortall state.

Lett mercie rule thyne infante reigne,
    'Twylle faste thye crowne fulle sure;
From race to race thy familie
    Alle sov'reigns shall endure:

ne] no   faste] secure

But yff wythe bloode and slaughter thou
   Beginne thy infante reigne,
Thy crowne uponne thy childrennes brows
   Wylle never long remayne.

CANYNGE, awaie! thys traytour vile
   Has scorn'd my power and mee;
Howe canst thou thenne for such a manne
   Intreate my clemencye?

My nobile leige! the trulie brave
   Wylle val'rous actions prize,
Respect a brave and nobile mynde,
   Altho' ynne enemies.

CANYNGE, awaie! By Godde ynne Heav'n
   Thatt dydd mee beinge gyve,
I wylle nott taste a bitt of breade
   Whilst thys Syr CHARLES dothe lyve.

By MARIE, and alle Seinctes ynne Heav'n,
   Thys sunne shall be hys laste.
Thenne CANYNGE dropt a brinie teare,
   And from the presence paste.

Wyth herte brymm-fulle of gnawynge grief,
   Hee to Syr CHARLES dydd goe,
And satt hymm downe uponne a stoole,
   And teares beganne to flowe.

Wee all must die, quod brave Syr CHARLES;
   Whatte bootes ytte howe or whenne;
Dethe ys the sure, the certaine fate
   Of all wee mortall menne.

Saye why, my frend, thie honest soul
   Runns overr att thyne eye;
Is ytte for my most welcome doome
   Thatt thou dost child-lyke crye?

Quod godlie CANYNGE, I doe weepe,
   Thatt thou so soone must dye,
And leave thy sonnes and helpless wyfe;
   'Tys thys thatt wettes myne eye.

Thenne drie the tears thatt out thyne eye
   From godlie fountaines sprynge;
Dethe I despise, and alle the power
   Of EDWARDE, traytor kynge.

Whan throgh the tyrant's welcom means
   I shall resigne my lyfe,
The Godde I serve wylle soone provyde
   For bothe mye sonnes and wyfe.

Before I sawe the lyghtsome sunne,
   Thys was appointed mee;
Shall mortall manne repyne or grudge
   Whatt Godde ordeynes to bee?

Howe oft ynne battaile have I stoode,
   Whan thousands dy'd arounde;
Whan smokynge streemes of crimson bloode
   Imbrew'd the fatten'd grounde:

How dydd I knowe thatt ev'ry darte,
   Thatt cutte the airie waie,
Myghte nott fynde passage toe my harte,
   And close myne eyes for aie?

And shall I nowe, forr feere of dethe,
  Looke wanne and bee dysmayde?
Ne! fromm my herte flie childyshe feere,
  Bee alle the manne display'd.

Ah, goddelyke HENRIE! Godde forefende,
  And guarde thee and thye sonne,
Yff 'tis hys wylle; but yff 'tis nott,
  Why thenne hys wylle bee donne.

My honest friende, my faulte has beene
  To serve Godde and mye prynce;
And thatt I no tyme-server am,
  My dethe wylle soone convynce.

Ynne Londonne citye was I borne,
  Of parents of grete note;
My fadre dydd a nobile armes
  Emblazon onne hys cote:

I make ne doubte butt hee ys gone
  Where soone I hope to goe;
Where wee for ever shall bee blest,
  From oute the reech of woe:

Hee taughte mee justice and the laws
  Wyth pitie to unite;
And eke hee taughte mee howe to knowe
  The wronge cause fromm the ryghte:

Hee taughte mee wythe a prudent hande
  To feede the hungrie poore,
Ne lett mye sarvants dryve awaie
  The hungrie fromme my doore:

And none can saye, butt alle mye lyfe
  I have hys wordyes kept;
And summ'd the actyonns of the daie
  Eche nyghte before I slept.

I have a spouse, goe aske of her,
  Yff I defyl'd her bedde?
I have a kynge, and none can laie
  Blacke treason onne my hedde.

Ynne Lent, and onne the holie eve,
  Fromm fleshe I dydd refrayne;
Whie should I thenne appeare dismay'd
  To leave thys worlde of payne?

Ne! hapless HENRIE! I rejoyce,
  I shalle ne see thye dethe;
Moste willynglie ynne thye just cause
  Doe I resign my brethe.

Oh, fickle people! rewyn'd londe!
  Thou wylt kenne peace ne moe;
Whyle RICHARD's sonnes exalt themselves,
  Thye brookes wythe bloude wylle flowe.

Saie, were ye tyr'd of godlie peace,
  And godlie HENRIE's reigne,
Thatt you dydd choppe youre easie daies
  For those of bloude and peyne?

Whatte tho' I onne a sledde bee drawne,
  And mangled by a hynde,
I doe defye the traytor's pow'r,
  Hee can ne harm my mynde;

choppe] exchange   sledde] sledge, gallows-cart

Whatte tho', uphoisted onne a pole,
  Mye lymbes shall rotte ynne ayre,
And ne ryche monument of brasse
  CHARLES BAWDIN's name shall bear;

Yett ynne the holie booke above,
  Whyche tyme can't eate awaie,
There wythe the sarvants of the Lorde
  Mye name shall lyve for aie.

Thenne welcome dethe! for lyfe eterne
  I leave thys mortall lyfe:
Farewell, vayne worlde, and alle that's deare,
  Mye sonnes and lovynge wyfe!

Nowe dethe as welcome to mee comes,
  As e'er the moneth of Maie;
Nor woulde I even wyshe to lyve,
  Wyth my dere wyfe to staie.

Quod CANYNGE, 'Tys a goodlie thynge
  To bee prepar'd to die;
And from thys world of peyne and grefe
  To Godde ynne Heav'n to flie.

And nowe the bell beganne to tolle,
  And claryonnes to sounde;
Syr CHARLES hee herde the horses feete
  A prauncyng onne the grounde:

And just before the officers,
  His lovynge wyfe came ynne,
Weepynge unfeigned teeres of woe,
  Wythe loude and dysmalle dynne.

663

Sweet FLORENCE! nowe I praie forbere,
   Ynne quiet lett mee die;
Praie Godde, thatt ev'ry Christian soule
   Maye looke onne dethe as I.

Sweet FLORENCE! why these brinie teeres?
   Theye washe my soule awaie,
And almost make mee wyshe for lyfe,
   With thee, sweete dame, to staie.

'Tys butt a journie I shalle goe
   Untoe the lande of blysse;
Nowe, as a proofe of husbande's love,
   Receive thys holie kysse.

Thenne FLORENCE, fault'ring ynne her saie,
   Tremblynge these wordyes spoke,
Ah, cruele EDWARDE! bloudie kynge!
   My herte ys welle nyghe broke:

Ah, sweete Syr CHARLES! why wylt thou goe,
   Wythoute thye lovynge wyfe?
The cruelle axe thatt cuttes thye necke,
   Ytte eke shall ende mye lyfe.

And nowe the officers came ynne
   To brynge Syr CHARLES awaie,
Whoe turnedd toe his lovynge wyfe,
   And thus toe her dydd saie:

I goe to lyfe, and nott to dethe,
   Truste thou ynne Godde above,
And teache thye sonnes to feare the Lorde,
   And ynne theyre hertes hym love:

saie] speech

Teache them to runne the nobile race
　　Thatt I theyre fader runne:
FLORENCE! shou'd dethe thee take——adieu!
　　Yee officers, leade onne.

Thenne FLORENCE rav'd as anie madde,
　　And dydd her tresses tere;
Oh! staie, mye husbande! lorde! and lyfe!—
　　Syr CHARLES thenne dropt a teare.

'Tyll tyredd oute wythe ravynge loud,
　　Shee fellen onne the flore;
Syr CHARLES exerted alle hys myghte,
　　And march'd fromm oute the dore.

Uponne a sledde hee mounted thenne,
　　Wythe lookes fulle brave and swete;
Lookes, thatt enshone ne moe concern
　　Thanne anie ynne the strete.

Before hym went the council-menne,
　　Ynne scarlett robes and golde,
And tassils spanglynge ynne the sunne,
　　Muche glorious to beholde:

The Freers of Seincte AUGUSTYNE next
　　Appeared to the syghte,
Alle cladd ynne homelie russett weedes,
　　Of godlie monkysh plyghte:

Ynne diffraunt partes a godlie psaume
　　Moste sweetlie theye dydd chaunt;
Behynde theyre backes syx mynstrelles came,
　　Who tun'd the strunge bataunt.

enshone] showed　　　　bataunt] a fictitious musical instrument

Thenne fyve-and-twentye archers came;
  Echone the bowe dydd bende,
From rescue of kynge HENRIES friends
  Syr CHARLES forr to defend.

Bolde as a lyon came Syr CHARLES,
  Drawne onne a clothe-layde sledde,
Bye two blacke stedes ynne trappynges white,
  Wyth plumes uponne theyre hedde:

Behynde hym fyve-and-twentye moe
  Of archers stronge and stoute,
Wyth bended bowe echone ynne hande,
  Marched ynne goodlie route:

Seincte JAMESES Freers marched next,
  Echone hys parte dydd chaunt;
Behynde theyre backs syx mynstrelles came,
  Who tun'd the strunge bataunt:

Thenne came the maior and eldermenne,
  Ynne clothe of scarlett deck't;
And theyre attendyng menne echone,
  Lyke Easterne princes trickt:

And after them, a multitude
  Of citizenns dydd thronge;
The wyndowes were alle fulle of heddes,
  As hee dydd passe alonge.

And whenne hee came to the hyghe crosse,
  Syr CHARLES dydd turne and saie,
O Thou, thatt savest manne fromme synne,
  Washe mye soule clean thys daie!

defend] prevent

Att the grete mynsterr wyndowe sat
    The kynge ynne myckle state,
To see CHARLES BAWDIN goe alonge
    To hys most welcom fate.

Soone as the sledde drewe nyghe enowe,
    Thatt EDWARDE hee myghte heare,
The brave Syr CHARLES hee dydd stande uppe,
    And thus hys wordes declare:

Thou seest mee, EDWARDE! traytour vile!
    Expos'd to infamie;
Butt bee assur'd, disloyall manne!
    I'm greaterr nowe thanne thee.

Bye foule proceedyngs, murdre, bloude,
    Thou wearest nowe a crowne;
And hast appoynted mee to dye,
    By power nott thyne owne.

Thou thynkest I shall dye to-daie:
    I have beene dede 'till nowe,
And soone shall lyve to weare a crowne
    For aie uponne my browe:

Whylst thou, perhapps, for som few yeares,
    Shalt rule thys fickle lande,
To lette them knowe howe wyde the rule
    'Twixt kynge and tyrant hande:

Thye pow'r unjust, thou traytour slave!
    Shall falle onne thye owne hedde—
Fromm out of hearyng of the kynge
    Departed thenne the sledde.

myckle] great

Kynge EDWARDE's soule rush'd to hys face,
   Hee turn'd hys hedde awaie,
And to hys broder GLOUCESTER
   Hee thus dydd speke and saie:

To hym that soe-much-dreaded dethe
   Ne ghastlie terrors brynge,
Beholde the manne! hee spake the truthe,
   Hee 's greater thanne a kynge!

Soe lett hym die! Duke RICHARD sayde;
   And maye echone oure foes
Bende downe theyre neckes to bloudie axe,
   And feede the carryon crowes.

And nowe the horses gentlie drewe
   Syr CHARLES uppe the hyghe hylle;
The axe dydd glysterr ynne the sunne,
   Hys pretious bloude to spylle.

Syrr CHARLES dydd uppe the scaffold goe,
   As uppe a gilded carre
Of victorye, bye val'rous chiefs
   Gayn'd ynne the bloudie warre:

And to the people hee dydd saie,
   Beholde you see mee dye,
For servynge loyally mye kynge,
   Mye kynge most rightfullie.

As longe as EDWARDE rules thys lande,
   Ne quiet you wylle knowe;
Youre sonnes and husbandes shalle bee slayne,
   And brookes wythe bloude shalle flowe.

You leave youre goode and lawfulle kynge,
  Whenne ynne adversitye;
Lyke mee, untoe the true cause stycke,
  And for the true cause dye.

Thenne hee, wyth preestes, uponne hys knees,
  A pray'r to Godde dydd make,
Beseechynge hym unto hymselfe
  Hys partynge soule to take.

Thenne, kneelynge downe, hee layd hys hedde
  Most seemlie onne the blocke;
Whyche fromme hys bodie fayre at once
  The able heddes-manne stroke:

And oute the bloude beganne to flowe,
  And rounde the scaffolde twyne;
And teares, enow to washe 't awaie,
  Dydd flowe fromme each mann's eyne.

The bloudie axe hys bodie fayre
  Ynnto foure parties cutte;
And ev'rye parte, and eke hys hedde,
  Uponne a pole was putte.

One parte dydd rotte onne Kynwulph-hylle,
  One onne the mynster-tower,
And one from off the castle-gate
  The crowen dydd devoure:

The other onne Seyncte Powle's goode gate,
  A dreery spectacle;
Hys hedde was plac'd onne the hyghe crosse,
  Ynne hyghe-streete most nobile.

Thus was the ende of BAWDIN's fate:
　Godde prosper longe oure kynge,
And grante hee maye, wyth BAWDIN's soule,
　Ynne heav'n Godd's mercie synge!

144. *Cumnor Hall*

THE dews of summer nighte did falle,
　The moone (sweete regente of the skye)
Silver'd the walles of Cumnor Halle,
　And manye an oake that grewe therebye.

Nowe noughte was hearde beneath the skies,
　(The soundes of busye lyfe were stille,)
Save an unhappie ladie's sighes,
　That issued from that lonelye pile.

Leicester, shee cried, is thys thy love
　That thou so oft has sworne to mee,
To leave mee in thys lonelye grove,
　Immurr'd in shameful privitie?

No more thou com'st with lover's speede,
　Thy once-beloved bryde to see;
But bee shee alive, or bee shee deade,
　I feare (sterne earle 's) the same to thee.

Not so the usage I receiv'd,
　When happye in my father's halle;
No faithlesse husbande then me griev'd,
　No chilling feares did mee appall.

I rose up with the chearful morne,
  No lark more blith, no flow'r more gaye;
And, like the birde that hauntes the thorne,
  So merrylie sung the live-long daye.

If that my beautye is but smalle,
  Among court ladies all despis'd;
Why didst thou rend it from that halle,
  Where (scorneful earle) it well was priz'de?

And when you first to mee made suite,
  How fayre I was you oft would saye!
And, proude of conquest—pluck'd the fruite,
  Then lefte the blossom to decaye.

Yes, nowe neglected and despis'd,
  The rose is pale—the lilly 's deade—
But hee that once their charmes so priz'd,
  Is sure the cause those charmes are fledde.

For knowe, when sick'ning griefe doth preye
  And tender love 's repay'd with scorne,
The sweetest beautye will decaye—
  What flow'ret can endure the storme?

At court I'm tolde is beauty's throne,
  Where everye lady 's passing rare;
That eastern flow'rs, that shame the sun,
  Are not so glowing, not soe fayre.

Then, earle, why didst thou leave the bedds
  Where roses and where lillys vie,
To seek a primrose, whose pale shades
  Must sicken—when those gaudes are bye?

gaudes] showy things

'Mong rural beauties I was one,
  Among the fields wild flow'rs are faire;
Some countrye swayne might mee have won,
  And thoughte my beautie passing rare.

But, Leicester, (or I much am wronge)
  Or tis not beautye lures thy vowes;
Rather ambition's gilded crowne
  Makes thee forget thy humble spouse.

Then, Leicester, why, again I pleade,
  (The injur'd surelye may repyne,)
Why didst thou wed a countrye mayde,
  When some fayre princesse might be thyne?

Why didst thou praise my humble charmes,
  And, oh! then leave them to decaye?
Why didst thou win me to thy armes,
  Then leave me to mourne the live-long daye?

The village maidens of the plaine
  Salute me lowly as they goe;
Envious they marke my silken trayne,
  Nor thinke a countesse can have woe.

The simple nymphs! they little knowe,
  How farre more happy's their estate—
—To smile for joye—than sigh for woe—
  —To be contente—than to be greate.

Howe farre lesse bleste am I than them?
  Dailye to pyne and waste with care!
Like the poore plante, that from its stem
  Divided—feeles the chilling ayre.

Nor (cruel earl!) can I enjoye
　　The humble charmes of solitude;
Your minions proude my peace destroye,
　　By sullen frownes or pratings rude.

Laste nyghte, as sad I chanc'd to straye,
　　The village deathe-bell smote my eare;
They wink'd asyde, and seem'd to saye,
　　Countesse, prepare—thy end is neare.

And nowe, while happye peasantes sleepe,
　　Here I set lonelye and forlorne;
No one to soothe mee as I weepe,
　　Save phylomel on yonder thorne.

My spirits flag—my hopes decaye—
　　Still that dreade deathe-bell smites my eare;
And many a boding seems to saye,
　　Countess, prepare—thy end is neare.

Thus sore and sad that ladie griev'd,
　　In Cumnor Halle so lone and dreare;
And manye a heartefelte sighe shee heav'd,
　　And let falle manye a bitter teare.

And ere the dawne of daye appear'd,
　　In Cumnor Hall so lone and dreare,
Full manye a piercing screame was hearde,
　　And many a crye of mortal feare.

The death-belle thrice was hearde to ring,
　　An aërial voyce was hearde to call,
And thrice the raven flapp'd its wyng
　　Arounde the tow'rs of Cumnor Hall.

The mastiffe howl'd at village doore,
   The oaks were shatter'd on the greene;
Woe was the houre—for never more
   That haplesse countesse e'er was seene.

And in that manor now no more
   Is chearful feaste and sprightly balle;
For ever since that drearye houre
   Have spirits haunted Cumnor Hall.

The village maides, with fearful glance,
   Avoide the antient mossgrowne walle;
Nor ever leade the merrye dance,
   Among the groves of Cumnor Halle.

Full manye a travellor oft hath sigh'd,
   And pensive wepte the countess' falle,
As wand'ring onwards they've espied
   The haunted tow'rs of Cumnor Hall.

145. *William Bond*

I WONDER whether the Girls are mad,
And I wonder whether they mean to kill,
And I wonder if William Bond will die,
For assuredly he is very ill.

He went to Church in a May morning
Attended by Fairies, one, two and three;
But the Angels of Providence drove them away,
And he return'd home in Misery.

He went not out to the Field nor Fold,
He went not out to the Village nor Town,
But he came home in a black, black cloud,
And took to his Bed and there lay down.

And an Angel of Providence at his Feet,
And an Angel of Providence at his Head,
And in the midst a Black, Black Cloud,
And in the midst the Sick Man on his Bed.

And on his Right hand was Mary Green,
And on his Left hand was his Sister Jane,
And their tears fell thro' the black, black Cloud
To drive away the sick man's pain.

O William, if thou dost another Love,
Dost another Love better than poor Mary,
Go and take that other to be thy Wife,
And Mary Green shall her Servant be.

Yes, Mary, I do another Love,
Another I Love far better than thee,
And Another I will have for my Wife;
Then what have I to do with thee?

For thou art Melancholy Pale,
And on thy Head is the cold Moon's shine,
But she is ruddy and bright as day,
And the sun beams dazzle from her eyne.

Mary trembled and Mary chill'd
And Mary fell down on the right hand floor,
That William Bond and his Sister Jane
Scarce could recover Mary more.

When Mary woke and found her Laid
On the Right hand of her William dear,
On the Right hand of his loved Bed,
And saw her William Bond so near,

The Fairies that fled from William Bond
Danced around her Shining Head;
They danced over the Pillow white,
And the Angels of Providence left the Bed.

I thought Love liv'd in the hot sun shine,
But O, he lives in the Moony light!
I thought to find Love in the heat of day,
But sweet Love is the Comforter of Night.

Seek Love in the Pity of others' Woe,
In the gentle relief of another's care,
In the darkness of night and the winter's snow,
In the naked and outcast, Seek Love there!

146. *Red Harlaw*

Now haud your tongue, baith wife and carle,
    And listen, great and sma',
And I will sing of Glenallan's Earl
    That fought on the red Harlaw.

The cronach 's cried on Bennachie,
    And doun the Don and a',
And Hieland and Lawland may mournfu' be
    For the sair field of Harlaw.

carle] man   cronach] piper's lament for the dead

They saddled a hundred milk-white steeds,
   They hae bridled a hundred black,
With a chafron of steel on each horse's head,
   And a good knight upon his back.

They hadna ridden a mile, a mile,
   A mile, but barely ten,
When Donald came branking down the brae
   Wi' twenty thousand men.

Their tartans they were waving wide,
   Their glaives were glancing clear,
The pibrochs rung frae side to side,
   Would deafen ye to hear.

The great Earl in his stirrups stood,
   That Highland host to see:
Now here a knight that 's stout and good
   May prove a jeopardie:

What wouldst thou do, my squire so gay,
   That rides beside my reyne,
Were ye Glenallan's Earl the day,
   And I were Roland Cheyne?

To turn the rein were sin and shame,
   To fight were wondrous peril;
What would ye do now, Roland Cheyne,
   Were ye Glenallan's Earl?

Were I Glenallan's Earl this tide,
   And ye were Roland Cheyne,
The spur should be in my horse's side,
   And the bridle upon his mane.

chafron] headpiece   branking] prancing   brae] hill   glaives]
swords   pibrochs] classical pipe music   stout] stalwart
the day] today

If they hae twenty thousand blades,
   And we twice ten times ten,
Yet they hae but their tartan plaids,
   And we are mail-clad men.

My horse shall ride through ranks sae rude,
   As through the moorland fern;
Then ne'er let the gentle Norman blude
   Grow cauld for Highland kerne.

★   ★   ★   ★   ★

kerne] cateran, vagabond

147. *The Three Sailors*

THERE were three sailors in Bristol city
   Who took a boat and went to sea.
But first with beef and captains biscuit
   And pickled pork they loaded she.

There was guzzling Jack and gorging Jimmy,
   And the youngest he was little Billy.
Now very soon they were so greedy
   They didn't have not one split pea.

Says guzzling Jack to gorging Jimmy,
   I am counfounded hung—ery.
Says gorging Jim to guzzling Jacky,
   We've no wittles so we must eat we.

Says guzzling Jack to gorging Jimmy,
　O gorging Jim, what a fool you be;
There 's little Bill, as is young and tender,
　We're old and tough, so let 's eat he.

O Bill, we're going to kill and eat you,
　So undo the button of your chemee.
When Bill he heard this information
　He used his pocket handkerchee.

O let me say my Catechism
　As my poor Mammy taught to me.
Make haste, make haste, says guzzling Jacky,
　While Jim pulled out his snickersnee.

So Billy went up to the main-top-gallant mast
　Where down he fell on his bended knee.
He scarce had said his Catechism
　When up he jumped: There 's land I see;

There 's Jerusalem and Madagascar,
　And North and South Amerikey;
Theres the British fleet a riding at Anchor
　With Admiral Napier, K.C.B.

So when they came to the Admirals vessel
　He hanged fat Jack and flogged Jimmy;
But as for little Bill, he made him
　The Captain of a Seventy-three.

Seventy-three] ship carrying 73 guns

148. *Stratton Water*

O HAVE you seen the Stratton flood
　　That 's great with rain to-day?
It runs beneath your wall, Lord Sands,
　　Full of the new-mown hay.

I led your hounds to Hutton bank
　　To bathe at early morn:
They got their bath by Borrowbrake
　　Above the standing corn.

Out from the castle-stair Lord Sands
　　Looked up the western lea;
The rook was grieving on her nest,
　　The flood was round her tree.

Over the castle-wall Lord Sands
　　Looked down the eastern hill:
The stakes swam free among the boats,
　　The flood was rising still.

What 's yonder far below that lies
　　So white against the slope?
O it 's a sail o' your bonny barks
　　The waters have washed up.

But I have never a sail so white,
　　And the water 's not yet there.
O it 's the swans o' your bonny lake
　　The rising flood doth scare.

The swans they would not hold so still,
    So high they would not win.
O it 's Joyce my wife has spread her smock
    And fears to fetch it in.

Nay, knave, it 's neither sail nor swans,
    Nor aught that you can say;
For though your wife might leave her smock,
    Herself she'd bring away.

Lord Sands has passed the turret-stair,
    The court, and yard, and all;
The kine were in the byre that day,
    The nags were in the stall.

Lord Sands has won the weltering slope
    Whereon the white shape lay:
The clouds were still above the hill,
    And the shape was still as they.

Oh pleasant is the gaze of life
    And sad is death's blind head;
But awful are the living eyes
    In the face of one thought dead!

In God's name, Janet, is it me
    Thy ghost has come to seek?
Nay, wait another hour, Lord Sands,—
    Be sure my ghost shall speak.

A moment stood he as a stone,
    Then grovelled to his knee,
O Janet, O my love, my love,
    Rise up and come with me!

win] reach, get

O once before you bade me come,
  And it 's here you have brought me!

O many 's the sweet word, Lord Sands,
  You've spoken oft to me;
But all that I have from you to-day
  Is the rain on my body.

And many 's the good gift, Lord Sands,
  You've promised oft to me;
But the gift of yours I keep to-day
  Is the babe in my body.

O it 's not in any earthly bed
  That first my babe I'll see;
For I have brought my body here
  That the flood may cover me.

His face was close against her face,
  His hands of hers were fain:
O her wet cheeks were hot with tears,
  Her wet hands cold with rain.

They told me you were dead, Janet,—
  How could I guess the lie?
They told me you were false, Lord Sands,—
  What could I do but die?

Now keep you well, my brother Giles,—
  Through you I deemed her dead!
As wan as your towers seem to-day,
  To-morrow they'll be red.

Look down, look down, my false mother,
    That bade me not to grieve:
You'll look up when our marriage fires
    Are lit to-morrow eve:

O more than one and more than two
    The sorrow of this shall see:
But it's to-morrow, love, for them,—
    To-day's for thee and me.

He's drawn her face between his hands
    And her pale mouth to his:
No bird that was so still that day
    Chirps sweeter than his kiss.

The flood was creeping round their feet,
    O Janet, come away!
The hall is warm for the marriage-rite,
    The bed for the birthday.

Nay, but I hear your mother cry,
    Go bring this bride to bed!
And would she christen her babe unborn,
    So wet she comes to bed?

I'll be your wife to cross your door
    And meet your mother's e'e.
We plighted troth to wed i' the kirk,
    And it's there you'll wed with me.

He's ta'en her by the short girdle
    And by the dripping sleeve:
Go fetch Sir Jock my mother's priest,—
    You'll ask of him no leave.

683

O it 's one half-hour to reach the kirk
   And one for the marriage-rite;
And kirk and castle and castle-lands
   Shall be our babe's to-night.

The flood 's in the kirkyard, Lord Sands,
   And round the belfry-stair.
I bade you fetch the priest, he said,
   Myself shall bring him there.

It 's for the lilt of wedding bells
   We'll have the hail to pour,
And for the clink of bridle-reins
   The plashing of the oar.

Beneath them on the nether hill
   A boat was floating wide:
Lord Sands swam out and caught the oars
   And rowed to the hill-side.

He 's wrapped her in a green mantle
   And set her softly in;
Her hair was wet upon her face,
   Her face was grey and thin;
And Oh! she said, lie still, my babe,
   It 's out you must not win!

But woe 's my heart for Father John
   As hard as he might pray,
There seemed no help but Noah's ark
   Or Jonah's fish that day.

The first strokes that the oars struck
   Were over the broad leas;
The next strokes that the oars struck
   They pushed beneath the trees;

The last stroke that the oars struck,
 The good boat's head was met,
And there the gate of the kirkyard
 Stood like a ferry-gate.

He's set his hand upon the bar
 And lightly leaped within:
He's lifted her to his left shoulder,
 Her knees beside his chin.

The graves lay deep beneath the flood
 Under the rain alone;
And when the foot-stone made him slip,
 He held by the head-stone.

The empty boat thrawed i' the wind,
 Against the postern tied.
Hold still, you've brought my love with me,
 You shall take back my bride.

But woe's my heart for Father John
 And the saints he clamoured to!
There's never a saint but Christopher
 Might hale such buttocks through!

And Oh! she said, on men's shoulders
 I well had thought to wend,
And well to travel with a priest,
 But not to have cared or ken'd.

And oh! she said, it's well this way
 That I thought to have fared,—
Not to have lighted at the kirk
 But stopped in the kirkyard.

thrawed] twisted about hale] haul

For it's oh and oh I prayed to God,
  Whose rest I hoped to win,
That when to-night at your board-head
  You'd bid the feast begin,
This water past your window-sill
  Might bear my body in.

Now make the white bed warm and soft
  And greet the merry morn.
The night the mother should have died,
  The young son shall be born.

149. *Duriesdyke*

THE rain rains sair on Duriesdyke
  Both the winter through and the spring;
And she that will gang to get broom thereby
  She shall get an ill thing.

The rain rains sair on Duriesdyke
  Both the winter and the summer day;
And he that will steek his sheep thereby
  He shall go sadly away.

Between Crossmuir and Duriesdyke
  The fieldhead is full green;
The shaws are thick in the fair summer,
  And three wellheads between.

Flower of broom is a fair flower,
  And heather is good to play.
O she went merry to Duriesdyke,
  But she came heavy away.

steek] enclose   shaws] small woods in hollows

It 's I have served you, Burd Maisry,
   These three months through and mair;
And the little ae kiss I gat of you,
   It pains me aye and sair.

This is the time of heather-blowing,
   And that was syne in the spring;
And the little ae leaf comes aye to red,
   And the corn to harvesting.

The first kiss their twa mouths had,
   Sae fain she was to greet;
The neist kiss their twa mouths had,
   I wot she laughed fu' sweet.

Cover my head with a silken hood,
   My feet with a yellow claith;
For to stain my body wi' the dyke-water
   God wot I were fu' laith.

He 's happit her head about wi' silk,
   Her feet with a gowden claith;
The red sendal that was of price
   He 's laid between them baith.

The grass was low by Duriesdyke,
   The high heather was red;
And between the grass and the high heather
   He 's tane her maidenhead.

They did not kiss in a noble house,
   Nor yet in a lordly bed;
But their mouths kissed in the high heather
   Between the green side and the red.

Burd] Maid   syne] then   fain] eager   greet] weep
wot] surely   dyke-] ditch-   happit] wrapped   sendal] silk

I have three sailing ships, Maisry,
   For red wheat and for wine;
The maintopmast is a bonny mast,
   Three furlongs off to shine.

The foremast shines like new lammer,
   The mizen-mast like steel:
Gin ye wad sail wi' me, Maisry,
   The warst should carry ye weel.

Gin I should sail wi' you, Lord John,
   Out under the rocks red,
It's wha wad be my mither's bower-maiden
   To hap saft her feet in bed?

Gin I should sail wi' you, Lord John,
   Out under the rocks white,
There's nane wad do her a very little ease
   To hap her left and right.

It fell upon the midwinter
   She gat mickle scaith and blame;
She's bound hersell by the white water
   To see his ships come hame.

She's leaned hersell against the wind,
   To see upon the middle tide;
The faem was fallen in the running wind,
   The wind was fallen in the waves wide.

There's nae moon by the white water
   To do me ony good the day;
And but this wind a little slacken,
   They shall have a sair seaway.

lammer] amber   Gin] if   mickle scaith] much harm   the
day] today

O stir not for this med, baby,
   O stir not at my side;
Ye'll have the better birth, baby,
   Gin ye wad but a little abide.

Gin ye winna cease for the pity of him
   O cease for the pity of me;
There was never bairn born of a woman
   Between the sea-wind and the sea:
There was never bairn born of a woman
   That was born so bitterly.

The ship drove hard upon the wind,
   I wot it drove full mightily;
But the fair gold sides upon the ship
   They were bursten with the sea.

O I am sae fain for you, Lord John,
   Gin ye be no sae fain
How shall I bear wi' my body,
   It is sae full of pain?

O I am sae fain of your body,
   Ye are no sae fain of me;
But the sails are riven wi' the wind
   And the sides are full of sea.

O when she saw the sails riven
   The sair pain bowed her back;
But when she saw the sides bursten
   I wot her very heart brak.

med] *here* account, reason

The wind waxed in the sea between,
　The rain waxed in the land;
Lord John was happit wi' saut sea-faem,
　Lady Maisry wi' sea-sand:
And the little bairn between them twa
　That was to her right hand.

The rain rains sair on Duriesdyke
　To the land side and the sea;
There was never bairn born of a woman
　That was born mair bitterly.

saut] salt

150. *Sir Halewyn*

SIR HALEWYN sang sae sweet and braw,
That nane that heard cud bide awa.

The King's young dochter heard him sing;
Her father lo'ed her abune a' thing.

She gaed to her father: Father o' mine,
Hae I leave to gae efter Sir Halewyn?

Na, lassie, na,—her father spak,—
There 's mony that gae, but few come back.

She gaed to her mither: Mither o' mine,
Hae I leave to gae efter Sir Halewyn?

Na, lassie, na,—her mither spak—
There 's mony that gae, but few come back.

She gaed to her sister: Sister o' mine,
Hae I leave to gae efter Sir Halewyn?

Na, sister, na,—her sister spak—
There 's mony that gae, but few come back.

She gaed to her brither: Brither o' mine,
Hae I leave to gae efter Sir Halewyn?

It 's ane to me: gang whaur you wud;
But see and no tine your maidenhude;
And wear your croon as a King's lass should.

She has risen and gane to her bed-chawmer,
And put on her brawest cleithin there.

What has she put on her fair bodie?
A sark, was finer than silk cud be.

What has she put on her best bodice?
A' stiff wi' gowden bands it is.

What has she put on her scarlet goon?
Tassels o' gowd a' hingin doon.

What has she put on her cloak sae feat?
A glistenin pearl at ilka pleat.

What has she set on her yallow hair?
A croon o' gowd that was heavy to wear.

She has gane into her father's sta',
And lowsed the fleetest horse o' them a'.

She has bestridden the horse sae guid,
And aye she sang as she rade through the wood.

tine] lose   sark] shift   gowden] golden   feat] trim

691

Half through the forest she has gane,
And has met Sir Halewyn ridin alane.

To a tree nearby his horse he tied;
The lassie, trummlin, grew flichtered and fleyed.

Greetin! quo' he, fairest o' fair!
Greetin! quo' he, broon een sae rare!
Come, sit you doon, unbind your hair.

Sae mony hairs as she unbound,
Sae mony tears fell to the ground.

And syne they rose and gaed awa,
Wi' mony a word atween thae twa.

Sae to a gallows-field they pass,
Whaur hung sae mony a bonnie lass.

He, turnin to his fere, quo' he:
Since a bonnier lass there canna be,
I'll let you wale the death you dee.

Gin I may choose hoo I shall dee,
I pray you, draw your swoord on me.

But first, your mantle lay aside;
A maiden's bluid may spatter wide.
'Twere shame your claes should a' be dyed.

But ere he cud his cloak undae,
His sindered heid before her lay;
His tongue begoud thae words to say:

trummlin] trembling   flichtered and fleyed] flustered and frightened
syne] then   fere] companion   wale] choose   begoud]
began

Gae to yon field o' bere;
Blaw on my horn sae clear,
That a' my friends may hear.

I winna gang among the bere,
Nor blaw upon your horn sae clear,
Nor heed the word o' a murderer.

Gae under the gallows-tree;
A pot o' salve you'll see:
Bring 't for my neck that's sae bluidie.

I winna gang to the gallows-tree,
Nor heal the neck, sae ill to see,
O' him wha wad hae slauchtered me.

By the hair she has grippit his bluidie heid,
And washed it clean that was sae reid.

She has bestridden her horse sae guid,
And aye she sang as she rade through the wood.

She has ridden half through the wood, and syne
She met the mither o' Halewyn:
Did my son come this wey, fair queyn?

Your son, Sir Halewyn, is a huntin gane!
In your life you'll never see him again.

Your son, Sir Halewyn, he is DEID!
Here in my lap I carry his heid;
Wi' his bluid is a' my bodice reid.

bere] barley

When her father's yett was near at han',
She blew her horn wi' the strength o' a man.

Her father heard the trumpet plain,
And was blithe that his lass was hame again.

In the muckle ha' they birled the wine,
And glowered on the heid o' Sir Halewyn.

yett] gate   muckle] great   birled] poured   glowered] stared

NOTES

ABBREVIATIONS

Blaikie MS	National Library of Scotland MS 1578
Bronson	B. H. Bronson, *The Traditional Tunes of the Child Ballads*, 3 vols., 1959–66
Bruce and Stokoe	J. C. Bruce and John Stokoe, *Northumbrian Minstrelsy*, 1882
Buchan	Peter Buchan, *Ancient Ballads and Songs of the North of Scotland*, 2 vols., 1828
Burns	James Kinsley, *The Poems and Songs of Robert Burns*, 3 vols., 1968
Child	F. J. Child, *The English and Scottish Popular Ballads* (1882–98), 5 vols., 1957 rpt.
Greig	Gavin Greig, *Folk Song of the North-East*, contributed to the *Buchan Observer* 1907–11
Greig MSS	Gavin Greig MSS, University Library, King's College, Aberdeen
Hastie MS	British Museum Add. MS 22307 (mainly Burns holographs, songs for *SMM*)
Herd	David Herd, *Ancient and Modern Scottish Songs* (1776), 2 vols., 1869 rpt.
Herd MS	British Museum Add. MS 22311
Jamieson	Robert Jamieson, *Popular Ballads and Songs from Tradition*, 2 vols., 1806
Jamieson–Brown MS	Edinburgh University Library Laing MS XIII 473, 'a faithful transcript of Popular Ballads, written from oral recitation [by his aunt Mrs Brown of Falkland] for his own amusement, by Mr R. Scott, Professor of Greek in King's College, Aberdeen. . . . Robert Jamieson, July 29, 1799'
Motherwell	William Motherwell, *Minstrelsy, Ancient and Modern*, 1827
N.L.S.	National Library of Scotland
Percy Folio	J. W. Hales and F. J. Furnivall, *Bishop Percy's Folio Manuscript*, 3 vols. and suppl., 1867–8
Percy, *Reliques*	H. B. Wheatley, *Reliques of Ancient English Poetry . . . by Thomas Percy* (1886), 3 vols., 1966
Pills	Thomas D'Urfey, *Wit and Mirth; or, Pills to Purge Melancholy* (1719), 6 vols., 1959 rpt.

Ritson–Tytler– Brown MS	Harvard College MS 25242. 12 (ballads sung by Mrs. Brown of Falkland, Aberdeenshire, late eighteenth century)
Scott	Sir Walter Scott, *Minstrelsy of the Scottish Border* (1802–3), ed. T. Henderson, 1931
SMM	James Johnson, *The Scots Musical Museum*, 6 vols., 1787–1803

1. Air and text, William Sandys, *Christmas Carols, Ancient and Modern*, 1833, pp. 123–5 and appendix no. 10. For a Scots variant see Greig, no. clx.

2. Text, Child, no. 22; B.M. MS Sloane 2593, f. 22b (fifteenth century).

3. Text, Joshua Sylvester, *A Garland of Christmas Carols*, 1861, pp. 50–2. A ballad on this theme is recorded in the sixteenth century. The surviving tunes are not necessarily older than the nineteenth century.

4. Air, Blaikie MS, no. 63, p. 21; text, Scott, pp. 580–2 ('given from a copy, obtained from a lady residing not far from Ercildoune [where Thomas Rymour lived in the thirteenth century], corrected and enlarged by one in Mrs. Brown's MSS').

5. Air, *SMM*, no. 370; text, Herd MS, p. 153.

6. Air, *SMM*, no. 411; text, Hastie MS, ff. 117–20^r (*Burns*, ii. 836–41).

7. Air and text, Child, v. 415 and ii. 61, transcripts of the Harris MS (Harvard). Given by Child in an appendix merely as an imperfect recollection of Percy's version; but see the important discussion in Bronson, ii. 37–8.

8. Text, Percy Folio, i. 166–73.

9. Text, Percy Folio, ii. 304 ff.

10. Text, Jamieson–Brown MS, pp. 34 ff.

11. Text, Jamieson, ii. 367–70. It is difficult to fit the words of **10** and **11** to the airs in the Ritson–Tytler–Brown MS.

12. Air, R. A. Smith, *The Scottish Minstrel*, 1820–4, iii. 92; text, Herd MS, pp. 166–8.

13. Text, Buchan, i. 24–7.

14. Text, Jamieson, ii. 187–90, 'from the recitation of Mrs. Brown'.

15. Air, Ritson–Tytler–Brown MS, p. 77; text, Jamieson–Brown MS, pp. 29 ff.

16. Text, Child, no. 36 (from the Skene MS, north of Scotland, 1802–3), with a line supplied from Skene's 'old lady's MS'.

17. Air, *Journal of the English Folk Dance and Song Society*, v (1947), 77; collected by P. N. Shuldham-Shaw from oral tradition in Unst. Text, Child, no. 19; collected in Shetland and first published in 1880.

18. Air, Child, v. 422 (with wrong title); text, Jamieson–Brown MS, pp. 31 ff., with a stanza supplied from Jamieson, ii. 194. I do not follow editors in marking a lacuna after stanza 17.

19. Air, *SMM*, no. 320; text, loc. cit., with additional lines from Motherwell, p. 162.

20. Air, Bruce and Stokoe, p. 61; text, Scott, pp. 473–6.

21. Air, G. R. Kinloch, *Ancient Scottish Ballads*, 1827, appendix to p. 195; text, Scott, pp. 349–50.

22. Text, Child, no. 47E; Alexander Laing's text, 1829, 'from the recitation of old people'.

23. Air, Motherwell, appendix no. 16; text, Herd MS, pp. 177–82. The second part *may* be an adaptation of a separate ballad.

24. Air, Motherwell, appendix no. 1; text, Harvard MS 25242. 12, i. 297–301 (Kinloch; 'from J. Kinnear, Stonehaven'), with four stanzas supplied from Motherwell, p. 93.

25. Text, Herd, i. 161–2, with a stanza supplied from the Ritson–Tytler–Brown MS, p. 7. On the problems raised by the music in the MS see Bronson, i. 334.

26. Text, Herd MS, pp. 182–5.

27. Air collected by Professor Otto Andersson in Orkney in 1938 and published, with text, in *Budkavlen*, xxvi (1947), 115; Mr. Francis Collinson's arrangement is followed here.

28. Air, Sir Walter Scott, *Poetical Works*, 1833–4, iii, facing p. 262; text, Scott, pp. 458–9. Not necessarily, as editors have assumed, a fragment with lacunae after stanzas 6, 8, and 12.

29. Air, C. J. Sharp, *English Folk-Song: Some Conclusions*, 1907, p. 63; text, Child no. 78A, first published in 1868 from oral tradition in Sussex.

30. Texts: (A) Greig, no. clvii, (B) Motherwell, pp. 287–90, communicated to Peter Buchan by James Nicol of Strichen. Despite a weak ending, B preserves the supernatural character of the father (*etin*, giant; title in Kinloch's *Ballads*). A is almost demythologized, but is still preferable to the long Peter Buchan version (Child, no. 41A) vulgarly spun out.

31. Air, Ritson–Tytler–Brown MS, p. 38; texts, Jamieson–Brown MS, pp. 11 ff.

32. Air, Greig MSS, iii. 118, 'sung by Mrs. Thain, New Deer'; text, Greig, no. lxxx.

33. Air and text, Bruce and Stokoe, pp. 31–3.

34. Air, Blaikie MS, no. 44, p. 16; text, Scott, pp. 340–1 (omitting a commonplace conclusion which Scott took from a stall print). Scott's text was provided by C. K. Sharpe of Hoddam.

35. Text, Motherwell, pp. 370–3.

36. Text, Percy Folio, i. 248–52. *Glasgerion*: probably Y Bardd Glas Keraint, Geraint the Blue (i.e. chief) Bard.

37. Text, Percy, *Reliques*, i. 87–96 (amended by Percy).

38. Text, Motherwell, pp. 327–35.

39. Air, *Burns*, ii. 678 (*SMM*); text, Harvard MS Eng. 512, pp. 151–8, no. 114. There are some doubts about the authenticity of the tune. There is an apparent lacuna after stanza 17; for singing, start again with the first part of the tune at 'O who will shoe my bony foot'.

40. Text, Percy Folio, ii. 271–8.

41. Air, *SMM*, no. 203; text, Percy, *Reliques*, iii. 91–100.

42. Air, Ritson–Tytler–Brown MS, p. 10 (I have followed Bronson's conjectural reading); text, Jamieson–Brown MS, p. 17.

43. Text, Child, no. 90A (from the Tytler–Brown MS).

44. Text, Skeat's transcript of a seventeenth-century broadside (Child, no. 81C).

45. Air, N.L.S. MS 843 (Sharpe), ff. 9ᵛ–10ʳ; text, C. K. Sharpe, *A Ballad Book* (1823), 1883, pp. 1 ff. (from Perthshire tradition).

46. Air, *SMM*, no. 535; text, Percy, *Reliques*, iii. 234–8.

47. Text, seventeenth-century broadside; Bodleian Library, Wood E. 25.

48. Text, Greig, no. cxvii.

49. Air, Ritson–Tytler–Brown MS, p. 48 (corrected); text, Jamieson–Brown MS, pp. 1 ff.

50. Air, Motherwell, appendix no. 26; text, ibid., pp. 88–92, from Perthshire tradition.

51. Text, Herd MS, pp. 224–6, 'copied from the mouth of a Milk Maid in 1771 by W. L.'.

52. Text, Scott, pp. 464–6, 'from the recitation of a lady nearly related' to Scott.

53. Text, Buchan, ii. 39 ff.

54. Air, Motherwell, appendix no. 18; text, ibid., pp. 193 ff., with a stanza interpolated from Buchan to clarify motive.

55. Text, Percy Folio, ii. 327–33.

56. Air, Ritson–Tytler–Brown MS, p. 31; text, Jamieson–Brown MS, p. 15, no. 6.

57. Air, Ritson–Tytler–Brown MS, p. 63 (I have followed Bronson's conjectural reading); text, Jamieson–Brown MS, p. 17.

58. Air, *Orpheus Caledonius* (1725), 1733, i. 109; text, Percy, *Reliques*, iii. 124–7.

59. Text, C. K. Sharpe, *A Ballad Book* (1823), 1883, p. 56, no. 19.

60. Air, Child, v. 412 (Harris MS); text, Jamieson, i. 66–72, 'taken down from the recitation of Mrs. Arrott'.

61. Text from Percy, *Reliques*, i. 82–4.

62. Sung by Jeannie Robertson, Aberdeen; collected by Hamish Henderson and transcribed by Francis Collinson, School of Scottish Studies, Edinburgh.

63. Air, *SMM*, no. 327; text, Child, no. 12A (McMath MS, eighteenth century).

64. Air and text, Thomas Ravenscroft, *Melismata. Musicall Phansies,* 1611, 'Country Pastimes', no. 20.

65. Air and text, *Pills*, iii. 37–9.

66. Air and text, *SMM*, no. 181. The seduction is 'explained' in a late English version—the lady was a gipsy maid (James Reeves, *The Everlasting Circle*, 1960, no. 61A).

67. Text, James Maidment, *A North Countrie Garland* (1824), 1884, p. 40.

68. Air, Child, v. 421 (Sharpe MS); text, Child, v. 261 (Sharpe).

69. Air, *SMM*, no. 434; text, Harvard MS 25242. 12, i. 237–51 (Kinloch), from the Mearns ('it is very popular in the North, and few milk-maids in that quarter, but can chaunt it to a very pleasant tune').

70. Air and text, G. R. Kinloch, *Ancient Scottish Ballads, recovered from Tradition and never before published*, 1827, appendix no. ix and pp. 25–8.

71. Air, Motherwell, appendix no. 10; text, Motherwell MS, Glasgow University Library, pp. 517–21, 'from the singing of Mrs. Storie of Lochwinnoch'. (Title of some versions, *The Broom o' the Cowdenknowes.*)

72. Air, *SMM*, no. 237 (*The Linkin Laddie*); text, Child, no. 241A (from the Skene MS, 1802–3). Stanzas 4 and 6 should perhaps be sung to the first part of the air, and stanzas 5 and 7 to the second.

73. Text, *Iacke of Newberie* (1596, 1626); Deloney's *Works*, ed. F. O. Mann, 1912, pp. 33–6. The surviving tunes are nineteenth century.

74. Air, Greig MSS, iv. 56; text, Greig, xciii B.

75. Text, Child, no. 89A (Tytler–Brown MS).

76. Air, *SMM*, no. 388; text, *A pretty Ballad . . . The tune is green sleeves* (broadside; Bodleian Library, Wood 401, fol. 95b).

77. Air, Ritson–Tytler–Brown MS, p. 91; text, Jamieson–Brown MS, pp. 24 ff.

78. Text, Greig, civ.

79. Air, Blaikie MS, p. 24, no. 75; text, N.L.S. Glenriddell MS xi. 78–9 (1791).

80. Text, Child, no. 91C (Tytler–Brown MS).

81. Air, Child v. 415 (Harris MS); text, Percy, *Reliques*, i. 98–102.

82. Air, W. Christie, *Traditional Ballad Airs*, i (1876), 60 (first part); text, Jamieson, i. 176 ff. (from Mrs. Brown).

83. Text, Jamieson, i. 151–4 (from Mrs. Brown).

84. Air, Joseph Ritson, *Scottish Songs* (1794), 1869 rpt., ii. 518; text, Percy, *Reliques*, ii. 228–31.

85. Air and text of *Waly, waly, Orpheus Caledonius* (1725), 1733, i. 70–3; text of ballad, Harvard MS 25242. 12, i. 99–102 (Kinloch). It is probable that the ballad is based on the older song, and sings to the same air. James, second Marquis of Douglas, repudiated his wife in 1681.

86. Air, Child, v. 421 (Harris MS); text, Child, no. 173G (from a manuscript 'copied by a granddaughter of Lord Woodhouselee, 1840–50'), with stanza 11 transferred from the end of the ballad.

87. Air, Greig MSS, i. 76; text, Greig, lx. Maggie who speaks from within the bower is an apparition.

88. Air, Alexander Campbell, *Albyn's Anthology*, i (1816), 34, sung by Dr. John Leyden (1797); text, Scott, pp. 342–5, 'from tradition'. 'In the interval betwixt death and interment the disembodied spirit is supposed to hover around its mortal habitation, and, if invoked by certain rites, retains the power of communicating, through its organs, the cause of its dissolution' (Scott).

89. Air and text, R. A. Smith, *The Scottish Minstrel*, 1820–4, v. 50.

90. Air, W. Chappell, *Popular Music of the Olden Time*, i (1855), 203; text, Percy, *Reliques*, iii. 135–7.

91. Air, Greig MSS, iv. 129; text, Greig, lxxxiv B.

92. Air and first stanza, *SMM*, no. 115; remainder of text, Herd MS, p. 97.

93. Air, *SMM*, no. 175 ('A Galick Air'); text, Jamieson, i. 129–34, 'taken down by Dr. Leyden from the recitation of a young lady (Miss Robson) of Edinburgh, who learned it in Teviotdale'.

94. Air, *SMM*, no. 221; text, Allan Ramsay, *The Tea-Table Miscellany* (1740 edn.), 1875 rpt., ii. 142–3.

95. Text, *The Brown Girl's Garland, Composed of Four extraordinary New Songs*; B.M. 11621. c. 3 (10). Eighteenth century.

96. Air and text, Bruce and Stokoe, pp. 25–9, with a defective stanza completed from a stall copy (Child, no. 211A).

97. Text, Herd MS, pp. 130–6. The historical reference is uncertain, and may be a fiction. Child suspected this to be a 'literary' ballad; but since a fragment survives in Scott's papers and Robert Riddell collected another imperfect version in the later eighteenth century (Child, no. 305), I take this to be a literary version of something more primitive.

98. Text, Child, no. 115; B.M. Sloane MS 2593, f. 14b (*c.* 1450).

99. Text, Jamieson, ii. 44–8 (from Mrs. Brown's recitation).

100. Text, Child's reconstruction (no. 116) from sixteenth-century printings, with some further emendations. (Child's completions of defective lines are not indicated here.)

101. Text, Skeat's transcript (Child, no. 119) of Cambridge University Library MS Ff. 5. 48, f. 128b (*c.* 1450).

102. Text, fifteenth-century (?) print in N.L.S., with missing passages supplied from Child's transcript (no. 117B) of Wynken de Worde's *Lytell Geste of Robyn Hode*. Numerals have been converted, and contractions expanded.

103. Air, Child, v. 419 (Sharpe MS); text, Scott, pp. 123–33. The battle was fought some thirty miles from Newcastle on 19 August 1388 between the Percys and James, Earl of Douglas.

104. Text, W. W. Skeat, *Specimens of English Literature 1394–1579*, 1879, pp. 67–75 (from Bodleian Library MS Ashmole 48; a sixteenth-century text of a fifteenth-century ballad). I have introduced capitals, expanded contractions and numerals, organized long couplets into quatrains, and repointed. A minstrel ballad, also referring to the Battle of Otterburn; probably that which moved Sir Philip Sidney's heart 'more than with a trumpet'. See Addison's critique, *Spectator*, nos. 70 and 74.

105. Text, Percy Folio, iii. 403–18. For the history of the Bartons, see Child, no. 167.

106. Air, *SMM*, no. 356; text, Allan Ramsay, *The Ever Green* (1724), 1875 rpt., ii. 190–6. This, says Ramsay, 'is the true old Ballad, never printed before, of the famous *John Armstrang* of *Gilnockhall* in *Liddisdale*, a Head of a numerous Clan and Faction, who used to pass over in Troops to *England*, making continual Incursions, and taking much Plunder in the bordering Parts. [He was] taken and executed, with many of his Followers . . . [by] *JAMES* the Vth, about the Year 1530. This I copied from a Gentleman's Mouth of the Name of *Armstrang*, who is the 6th Generation from this *John*.'

107. Air, George Thomson, *A Select Collection of Original Scotish Airs*, iv (1805), 162; text, Scott, pp. 381–2, 'obtained from recitation in the forest of Ettrick' and supposedly relating to the execution of Cockburn of Henderland by James V in 1529.

108. Text, Percy Folio, ii. 217–26. The banished Earl of Northumberland was delivered by the Armstrongs to the Scots regent in December 1569 and imprisoned in Lochleven Castle until June 1572. Although his countess paid ransom, he was held at Berwick and beheaded at York on 27 August 1572.

109. Air, Motherwell, appendix no. 22; text, Harvard MS 25242. 12, vii. 28–37 (Kinloch; from oral tradition), with a final stanza from Kinloch's *Ballads* (Child, no. 114D).

110. Air and refrain, Alexander Campbell, *Albyn's Anthology*, ii (1818), 30 (sung by Robert Shortreed, Liddisdale, in 1816); text, Child, no. 185, from the Percy Papers (1775).

111. Text, Scott, pp. 162–9. The ballad may commemorate an escapade of 1582.

112. Air and text, Burns, ii. 618–20 (*SMM*). Collected and probably revised by Burns. Geordie may have been the sixth Earl of Huntly who rose against James VI in 1589, was imprisoned as a traitor, and later freed.

113. Text, Scott, pp. 179–90, probably substantially amended. The air in Campbell, *Albyn's Anthology*, is dubious. The ballad commemorates an event of 1596.

114. Air and text from Alexander Campbell, *Albyn's Anthology*, ii (1818), 28 ff. (sung by Thomas Shortreed, Liddisdale).

115. Text, George Caw, *The Poetical Museum*, 1784, pp. 193–200.

116. Air, *SMM*, no. 303; text, Hastie MS, f. 60. Collected by Burns 'from oral tradition in Ayrshire', and I suspect revised by him.

117. Air and text, *SMM*, no. 579; perhaps collected by Burns.

118. Air, Bruce and Stokoe, p. 42; text, transcript of the Telfer MS (from oral tradition, 1824).

119. Air, *The Caledonian Pocket Companion*, v (1753), 26; text, Child, no. 214A (from Principal Robertson's copy sent to Percy). The musical tradition is complex (see Bronson, iii. 314).

120. Air and text, *Orpheus Caledonius*, 1733, ii. 110.

121. Air and text A, *Orpheus Caledonius*, 1733, ii. 8; text B, John Finlay, *Scottish Historical and Romantic Ballads*, 1808, ii. 21–3. James Stewart of Doune became Earl of Moray, following his marriage, in 1581. He supported the rebel Bothwell. Moray's enemy the Earl of Huntly was commissioned in 1592 to bring him in for trial, but burnt his house and slew him.

122. The Macintoshes avenged Moray (see **121**) by invading Huntly's estates in 1592, but were overtaken and put to flight. Text, Alexander Laing, *The Thistle of Scotland*, 1823, p. 106.

123. Air, Joseph Ritson, *Scotish Songs* (1794), 1869 rpt., ii. 362; text, *Edom of Gordon; An Ancient Scottish Poem. Never before printed*, Glasgow, 1755. Relating an incident (1571) in the feud between Sir Adam Gordon of Auchindoun (the queen's lieutenant-deputy in the north) and the Forbeses.

124. Text, Buchan, i. 56 ff. John Kincaid's wife and the nurse were executed at Edinburgh on 5 July 1600.

125. Air, Blaikie MS, p. 19, no. 55 (entitled *The King of Fairies*); text, Child, no. 195A (from George Paton's MS, 1778).

126. Air, Greig MSS, iv. 6; text, Motherwell, pp. 167–72. The ballad relates events of 1630.

127. Air, current tradition; text, Greig, lviii. The Duke of Argyll was commissioned in 1640 to take arms against the Earl of Airlie, an enemy to the covenant. (The Earl's son Lord Ogilvie and his family were not at Airlie when it was pillaged.)

128. Air, *SMM*, no. 128; text, C. K. Sharpe, *A Ballad Book* (1823), 1883, p. 62. Probably relating to the plague of 1645–7.

129. Air and text collected and transcribed by Mr. Francis Collinson in 1953; given here, with permission, from the archive of the School of Scottish Studies, Edinburgh.

130. Air, Robert Chambers, *Twelve Romantic Scottish Ballads*, 1844, p. 26 ('Earlistoun'); text, Scott, pp. 271–81. The battle was fought between the Duke of Monmouth and the Covenanters on 23 June 1679; the Covenanters were routed. The stanzas on Claverhouse are manifest nonsense.

131. Air and text, *SMM*, no. 266. Romantically attributed with
132 to James V of Scotland.

132. Air and text, *Orpheus Caledonius* (1725), 1733, i. 95–8.

133. Air, *SMM*, no. 365; text, Hastie MS, f. 89; collected and probably revised by Burns.

134. Air, Child, v. 424 (from W. Walker, Aberdeen); text, Buchan, i. 278–80, with the refrain adapted to fit the air.

135. Air, *SMM*, no. 379; text, Hastie MS, f. 101. Collected and probably revised by Burns. (*Burns*, iii. 1404.)

136. Text, B.M., Roxburghe Ballads, iii. 230.

137. Text and air, *Pills*, v. 77–80.

138. Text, B.M., Bagford Ballads, ii. 155.

139. Text, B.M., Douce Ballads, i. 39a.

140. Air and text, *Pills*, v. 46–8.

141. Text, Nottingham University Library, Broadsides, 118/B2.

142. Text, *The Curiosities of Street Literature*, 1871, p. 195.

143. By Thomas Chatterton (1752–70). Text, 1772 edn.

144. By William Julius Mickle (1735–88). Text (1784), *The Oxford Book of Eighteenth Century Verse*, no. 329.

145. By William Blake (1757–1827). Text, *Complete Writings*, ed. Geoffrey Keynes, 1966, pp. 434–6.

146. By Walter Scott (1771–1832); a 'fragment of minstrelsy' sung by old Elspeth in *The Antiquary* (1816), ch. xl.

147. By W. M. Thackeray (1811–63). Text, *Letters and Private Papers*, ed. G. N. Ray, ii (1945), 484–5.

148. By Dante Gabriel Rossetti (1828–82). Text, *Collected Works*, 1886, i. 274–9.

149. By Algernon Charles Swinburne (1837–1909); written *c.* 1859. Text reconstructed by Anne Henry Ehrenpreis from the portions of the MS in Harvard College Library and the British Museum (*Huntington Library Quarterly*, xii (1958), 354–62).

150. By Sir Alexander Gray (1882–1968). Text, *Sir Halewyn. Examples in European Balladry and Folk Song*, 1949; a version of the Dutch *Heer Halewyn*.

INDEX OF TITLES

INDEX OF TITLES

INDEX OF TITLES

OXFORD

MORE OXFORD PAPERBACKS

Details of a selection of other books follow. A complete list of Oxford Paperbacks, including The World's Classics, Twentieth-Century Classics, OPUS, Past Masters, Oxford Authors, Oxford Shakespeare, and Oxford Paperback Reference, is available in the UK from the General Publicity Department, Oxford University Press (JN), Walton Street, Oxford OX2 6DP.

In the USA, complete lists are available from the Paperbacks Marketing Manager, Oxford University Press, 200 Madison Avenue, New York, NY 10016.

Oxford Paperbacks are available from all good bookshops. In case of difficulty, customers in the UK can order direct from Oxford University Press Bookshop, 116 High Street, Oxford, Freepost, OX1 4BR, enclosing full payment. Please add 10 per cent of published price for postage and packing.

THE NEW OXFORD BOOK OF
EIGHTEENTH-CENTURY VERSE

Chosen and Edited by Roger Lonsdale

'a major anthology: one of the best that Oxford has ever produced' *The Times*

'a major event . . . forces a reappraisal of what 18th-century poetry is' *Sunday Times*

'the most important anthology in recent years' *The Economist*

'indispensable' Kingsley Amis

THE NEW OXFORD BOOK OF LIGHT VERSE

Chosen by Kingsley Amis

'extremely funny and absorbing . . . a reflection, of course, of the sureness of Amis's taste' *Times Literary Supplement*

'very comprehensive and enjoyable' *Observer*

'Full of good stuff.' *New Statesman*

THE OXFORD BOOK OF CONTEMPORARY
VERSE, 1945–1980

Compiled by D. J. Enright

This anthology offers substantial selections from the work of forty British, American, and Commonwealth poets who have emerged and confirmed their talents since 1945.

'There is more pithy and Johnsonian good sense in his short introduction than in all the many books that have been written about modern poetry . . . one of the best personal anthologies I have come across.' John Bayley in the *Listener*

THE OXFORD BOOK OF DREAMS

Chosen by Stephen Brook

Drawing on the dream material of a variety of novelists, poets, playwrights, and diarists, this anthology explores the dream experience in literature from pre-Christian times to the present day.

'Anthologies which transcend themselves . . . (are) very rare, but Stephen Brook's *Oxford Book of Dreams* is of their number.' *New Statesman*

THE OXFORD BOOK OF LITERARY ANECDOTES

Edited by James Sutherland

'A heavenly book . . . cannot be too warmly recommended.'
Michael Ratcliffe in *The Times*

'Full of delights . . . all the pleasures of wit, malice, affection,
and memorable conversation.' *Daily Telegraph*

'As long as books are read for pleasure, stories like those
collected here will continue to delight.' *Listener*

'Lovely collection . . . of stories that amuse and warm and
which display writers in all their vanity, their greed, their mod-
esty, their humiliations, their complacency, their wit.' *Country
Life*

THE OXFORD BOOK OF SATIRICAL VERSE

Chosen by Geoffrey Grigson

'one of the best anthologies by the best modern anthologist.'
New York Review of Books

'an immense treasury of wit, exuberance, controlled malice
and uncontrolled rage.' *Times Literary Supplement.*

THE NEW OXFORD BOOK OF
CHRISTIAN VERSE

Chosen and edited by Donald Davie

What is meant by Christian verse? What must there be in a passage of verse that gives us the right to call it 'Christian'? These are the questions discussed in Professor Davie's illuminating introduction and answered implicitly on every page of his collection of over 260 poems.

The anthology ranges from the Anglo-Saxon to the works of the modern poets. In a choice of poems that will delight and surprise, Australian and American poetry appears alongside English, Anglo-Irish, Scottish and Anglo-Welsh. Several women poets, including the Elizabethan Countess of Pembroke and Emily Dickinson, are represented as fully as the four men whom Davie offers as 'the masters of the sacred poem in English': George Herbert, Henry Vaughn, Christopher Smart, and William Cowper. A large number of congregational hymns are also included.

'a tremendous achievement'
Methodist Recorder

THE OXFORD BOOK OF SHORT STORIES

Chosen by V. S. Pritchett

'by a writer with a distinctive and distinguished taste . . . could hardly have been done better' *Sunday Times*

V. S. Pritchett, one of our greatest living short-story writers, has chosen some forty stories, written in the English language, to produce a collection that successfully displays the wealth and variety of an art that spans some 200 years.

'(a) treasure trove of an anthology . . . marvellous . . . . The enormous variety of tone and intention allows each story to make its own impact without detracting from that of those that precede and follow it.' *Times Educational Supplement*

TWENTIETH-CENTURY CLASSICS

THE OXFORD BOOK OF SHORT POEMS

Chosen and Edited by P. J. Kavanagh and James Michie

P. J. Kavanagh and James Michie have chosen the best poems in English of less than 13 lines in length for this unique and exciting anthology.

'One of the best of Oxford anthologies and a wonderful literal demonstration of Pound's remark about poetry being a matter of gists and piths.' *Guardian*

'delightful and unexpected' *Sunday Times*

'an excellent anthology' *British Book News*

THE OXFORD BOOK OF VERSE IN ENGLISH TRANSLATION

Chosen and Edited by Charles Tomlinson

Our vast and often neglected literature of poetic translation is represented in this anthology by some 600 poems or extracts ranging from Gavin Douglas's *Aeneid* in the early sixteenth century to Ezra Pound's versions of classical Chinese and Elaine Feinstein's translations from the Russian of Marina Tsvetayeva.

'a treasure house packed with fresh surprises' *Books and Bookmen*

'serious, innovatory, large in its scope and meticulously edited . . . deserves high praise' *London Review of Books*

THE OXFORD BOOK OF APHORISMS

Chosen by John Gross

This anthology demonstrates to the full just how rewarding an art-form the aphorism can be, and just how brilliantly the aphorist can lay bare the ironies of existence.

'an entertaining, thoughtful, splendidly varied and adventurous collection' Kingsley Amis

'an admirable compilation' Anthony Burgess

'fascinating . . . (the reader) will experience the delight of having his worst fears for the human race confirmed with brevity and style' Quentin Crisp

THE OXFORD BOOK OF DEATH

Chosen and edited by D. J. Enright

D. J. Enright has chosen a selection whose range of conjecture, opinion, and emotion, from ancient times to the present, from East to West, is vast and in various ways inspiring.

'only the most flint-hearted of readers could fail to be absorbed, illumined, and even cheered by it' *New Yorker*

'Enright's anthology is an excellent one . . . he has gathered a fine harvest and cleverly kept melancholy in check.' *Guardian*

THE OXFORD BOOK OF AGES

Chosen by Anthony and Sally Sampson

'a delightful anthology of quotations from all sorts of men and women on the peculiarities of being a mortal human being at any moment between the ages of zero and a hundred . . . richly suggestive compilation.' *Sunday Telegraph*

This original anthology brings together the wit and wisdom of some of the more remarkable figures on the social scene, past and present, to reveal a kaleidoscope of opinions about every age of life from birth to 100.

After reading these pages you may be encouraged to proclaim your age—or hide it. Whatever you decide, you will know you are in good company.

THE OXFORD BOOK OF WAR POETRY

Chosen and edited by Jon Stallworthy

'full of good things . . . many old favourites . . . and quite a few genuine surprises' Vernon Scannell, *Guardian*

There can be no area of human experience that has generated a wider range of feeling than war: hope and fear; exhilaration and humiliation; hatred and love. Man's early war-songs were generally exhortations to action, or celebrations of action. More recently, war poetry has been implicitly, if not explicitly, anti-war as poets more and more have responded to 'man's inhumanity to man'—and to women and children.

This great shift in social awareness is revealed in the 250 poems included in this anthology. The selection is arranged chronologically by conflict, to produce a history of warfare as seen by the most eloquent observers and chroniclers. After an unsparing scrutiny of two World Wars and Vietnam, violence in Northern Ireland and El Salvador, the anthology ends with chilling visions of the 'Next War'.